T0189280

Communications in Computer and Information Science 2022

Rationale

The CCIS series is devoted to the publication of proceedings of computer science conferences. Its aim is to efficiently disseminate original research results in informatics in printed and electronic form. While the focus is on publication of peer-reviewed full papers presenting mature work, inclusion of reviewed short papers reporting on work in progress is welcome, too. Besides globally relevant meetings with internationally representative program committees guaranteeing a strict peer-reviewing and paper selection process, conferences run by societies or of high regional or national relevance are also considered for publication.

Topics

The topical scope of CCIS spans the entire spectrum of informatics ranging from foundational topics in the theory of computing to information and communications science and technology and a broad variety of interdisciplinary application fields.

Information for Volume Editors and Authors

Publication in CCIS is free of charge. No royalties are paid, however, we offer registered conference participants temporary free access to the online version of the conference proceedings on SpringerLink (http://link.springer.com) by means of an http referrer from the conference website and/or a number of complimentary printed copies, as specified in the official acceptance email of the event.

CCIS proceedings can be published in time for distribution at conferences or as post-proceedings, and delivered in the form of printed books and/or electronically as USBs and/or e-content licenses for accessing proceedings at SpringerLink. Furthermore, CCIS proceedings are included in the CCIS electronic book series hosted in the SpringerLink digital library at http://link.springer.com/bookseries/7899. Conferences publishing in CCIS are allowed to use Online Conference Service (OCS) for managing the whole proceedings lifecycle (from submission and reviewing to preparing for publication) free of charge.

Publication process

The language of publication is exclusively English. Authors publishing in CCIS have to sign the Springer CCIS copyright transfer form, however, they are free to use their material published in CCIS for substantially changed, more elaborate subsequent publications elsewhere. For the preparation of the camera-ready papers/files, authors have to strictly adhere to the Springer CCIS Authors' Instructions and are strongly encouraged to use the CCIS LaTeX style files or templates.

Abstracting/Indexing

CCIS is abstracted/indexed in DBLP, Google Scholar, EI-Compendex, Mathematical Reviews, SCImago, Scopus. CCIS volumes are also submitted for the inclusion in ISI Proceedings.

How to start

To start the evaluation of your proposal for inclusion in the CCIS series, please send an e-mail to ccis@springer.com.

Richard Chbeir · Djamal Benslimane ·
Michalis Zervakis · Yannis Manolopoulos ·
Ngoc Thanh Ngyuen · Joe Tekli
Editors

Management of Digital EcoSystems

15th International Conference, MEDES 2023
Heraklion, Crete, Greece, May 5–7, 2023
Revised Selected Papers

 Springer

Editors
Richard Chbeir 🆔
University of Pau & Pays de l'Adour
Anglet, France

Djamal Benslimane 🆔
Claude Bernard University Lyon 1
Villeurbanne Cedex, France

Michalis Zervakis 🆔
Technical University of Crete
Chania, Greece

Yannis Manolopoulos 🆔
Open University of Cyprus
Nicosia, Cyprus

Ngoc Thanh Ngyuen 🆔
Wroclaw University of Science
Wroclaw, Poland

Joe Tekli 🆔
Lebanese American University
Byblos, Lebanon

ISSN 1865-0929 ISSN 1865-0937 (electronic)
Communications in Computer and Information Science
ISBN 978-3-031-51642-9 ISBN 978-3-031-51643-6 (eBook)
https://doi.org/10.1007/978-3-031-51643-6

This Springer imprint is published by the registered company Springer Nature Switzerland AG
The registered company address is: Gewerbestrasse 11, 6330 Cham, Switzerland

Paper in this product is recyclable.

Preface

Today's world is highly technically and technologically connected!! Entities such as organizations, services, components, and systems are engaged in all forms of interactions mimicking the social world of humans. Commonly referred to as a digital ecosystem, this latter includes different producers of data (the Web, Internet of Things, Sensors, etc.), consumers of data (end users, applications, systems, etc.), networking capabilities to ensure data transfer and sharing, data-enabled services, processes (including AI and Big Data), deployment infrastructures (e.g., Cloud computing), processing capabilities, and visualization and reporting facilities. Services underpinning such ecosystems expose different self-capabilities such as self-management, self-healing, and self-configuration and at the same time satisfy non-functional requirements such as performance, security, and data privacy.

During the past years, the International Conference on ManagEment of Digital EcoSystems (MEDES) has become one of the most important international scientific events bringing together researchers, developers, and practitioners to discuss the latest research issues and experiences in developing advanced solutions that will help to design, deploy, exploit, and tune emerging ecosystems. MEDES acts as a hosting platform for a diverse community from academia, research laboratories, and industry interested in exploring the manifold challenges and issues related to web technologies and resource management of Digital Ecosystems and how current approaches and technologies can be evolved and adapted to this end.

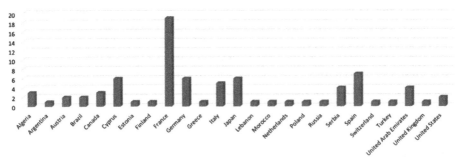

Fig. 1. Countries of PC members of MEDES 2023.

This year, we received 52 submissions out of which 29 full papers were accepted for inclusion in the conference proceedings. Using a single-blind review, each paper was evaluated by 3 reviewers at least. The accepted papers cover a number of broad research areas on both theoretical and practical aspects of Emerging Digital Ecosystems. These papers were categorized in the following sessions: Design Issues & BlockChain, Query

Processing and Visualization, Learning Issues, Digital Twin and Security, Architecture Technologies, Time and Text Management, Services and Systems, and Business and Communication Technologies. MEDES 2023 took place in hybrid mode: with both physical and online participation. Despite the improvement of public health conditions in several countries allowing lifting of travel restrictions, a good number of well-established conferences, including MEDES, have had to wrestle with the limited number of submissions (many people who prefer in-person events have alerted us about their worries and did not submit their work).

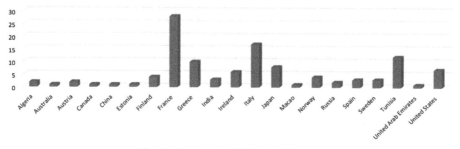

Fig. 2. Countries of Submitted Papers.

Commonly with IDEAS 2023, this year MEDES invited 4 well-known keynote speakers:

- Schahram Dustdar (TU Wien, Austria), who delivered a lecture on "Learning and reasoning for distributed computing continuum ecosystems",
- Ernesto Damiani (Khalifa University, UAE), who delivered a talk on "Blockchain Based Federated Learning for Collaborative Research: The MUSA approach",
- Ioannis Tsamardinos (University of Crete, Greece), who delivered a talk on "Automated Machine Learning for Knowledge Discovery", and
- Marios Dikaiakos (University of Cyprus, Cyprus), who delivered a lecture on "From Fake News to Foreign Information Manipulation and Interference: Considerations on Threats, Mechanisms & Mitigation"

Also, a tutorial on "Parallel and Distributed Data Series Processing" was provided by Panagiota Fatourou (University of Crete, Greece) and a special plenary session under the umbrella of "Diversity & Inclusion" was provided by Eirini Ntoutsi (Bundeswehr University Munich, Germany).

We would like to thank our invited guests and keynotes for their contribution to the success and sustainability of MEDES. We would like to thank all authors for submitting their papers to MEDES 2023 and we hope they will submit their research papers again in the future. We express our gratitude to all the Program Committee members who provided high-quality reviews. Finally, we would like to thank our sponsors: Springer, ACM SIGAPP, ACM SIGAPP.FR, and IFIP WP 2.6 for their regular support. Last but not least, we would like to thank the local organizers for their support.

This year, we have two special issues in the following journals: WWW Journal by Springer, and SN Computer Science by Springer. Finally, we hope the conference attendees enjoyed the technical program, informal meetings, and interaction with colleagues from all over the world. We hope that next year, despite the pandemic – if it still exists globally – the conditions will allow us to turn again to exclusively physical conference organization.

January 2024

Djamal Benslimane
Michalis Zervakis
Richard Chbeir
Yannis Manolopoulos
Ngoc Nguyen
Joe Tekli

Organization

General Chairs

Richard Chbeir   Université de Pau et des Pays de l'Adour, France
Djamal Benslimane   Lyon 1 University, France
Michalis Zervakis   Technical University of Crete, Greece

Program Chairs

Yannis Manolopoulos   Open University of Cyprus, Cyprus
Ngoc Nguyen   Wroclaw U. of Science & Tech., Poland
Joe Tekli   Lebanese American University, Lebanon

Tutorial Chair

Claudio Silvestri   Ca' Foscari University of Venice, Italy

Diversity, Equity and Inclusion Chairs

Sana Sellami   Aix Marseille University, France
Panagiota Fatourou   University of Crete, Greece

Workshop/Special Tracks Chairs

Ejub Kajan   State University of Novi Pazar, Serbia
Zakaria Maamar   University of Doha for Science and Technology, Qatar

PhD Student Track Chairs

Allel Hadjali   Ensma, France
Khouloud Salameh   American University of Ras Al Khaimah, UAE

Publicity/Social Media Chairs

Antonio M. Rinaldi	University of Naples Federico II, Italy
Theodoros Tzouramanis	University of Thessaly, Greece

Publication Chair

Karam Bou-Chaaya	Expleo Group, France

Webmaster

Elie Chicha	Université de Pau et des Pays de l'Adour, France

International Program Committee Members

Adel Alti	Ferhat Abbas University of Setif, Algeria
Hassan Badir	ENSA of Tangier, Morocco
Maxim Bakaev	Novosibirsk State Technical University, Russia
Luciano Baresi	Polytechnic University of Milan, Italy
Khalid Benali	University of Lorraine, France
Amel Benna	Research Center on Scientific and Technical Information, Algeria
Djamal Benslimane	University Lyon 1, France
Morad Benyoucef	University of Ottawa, Canada
Christoph Bussler	Bosch, USA
Richard Chbeir	Université de Pau et des Pays de l'Adour, France
Elie Chicha	Université de Pau et des Pays de l'Adour, France
Antonio Corral	University of Almeria, Spain
Francisco Jose Dominguez Mayo	University of Seville, Spain
Schahram Dustdar	Vienna University of Technology, Austria
Jutta Eckstein	IT Communication, Germany
Karam Bou Chaaya	Expleo Group, France
Anna Formica	Institute for System Analysis and Informatics, Italy
Daniela Godoy	National University of Central Buenos Aires, Argentina
Francesco Guerra	University of Modena and Reggio Emilia, Italy
Hao Han	Konica Minolta, Japan
Ramon Hermoso	University of Zaragoza, Spain

Sergio Ilarri	University of Zaragoza, Spain
Hiroshi Ishikawa	Tokyo Metropolitan University, Japan
Mirjana Ivanovic	University of Novi Sad, Serbia
Adel Jebali	Concordia University, Canada
Ejub Kajan	State University of Novi Pazar, Serbia
Epaminondas Kapetanios	University of Hertfordshire, UK
Alexander Knapp	University of Augsburg, Germany
Harald Kosch	University of Passau, Germany
Anne Laurent	University of Montpellier, France
Sylvain Lefebvre	Toyota, TMC, France
Zakaria Maamar	Zayed University, UAE
Yannis Manolopoulos	Open University of Cyprus, Cyprus
Santiago Melia	University of Alicante, Spain
Tommi Mikkonen	University of Helsinki, Finland
Ngoc-Thanh Nguyen	Wroclaw University of Science and Technology, Poland
Gunnar Piho	Tallinn University of Technology, Estonia
Thomas Richter	Rhein-Waal University of Applied Sciences, Germany
Khouloud Salameh	American University of Ras Al Khaimah, UAE
Imad Saleh	Université Paris 8, France
Rodrigo Santos	Federal University of the State of Rio de Janeiro, Brazil
Lionel Seinturier	University of Lille, France
Sana Sellami	Aix Marseille University, France
Benkrid Soumia	Higher National School of Computer Science, Algeria
Yasufumi Takama	Tokyo Metropolitan University, Japan
Joe Tekli	Lebanese American University, Lebanon
Caetano Traina	University of São Paolo, Brazil
Chrisa Tsinaraki	Technical University of Crete, Greece
Masashi Tsuchida	Tokyo Metropolitan University, Japan
Marco Viviani	University of Milano-Bicocca, Italy
Michael Weiss	Carleton University, Canada
Erik Wilde	CA Technologies, Switzerland
Tulay Yildirim	Yildiz Technical University, Turkey
Nicola Zannone	Eindhoven University of Technology, The Netherlands
Gefei Zhang	University of Applied Sciences Berlin, Germany
Qiang Zhu	University of Michigan – Dearborn, USA

Sponsors

Springer

Connected Environment & Distributed Energy Data Management Solutions Research Group

The ACM Special Interest Group on Applied Computing

The French Chapter of the ACM Special Interest Group on Applied Computing

International Federation for Information Processing Working Group 2.6

Contents

Learning Issues

Services and Systems

Business and Communication Technologies

Digital Twin and Security

Architecture Technologies

Time and Text Management

Invited Paper

Design Issues & BlockChain

Using Focused Crawlers with Obfuscation Techniques in the Audio Retrieval Domain

Domenico Benfenati, Marco Montanaro⬤, Antonio M. Rinaldi(✉),
Cristiano Russo⬤, and Cristian Tommasino⬤

Department of Electrical Engineering and Information Technology,
University of Naples Federico II, Via Claudio, 21, 80125 Naples, Italy
{domenico.benfenati,marco.montanaro,antoniomaria.rinaldi,
cristiano.russo,cristian.tommasino}@unina.it

Abstract. The detection of intellectual property violations in multimedia files poses a critical challenge for the Internet infrastructure, particularly in the context of very large document collections. The techniques employed to address these issues generally fall into two categories: proactive and reactive approaches. In this article we propose an approach that is both reactive and proactive, with the aim of preventing the deletion of legal uploads (or modifications of such files, such as remixes, parodies, and other edits) due to the presence of illegal uploads on a platform. We have developed a rule-based, obfuscating focused crawler that can work with files in the Audio Information Retrieval domain. Our model automatically scans multimedia files uploaded to a public collection only when a user submits a search query. We present experimental results obtained during tests on a well-known music collection, discussing the strength and efficiency of specific combinations of Neural Network-Similarity Scoring solutions.

Keywords: Audio retrieval · Deep Neural Networks · Web Crawling · Information Retrieval

1 Introduction

The web allows for efficient sharing of multimedia content across devices, but it does not prioritize the security of transmitted data. This includes the sharing of copyright-protected data, difficult to monitor due to a lack of cohesive laws on Intellectual Property protection [1] and the complexity of overseeing large amounts of data transmitted in a distributed manner. One way to prevent IP infringement is to include a digital signature or watermark [2,3] in multimedia files using unique keys.

Our approach employs the original data of protected multimedia files instead, only storing information relevant to indexing audio files, leaving the original data unchanged. It uses a focused web crawler to gather information related to multimedia files hosted on the net. Focused Crawlers [4] are specialized Web Crawlers that deal with specific topics or parts of the known web. They implement a page

R. Chbeir et al. (Eds.): MEDES 2023, CCIS 2022, pp. 3–17, 2024.
https://doi.org/10.1007/978-3-031-51643-6_1

filtering mechanism based on a given topic as their On-Line Selection Policy to analyze a section of the web. Our focused crawler operates in the domain of Multimodal Content-Based Information Retrieval, which involves searching for information in the form of multimedia data, including typed text, audio tracks, or metadata [5]. Its goal is to determine the relevance of retrieved documents to the end user's objectives. Since we're interested in the obfuscation of potentially illegal results, our Crawler uses Deep Neural Networks to show only audio tracks deemed legal when compared to a Copyright-protected reference collection. Intellectual Property laws present several issues related to the ambiguity of judiciary[1] texts [1], which requires research into less strict mechanism used for verifying the integrity of online data. This activity could be seen as a recommendation task [6]. Searches executed via our implementation of the focused crawler also perform Adversarial Information Retrieval tasks. This means that the system retrieves data that will be purposefully hidden from the user in response to a query. The peculiarity of our approach is the fact that it can work in an obfuscating manner - rather than deleting illegal files, our system stores an abstract representation of the relevant subset of files that must be hidden from the user. The retrieved illegal data is used to improve the detection capabilities of the implemented DNNs, in order to discover more complex illegal audio data. By doing so, server administrators for large document collections and website owners can automate the manual monitoring of illegal content on their platforms, which otherwise would require them to pay for or to develop costly DRM (Digital Rights Management) software [7] or to analyze and act upon legally ambiguous uses of Copyright-protected content [8]. An innovative approach for similarity mapping among audio tracks has been implemented in this article. The approach is based on Deep Neural Networks, which offer several advantages compared to classical Machine Learning techniques [9]. The neural networks under study are the Convolutional Neural Networks and the Recurrent Neural Networks. While CNNs must compute from scratch the input at each execution cycle, RNNs can maintain information relative to a prior cycle, using it to further acquire new information from the input data for following cycles. The similarity check executed in our work uses a vector of features [10] extracted from the original audio tracks via segmentation and frequency filters. The extracted features are the Mel-filtered Cepstral Coefficients [11]. MFCCs are representations of the power spectrum of a given signal and are used to obtain the visual representation of audio tracks. We discuss their definition in Sect. 3.2.

This article is organized as follows: examples from literature for the treatment of Audio Information are presented in Sect. 2, like systems for digital watermarking, focused crawlers, systems operating Machine Learning and DNNs; in Sect. 3 we show the proposed system, its components and behavior; some test cases and criteria for evaluating the effectiveness and goodness of the system are shown in Sect. 4; finally, conclusions on the results of our work and possible improvements to our model are shown in Sect. 5.

---

[1] http://www.oecd.org/sti/ieconomy/KBC2-IP.Final.pdf.

2   Related Works

While Focused Web Crawling has been studied for years, Audio Recognition has only recently been the subject of research, partly because of the improvements in the field of DNNs. This led to several techniques being developed for data retrieval from the web and for the analysis and recognition of audio tracks. Capuano et al. [12] proposed an ontology-based approach for the development of a focused crawler in the cultural heritage domain. They showed how Linked Open Data and the use of Semantic Web can be exploited to improve the performance of an information retrieval task from the point of view of semantics. Knees, Pohle et al. [13] presented an approach for building a search engine which is optimized for large scale audio repositories. Their focused crawler uses information obtained from metadata of the downloaded multimedia files to categorize their host web pages. Potentially useless data, like year of publishing or sources, is discarded from the computation. Violation of intellectual property over multimedia files is a complex issue. There are various techniques that can be used to protect rights, such as approaches based on digital Watermarks. Kim [14] proposes a method to detect illegal copies of protected images, reducing them to an 8×8 pixel representations by calculating the average of their intensity, applying a discrete cosine transforms and inferring AC coefficients as discriminant. These coefficients can be used to detect similarity between the reference picture and the illegal copies. Dahr and Kim [15] propose a watermarking system in the field of Audio Information Retrieval. The watermark is applied to the content of the track itself on its amplitude peaks using Fast Fourier Transforms of the original data. As the peaks do not change when the pitch or tempo of the track is modified, the watermark is shielded from manipulation. It can also be extracted from the signal mix by applying the right cryptographically secure key. A focal point of our approach is the use of Deep Neural Networks to extract feature vectors from audio tracks. Several techniques can be used to monitor the similarity between different features, feature manipulation and extraction from the original audio data thanks to Machine Learning techniques. Some methods implement non-supervised learning approaches to solve the issue of Audio Similarity. Henaff et Jarrett [16] codified audio tracks using some base functions, using Support Vector Machines to classify their outputs. Guo et Li [17] also use binary SVM methods, formulating a metric called Distance-From-Boundary to determine similarity. DNNs used in the field of Audio Classification generally adopt supervised learning approaches, where Deep Learning techniques are used to extract feature vectors from the original audio files. The vectors are used in Classification or Similarity Checking tasks. Rajanna et al. [18] compare Neural Networks techniques with classical Machine Learning ones when used in the Audio Classification domain, reaching the verdict that DNNs obtain, on average, the best results. After a preliminary computation of the input data and having extracted the Mel Frequency Cepstral Components [11] from target audio files, their proposed Neural Network is trained using Manifold Learning, a technique that diminishes the dimensionality of the problem. Sets of feature vectors are highly valuable for characterizing audio files, whether it involves solving similarity checking or classification problems or performing dimensionality reduction in a DNN-based task. There is no catch-all kind of feature to extract, as it heavily depends on the kind of model used in feature extraction. Several techniques are described in literature, like the studies made by Safadi et al. [19]. DNNs are heavily specialized for feature vector extractions, which can be used to uniquely represent audio files. Becker et al. [20] explore Feature Extraction functionalities of DNNs in the audio domain using a technique called Layer-Wise Relevance Propagation. This method identifies relevant characteristics of a given DNN when the input data exhibits a specific signal shape. Our approach to feature extraction is innovative as we employ Transfer Learning from the visual to the audio domain. Traditional Transfer Learning methods associate trained weights with relevant fields. For instance, a Neural Network trained on pictures from a different domain can be used to classify elements within a picture. However, Transfer Learning can be extended to address tasks across completely different domains, such as using visual domain training to tackle audio domain tasks. For instance, Mun and Shon [21] explored Acoustic Scene Classification by training a DNN on Visual Object Classification and then applying the obtained matrices in the audio domain. Our method uses DNNs trained on standard visual classification problems, treating them as feature extraction tools in the visual domain. These DNNs operate on audio tracks transformed into their visual representations.

3   The Proposed System

A Rule-Based, Obfuscating Focused Crawler has been developed as a software system with various modules that work together to provide capabilities for generalization and extensibility. The system includes a graphic interface, a Crawling Component for downloading files, an Indexing Component for working with metadata, a Referential Document Collection of illegal audio files, a Neural Network for extracting feature vectors from reference audio files and a Scoring Module for calculating a Combined Similarity Score based on scores from other modules. The system starts in an idle state and waits for a user query. The query can be sent via the GUI and is used to initialize the Crawling process on a document collection, either hosted locally or on the internet. The Web Crawler is implemented as an instance of Apache Nutch[2] and the crawling and indexing submodules can be called by external programs using a Python API. The target website must respond to data requests and Nutch must follow the principle of politeness by not overloading the website with a high number of requests. It abides by the crawling protocols imposed by the website owner, as found in the *robots.txt* file and must identify itself as a web crawler to the website. The Nutch Crawler performs a preliminary filtering of obtained data. Contents from the downloaded pages are analyzed to locate all files with the ".mp3" file extension, the only ones we're interested in keeping in the local storage. Depending on the depth level requested, Nutch could further explore the web pages it has

---

[2] http://nutch.apache.org/.

found by browsing the hyperlinks in the last visited page, or in the subfolders of a local repository. The system proceeds with the analysis of the relevant retrieved audio files. These are indexed on an instance of Apache Solr[3] according to the metadata extracted from each file by the Nutch Crawler. The system compares the metadata contained in the files retrieved by the Crawler with the metadata contained in the files from the reference collection to obtain Textual Similarity Scores for each file pair. The score is calculated based on the semantic distance between words contained in the metadata of each pair of files, using Cosine Similarity. If an audio file contains an empty field, the system ignores the contribution by that tag to Cosine Similarity. The files are converted to .wav, filtered to obtain a visual representation using MFCCs and sent to a Feature Vector Extraction and Comparison module, which is composed of a trained neural network used to extract feature vectors. These vectors are then compared to the feature vectors obtained from the audio files of the reference collection using Cosine Similarity. The system can be executed sequentially or in parallel, in which case the two scores are computed simultaneously. The system sends the Textual and Feature Similarity Scores to the Scorer module for the relevant pairs of audio files under analysis and those present in the reference collection. For each pair, the system calculates a Combined Similarity Score using various methods (Weighted Sum, OWA Operator, Textual-Feature Sequential Score). The Combined Similarity Score is compared to a threshold determined from the analysis results. If any pair's score exceeds the threshold, the analyzed file is flagged as potentially illegal. Metadata and Feature Vector of the flagged file are stored in the reference collection to enhance system recognition. The raw data of the flagged file is obfuscated instead of being deleted, allowing future resolution of potential disputes. Once all Combined Similarity Scores are obtained, the system selects which files to display based on user queries, hiding flagged illegal files from public view. All files in the Reference Collection are already flagged as illegal and not shown to users to avoid including them in query results.

3.1 Crawling Phase

The Graphic User Interface lets users input their queries and specify parameters for the Crawling and Scoring phases for system administrators. The parameters are the initial Seed, which can be either the base URL of a web page or the path of a directory that the Crawler will scan; space separated Query Keywords to search for in the main fields of files to be indexed; a checkbox for the use of a Blacklist, containing Keywords that must not be included in the results, and its path. Apache Nutch initializes Crawling threads once the user clicks on the "Begin Crawl" button. The GUI sends a signal to Apache Nutch and Apache Solr using the Python libraries *nutch-api* and *subprocess*. The former sends special commands to the Nutch Server instance executing in the background, which consists of information pertaining to the instantiated Solr Server that will receive data to index and parameters to set up the Crawler, such as the number of rounds

---

[3] https://lucene.apache.org/solr/.

or a stopping criterion. By default, the Crawler will only save files from the main page or directory selected and in the first pages or subdirectories available. The GUI interacts with the *crawlerlogic* module, which checks and assigns Legality Flags and Legality Scores for a given audio file once found. The Crawling phase returns .mp3 audio files. They contain information stored as metadata, such as Author, Title, Release Date and so on. The tags are extracted using a software tool called *Apache Tika*. The metadata is used to calculate Textual Similarity Scores between the analysed audio file and a subset of elements taken from a reference collection through their Cosine Similarity, given by the formula:

$$cosineSimilarity(a, b) = \frac{\vec{a} \cdot \vec{b}}{\| \vec{a} \| \times \| \vec{b} \|} \tag{1}$$

Vectors $\vec{a}$ and $\vec{b}$ must contain elements of the same type. In the case of Textual Similarity Scores, the two vectors are lists of strings, which map to the tags in metadata. The maximum score is given when both audio tracks have the same metadata, while its minimum is given when they contain no shared keyword in their tags. All Textual Similarity Scores computed between pairs of audio files are stored in memory and sent to the Scorer module. Audio tracks obtained during the Crawling phase cannot be directly used with the implemented DNNs, as the Networks have been trained to work in a visual domain. A visual representation of the tracks is needed to extract their feature vectors. Audio data must first be converted from .mp3 to .wav file extension. We also extract only 30 s of the transformed audio file to reduce DNN input dimensionality. For shorter files, appropriate padding is inserted at the end. The modified file can then be processed to obtain its visual representation, which is characterized by the Mel Frequency Cepstral Coefficients.

3.2 Mel Frequency Cepstral Components

A crucial contribution in the field of study for optimal description in the Audio Recognition domain came from Davis and Mermelstein's formulation of their Mel Frequency Cepstral Coefficients [11]. These are numeric values that are unique for each audio track, which make up their Mel Frequency Cepstrum. A Cepstrum [22] is the result of a mathematical transform in Fourier Analysis. It allows us to study phenomena relative to periodic signals by analyzing their spectral components. A mel is a unit of measurement for the perceived acoustic intonation of one tone, appropriately scaled to consider the sensibility of human hearing. An MFC is a special kind of representation of the frequency spectrum of a signal once a logarithmic transform has been applied on the spectrum. In order to obtain its Mel Components, the audio file must be transformed using a chain of triangular filter, as shown in Fig. 1. The distance between two filters is such that the central frequency of the preceding filter is equal to the source frequency of the following filter. The response of each filter increases in strength from its source to its center and then decreases to zero on its end frequency. Following this step, a Discrete Cosine Transform is applied to the filtered signal with the aim of decorrelating the coefficients obtained from the sequence of filters. The decorrelated coefficients are the mel components we were looking for. In Fig. 1 we also show an example of MFCC acquisition from an audio signal. The formula that Davis and Mermelstein came up with to compute MFCCs takes into account a sequence of 20 triangular filters:

$$MFCC_i = \sum_{k=1}^{20} X_k cos[i(k - \frac{1}{2})\frac{\pi}{20}], \ i = 1, 2, \cdots, M \qquad (2)$$

where M is the number of coefficients to retrieve from the signal and X_k is the logarithm of the output of the k-th filter.

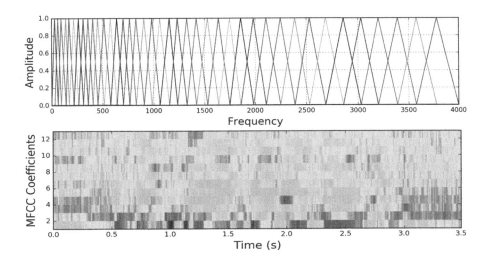

Fig. 1. A Mel Filter Bank and Obtained MFCCs.

3.3   Feature Extraction Phase

The Extraction of a Feature Vector is initiated once the visual representations of the audio files have been obtained. These images are the inputs of one of the implemented Neural Networks, which have been trained to predict the musical genre of a track. The chosen Network must be pre-trained on an annotated reference collection. The focal point of our work is the goodness of the extracted high-level features, which in turn determine how well they can identify matching audio tracks. The hidden layer before the Classification output layer is extracted from the Network. This hidden layer's matrix is much bigger than all preceding ones to include as much information obtained from low level features as possible. Its output is a feature vector unique to a single audio file, which can be compared with other reference files to assess its legality. Comparing coherent features on a large set of files is necessary to identify matching copies of illegal audio files, even if they have been modified. In this work, we used the following neural networks: for convolutional neural networks, we chose VGG-16[4], ResNet [23], a Monodimensional VGG-16 and a ad-hoc Small Convnet with a reduced number of layers, while for recurrent neural networks we implemented a Long-Short Term Memory network [24]. The networks have been modified by adding a batch normalization layer, which lowers convergence time for classification problems. The VGG-16 and ResNet Networks have been pre-trained using predefined weights, extracted from the Imagenet Dataset[5]. Transfer Learning allows us to use information acquired to solve a given problem in order to find a solution for an entirely different one. In this case, the weights computed over Imagenet can be used to distinguish different object classes in a picture. The knowledge acquired by the way individual objects contrast with the background with their edges and shapes generates weights which can be used to find discontinuities in the pictures. This discriminating capability of the Neural Network can be used in the analysis of a visual representation of the power spectrum of an audio file, as shown in Fig. 1. Since the minimum input matrices for our networks must be $32 \times 32 \times 3$ in size, the representations of audio signals have been enlarged by sampling at mel frequencies much higher than those of the original signals. The GTZAN library[6] has been used as the training dataset. It contains 1.000 audio files, each 30 s long and divided into 10 different musical genres. Their original file extension is .au and they were transformed into .wav files before being fed to the DNNs. Audio file representations are inserted as input for the chosen Neural Network and activations from the network's final hidden layer are taken as output. The obtained feature vector is unique for the neural network and analyzed audio file pair. However, if the file is very similar to another reference audio file, even assuming modifications in pitch, tone, volume, duration etc., their feature vectors will be very similar. A Feature Similarity Score computed between each pair of analyzed-reference files determines how similar the two files appear to be.

3.4 Scoring and Evaluation Phase

The Scorer Module computes the Textual and Feature Similarity Scores, then turns them into a Combined Similarity Score. Three different combinations have been implemented:

i) **Sum of the Scores:** both Textual and Feature Scores are multiplied by predetermined weights, then summed up. The reference file with the corresponding highest Combined Similarity Score is reported for a given file under analysis, using the formula:

$$f * score_{feature}(a) + t * score_{textual}(a); \tag{3}$$

---

[4] https://www.robots.ox.ac.uk/~vgg/research/very_deep/.
[5] http://www.image-net.org/.
[6] https://www.kaggle.com/andradaolteanu/gtzan-dataset-music-genre-classification.

ii) **Ordered Weighted Average Operator over Feature Similarity Scores:** Textual Similarity Scores of an analyzed file are normalized in relation to all reference files, ensuring a unitary sum. This normalized score is multiplied by the Feature Similarity Score for each reference file. The reference file with the highest cumulative score is identified as the most similar to the analyzed file. The formula for this mode is the following:

$$score_{feature}(a) * \frac{score_{textual}(a)}{\sum_i score_{textual}(a)}; \qquad (4)$$

iii) **Sequential Textual-Feature Score:** a preliminary check is performed on the Textual Score only for each reference file, ignoring reference files with a Textual Similarity Score lower than a threshold. All files who scored higher are kept as the new reference collection, and the Feature Similarity Score is computed. The file with the highest Feature Similarity Score among the filtered set is considered the most similar. The formula for this mode is the following:

$$if\ score_{textual}(a) > THRESHOLD \mapsto score_{feature}(a);\ else\ 0. \qquad (5)$$

All the scores are saved in their own variables. These can be extracted from results and analyzed by the system administrator to choose which combination has the best results for the collection. By default, the system uses the Sum of the Scores mode. Depending on the scoring function being used, different thresholds must be considered when determining file illegality. For example, the OWA Operator has much lower scores as output compared to the other two, meaning it requires much more accurate thresholding. Sum of the Scores can be heavily influenced by the weights f e t. Sequential Scoring tends to ignore files with no tags attached. Tuning of the thresholding is done through several tests on subsets of the original data and must be performed according to the Scoring system on a subset of the reference collection.

4   Results Evaluation

There are several challenges brought up by the Results Evaluation Phase. One challenge is the granularity of the solution, where the system flags a file as illegal if it's similar to any file from the reference collection. This can lead to false positives among the results, with several files marked as illegal even if no exact copy exists within the reference collection. To address this, the system was tested in two ways: the first test was to identify which of the illegal (modified) audio tracks in the collection are recognized by the system, without considering whether there is an exact copy of those in the reference collection. The second test was to identify the specific audio track being copied by the illegal ones, which can be used as a metric for the system's Adversarial Crawling capabilities. Another challenge comes from the choice of the values of thresholds and weights for the Scorer. Each operator computing a Combined Similarity Score requires a fine tuning of its weights in order to solve all ambiguities in illegality flagging.

Some combination of the weights may make Textual or Feature Scores much more important than the other, and thus creating false positives or false negatives in the results. Weights and thresholds have been identified for each Neural Network/Combined Similarity Scorer after having a set of initial experiments on part of the test dataset. The tests have been executed on a reference collection composed of audio files from the Free Music Archive library. The files have been downloaded from the "medium" sized archive[7] which contains 30 s long 25.000 audio tracks, divided in 16 different musical genres, weighting 22 Gigabytes. The collection has been stored locally to prevent overloading the FMA Web Server, but the tests can be replicated online.

4.1   Accuracy Tests on Illegal Files

In this test we assess how well the system can deal with illegal files. The system must find illegal files among legal uploads without any prior knowledge of their characteristics and classify them correctly comparing them to the reference files. The test was executed on a collection of 7049 audio tracks from the FMA archive. The system is able to locate rule violations while searching for files using keywords from user queries by applying Cosine Similarity to dictionaries of metadata. The user cannot see the obfuscated (illegal) results, but only the portion of files that the system deemed legal at query time. The steps for feature evaluation are the following: the implemented Neural Networks have been trained on a set of audio tracks, divided by genre, taken from the GTZAN collection. The tracks have first been converted from the .au to the .wav file type; several "illegal" audio tracks have been produced by taking some of the files from the reference collection and randomly applying changes in pitch and volume, and then added to the audio collection; the final MaxPooling layer of each Neural Network has been computed at Feature Extraction time for each of the tested audio files, in order to use them to check file similarity when comparing them to the files in the reference collection. A similar procedure has been applied on the equivalent LSTM layer for the implemented Recurrent Neural Network, and its output has been used to check file similarity; each Neural Network returned a Feature Descriptor Vector for each file. Said descriptors have been compared to each other using Cosine Similarity. The adopted metric for evaluating the goodness of our tests is the F1-Measure. It has been adapted to an adversarial retrieval task as:

$$F1(j) = \frac{2}{\frac{1}{r(j)} + \frac{1}{P(j)}} \tag{6}$$

where j is the rank of the j-th retrieved document, $r(j)$ is the Recall at the j-th ranked document, $P(j)$ is the Precision at the j-th rank in the results. Note that in the test all illegal documents of the collection have been searched in a single query ("*"). This lets us evaluate the chance that any of the illegal files, which may or may not have been modified and can all be returned during hypothetical searches on more specific terms, could possibly be ignored by the system during

---

[7] https://github.com/mdeff/fma.

its obfuscating phase. Given the goal of our test, the way the system computes the F1-Measure differs from its standard definition. While relevant documents would increase the F1-Measure and the illegal documents would decrease it, in our test all documents pertain to the same class and we are interested in obfuscating documents that could be relevant, but also illegal when compared to the reference files, which are our pre-established rules. Because of that, the system computes the F1-Measure by finding all illegal documents and considering retrieved non-illegal documents as "not relevant". All retrieved and presumed illegal documents are instead considered "relevant" if the right corresponding reference document has been found. In this test, both textual and feature evaluation have the same importance ($t = 0 : 5; f = 0 : 5$). The total number of indexes files is 7094 non modified files, 1137 modified files and 855 reference files. Illegal, modified files are composed of 855 audio tracks. Their metadata has been modified by either removing or renaming Album, Title and Author fields, while the track has been modified in pitch and volume. Because the search only concerns the illegally modified files, the ground truth vector for this test contains only positive values, stored as 1 s. We do this as each one of the analyzed documents in this test is already relevant to the obfuscating search. The prediction vector can be obtained by combining the searches for all the combinations of modified files. After executing the test, it contains 1 s for each illegal file that has been correctly identified as illegal, and 0 s for each illegal file incorrectly identified as legal or if the reference file most similar to the file under analysis is not the original reference file from which we derived the modified one. Test results are shown in Table 1 and in Fig. 2. The total number of correctly identified files has been calculated in two ways, for each calculation method: by identifying only file illegality, ignoring which reference file corresponds to the illegal one and then testing the similarity score to a single predefined threshold. The three thresholds have been averaged over several preliminary experiments. The choice of thresholds is an important and discriminating factor in determining file illegality. Choosing a single threshold value for all Combined Similarity Scores, as done in this example, allows us to compare all methods at the same time, but it is not the best way to understand the strengths of each Network/Scorer combination. Different neural networks return different Feature Vectors, meaning Feature Similarity Scores

Table 1. Results of the First Test

885 Tested Files over 1137 Illegal Files	small convnet	ResNet	LSTM	vgg16	vgg161d
sum, correctly identified	432	505	427	**566**	380
sum (> 0.5)	427	499	418	**555**	378
sum Recall	0.50256 - 0.49941	0.59064 - 0.58362	0.49941 - 0.48888	**0.66198 - 0.64912**	0.44444 - 0.44210
sum Macro-Average F1	0.33566 - 0.33307	0.37132 - 0.36853	0.33307 - 0.32835	**0.39831 - 0.39361**	0.30769 - 0.30656
owa, correctly identified	258	422	188	**481**	169
owa (> 0.00075, as measured on 1137 samples)	155	422	12	**481**	66
owa Recall	0.30175 - 0.18128	0.49356 - 0.49356	0.21988 - 0.01403	**0.56257 - 0.56257**	0.19766 - 0.07719
owa Macro-Average F1	0.23180 - 0.15346	0.33046 - 0.33046	0.18024 - 0.01384	**0.36002 - 0.36002**	0.16503 - 0.07166
sequential, correctly identified	168	148	118	**288**	81
sequential (> 0.35)	73	148	9	**287**	21
sequential Recall	0.19649 - 0.08538	0.17309 - 0.17309	0.13801 - 0.01008	**0.33684 - 0.33567**	0.09473 - 0.024561
sequential Macro-Average F1	0.16422 - 0.07866	0.14755 - 0.14755	0.12127 - 0.01052	**0.25196 - 0.25131**	0.08653 - 0.02397

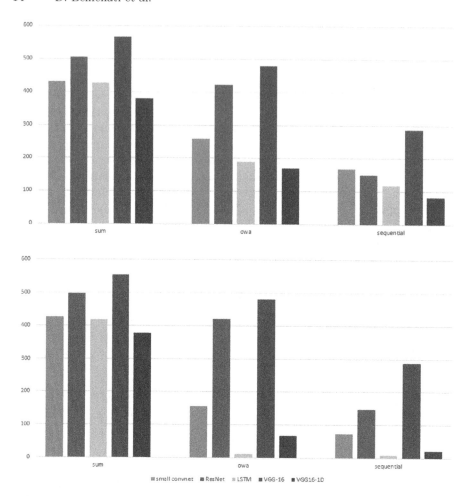

Fig. 2. Results for the Accuracy Test on Illegal Files. 1) Absolute File Illegality Results; 2) Results with Thresholding.

vary depending on the method. For example, even though LSTM seems to be the worst of all the implemented Networks, it could still obtain better results by lowering threshold values in accordance with the lower scores obtained from feature extraction. Secondly, we tried to check whether illegal files did match their original reference files. The filename (not the Title) of the original audio has been altered for both illegal modifications and reference files, and a second evaluation of the results has taken place by checking whether the two files shared filenames. Data shown in the same table cell map to the absolute illegality test and the reference file matching test, respectively. The Micro Average F1-Measure has been computed by the testing module to assign equal importance to each analyzed file. We consider a single class in our Precision/Recall calculations for illegal files, ignoring the class of legal files. The Precision score for correctly and incorrectly classified documents equals 0 and 1, respectively. The second experiment has been executed including the class of legal files. The Recall for illegal documents which have been correctly identified as illegal is the same value as the Micro Average F1-Measure. The test shows us that, given a unique threshold and ignoring other issues related to the number of illegal and reference files or to training and feature extraction times for neural networks, VGG-16 is the best performing model on all the given tests when we are just trying to identify illegal files. This doesn't mean that VGG-16 is the best network for our system, but that is best suited for extracting unique information regarding input audio files when compared to the others. VGG16-1D has obtained much worse results when looking at the obtained values, while the Small Convnet, despite middling results, could converge to a solution in less time compared to the other network using less computational resources. This means that it could be a good fit if our crawler were to be executed on a personal computer instead of a server. ResNet returned outstanding results, but it also required greater execution time and computational resources from the server, making it impractical for a hypothetical deployment of the system.

5 Conclusions

In this paper we have proposed a rule-based focused crawler system that extracts high-level features from audio files using deep neural networks and searches for information on the web or local repositories. The system obfuscates retrieved data deemed illegal and improves its reference audio collection with data from illegal files through user feedback. The system is scalable and efficient in distinguishing legal files from illegal copies. Our results show a method for search engines to show only legal results to the end user while keeping information about potentially illegal files in the form of an abstract representation of the files. The system uses VGG-16 and ResNet-50 neural networks and transfer learning to extract representative feature vectors. Possible improvements to the approach include increased computational resources, extended pre-training and training epochs, distributed architectures, and using better GPUs. The system aims to find feature vectors that are specific enough given the available resources and imposed rules and other kind of information also for visualization [25–27]. It also addresses the issue of copyright violation by allowing the upload of content while automatically checking potentially harmful uploads.

Acknowledgments. We acknowledge financial support from the project PNRR MUR project PE0000013-FAIR.

References

1. Oppenheim, C.: Copyright in the electronic age. Office For Humanities Communication Publications-Oxford University Computing Services, pp. 97–112 (1997)
2. Sumanth, T., et al.: A new audio watermarking algorithm with DNA sequenced image embedded in spatial domain using pseudo-random locations. In: 2018 Second International Conference on Electronics, Communication and Aerospace Technology (ICECA), pp. 1813–1817. IEEE (2018)
3. Nair, Birajdar: Audio watermarking in wavelet domain using Fibonacci numbers. In: 2016 International Conference on Signal and Information Processing, pp. 1–5. IEEE (2016)
4. Kumar, et al.: A survey of web crawlers for information retrieval. Wiley Interdisc. Rev. Data Min. Knowl. Discov. **7**(6), e1218 (2017)
5. Bokhari, Hasan: Multimodal information retrieval: challenges and future trends. Int. J. Comput. Appl. **74**(14) (2013)
6. Moscato, V., Picariello, A., Rinaldi, A.M.: A recommendation strategy based on user behavior in digital ecosystems, pp. 25–32 (2010)
7. Van der Ende, et al.: Estimating displacement rates of copyrighted content in the EU (2014)
8. Sturm, et al.: Artificial intelligence and music: open questions of copyright law and engineering praxis. In: Arts, vol. 8, p. 115. Multidisciplinary Digital Publishing Institute (2019)
9. Liu, W., et al.: A survey of deep neural network architectures and their applications. Neurocomputing **234**, 11–26 (2017)
10. Wold, et al.: Content-based classification, search, and retrieval of audio. IEEE Multimed. **3**(3), 27–36 (1996)
11. Davis, Mermelstein: Comparison of parametric representations for monosyllabic word recognition in continuously spoken sentences. IEEE Trans. Acoust. Speech Signal Process. **28**(4), 357–366 (1980)
12. Capuano, A., Rinaldi, A.M., Russo, C.: An ontology-driven multimedia focused crawler based on linked open data and deep learning techniques. 1–22 (2019)
13. Knees, et al.: A music search engine built upon audio-based and web-based similarity measures. In: Proceedings of the 30th Annual International ACM SIGIR Conference on Research and Development in Information Retrieval, pp. 447–454 (2007)
14. Kim, C.: Content-based image copy detection. Signal Process. Image Commun. **18**(3), 169–184 (2003)
15. Dhar, Kim: Digital watermarking scheme based on Fast Fourier transformation for audio copyright protection. Int. J. Secur. Appl. **5**(2), 33–48 (2011)
16. Henaff, et al.: Unsupervised learning of sparse features for scalable audio classification. In: ISMIR, vol. 11, p. 2011. Citeseer (2011)
17. Guo, Li: Content-based audio classification and retrieval by support vector machines. IEEE Trans. Neural Netw. **14**(1), 209–215 (2003)
18. Rajanna, A.R., et al.: Deep neural networks: a case study for music genre classification. In: 2015 IEEE 14th International Conference on Machine Learning and Applications (ICMLA), pp. 655–660. IEEE (2015)
19. Safadi, et al.: Descriptor optimization for multimedia indexing and retrieval. Multimed. Tools Appl. **74**(4), 1267–1290 (2015)
20. Becker, S., et al.: Interpreting and explaining deep neural networks for classification of audio signals. arXiv preprint arXiv:1807.03418 (2018)

21. Mun, et al.: Deep neural network based learning and transferring mid-level audio features for acoustic scene classification. In: 2017 IEEE International Conference on Acoustics, Speech and Signal Processing (ICASSP), pp. 796–800. IEEE (2017)
22. Bogert, B.P.: The quefrency alanysis of time series for echoes; cepstrum, pseudo-autocovariance, cross-cepstrum and saphe cracking. In: Time Series Analysis, pp. 209–243 (1963)
23. He, et al.: Deep residual learning for image recognition. In: Proceedings of the IEEE Conference on Computer Vision and Pattern Recognition, pp. 770–778 (2016)
24. Sak, et al.: Long short-term memory recurrent neural network architectures for large scale acoustic modeling (2014)
25. Caldarola, E.G., Picariello, A., Rinaldi, A.M.: Big graph-based data visualization experiences: the wordnet case study, pp. 104–115 (2015)
26. Caldarola, E.G., Picariello, A., Rinaldi, A.M.: Experiences in wordnet visualization with labeled graph databases. Commun. Comput. Inf. Sci. **631**, 80–99 (2016)
27. Purificato, E., Rinaldi, A.M.: Multimedia and geographic data integration for cultural heritage information retrieval. Multimed. Tools Appl. **77**, 27447–27469 (2018)

A Social BPM Approach to Deal with Agility

Mehran Majidian Eidgahi[1]([✉])[iD], Sina Namaki Araghi[4][iD], Dominik Bork[2][iD], Anne-Marie Barthe-Delanoë[1][iD], Guillaume Mace-Ramete[3][iD], and Frederick Benaben[1][iD]

[1] Centre de Génie Industriel, Université Toulouse – Mines Albi, Campus Jarlard, Route de Teillet, 81000 Albi, France
{Mehran.Majidian,anne-marie.barthe,Frederick.BENABEN}@mines-albi.fr
[2] TU Wien, Vienna, Austria
dominik.bork@tuwien.ac.at
[3] Iterop - Dassault Systèmes, 1 bis rue Antoine Lavoisier, 31770 Colomiers, France
Guillaume.MACE-RAMETE@3ds.com
[4] Laboratoire Génie de Production de l'École Nationale d'Ingénieurs de Tarbes (LGP-INP-ENIT), Université de Toulouse, 65016 Tarbes, France
sina.namakiaraghi@enit.fr

Abstract. Business Process Management (BPM) takes care of the business process (BP) lifecycle using different technologies in organizations to provide value-added services or products for end-users. Although today's fast-changing business world poses vast variants of business processes (BPs) alongside uncertainty. This situation requires an agile BPM to manage, maintain, and execute different variants of a BP as well as deal with uncertainties and changes. One of the emphasises of agile BPM is involving stakeholders in the BP lifecycle, which requires a standard approach for all stakeholders to have quick and efficient access to the BP lifecycle to prevent problems like cultural resistance. In order to reach a standard approach, social BPM is an emerging concept that can help the easy and efficient involvement of stakeholders in the BP lifecycle. By inspiring form social BPM, this paper propose a new social media-based BPM platform to deal with different varieties of BP and uncertainties by integrating stakeholders in the BP lifecycle. While the platform eases communication, information exchange, and decision-making among stakeholders; it also eliminates the exchange between design-time and run-time while a change occurs by merging design-time and run-time.

Keywords: BPM · agile BPM · Social BPM · Business Process Management

1 Introduction

Business Process Management (BPM) deals with the business process (BP) lifecycle and technologies in organizations willing to drive their business based on the underlying processes they perform to provide services or products with value

R. Chbeir et al. (Eds.): MEDES 2023, CCIS 2022, pp. 18–31, 2024.
https://doi.org/10.1007/978-3-031-51643-6_2

for end-users [1,2,10,17]. While BPM can provide significant benefits, such as increased efficiency and productivity, it also faces a number of social and business problems that need to be addressed.

In terms of societal issues, today's businesses rely heavily on their ability to respond to changes that are not only foreseen, but also unexpected. For example, as organizations introduce new technologies, systems, and tools to their processes, they must ensure that those changes are integrated smoothly, reactively, and effectively. Failure to manage changes reactively and effectively can result in disruptions to processes, increased costs, and delays in achieving business objectives [4–7]. Another issue concerns employees who resist changes. This resistance is mostly because of the effort required to adapt to changes, and based on this, the employee finds changes to processes disruptive and unsettling. Organizations need to minimize the required effort in adapting to changes for employees by providing the necessary support and resources as well as involving them in process change [3,8]. As a result, BPM has long focused on agility in order to be ready for either foreseen or unpredicted uncertainties and changes.

Technology limitations were one of the first main challenges of BPM business issues. Lack of flexibility in tools and systems was an inhibiting factor in performing changes to BPs. Organizations had to rely on IT professionals to implement changes, which was often time-consuming and expensive [13]. BPM orchestrators were not exempt from this problem. BPM orchestrators are used by businesses to design, execute, and monitor BPs. Solutions to societal concerns were presented, but they required a BPM orchestrator to implement the solutions while ensuring that processes are efficient, effective, and responsive to changing business demands. Despite advancements in technology and the emergence of agile orchestrators, there are still challenges, such as the system's complexity, the need for robust governance, and interaction with other systems and applications which complicate the redesign stage of BP's lifecycle.

This research project attempts to answer the following research question in order to address the aforementioned challenges:

1. **How might tools and technology bring agility to BPs and BPM orchestrators?**

In the remaining of the paper, the basic concepts related to BPM, agile BPM and Social BPM are presented in Sect. 2. Moreover, in Sect. 3, a new social-based BPM platform is introduced followed by a use case in Sect. 4. Eventually, the conclusion of this paper is available in Sect. 5.

2 Background

2.1 BPM

Before digging more into the agile BPM idea, it is necessary to understand what BPM is and how it addresses BP-related issues. The idea of agility and its current state in the literature must then be understood. After all, it is possible to understand the correlation between BP's lifecycle and agility.

To handle all of the many lifecycles of BPs, BPM employs several methodologies and tools offered by various disciplines and technologies. Several phases of the BPM lifecycle are identified in the literature. Based on an examination of the many proposed phases and our best understanding, the BPM lifecycle may be divided into two primary looping phases that incorporate the phases presented in the literature: design-time and run-time [1,2,10,17]. Each has a definition, which may be found below:

- **Design-time:** It is the time in which BPs are identified, designed, reviewed, validated, and represented by business process models. The models are then set with technical information according to the business's objectives and goals. BPs redesign and adjustment occur in this time.
- **Run-time:** It is the time in which BPs are run based on the prepared business process model. Meanwhile, BPs are controlled and monitored. Basically the step where BPs are turned into workflows.

Figure 1 demonstrates how design-time and run-time embed the other BPM lifecycles mentioned in the literature.

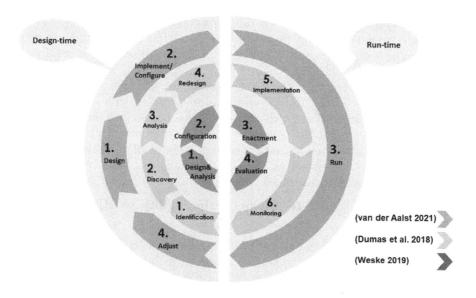

Fig. 1. Different BPM lifecycle proposals

In business process modeling language, many ways (Imperative, Declarative) are presented to handle BPs throughout their lifecyle. Each of these techniques has advantages and shortcomings that make it appropriate for certain types of BP (highly repetitive, highly dynamic) [14]. Responding to changes in traditional BPM techniques also necessitates a mass interaction between design-time and run-time, which takes time and effort. As a result, agile BPM is essential to make BPM capable of coping with various BP kinds and changes in a reactive and effective manner.

2.2 Agile BPM

Agility is a reactive and efficient process of discovering changes and deciding on and implementing a response strategy [5–7,18]. Agility has been explored and developed in a variety of industries, including manufacturing, software development, and corporate management. But, to the best of our knowledge, there are three major abstraction levels in agility: **discovering** a change [7], **deciding** a response strategy [11], and **implementing** the chosen strategy [7].

The recent abstraction levels remained the basics for agile BPM as well. Agile BPM is an approach to BPM that emphasizes flexibility, collaboration, and continuous improvement. It is a response to the increasing complexity and dynamism of today's business environment, which requires organizations to be more adaptable and responsive to changes. The agile BPM approach borrows principles and practices from Agile software development and applies them to BPM [16]. One of the key characteristics of agile BPM is the focus on collaboration and teamwork. Agile BPM emphasizes the involvement of all stakeholders in the BPM process, including business users, IT staff, and other relevant parties. This collaborative approach is designed to ensure that BPM processes are aligned with business needs and that they can be adapted quickly and efficiently in response to changing requirements [4]. Despite the fact that agile BPM emphasizes incorporating stakeholders in orchestrating BPs, or, to put it another way, socializing BPs, it remains a difficulty [9].

There are a variety of agile BPM solutions available, ranging from software tools and platforms to consulting services and training programs. Agile BPM solutions typically include features for collaboration and teamwork, enabling stakeholders from across the organization to participate in the BPM process. This collaboration is designed to ensure that BPM processes are aligned with business needs and that they can be adapted quickly and efficiently in response to changing requirements. Some of these agile BPM solutions are Iterop - Dassault Systèmes[1], Camunda BPM[2], Appian[3], AgilePoint NX[4], Bizagi BPM[5].

2.3 Social BPM

Social BPM is an approach to business process management that incorporates social media and collaboration technologies into the design, execution, and monitoring of BPs to facilitate stakeholders engagement. This approach enables organizations to improve communication, collaboration, and knowledge sharing among employees, customers, and partners [3,12]. Given the capabilities of

---

[1] https://iterop.3ds.com/.
[2] https://camunda.com.
[3] https://www.appian.com/.
[4] https://agilepoint.com/.
[5] https://www.bizagi.com/.

Social BPM, it can be seen as an effective solution to address the challenge of integrating social elements into agile BPM, particularly in the context of socializing BPs.

Several studies have explored the benefits and challenges of Social BPM. For example, Social BPM can lead to increased collaboration and process visibility, as well as improved process efficiency and flexibility. However, there are challenges such as privacy and security concerns, cultural resistance, and difficulty in measuring the impact of social media on business processes [15].

Some studies examined the role of social media in the design and execution of business processes. They found that social media can be used to support collaboration, knowledge sharing, and feedback gathering throughout the process lifecycle. However, the studies also identified challenges related to the integration of social media into existing process management systems [3].

Despite the fact that there are good contributions in BPM and agile BPM to cope with uncertainties and changes, they often target only one phase of the BPM lifecycle (design-time or run-time). As a result, the other phase remains an impediment to achieving the desired agility. Our proposal to address both phases in BP's lifecycle is to merge design-time and run-time. This proposal eliminates the need for design-time and run-time compromises, allowing the system to coordinate the BPs on the fly and respond to changes reactively and effectively. Employing such a concept makes coordinating the BPs easier by removing the complexity and allows stakeholders to participate in the design and orchestration of the BPs. Following the preparation of the potential of including stakeholders in the BP lifecycle, it is necessary to optimize this engagement by making it easier and more efficient. This entails establishing a simple and personalized access to all BPs relevant to a single person. Social BPM and social media can help with this by introducing thoughts and tools.

3   Proposal

A Social agile BPM tool has been designed to address the aforementioned challenges of agile BPM while also utilizing the advantages of Social BPM. The primary goal of this platform is to include the corresponding stakeholders of each BP in the design and execution of the BP on the fly. This platform is a proposal to combine the design-time and run-time in BPM and make it easier to respond to potential changes. By incorporating the stakeholders of each BP in the process, stakeholders are kept up to date on the present state of BP and are made available in case of required action to possible changes.

3.1   Features and Capabilities

Here the platform's key features and capabilities are listed. It is a text-based platform inspired by Twitter and Instagram. The platform includes the four concepts listed below to let stakeholders design and execute the BPs at the same time. The following are four main concepts and their definitions:

- **Post:** It is intended to define, initiate, and announce a new BP. Groups or individuals involved should be tagged here. It may also include keywords that provide further information about the BP.
- **Comment:** It is a way for users' communication to shape and run the BP by users.
- **Reaction:** It is a way of validating, rejecting, and deferring a post and assigned tasks.
- **Notification:** It is a way of either asking people to respond to a post or notifying them of a new post or task.

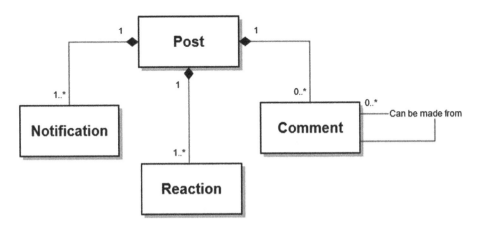

Fig. 2. Four main concepts of platform

Relations between concepts are depicted in Fig. 2. Figure 3 also depicts the metamodel of links between the notions of BPM design-time, BPM run-time, and the Social-Media (SM) platform concepts. In other words, it explains how platform concepts enable users to design and orchestrate BPs at the same time and merge design-time and run-time. The classes in the SM platform's package are previously discussed. The classes that may handle a BP are chosen at the maximum degree of granularity in the Design-time and Run-time packages. The Design-time package includes the Process class as a parent and the Event, Gateways, and Task classes as children, which would not exist without the Process class. There are three classes in the Run-time package: Execution Context, Token, and Participant. By completing each other, these three classes orchestrate the process.

Each user has a profile that includes information like supervisors, working department, and competency. These details aid in involving the appropriate users who can contribute to the design and orchestration of the BP. Any individual can also begin a new BP by creating a new post. Users who were involved in the process should be specified, and keywords related to the process should be marked in the post. Based on their user profile and the context of the process,

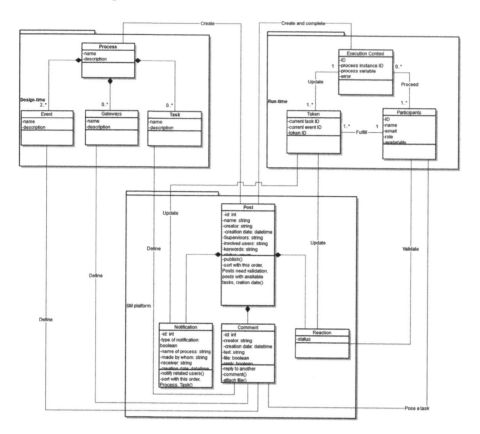

Fig. 3. Relationships between design-time, run-time and platform's concepts

involved persons are classified as creators, controllers, or contributors with the following definitions:

- **Creator:** It is the user who creates a new post.
- **Controller:** It is the user who has the authority to react to and validate the post as well as assign tasks to resources.
- **Contributor:** It is the user who can only track and comment on posts.

As soon as a user creates a new post, then the orchestrator notifies the potential controllers to react to the process. Acceptance, Refusal, or Postponement are all possible responses. A single rejection leads to the termination of the process, while unanimous acceptance from all controller users validates the procedure and distributes it to contributors. Next, to complete the process, users begin communicating under the post via comments. This communication might include posing or recommending a task to someone, as well as sub-objectives for the process. Figure 4 depicts the BPMN model of the process by which a post on the platform can be finished. The key goal in creating the User Interface (UI) was to give users fast access to all related posts as well as the ability to create new ones without losing the post's progress information. To do so, utilize the "Add an Objective" button at the top center of the UI's main page to create a new post, which is then followed by previously launched user-involved posts. Posts are ordered by the date they were made, but users may filter by the posts they created, controlled, or contributed to. The notification bar is located at the top right of the UI. The notification bar alerts users to new postings or tasks that have been assigned to them. By clicking on a notification that requires validation, a new window appears with the option to react to the notification. Figure 5 depicts the UI schema and concepts placement.

4   Case Study

A procedure for publishing a paper case study is described below to validate the platform's functionality. A sequence diagram of this case study depicting the concepts and various users is depicted in Fig. 6. This scenario may be thought of in two stages: before and after validation. The phase before validation is largely concerned with BPM design-time, whereas the phase after validation is concerned with BPM design-time BPM and run-time and demonstrates how they are merged.

In the stage before validation, a creator starts a new post to begin the process of publishing a paper, noting the persons involved and relevant keywords. After establishing a new page for the post, the system notifies controllers to validate the post. Each Controller authenticates the post, and the system then shares it with contributors.

Then in the stage after validation, contributors communicate with one another by commenting on the post about their experience with the conference. Controllers then assign two tasks: verifying the conference format and providing the first draft in two weeks. Considering the previously indicated task priority, the system will first alert the inventor to confirm the conference format. The system will then alert the next task, which is composing the first draft in two weeks, when the previous task has been validated by the inventor. Controllers get notifications after each task is completed. Meanwhile, contributors propose writing the paper on overleaf and inviting others. The system notifies the controllers of this suggestion and requests that it be validated. Controllers approve

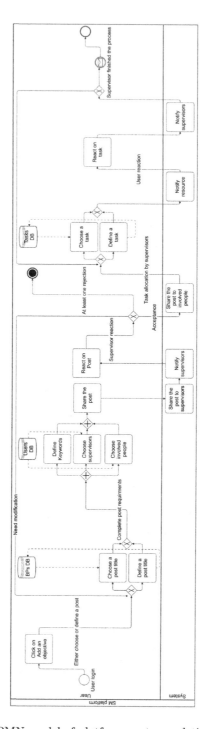

Fig. 4. BPMN model of platform post-completion process

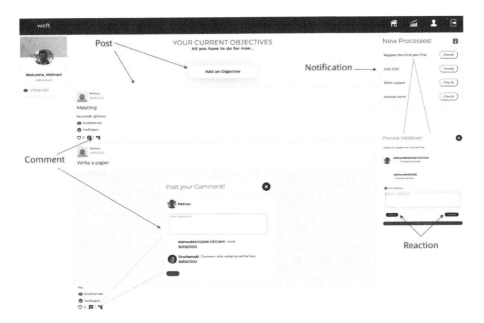

Fig. 5. Location of concepts on platform

the suggestion, and it is assigned as a new task. The system will inform the creator of this new task. By replying to the associated comment, the creator uploads the initial draft. When controllers are alerted of a completed task, they examine it and upload their feedback file by replying to the comment and asking the creator to change it. When alerted of a new revising job, the creator revises and uploads the revised version in the comments by answering. Controllers re-review and accept the article when it has been modified. Controllers request that the document be submitted by accepting it. Creator is notified of this new task and has submitted the paper. The controllers are notified, and after checking the procedure, they terminate the post. Following all, the end of the post is announced to all parties concerned.

The only persons who can contribute to the advancement of the process are involved in the post, as specified in the case study description. This capability makes the responsible persons constantly ready to participate in the process while also keeping them up to speed on the status of the process by notifying critical events and tracking the progress of the post clearly and simply.

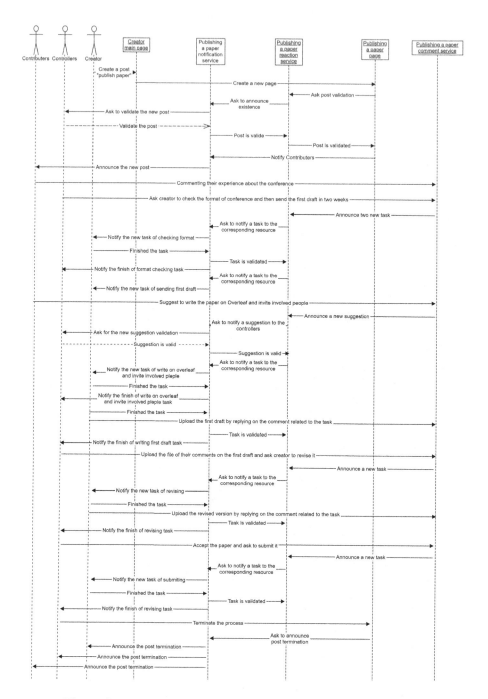

Fig. 6. A sequence diagram of case study scenario on the platform

5   Conclusion

Developing strategies that deal with uncertainties and adapt to changes efficiently is necessary to survive in a rapidly changing business. Developing strategies that deal with uncertainties and adapt to changes efficiently is necessary to survive in a rapidly changing business. Agility responds to this necessity by providing the capability of responding to changes reactively and efficiently. Considering this, agile BPM tries to bring agility to BPs through its related methodologies. Despite the agile BPM contributions to the phases of the BP lifecycle, the exchange between design-time and run-time while a change occurred still remained a difficulty. This difficulty became more important with the emphasis of agile BPM on involving stakeholders in the BP lifecycle because the exchange process is complex and requires specialized knowledge.

This paper proposes a novel platform that addresses the aforementioned difficulty by merging design-time and run-time. The next step was to effectively and efficiently involve stakeholders in the BP lifecycle, while each BP is related to a person or group of people and unrelated to others. After involving the related people in the corresponding BP, it's necessary to ensure that the involved people efficiently track the corresponding BP and stay updated. Social BPM facilitates involving related people and tracking the BPs by proposing technology and concepts that provide the foundation for cooperation, knowledge sharing, and decision-making. So the proposed social-based BPM platform was built using social BPM.

All stakeholders gather around on the platform to design and orchestrate the BPs simultaneously on the fly. Stakeholders involve in their corresponding BPs based on their profile information. By using the provided communication facilities and targeted notification, stakeholders design, orchestrate, and track the BPs. The absence of restrictions on the number of actors in each involved people category, the possibility to continue the process under the post without limitation, and regular updating of actors bring scalability to the platform to handle large and complex BPs.

As a perspective for future work, the platform may profit from artificial intelligence (AI) in many ways. The platform provides the possibility of stakeholders engagement in the BP lifecycle, while AI can optimize this engagement by assisting stakeholders. AI may be able to help in a variety of ways, including detecting similarities between previous and new BPs, suggesting tasks in design and orchestration, distributing tasks among resources, recommending the appropriate involved people, and using speech-to-text mining to add the ability of audio comments. These recent ways reduce effort and save time for stakeholders in designing and orchestrating BPs. So stakeholders will have more potential to contribute to more BPs or more engagement in the current ones.

References

1. van der Aalst, W.M.P.: Business process management: a comprehensive survey. Int. Scholarly Res. Not. **2013** (2013)
2. van der Aalst, W.M.P., van Hee, K.M.: Workflow Management: Models, Methods, and Systems. Cooperative Information Systems, MIT Press, Cambridge (2002)
3. Ariouat, H., Hanachi, C., Andonoff, E., Bénaben, F.: A conceptual framework for social business process management. In: Zanni-Merk, C., Frydman, C.S., Toro, C., Hicks, Y., Howlett, R.J., Jain, L.C. (eds.) Knowledge-Based and Intelligent Information & Engineering Systems: Proceedings of the 21st International Conference KES-2017, Marseille, France, 6–8 September 2017. Procedia Computer Science, vol. 112, pp. 703–712. Elsevier (2017). https://doi.org/10.1016/j.procs.2017.08.151
4. Badakhshan, P., Conboy, K., Grisold, T., vom Brocke, J.: Agile business process management: a systematic literature review and an integrated framework. Bus. Process. Manag. J. **26**(6), 1505–1523 (2020). https://doi.org/10.1108/BPMJ-12-2018-0347
5. Barthe-Delanoë, A.M., Montarnal, A., Truptil, S., Benaben, F., Pingaud, H.: Towards the agility of collaborative workflows through an event driven approach. Int. J. Disaster Risk Reduction **28**, 214–224 (2018). https://doi.org/10.1016/j.ijdrr.2018.02.029. https://hal-mines-albi.archives-ouvertes.fr/hal-01724575
6. Barthe-Delanoë, A., Truptil, S., Bénaben, F., Pingaud, H.: Event-driven agility of interoperability during the run-time of collaborative processes. Decis. Support Syst. **59**, 171–179 (2014). https://doi.org/10.1016/j.dss.2013.11.005
7. Bénaben, F., Mu, W., Boissel-Dallier, N., Barthe-Delanoë, A., Zribi, S., Pingaud, H.: Supporting interoperability of collaborative networks through engineering of a service-based mediation information system (MISE 2.0). Enterp. Inf. Syst. **9**(5–6), 556–582 (2015). https://doi.org/10.1080/17517575.2014.928949
8. vom Brocke, J., Rosemann, M. (eds.): Handbook on Business Process Management 2, Strategic Alignment, Governance, People and Culture, 2nd edn. International Handbooks on Information Systems. Springer, Cham (2015). https://doi.org/10.1007/978-3-642-45103-4
9. Bruno, G., et al.: Key challenges for enabling agile BPM with social software. J. Softw. Maintenance Res. Pract. **23**(4), 297–326 (2011). https://doi.org/10.1002/smr.523
10. Dumas, M., Rosa, M.L., Mendling, J., Reijers, H.A.: Fundamentals of Business Process Management, 2nd edn. Springer, Cham (2018). https://doi.org/10.1007/978-3-662-56509-4
11. Gong, Y., Janssen, M.: Agent-based simulation for evaluating flexible and agile business processes: separating knowledge rules, process rules and information resources. In: Barjis, J. (ed.) EOMAS 2010. LNBIP, vol. 63, pp. 41–58. Springer, Heidelberg (2010). https://doi.org/10.1007/978-3-642-15723-3_4
12. Kocbek, M., Jošt, G., Polančič, G.: Introduction to social business process management. In: Uden, L., Heričko, M., Ting, I.-H. (eds.) KMO 2015. LNBIP, vol. 224, pp. 425–437. Springer, Cham (2015). https://doi.org/10.1007/978-3-319-21009-4_33
13. Lacity, M.C., Willcocks, L.P.: An empirical investigation of information technology sourcing practices: lessons from experience. MIS Q. **22**(3), 363–408 (1998). https://misq.org/an-empirical-investigation-of-information-technology-sourcing-practices-lessons-from-experience.html

14. Pichler, P., Weber, B., Zugal, S., Pinggera, J., Mendling, J., Reijers, H.A.: Imperative versus declarative process modeling languages: an empirical investigation. In: Daniel, F., Barkaoui, K., Dustdar, S. (eds.) BPM 2011. LNBIP, vol. 99, pp. 383–394. Springer, Heidelberg (2012). https://doi.org/10.1007/978-3-642-28108-2_37

15. Prodanova, J., Looy, A.V.: How beneficial is social media for business process management? A systematic literature review. IEEE Access **7**, 39583–39599 (2019). https://doi.org/10.1109/ACCESS.2019.2903983

16. Thiemich, C., Puhlmann, F.: An agile BPM project methodology. In: Daniel, F., Wang, J., Weber, B. (eds.) BPM 2013. LNCS, vol. 8094, pp. 291–306. Springer, Heidelberg (2013). https://doi.org/10.1007/978-3-642-40176-3_25

17. Weske, M.: Business Process Management - Concepts, Languages, Architectures, 2nd edn. Springer, Cham (2012). https://doi.org/10.1007/978-3-642-28616-2

18. Zhang, D.: Web services composition for process management in e-business. J. Comput. Inf. Syst. **45**(2), 83–91 (2005). https://doi.org/10.1080/08874417.2005.11645834. https://www.tandfonline.com/doi/abs/10.1080/08874417.2005.11645834

Exploring the Benefits of Blockchain-Powered Metadata Catalogs in Data Mesh Architecture

Anton Dolhopolov[✉], Arnaud Castelltort, and Anne Laurent

LIRMM, Univ. Montpellier, CNRS, Montpellier, France
{anton.dolhopolov,arnaud.castelltort,anne.laurent}@lirmm.fr

Abstract. The Data Mesh architecture is gaining popularity as a new approach to data management within modern organizations. A key component of this architecture is the metadata catalog, which provides a centralized repository for documenting and discovering data products across different teams. However, maintaining an accurate and secure catalog in the context of this architecture is challenging. In this paper, we explore the benefits of using blockchain technology to power the metadata catalog in a Data Mesh architecture. Indeed, blockchain provides a decentralized and immutable ledger that can help to ensure the accuracy and consistency of metadata across different teams. It provides a secure and transparent way of tracking changes and access to the metadata. We discuss the potential advantages of using blockchain for metadata catalog, including data security, data provenance, and data ownership. We also examine the potential challenges and limitations of using blockchain technology in the context of Data Mesh architecture. Overall, we argue that blockchain-powered metadata catalogs have the potential to enhance the efficiency and reliability of data management in a Data Mesh.

Keywords: Metadata · Blockchain · Data Mesh · Data Governance

1 Introduction

Over the last 30 years research and industry came up with different approaches of building analytical systems. *Data warehouse* [8] was the first paradigm of its kind, tailored to analyzing mainly the structural data: relational databases, XML files, tabular data. It focuses on calculating statistical information over large amounts of data and then constructing multidimensional cubes. Then *slice-and-dice* or *drill-down* operations are used for fast navigation over computed values.

Data lake [11] was the second paradigm that went further into analyzing all kinds of data: structured, semi-structured, and unstructured. But the most significant change was collecting raw data, without preliminary schema enforcement. It is known as *schema-on-read*: when the final shape of data is determined only at the analysis phase, not before storing it. It gives a way to apply various types of analyses at different times, potentially extracting distinct insights.

R. Chbeir et al. (Eds.): MEDES 2023, CCIS 2022, pp. 32–40, 2024.
https://doi.org/10.1007/978-3-031-51643-6_3

Data mesh [3] is the most recent paradigm, which goes further into changing the way modern data platforms are built. Previous generations focused on creating big data monoliths, where separated teams work on disjoint parts of a global IT system: operational applications on one side, and analytical data platform on another. The mesh stipulates the organizational change towards decentralization in the first place and adapts bounded business contexts for building both operational and analytical products by joint teams of engineers.

The key element of building any kind of data platform is a metadata management system [14]. It is necessary for preventing the formation of *data swamps*, which can easily happen when collecting large amounts of data. Most of the time, metadata management involves dealing with data cataloging (necessary for querying and discovery), data schemes, lineage, quality rules definition, technical and semantical information, etc. It can also integrate user activity tracking, security and privacy rules, and other policies.

Blockchains are well suited for developing solutions aimed at privacy, audibility, tamper-proof storage, and trust verification. It makes the technology applicable in the industries like finance, healthcare, or Internet-of-Things (IoT) [1]. Some recent research also attempted to implement metadata management by using the blockchain. In [4,9] authors use it for provenance metadata registration, sensitive data access verification, and tracking. [12] proposes methods for preventing information leakage through metadata sharing. [10] considers the Hadoop Distributed File System (HDFS) platform environment and moves the central metadata node to a distributed network, while [5] offers a general model for deploying metadata using the blockchain.

In this paper, we review the Data Mesh architecture and point out the problems of centralized metadata systems. We compare the decentralization options to the properties of a blockchain solution and show, that the latter offers a range of benefits for implementing the catalog, but brings its own set of constraints.

2   Data Mesh Application for Inter-organizational Work

2.1   Data Mesh Definition

Data Mesh helps to develop and deploy new services and products without facing administrative and communication delays. It proclaims the idea of data platform decentralization, just like microservice architecture is used for the application platform. The core principles adapt a domain-driven design around data and code, not just a single functional code part. In [3] authors define the following principles: 1) distributed data domains; 2) data-as-a-product; 3) self-serve infrastructure platform; 4) federated computational governance.

2.2   Running Example

To illustrate the mesh, we show a running example of a video-service company that comprises Human Resources, Sales, and Studio Production departments which are equivalent to different domains. Figure 1 shows its main components. For simplification, we assume that each team manages a single data domain.

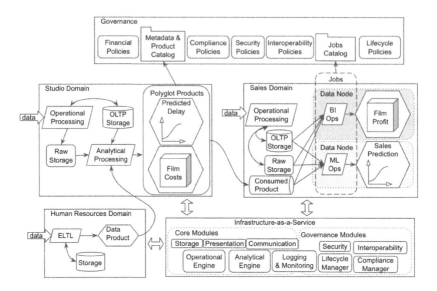

Fig. 1. Data mesh running example architecture overview.

In this example, the Studio team is occupied with both transactional and analytical online processing (OLTP and OLAP). The domain output can be one or more polyglot data products, that is actual or derived data (e.g. IoT events, business intelligence cubes, machine learning models) published for use by any other domain or the end user.

Since there are a lot of products produced by a number of teams, it is a good practice to register them in the Product (data) Catalog alongside metadata describing their owner, purpose, lineage, mode of use, etc. In our case, the product is consumed by the Sales team, which also operates its own OLTP and OLAP.

By consuming Studio reports, Sales will improve the delivered value from data and potentially enhance the number of published products. Because different teams may apply similar and configurable computation over data, we could also have a Jobs (processing) Catalog that assembles common data operations and helps to create new products.

The common infrastructure platform provides another abstraction layer over the computing platform. It helps to put in place monitoring and automatic control execution on all domains at once, to provide service communication interoperability and avoid resource provisioning overhead when working with different technological stacks. In modern days, cloud providers (e.g. Microsoft Azure, Amazon Web Services) can be seen as good candidates for such a platform.

The federated computational governance is necessary for well-coordinated work and automated enforcement of mesh policies. Here governance is a collection of policies, standards, objectives, metrics, and roles aimed to maximize the value of data. Metadata management is one of its key elements. Product Catalog and Jobs Catalog can be seen as management system replacements. The policies can state the requirement of registering all the necessary information about the code and data products to the catalogs for improving the platform.

2.3   Implementing Inter-organizational Collaboration

Distributed domains architecture opens a way for cross-organizational interaction when data from a company can be used by another one. Data mesh supports the implementation of business processes for storing and exchanging data in a decentralized environment with loosely connected collaborating domains or even organizations. In our scenario, we could have dozens of Studio domains (e.g. fiction, documentary, educational) that are dedicated to the production of different video content. In fact, each Studio could operate independently. But on the scale of large enterprises, connecting a big number of such independent domains created around the bounded business context will form a global data mesh.

Next, we review the challenges of implementing metadata systems.

3   Challenges of Metadata Management in Data Mesh

Previously we saw the core principles of the data mesh architecture. Although it promises to improve the performance of large enterprises, it also brings a set of challenges necessary to resolve.

3.1   Metadata Catalog as a Governance Machinery

The main aspect of coordinating the distributed environment is well-established governance. Generally, governance has a lot of important elements, but we focus on metadata management further.

Metadata systems help users to discover, understand, and use data produced by the organization. In our previous example, Sales and Studio teams are responsible for creating and managing the data products, including their metadata. But in the literature [2,6,7,15,16], such systems are built as a centralized repository that contains information on all the data available in the platform. A single metadata repository implies governance centralization with issues like a single point of failure (SPoF) [10], single source of truth (SSoT) [9], or product upgrade delays [13]. It becomes even more difficult to operate in a cross-organization environment since it is not clear who and how owns and operates such catalogs.

3.2   Metadata Catalog Decentralization Requirements

Metadata catalog decentralization is a solution that removes the SPoF by tolerating domain failures. But it also must conform to a list of requirements.

First, the different domains must be interoperable and implement common taxonomies, definitions, ontologies, etc. Otherwise, it will add unnecessary complexity and cause operating miscomprehension.

Second, we should have ways to verify, audit, and define the rules for sensitive (meta)data access. Immutable data structures are essential in these scenarios. In highly regulated fields (e.g. finance) it is of great importance to have security methods for preventing and prosecuting illegal activities. In an inter-organization collaboration, the verification process also helps to handle issues related to SSoT.

Third, as with the evolutionary nature of enterprise processes, we should be able to upgrade the active policies in place without interrupting the whole system. The situation when all domain teams declare and start using the new system rules is highly unlikely and error-prone. Thus, the system upgrade to a new set of rules should be automatic and without human intervention.

Next, we describe our research work for implementing these requirements.

4   Research Contribution

In Sect. 2, we saw how the data mesh could be used for cross-organization projects, and in Sect. 3 we saw some challenges associated with it. In this section, we provide our research contribution to solving these issues.

First, we make a renewed view of data mesh governance options by defining 3 formal types of metadata catalogs: centralized, distributed, and decentralized.

Second, we show how blockchain technology fulfills the requirements for building a distributed Type II metadata catalog and describe its application with our updated, blockchain-based running example.

The section concludes with some new challenges and potential solutions.

4.1   Defining the Data Mesh Governance Types

On one side, centralized governance dictates how each domain should function, which defeats the goals of data mesh in the first place. On the other side, interoperability is a big challenge of complete decentralization. In Fig. 2, we define the data mesh governance scale that helps to understand better how we can configure and build our metadata catalog. The horizontal axis shows the proposed deployment modes ranging from centralization (left) to decentralization (right).

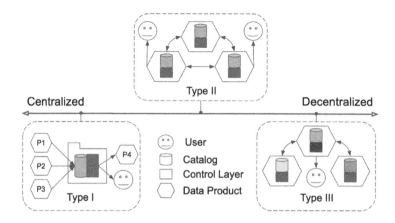

Fig. 2. Data Mesh Governance Scale

Type I - Centralized Metadata Catalog. The centralized catalog implies that a set of all metadata records $m_1, ...m_n = M$ is stored in a single repository C. Upon the release of a data product p_x, the new metadata record m_x is pushed to the repository in order to make the product discoverable and accessible by other domains. To have control over the records, a repository operator can define the visibility map function $v : (u, m) \rightarrow \{1, 0\}$, and the access function $a : (u, m) \rightarrow \{Read, Write, Delete\}$ that are associated with user profiles U.

In total, metadata catalog is defined as $C = \{P, M, U, d_m, v_m, a_m\}$, where:

- P is a set of data products
- M is a set of metadata records
- U is a set of catalog users
- $d_m : P \rightarrow M$ is a function returning the metadata of a product (description)
- $v_m^u : U \times M \rightarrow \{1, 0\}$ is a function returning a visibility map for pairs (u, m)
- $a_m^u : U \times M \rightarrow \{Read, Write, Delete\}$ is a function returning a permissions map for pairs (u, m).

Type II - Distributed Metadata Catalog. The middle state between Type I and Type III is a distributed catalog. There is no central repository and each domain d hosts a complete copy r of the metadata catalog on a dedicated metadata node n which resolves the SPoF problem. Meanwhile, there must be a peer-to-peer (P2P) system that keeps the data in sync across all nodes and the contracts or techniques T defined for enforcing the unified behavior B to be followed by all participants.

The shared catalog is $C = \{P, M, U, B, D, R, N, T, d_m, v_m, a_m, t_b, s_r\}$, where:

- D is a set of data domains
- B is a set of unified governing policies (behaviors)
- R is a set of metadata catalog replicas
- N is a set of metadata nodes that host the replicas
- T is a set of techniques (contracts) that enforce the policies
- $t_b : D \times N \times B \rightarrow T$ is a function returning a contract map for triples (d, n, b)
- $s_r : R \times R \rightarrow \{1, 0\}$ is a function returning the consistency state map for any two given replicas (synchronization state).

Type III - Decentralized Metadata Catalog. The decentralized catalog is the case where each domain (or a subset of domains) uses different technologies and policies for managing its catalogs. Each team independently owns and serves the (meta)data products, and in order to provide discoverability and querying one must interlink its metadata with other domain's metadata. It can be the case that n given domains can configure a shared distributed catalog, but also have their own private catalogs in parallel.

Therefore, the metadata catalog $\mathcal{C}$ is defined as:

- $\mathcal{C} = \bigcup_{i=1,n_d} C_i$ with C_i being the catalog associated with $D_i \subset \mathcal{D}$ and $D_i \neq \emptyset$
- $\mathcal{D} = \bigcup_{j=1,n_d} d_j$ is a set of all data domains
- $l : M \times M \rightarrow \{1, 0\}$ is a function establishing the link presence or absence between a pair of metadata records.

4.2 Blockchain-Powered Type II Metadata Catalog

Metadata catalog distribution comes with requirements such as consistency, immutability, auditing, versioning, and access control. Distributed databases have been a subject of research and industrial use for a long time. But their main drawback is a lack of trust verification methods in a multi-party environment.

At the same time, blockchain research demonstrates that we can use it within a virtual organization (VO) for implementing a joint project [4] or data exchange process with traceability and accountability [9]. For instance, VO can be formed by distributed data domains for inter-organizational collaboration.

Benefits of Using Blockchain. Blockchains possess a number of characteristics that fit the needs for implementing the Type II metadata catalog.

Blockchain benefits from the immutable append-only ledger that can store the metadata records M permanently and gives records version history. The blocks hashing function adds a trust component that is essential for verification and auditing. The network nodes can hold a ledger copy with all the records. It can be seen as equal to metadata nodes N that store the replicas R.

The implementation of smart contracts enforces the automatic execution of the globally defined, unified governing policies (a set of techniques T).

The distributed consensus algorithm that guarantees ledger synchronization is a form of consistency function s_r. Upon the business process evolution, it also provides a way to make an automatic upgrade to the new set of policies B'.

Blockchains can also be classified as public or private. Public ones make no assumption about the identities of the network users meaning that all participants are anonymous and equal: they have the same rights and can perform the same functions. It makes the network more vulnerable to malicious activities.

By contrast, private blockchain gives more control over the users. The bad actors can be identified and access can be denied since the identities are known in advance. Therefore, it is more favorable compared to a public one as it supports the implementation of visibility and access functions (v_m^u and a_m^u).

Blockchain Catalog Running Example. Our new diagram of the distributed metadata catalog is shown in Fig. 3. It runs on a permission-based (private) blockchain network of independent domain nodes that form a shared metadata mesh. A (domain) metadata node can be seen as the most granular unit of catalog deployment. This unit is defined as a part of the data infrastructure code. In some sense, metadata is equivalent to the special form of a data product. In our running example, a Studio domain can have multiple data nodes where each node can serve one or more polyglot data products. The Studio team can run multiple data nodes and metadata nodes simultaneously.

When a new product is released or updated, its metadata has to be registered in the catalog. Upon a data node start-up, a special middleware can verify whether the hosted product metadata is present and run the corresponding smart contract if necessary. If a new record is added, it will be replicated in the network following the distributed consensus algorithm.

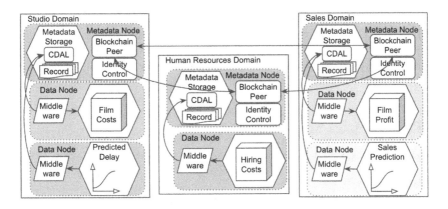

Fig. 3. Blockchain-based Type II metadata catalog running example overview.

Blockchain Peer is an application abstraction responsible for peer-to-peer communication, data synchronization, and consensus. Identity Control abstract defines the participants, roles, and permissions used to manage access to the chain data. It might be useful when access to the published metadata has to be limited, for instance, inter-organization access would be more restrictive rather than intra-organization. Metadata Storage is the medium of storage, the actual blockchain, replicated across all the network nodes. It has a Chain Data Access Layer (CDAL) that is responsible for writing and reading the data to the chain. It is based on a smart contract code. Records in the chain represent the data products metadata: product name, location, owner, format, access flow, etc.

Challenges of Using Blockchain. Although the blockchain unlocks a number of benefits, it comes with challenges. The append-only ledger keeps the whole history of each metadata record. Therefore, it raises two obvious concerns: querying performance and storage capacity.

First, in a catalog with a lot of similar or nearly identical records, it can result in bad querying performance since the system has to process a larger amount of data compared to the case of storing only the latest record versions.

Second, big number of data products and the duplication of metadata records can result in the exponential growth of the catalog size. It may become especially problematic when a new node joins the mesh and has to download all records.

Some potential solutions for these issues are to use the pruned nodes for reducing the storage by keeping the latest ledger segments and to build the "world state" database, as in Hyperledger Fabric, for improving querying performance.

5 Conclusions and Further Research

In our proposal, we demonstrated the main elements of data mesh architecture and distributed metadata catalog. We explored the theoretical benefits of doing the distribution through a private permission-based blockchain network.

Our further work will focus on implementing the proposed Type II block-chain-based architecture and its comparison to other solutions for the outlined challenges. Particularly, we will investigate a construction process of a Type III metadata catalog on top of property graph technologies by estimating the discoverability and querying issues caused by partitioning the underlying graph.

References

1. Casino, F., Dasaklis, T.K., Patsakis, C.: A systematic literature review of block-chain-based applications: current status, classification and open issues. Telemat. Inform. (2019)
2. Chessell, M., Jones, N.L., Limburn, J., Radley, D., Shan, K.: Designing and operating a data reservoir. In: IBM Redbooks (2015)
3. Dehghani, Z.: Data Mesh: Delivering Data-Driven Value at Scale. O'Reilly (2022)
4. Demichev, A., Kryukov, A., Prikhodko, N.: The approach to managing provenance metadata and data access rights in distributed storage using the hyperledger blockchain platform. In: Ivannikov Ispras Open Conference. IEEE (2018)
5. García-Barriocanal, E., Sánchez-Alonso, S., Sicilia, M.-A.: Deploying metadata on blockchain technologies. In: Garoufallou, E., Virkus, S., Siatri, R., Koutsomiha, D. (eds.) MTSR 2017. CCIS, vol. 755, pp. 38–49. Springer, Cham (2017). https://doi.org/10.1007/978-3-319-70863-8_4
6. Hai, R., Geisler, S., Quix, C.: Constance: an intelligent data lake system. In: Proceedings of the 2016 International Conference on Management of Data (2016)
7. Halevy, A.Y., et al.: Managing Google's data lake: an overview of the goods system. IEEE Data Eng. Bull. **39**(3), 5–14 (2016)
8. Inmon, W., Strauss, D., Neushloss, G.: DW 2.0: The Architecture for the Next Generation of Data Warehousing. Elsevier (2010)
9. Koscina, M., Manset, D., Negri-Ribalta, C., Perez, O.: Enabling trust in healthcare data exchange with a federated blockchain-based architecture. In: International Conference on Web Intelligence-Companion Volume (2019)
10. Kumar, D.S., Rahman, M.A.: Simplified HDFS architecture with blockchain distribution of metadata. Int. J. Appl. Eng. Res. (2017)
11. Laurent, A., Laurent, D., Madera, C.: Data Lakes, Chapter 1, Introduction to Data Lakes: Definitions and Discussions, vol. 2. Wiley (2020)
12. Liu, L., Li, X., Au, M.H., Fan, Z., Meng, X.: Metadata privacy preservation for blockchain-based healthcare systems. In: Bhattacharya, A., et al. (eds.) DASFAA 2022. LNCS, vol. 13245, pp. 404–412. Springer, Cham (2022). https://doi.org/10.1007/978-3-031-00123-9_33
13. Majchrzak, J., Balnojan, S., Siwiak, M., Sieraczkiewicz, M.: Data Mesh in Action. Manning Publishing (2022)
14. Sawadogo, P., Darmont, J.: On data lake architectures and metadata management. J. Intell. Inf. Syst. **56**(1), 97–120 (2021)
15. Sawadogo, P.N., Darmont, J., Noûs, C.: Joint management and analysis of textual documents and tabular data within the AUDAL data lake. In: Bellatreche, L., Dumas, M., Karras, P., Matulevičius, R. (eds.) ADBIS 2021. LNCS, vol. 12843, pp. 88–101. Springer, Cham (2021). https://doi.org/10.1007/978-3-030-82472-3_8
16. Zhao, Y.: Metadata management for data lake governance. Ph.D. thesis, Univ. Toulouse 1 (2021)

Preventing Data-Security Breaches
and Patient-Safety Risks
in Cross-Blockchain e-Healthcare Systems

Aleksandr Kormiltsyn[1]([✉]), Alex Norta[2,3], Sanam Nisar[4], and Vimal Dwivedi[4]

[1] Department of Software Science, Tallinn University of Technology, Tallinn, Estonia
alexandrkormiltsyn@gmail.com
[2] Tallinn University, Tallinn, Estonia
alex.norta.phd@ieee.org
[3] Dymaxion OÜ, Tallinn, Estonia
[4] University of Tartu, Tartu, Estonia
sanisa@taltech.ee

Abstract. Blockchain-based person-centric services aim to solve main healthcare problems such as high costs and low service availability. The complex architecture of integrated blockchain systems results in additional risks related to personal data misuse and patient safety. Self-sovereign identity (SSI) provides security for health data in blockchain-based systems by giving individuals control over the information they use to prove who they are. However, in cross-organizational healthcare processes, humans and smart devices collect and share health data that require strong authentication mechanisms. In this research, we integrate multi-factor self-sovereign identity authentication (MFSSIA) into healthcare services to enable secure cross-blockchain communication between human and non-human stakeholders. The solution focuses on risks for patient safety and personal data misuse and proposes a secure data exchange for different blockchain-based healthcare systems without any central authority.

Keywords: Blockchain · multi-factor · identity · authentication · self-sovereign · smart contract · legal relevance · e-health · security risks · patient safety

1 Introduction

In our previous research [9,10,12], we propose blockchain as a technology that improves person-centric healthcare processes and solves problems in healthcare, such as high costs and low service availability. At the same time, the proposed solution does not include a mechanism to prevent data security- and patient-safety risks. Healthcare data is sensitive, and personal-data legal restrictions are based on data-processing logic, such as the general data protection regulation

(GDPR[1]). Person-centric healthcare is based on cross-organizational processes that involve different organizations and stakeholders supporting the person in the healthcare service provision using personal data for their benefit. The main principle of personal health records (PHR) infers a person is the author and owner of his/her medical data that can be shared with other individuals, including healthcare professionals, or automated clinical decision-support services.

In [25], the authors state an increase in adapting e-health leads to patient safety- and health-data misuse risks that are not well known. Research [24] states that self-sovereign identity (SSI) solutions can counter patient information privacy and security threats in healthcare systems. Health-data misuse in e-health systems results, e.g., in health risks link to the inappropriate usage of medications [28]. Patient safety is a critical component of the quality of healthcare [20] and aims to prevent and reduce risks, errors, and harm that occur to patients while providing healthcare [7]. As the healthcare domain greatly impacts the physical person's health, it is not enough to focus only on data-security risks in blockchain-based systems.

Self-sovereign identity (SSI) reduces privacy data risks in e-health systems, and blockchain technology supports person-centric healthcare services. However, there is a state-of-the-art gap in defining security and conflict-resolution methods for person-centric cross-organizational processes in e-health, where personal data is shared between different human- and non-human agents. In this paper, we focus on both security- and patient safety risks in blockchain-based healthcare systems. The main research question is how to specify cross-organizational processes for handling PHR and electronic health records (EHR) dynamically and securely in distributed patient-centric systems. The explanation of EHR assumes a creation and maintenance by medical professionals. To establish a separation of concerns, we deduce the following sub-questions to answer the main one. What is the smart-contract language that enables the data-sharing process to support privacy? After defining the cross-organizational smart contracting data process to enable data sharing in decentralized e-health, we focus on security. What is the security component of the e-health cross-organizational data-sharing process to prevent data-security risks? We propose using a trustful and decentralized authentication mechanism such as the one defined in [19], multi-factor self-sovereign identity authentication (MFSSIA) for interoperability in the cross-organizational processes between different blockchain-based healthcare systems. MFSSIA is important for establishing trust between systems, devices, organizations, and humans for the emerging machine-to-everything (M2X) economy [13]. Thus, the M2X Economy results from interactions, transactions, collaborations, and business enactments among humans, autonomous and cooperative smart devices, software agents, and physical systems. The corresponding ecosystem is formed by automated, globally-available, heterogeneous socio-technical e-governance systems with loosely coupled, P2P-resembling network structures. It is characterized by its dynamic, continuously changing, interoperable, open,

---

[1] https://gdpr-info.eu/.

and distributed nature. Thereby, the M2X Economy employs concepts such as cyber-physical systems, the Internet of Things, and wireless sensor networks.

The remainder of the paper is structured as follows. Section 2 introduces a running case and background preliminaries. Next, Sect. 3 defines the cross-organizational data-sharing process. Next, Sect. 4 focuses on the security component and integration of MFSSIA into the data-sharing process. In Sect. 5, we present and discuss a proof-of-concept prototype. Finally, Sect. 6 ends this paper with conclusions and future work.

2 Running Case and Preliminaries

In this section, we provide the essential information that helps the reader to better understand the context of our research. Section 2.1 presents a running case illustrating the privacy conflict example. Next, Sect. 2.2 explains the base concepts used in the research.

2.1 Running Case

Figure 1 describes the running case in the cancer-prevention domain. While the most commonly used clinical outcome measures by physiotherapists are pain, range of motion, and strength, the patient-goal domains are identified as physical activity, quality of the workplace, and sleep. Such a difference is explained by the fact that The Patient Specific Functional Scale [29] comparison between individuals is difficult and thus, patient-goal domains cannot be measured. Suppose a patient monitors himself at home with autonomous devices such as a smartwatch and components of a smart home such as air- and water quality sensors, these devices collect data about a patient's activities and ecological environment as the devices communicate with each other sharing the data.

This data is collected continuously, enabling a feedback loop for a healthcare professional who monitors the patient. In parallel, during the patient visit to a doctor, the latter creates EHR data that include laboratory test results and anamnesis. Both healthcare professionals and a doctor have access to EHR. After treatment is performed, a healthcare specialist and general practitioner send medical reports to the insurance provider requesting claims. The medical reports differ because the data available for the healthcare professional includes PHR and continuous feedback from the patient. This improves the health-context understanding and results in personalized care the healthcare professional provides. For the doctor, only EHR is available and thus, his focus is on employing conventional Western allopathic school medicine for treatment that relies primarily on administering medications.

Both general practitioners and healthcare professionals share collected medical data to request compensation from the insurance provider. The latter can misuse shared health data according to business needs that violates the patient's privacy. Such a gap complicates the usage of new cross-organizational medical services based on the PHR processing and a feedback loop that can potentially improve the current healthcare system. Feedback loop communications between patients and specialists are an iterative process where patient feedback provides input for healthcare professional decisions.

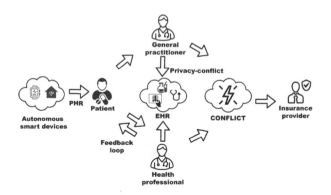

Fig. 1. Conflicts and security risks in the EHR and PHR processing.

The patient faces privacy conflicts as his data can be stolen due to a lack of security in either wearables, or different applications. After the patient shares this PHR data with the family doctor, the latter can use the data in the internal processes of the healthcare provider, e.g., for reporting, statistics, and research. These processes may include external stakeholders such as the national statistics department, private research companies, or private companies specializing in reporting services. As such, processes are not transparent for the patient, and as a consequence, inappropriate use of PHR data may occur.

In our paper, we focus on conflicts when integrating PHR and EHR. First, privacy conflicts occur when the patient collects data during home monitoring. The use of wearable devices and PHR systems that store collected data can be vulnerable to stealing data from unauthorized persons. A privacy conflict occurs after PHR is shared with a family doctor, integrated with EHR, and then shared by the doctor with external stakeholders. The internal processes of healthcare providers are not transparent to the patient and result in an inappropriate use of the patient's information.

2.2   Preliminaries

We assume that the decentralized patient-centric e-health process runs on a blockchain system, which is a distributed ledger that allows participants to write and update records on a ledger while cryptography ensures the records stored remain the same once added [26]. Records are added to the ledger as hashed transactions and grouped in blocks. Each block is cryptographically linked to the next block, and the records in the ledger are immutable. Smart contracts are computer programs supported by blockchain technologies [17], stored and executed on blockchain nodes. According to [2], common blockchain platforms are Ethereum[2], Cardano[3], Polkadot[4], etc.

In a blockchain-based e-health system, secure data sharing may be enabled by a system such as MFSSIA [19] that offers self-sovereign, configurable multi-challenge set identity authentications managed with means of smart-contract blockchain technologies for devices, organizations, systems, and humans.

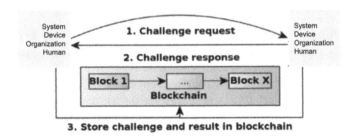

Fig. 2. Conceptual depiction of the MFSSIA lifecycle for challenge-response management.

In Fig. 2, the depiction illustrates the challenge/response-lifecycle management conceptually. Both challenges issued and the corresponding responses are recorded on a blockchain. Either the evaluation of the responses fails, or they are correct responses for a successful evaluation. The chosen challenge set depends on the use case, the required security level, and the threat level of the involved entities.

An IoT device can securely authenticate its identity via MFSSIA to join a system through various methods. There are several methods for secure data sharing. In Pre-shared keys (PSK) [5], devices are provisioned with a unique secret key, which is also known by the system they intend to join. During the authentication process, the device and the system use this pre-shared key to prove their identity to each other. This method is relatively simple but can be vulnerable if the keys are not managed securely.

In Public Key Infrastructure (PKI) [15], devices are issued as digital certificate signed by a trusted Certificate Authority (CA). The certificate contains the device's public key and other identifying information. The system verifies the device's identity by validating the certificate and then uses public key cryptography for secure communication.

Device attestation is used to verify the hardware and software integrity of the device. It often involves a hardware-based root of trust, such as a Trusted Platform Module (TPM) [8] or a secure element, which stores unique cryptographic keys and securely performs cryptographic operations. The device generates an

---

[2] https://www.ethereum.org/.
[3] https://cardano.org/.
[4] https://polkadot.network/.

attestation report, which is then verified by the system to ensure the device is genuine and has not been tampered with.

In Token-based authentication, devices use tokens, such as OAuth [23] or JWT [22], to authenticate themselves. The device first obtains a token from an authentication server by providing its credentials (e.g., username and password, client ID, and secret). The token is then used to access the system securely. The system verifies the token's validity before granting access.

Two-factor authentication (2FA) [27] combines two different factors to authenticate the device, such as something the device knows (a password or pre-shared key) and something the device has (a cryptographic key or digital certificate). By requiring two factors, the security of the authentication process is significantly improved. To ensure the security of IoT devices and the systems they join, it's crucial to use strong encryption, keep software and firmware up-to-date, and follow best practices for secure device management.

MFSSIA enables cross-blockchain interoperability by utilizing blockchain oracles to evaluate blockchain-stored responses to the challenge set. The oracles are digital agents that aim to fetch external world information into a blockchain. Data from various sources are then submitted to the blockchain as transactional data [4], e.g., blood pressure monitors, PHR, EHR, etc. Thus, oracles are used as data feeds for real-world information to be queried by smart contracts running on blockchains and by pushing data into data sources from the blockchains themselves [21].

The challenge sets in MFSSIA are stored in a decentralized knowledge graph (DKG[5]). In DKG, information is stored as a graph of entities and relationships that are relevant to a specific domain or organization. DKG provides immutable, queryable, and searchable graphs that can be used across different applications to create a unified view of a highly decentralized data landscape.

To evaluate the provided running case, we design a formal Colored Petri Nets (CPN) [6,16] model to detect and eliminate eventual design flaws, missing specifications, security, and privacy issues. A CPN is a graphical-oriented language for the design, specification, simulation as well as verification of systems. CPN describes a bipartite graph comprising places, transitions, arcs, and tokens. Places may hold multiple tokens with color, i.e., attributes with values. Transitions fire when all input places hold the required sets of tokens and produce condition-adhering tokens into output places [14]. We use CPN ML functional programming language as a formal equivalent to smart contracts.

3 e-Health Smart-Contract Data-Sharing Process

First, we define the smart contracting healthcare data process through our proposed smart legal contract markup language (SLCML) [1]. The SLCML is a semantically rich, process-driven, and formally verifiable language that allows programmers to configure smart contracts (SC)) based on their knowledge and

---

[5] https://docs.origintrail.io/general/dkgintro.

understanding. The main difference in the method used to create SLCML is the occurrence of process views [3] for corresponding collaborating organizations to define contractual consensus during the collaboration-setup phase. These process views are subsets of larger in-house processes, the extensions of which are kept hidden from the counterparty to protect privacy, business secrets, and so on.

To protect the safety of collaborating parties, an SC must be legally binding and written in a programming language that contains all of the necessary legal elements. The legal elements described in the SLCML are defined in the code extract shown in Listing 1.1. The element role in Line 4 defines the role of the parties to the contract; the patient and insurance provider. Line 5 of Listing 1.1 defines the contractual considerations and the variable types. The value of minOccurs and maxOccurs in Line 5 represents the amount of consideration required for a legally binding smart contract. Line 6 defines the terms_and_conditions element that specifies the SC's terms and conditions. The contracting party's description is defined on Line 7 of Listing 1.1, followed by the customer type company_info that includes the contracting party's name, type of legal organization, and company contact information. A link is provided to the complete SLCML schema[6].

Listing 1.1. Upper layer of the smart-contract schema.

```
<xs:element name="contract">
    <xs:complexType>
        <xs:sequence>
            <xs:element name="role"
                type="variables_def_section"
                minOccurs="0" maxOccurs="unbounded"/>
            <xs:element name="consideration"
                type="variables_def_section"
                minOccurs="1" maxOccurs="unbounded"/>
            <xs:element name="terms_and_conditions"
                type="terms_and_condition_definition"
                minOccurs="0" maxOccurs="unbounded"/>
            <xs:element name="party" type="company_info"
                maxOccurs="unbounded" />
            <xs:element name="mediator" type="company_info"
                minOccurs="0" maxOccurs="unbounded" />
        </xs:sequence>
            <xs:attribute name="contract_id" type="xs:ID" />
            <xs:attribute name="global_language"
                type="xs:string" />
            <xs:attribute name="web_service_uri"
                type="xs:string" />
    </xs:complexType>
</xs:element>
```

---

[6] shorturl.at/uBHR6.

Following that, SLCML is used to configure the contracting parties' rights and obligations for the healthcare running case. Due to page constraints, we do not demonstrate the entire SLCML code in the paper and refer the reader to the link for the complete code[7]. Listing 1.2 defines the fundamental contractual elements required for any legally binding health-oriented smart contract.

Listing 1.2. Contract instantiation for the healthcare safety risk.

```
<contract contract_id="Id1">
        <party address="03_m6">
            <name> Patient </name>
            <role> Patient Data owner </role>
        </party>
        <party address="31_x7">
            <name> Family doctor </name>
            <role> Healthcare provider </role>
        </party>
        <party address="31_x7">
            <name> Insurance provider </name>
            <role> Healthcare providers </role>
        </party>
        <consideration>
            EHR and PHR records
        </consideration>
        <terms_and_conditions/>
        <obligation/> <right/> <prohibitions/>
    </contract>
```

Listing 1.3. Compensation for data breaches.

```
<right_rule tag_name ="Data_breaches" rule_id ="0002"
changeable ="true" monetary ="false">
<state> enabled </state>
<parties>
    <beneficiary> Patient (03 m6 ) </beneficiary>
    <obligor> family doctor (31 x7) </obligor>
    <third_party> Insurance provider </third_party>
</parties >
<right_type>
    <conditional_right> claim </conditional_right>
</right_type>
<precondition>
    act1 (signed)& EHR & PHR (transferred)
</precondition>
<performance_type>
    Patient data privacy (data breaches)
```

---
[7] shorturl.at/uBHR6.

```
</performance_type>
<action_object>
    privacy of EHR and PHR records
</action_object>
<rule_conditions> deadline (date) </rule_conditions>
<remedy> pen (amount, 31 x7) </remedy>
</right_rule >
```

Listing 1.3 depicts a doctor's and patient's commitment to compensate if privacy is compromised for health records. The obligation has a name and a unique ID that is used to track performance. This obligation is classified as monetary due to the focus on economic-or financial consequences. Line 3 begins the obligation state, indicating that the doctors and insurance providers collect patient health records through wearable devices and PHR systems and are responsible for patient data safety.

The family doctor is the obligor and is responsible for carrying out the obligation stated in Line 6. Line 5's obligations benefit the patient assuming the insurance provider is an involved intermediary or arbitrator, as indicated by Line 7. The family doctor is expected to act by collecting patient health data, and the to-do obligation (Line 10) specifies the legal consequences. Line 12 implies the obligations for which the patient, family doctor, and insurance provider sign contracts (Act 1); the insurance provider receives health data from the family doctor. The performance type (Line 13) refers to the patient data that must be transferred from the family doctor's blockchain address to the insurance provider's address. In addition, the performance object (Line 14) is defined as qualified EHR and PHR health data for which a doctor and insurance provider is obligated to data privacy within a specific time frame. Line 15 specifies the privacy safety condition, while the rule conditions specify the data safety conditions. Finally, the obligation is amended to include a mention of the existence of a remedy if privacy is compromised (Line 17). If the family doctors and insurance provider fail to secure privacy within the specified time frame, the patient may ask for a penalty.

4   MFSSIA Integration

First, we define the architecture of the decentralized e-health system's prototype in Fig. 3. The proposed system has three layers: orchestration, choreography, and DAOs. The orchestration layer communicates with stakeholder legacy systems, such as patients-, hospitals-, healthcare providers- and insurance systems. We assume stakeholder systems can be built on different blockchains such as Ethereum, Tezos[8], and so on. The orchestration layer enables the communication between these systems, while the choreography layer integrates the different blockchain-based systems to enable cross-organizational processes. In our

---

[8] https://tezos.com/.

proofs-of-concept, we use Polkadot[9] for integrating the respective stakeholder blockchains. Finally, occurring conflicts in the cross-organizational process are propagated to the DAO layer that implements the conflict resolution- and voting mechanisms.

Fig. 3. Architecture layers of a proof-of-concept prototype.

In Fig. 4, we depict the integration of MFSSIA to the choreography layer of the decentralized e-health system where data sharing occurs in the cross-organizational processes. To set up the connection between different stakeholders, i.e., the hospital and insurance provider of the running case in Sect. 2.2, the requested party provides a challenge set. Then the target party sends corresponding responses back. If these responses are matched with challenge sets, then the connection between systems can be established. We refer interested details to [19] for further details about challenge/response-lifecycle management.

MFSSIA is integrated into the automated cross-organizational process implemented with SCs; therefore, the patient's health data is checked before sharing. As a patient owns the health data, MFSSIA checks the patient's permission before data can be shared between a hospital and the insurance provider. Thus, MFSSIA is used as a low-level authentication mechanism that confirms that only authenticated parties are involved in the cross-organizational process.

In the context of the e-health blockchain-based systems MFSSIA is an essential security component that provides a decentralized way of authentication when data is shared via oracles by the smart contracts with the different stakeholders.

---

[9] https://polkadot.network.

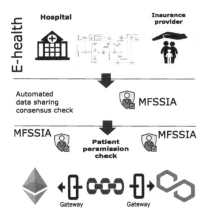

Fig. 4. SC health data sharing process.

5   Evaluation and Discussion

First, we implement the running case defined in Sect. 5.1 based on the architecture defined in Fig. 3. Next, Sect. 5.2 provides the implementation of the MFSSIA framework. Finally, Sect. 5.3 discusses the formal evaluation of the provided running case with CPN Tools.

5.1   E-Health Data Sharing Process Proof-of-concepts Prototype

The implementation[10] of the proof-of-concept prototype for the e-health data-sharing process is presented in [18]. In our context, we propose the usage of Ethereum SCs for the patient-, hospital- and healthcare professional systems and Polygon[11] SCs for the insurance-provider system. The Polygon network uses a high-throughput blockchain with consensus provided by a group of block producers selected by stakeholders at each checkpoint. A proof-of-stake (PoS) layer is used to validate blocks and periodically posts proofs of block producers to the Ethereum mainnet. To enable interoperability between different blockchain-based systems, we use Polkadot[12] that enables scalability by allowing specialized blockchains to communicate with each other in a secure, trust-free environment. Polkadot is a foundational layer of a decentralized web, where users control their data and are not limited by trust bounds within the network.

5.2   MFSSIA Implementation

Our proof-of-concept prototype[13] comprises two decentralized applications (dApps) that establish a connection with each other. The integration is enabled

---

[10] https://github.com/sanamnisarmalik/hprivacyconflictresolutionbyblockchain.
[11] https://polygon.technology.
[12] https://polkadot.network/.
[13] https://github.com/ONTOCHAIN/MFSSIA.

by the iExec Oracle Factory[14] used to implement iExec oracles for retrieving the data from DKG and deciding on the connection establishment possibility. The SCs for multi-factor authentication use an RPC interface exposed to external systems, which is a standard way of communication with SCs by off-chain applications. Oracles use REST API to retrieve the required information from a DKG node. This communication occurs with the support of a DKG rest client that encapsulates the logic for building and sending the HTTP requests to DKG and receiving and parsing the response in JSON format. The DKG node contains the domain knowledge, including the business contract, security license, gateway, and challenge sets. This domain knowledge is based on the MFSSIA ontology mapped to JSON structures supported by the DKG. The challenge-set marketplace is a separate front-end application deployed outside the AWS infrastructure. We provide the more detailed implementation of MFSSIA in our previous research [19].

5.3   Formal Cross-Organizational e-Health Data Sharing Process Evaluation with CPN

We expand the collaboration scenario of Sect. 2 for a CPN simulation and evaluate our model[15] in two ways. First, we perform a simulation in CPN Tools to ensure that all initial tokens reach the unique end state of the model. Then, we perform the state-space analysis[16] for the external layer of the model showing the absence of deadlocks to always reach a given end state and the guaranteed delivery of a given service [6]. In the evaluation result, we do not discover deadlocks and data leaks. The CPN *External Layer* represents a cross-organizational process that outsources a subset of its functions to the stakeholders' internal processes. Each internal process in the CPN model has a unique start place and a unique end place with one token in the start place (all other places are empty). The complete evaluation description is provided in the technical report [11].

6   Conclusion and Future Work

In this paper, we research integrating multi-factor challenge set self-sovereign identity authentication to prevent data-security breaches and patient-safety risks in cross-blockchain e-healthcare systems. The cross-organizational e-healthcare data-sharing process is evaluated with CPN state-space analysis and proof-of-concept prototype.

The specification of the cross-organizational process for handling PHR and EHR is defined through our existing proposed smart-legal-contract markup language. After defining the cross-organizational smart contracting data process to enable data sharing in the decentralized e-health running case, we focus on the security component in these process systems requiring a layered architecture. The

---

[14] https://oracle-factory.iex.ec/gallery.
[15] https://goo.by/JOQJ8.
[16] https://goo.by/id6cP.

legacy systems are presented in the orchestration layer, and cross-organizational processes are in the choreography layer. The security component is MFSSIA that manages the evaluations of challenge-response lifecycles to enable trust in the data sharing between different stakeholders in the cross-organizational e-health process.

There are limitations in our research. First, we have not implemented the integration of MFSSIA and the cross-organizational data-sharing process. The challenge sets for e-healthcare are not defined in detail. Future work is related to integrating MFSSIA into the cross-organizational data-sharing process and extending the MFSSIA challenge sets in a corresponding marketplace related to e-healthcare data sharing.

References

1. Dwivedi, V., Norta, A., Wulf, A., Leiding, B., Saxena, S., Udokwu, C.: A formal specification smart-contract language for legally binding decentralized autonomous organizations. IEEE Access **9**, 76069–76082 (2021). https://doi.org/10.1109/ACCESS.2021.3081926
2. Erol, I., Oztel, A., Searcy, C., Medeni, İT.: Selecting the most suitable blockchain platform: a case study on the healthcare industry using a novel rough MCDM framework. Technol. Forecast. Soc. Chang. **186**, 122132 (2023)
3. Eshuis, R., Norta, A., Kopp, O., Pitkänen, E.: Service outsourcing with process views. IEEE Trans. Serv. Comput. **8**(1), 136–154 (2015). https://doi.org/10.1109/TSC.2013.51
4. Ezzat, S.K., Saleh, Y.N., Abdel-Hamid, A.A.: Blockchain oracles: state-of-the-art and research directions. IEEE Access **10**, 67551–67572 (2022)
5. Housley, R., Hoyland, J., Sethi, M., Wood, C.: RFC 9257 guidance for external pre-shared key (PSK) usage in TLS (2022)
6. Jensen, K., Kristensen, L.M.: Coloured Petri Nets: Modelling and Validation of Concurrent Systems. Springer Science & Business Media, Cham (2009)
7. Jha, A.: Patient safety-a grand challenge for healthcare professionals and policymakers alike. In: Roundtable at the Grand Challenges Meeting of the Bill & Melinda Gates Foundation (2018)
8. Jha, D.N., Lenton, G., Asker, J., Blundell, D., Wallom, D.: Trusted platform module-based privacy in the public cloud: challenges and future perspective. IT Prof. **24**(3), 81–87 (2022)
9. Kormiltsyn, A.: A systematic approach to define requirements and engineer the ontology for semantically merging data sets for personal-centric healthcare systems
10. Kormiltsyn, A., Norta, A.: Dynamically integrating electronic - with personal health records for ad-hoc healthcare quality improvements. In: Alexandrov, D.A., Boukhanovsky, A.V., Chugunov, A.V., Kabanov, Y., Koltsova, O. (eds.) DTGS 2017. CCIS, vol. 745, pp. 385–399. Springer, Cham (2017). https://doi.org/10.1007/978-3-319-69784-0_33
11. Kormiltsyn, A., Norta, A.: Formal evaluation of privacy-conflict resolution for integrating personal-and electronic health records in blockchain-based systems. Technical report (2022)
12. Kormiltsyn, A., Udokwu, C., Karu, K., Thangalimodzi, K., Norta, A.: Improving healthcare processes with smart contracts. In: Abramowicz, W., Corchuelo, R. (eds.) BIS 2019. LNBIP, vol. 353, pp. 500–513. Springer, Cham (2019). https://doi.org/10.1007/978-3-030-20485-3_39

13. Leiding, B., Sharma, P., Norta, A.: The machine-to-everything (m2x) economy: business enactments, collaborations, and e-governance. Fut. Internet **13**(12), 319 (2021)

14. Mahunnah, M., Norta, A., Ma, L., Taveter, K.: Heuristics for designing and evaluating socio-technical agent-oriented behaviour models with coloured petri nets. In: 2014 IEEE 38th International Computer Software and Applications Conference Workshops (COMPSACW), pp. 438–443. IEEE (2014)

15. Maldonado-Ruiz, D., Torres, J., El Madhoun, N., Badra, M.: Current trends in blockchain implementations on the paradigm of public key infrastructure: a survey. IEEE Access **10**, 17641–17655 (2022)

16. Morel, G., Valckenaers, P., Faure, J.M., Pereira, C.E., Diedrich, C.: Manufacturing plant control challenges and issues. Control. Eng. Pract. **15**(11), 1321–1331 (2007)

17. Nguyen, G.T., Kim, K.: A survey about consensus algorithms used in blockchain. J. Inf. Process. Syst. **14**(1) (2018)

18. Nisar, S.: Defining blockchain-based techniques for privacy conflict-resolution in cross-organizational processes for e-health systems. Master's thesis, University of Tartu, Faculty of Science and Technology Institute of Computer Science (2022)

19. Norta, A., Kormiltsyn, A., Udokwu, C., Dwivedi, V., Aroh, S., Nikolajev, I.: A blockchain implementation for configurable multi-factor challenge-set self-sovereign identity authentication

20. Reis, C.T., Paiva, S.G., Sousa, P.: The patient safety culture: a systematic review by characteristics of hospital survey on patient safety culture dimensions. Int. J. Qual. Health Care **30**(9), 660–677 (2018)

21. Riley, L.: Universal DLT interoperability is now a practical reality (2021)

22. Saeed, L., Abdallah, G.: Security with JWT. In: Pro Cloud Native Java EE Apps: DevOps with MicroProfile. Jakarta EE 10 APIs, and Kubernetes, pp. 293–308. Springer, Cham (2022). https://doi.org/10.1007/978-1-4842-8900-6_11

23. Sharif, A., Carbone, R., Sciarretta, G., Ranise, S.: Best current practices for OAuth/OIDC native apps: a study of their adoption in popular providers and top-ranked android clients. J. Inf. Secur. Appl. **65**, 103097 (2022)

24. Shuaib, M., Alam, S., Alam, M.S., Nasir, M.S.: Self-sovereign identity for healthcare using blockchain. Mater. Today: Proc. (2021)

25. Stevens, W.J.M., van der Sande, R., Beijer, L.J., Gerritsen, M.G., Assendelft, W.J.: ehealth apps replacing or complementing health care contacts: scoping review on adverse effects. J. Med. Internet Res. **21**(3), e10736 (2019)

26. Swan, M.: Blockchain: Blueprint for a New Economy. O'Reilly Media Inc, Sebastopol (2015)

27. Tirfe, D., Anand, V.K.: A survey on trends of two-factor authentication. In: Sarma, H.K.D., Balas, V.E., Bhuyan, B., Dutta, N. (eds.) Contemporary Issues in Communication, Cloud and Big Data Analytics. LNNS, vol. 281, pp. 285–296. Springer, Singapore (2022). https://doi.org/10.1007/978-981-16-4244-9_23

28. Vignot, S., et al.: Collaboration between health-care professionals, patients, and national competent authorities is crucial for prevention of health risks linked to the inappropriate use of drugs: a position paper of the ansm (agence nationale de sécurité du médicament et des produits de santé). Front. Pharmacol. **12**, 635841 (2021)

29. Westaway, M.D., Stratford, P.W., Binkley, J.M.: The patient-specific functional scale: validation of its use in persons with neck dysfunction. J. Orthop. Sports Phys. Therapy **27**(5), 331–338 (1998)

Query Processing and Visualization

Towards a Data Provenance Collection and Visualization Framework for Monitoring and Analyzing HPC Environments

Nitin Sukhija[1]([✉]) [ID], Elizabeth Bautista[2] [ID], Adam Schultz[2] [ID],
Cary Whitney[2] [ID], and Thomas Davis[2] [ID]

[1] Slippery Rock University, Slippery Rock, PA, USA
`nitin.sukhija@sru.edu`
[2] NERSC, Lawrence Berkeley National Laboratory, Berkeley, CA, USA
`{ejbautista,aschultz1054,CLWhitney,tadavis}@lbl.gov`

Abstract. Today, the High Performance Computing (HPC) landscape is growing and evolving rapidly and is catalyzing innovations and discoveries to new levels of power and fidelity in a multitude of domains. With this rapid evolution and integration of heterogeneous architectures, technologies and software models underlying HPC infrastructure, managing the confidentiality, integrity, reliability and availability of these complex systems has become extremely challenging. Thus, many research efforts are focusing on monitoring solutions for collecting, correlating and analyzing health metrics and events data for achieving HPC facilities operational efficiency. Data provenance and its sources (such as metadata, lineage) empowers monitoring and event management solutions with capabilities of verification and historical evidence for identifying and troubleshooting HPC infrastructure issues and for forecasting and gaining meaningful insights about the data transformations. In this preliminary work, we present a data provenance collection and visualization infrastructure integrated with the Operations Monitoring and Notification Infrastructure (OMNI) data warehouse at Lawrence Berkeley National Laboratory's (LBNL) National Energy Scientific Computing Center (NERSC) that has implemented Apache Hop, Neo4j and Grafana Loki for automated root cause analysis and visualization in the face of a computational center's and users' critical needs. Moreover, herein we also present several cases illustrating the benefits of employing the proposed framework using 600K concatenated JSON system events and health metrics datasets originating from the Perlmutter computational system, to aid in collection, analysis and visualization of the gathered data provenance. We further elucidate the advantages of this preliminary framework towards reducing the time for detecting and responding to computational center critical issues caused due to physical and cyber threats.

Keywords: High Performance Computing · Availability · Fault Tolerance · Reliability · Big Data · Monitoring · Root Cause Analysis · Provenance

R. Chbeir et al. (Eds.): MEDES 2023, CCIS 2022, pp. 57–72, 2024.
https://doi.org/10.1007/978-3-031-51643-6_5

1   Introduction

The enormous computational power enabled by today's supercomputers is catalyzing research and innovation in many scientific and business domains. Given, the high-performance computing (HPC) achieved its next major milestone of exaflop capabilities (10^{18} floating point operations per second (FLOPS)), the management and monitoring of the scale and complexity of hardware and software components comprising such computing systems is becoming exceedingly difficult. Moreover, this monumental task becomes even more intricate with the exponential amount of metrics and event data generated for determining the health of such complex systems, leading to operational fatigue. The timely monitoring of the status and functionality of the exascale HPC facilities necessitates storing, managing, and analyzing such diverse and extreme scale data to aid operations teams for efficiently handling potential problems and for decreasing Mean Time to Repair (MTTR). Thus, maintaining reliability and availability of such complex computing facilities is becoming extremely challenging and requires significant new research and solutions for reducing response time to resolve failures, enhancing operational efficacy [14].

Given the inexorable proliferation in the hybrid computing models and usage of automation and orchestration systems encompassing modern computational facility operations, both the collection and traceability of the computing systems and the underlying infrastructure data along with environment data is of paramount importance. The collection and traceability capabilities facilitate root cause analysis in real-time reducing response time or downtime due to physical and cyber threats. Data provenance (meaning metadata and lineage), aids in resolving problems by facilitating knowledge about the origins of data, usage, and variation, thus enabling the tracing of the problem symptoms and root causes [18]. Therefore, data provenance is extremely significant in gaining meaningful insights about potential threats or problems in dynamically changing high performance computing environments. However, utilizing data provenance for reducing time to repair requires a monitoring framework that provides a comprehensive view of the underlying computing infrastructure with capabilities of gathering and collection of data. Additionally, the monitoring framework should also enable visualization of the origins of the data that will aid the computational staff to perform root cause analysis in near real-time by transforming and correlating alerts and notifications via single pane of glass dashboards leading to informed operational decisions [13]. Thus, a real time monitoring framework with data provenance collection and visualization capabilities facilitates increased operational intelligence in HPC facilities for prioritizing and responding to the potential critical faults or service level exceptions.

The Operations Monitoring and Notification Infrastructure (OMNI) [8] is one of such comprehensive monitoring and event management solutions that is being implemented and deployed by Lawrence Berkeley National Laboratory (hereafter referred to Berkeley Lab) for achieving operational excellence at the National Energy Research Scientific Computing Center (NERSC). In our previous work, we presented multiple open source technologies and frameworks encompassing

OMNI infrastructure, such as, Prometheus [4], Grafana and ServiceNow [5] that enables in collection of the real-time time-series monitoring data from various sources including pre-exascale computing systems at NERSC, computational infrastructure, environmental sensors, mechanical systems and more. In this preliminary work, we seek to expand on our existing OMNI infrastructure, through providing a comprehensive data provenance collection and visualization framework which specializes in illuminating insights into the historical perspective of system generated events and related environmental telemetry metadata, ultimately aiding in the troubleshooting of critical system faults which commonly plague HPC facilities.

Given computing facilities face exponential amounts of events generated across such underlying infrastructure, automated root cause analysis and visualization is required for proactive alert monitoring to reduce events noise and predictive intelligence, thus achieving operational efficiency in such changing high performance environments. The proposed data provenance collection and visualization infrastructure is motivated by the need for high availability and automated operational Intelligence for current and future computing systems at NERSC. *The key contributions of this preliminary research are:* 1) a data provenance collection and visualization infrastructure integrated with OMNI that implements and deploys open source tools such as, Apache Hop: an open-source data orchestration platform for collecting and processing fine grained metadata [1], Neo4j: a graph database management system to ingest such metadata [2], lineage, and provenance data for gaining an increased visual understanding of system changes and Grafana Loki: a log aggregation system which compiles syslog information originating from all NERSC computing systems [7]; and 2) early results that provide a preliminary benefit analysis of the framework using 600K compressed JSON syslog and telemetry datasets from the Perlmutter Computational system at NERSC [3].

The rest of the paper is organized as follows. A review of OMNI, the computational center monitoring and management infrastructure, Data Provenance, and related work is presented in Sect. 2. Our proposed data provenance collection and visualization infrastructure as well as the use cases and experimental results are presented in Sects. 3 and 4, followed by the conclusions and possible future directions in Sect. 5.

2   Background

2.1   Operations Monitoring and Notification Infrastructure (OMNI)

NERSC's Perlmutter system has the potential to significantly provide more diagnostic data than any of their previous systems. Perlmutter is producing an average of 100k–400k lines of logs and metric data points per second. The Operations team leverages this data to perform real-time monitoring of the system to respond to issues quickly, identify root causes as they occur and provide additional after incident analysis to improve performance of the system availability and staff responsiveness. The Operations Monitoring and Notification Infrastructure (OMNI) serves as the data collection warehouse, not only for Perlmutter data, but heterogeneous data from the entire facility. OMNI is designed to be scalable and robust to accommodate large data streams. Data is streamed into a VictoriaMetrics [6] time-series database where metrics are stored and queried for analysis. VictoriaMetrics can collect from 450K to 40 million data points per second depending on the speed of the source and type of data. Multiple virtual servers on OMNI support visualization of the data with a Grafana Enterprise front end. To analyze logs and events, Loki is used as a log aggregation tool to analyze real time data and provide insights like thresholds for alerting and notification. Moreover, the incident management platform like ServiceNow [5] facilitate creation of tickets automatically from alerts that are generated when thresholds occur. OMNI data and tools have transformed data into providing critical insight into the health and performance of the systems and facility. OMNI stores an average of 85 TB of data monthly depending on the type of data, the data owner's requirements and the density of the data.

2.2   The Need of Provenance in HPC Monitoring and Management

Given the scale and complexity of the computational systems, the provenance becomes increasingly important for ensuring the fidelity of data in dynamically changing high performance computing ecosystems. Provenance facilitates assessment of authenticity to enable trust and reproducibility for tracking data issues, performing impact analysis in event of system failures, or accidental human errors. The provenance research encompasses two granularities: 1) coarse-grained (or workflow) provenance reflecting the functional model of workflow systems, and 2) data (or fine-grained) provenance capturing the transformations to tuples on the data [18]. The workflow provenance is too coarse-grained to aid in troubleshooting problems while the fine grained data provenance enables capturing the lineage of the data item over its life cycle for monitoring, analyzing, and debugging complex and large scale data pipelines. With the increase in the heterogeneity of the modern computational centers, the volume, variety, value, velocity, and variability of the event data has also reached an exponential scale. Moreover, with the increase in the generation of the health and events data, the metadata pertaining to the data origin and the lifecycle of data also increases in complexity leading to operational challenges with respect to interpretation and investigation of such gathered data. Furthermore, maintaining HPC systems necessitates a careful analysis of operational provenance data to manage current issues and mitigate future incidents. Having robust failure detection and prediction schemes is often not enough and doesn't fully aid in answering how these issues occurred or why they were caused. Traditional root cause analysis processes aid us in answering these questions but are typically riddled with inefficiencies which can become exacerbated when working in environments that handle large volumes of data [8]. Thus, a monitoring and event management solution with data provenance collection and visualization platform is required to resolve critical infrastructure performance issues and to achieve high availability of the HPC Facility services via the root cause incidents detection and automated remediation.

2.3   Related Work

Over years various data provenance systems have been proposed and employed in the computational environments [12]. Moreover, many studies involving visualization of provenance have been researched and reported. However, only a few studies published illustrate the integration of the data provenance collection and visualization with real-time monitoring and event management to provide a comprehensive solution for dynamically changing heterogeneous computing environments. Many provenance systems proposed and designed such as PASSv2 [16], ES3 [11] and many others [15] are limited by the complexity and the scale of todays HPC environments. The authors in [9] presents visualization techniques created for exploring and explaining of provenance of large scale network datasets. Other study following an adaptive workflow monitoring approach was reported by authors in [17] that utilizes a human-in-the-loop and provenance data monitoring to support users in analyzing the evolution of key parameters and determining the data reduction in scientific workflows. However, the in-situ visualization still needs to be addressed the above approach. A lightweight provenance service (LPS) for HPC was designed and implemented by authors in [10], where systemwide provenance was generated using operating system kernel and environmental variables and visualized using d3.js. In comparison to the above mentioned work, our preliminary framework introduces a data provenance and visualization platform employing Apache Hop and Neo4j resources integrated with OMNI infrastructure to overcome limitations of current monitoring solutions. With the introduction of a graph database system such as Neo4j, which can efficiently store and analyze large volumes of data, we can quickly create representations or visualizations of operational provenance data to easily trace where issues are originating from as well as how other issues are related to each other. When needs for an automated system that can easily process and create graph visualizations arise, we introduce a data orchestration platform such as Apache Hop to easily process the incoming provenance data and create an output Neo4j graph representation. Through applying our framework to NERSC Perlmutter's syslog and telemetry data, we were able to prioritize punctuality in retrieving impactful graph visualizations quickly, even while processing large amounts of data, by exploiting the implicit parallelization of subprocesses in our Apache Hop pipelines. Our graph outputs offer as coarse or fine-grained of an analysis as needed, to further aid understanding of the data during any stage of the root cause analysis process. With further metadata on the temperature, pressure, voltage, or fan/pump speed for any system we can further aid the root cause analysis process by using other metrics to reinforce our prediction.

3 Data Provenance Collection and Visualization Framework

This section illustrates the design and architecture of our data provenance collection and visualization framework (shown in Fig. 1) integrated with OMNI to provide a comprehensive monitoring and analysis of our HPC environment within NERSC. Our framework employs Apache Hop and Neo4j, both open source, for metadata collection and root cause analysis. Apache Hop acts as an orchestration and metadata collection tool that allows users to create workflows (a sequential set of connected steps or phases that generally orchestrate the overall data integration task), and pipelines (sub-processes which transform raw data into useable insights) all while prioritizing native metadata (provenance) support, and rich logging capabilities, which can better determine the root of an issue. We further improve the benefits of metadata collection for root cause analysis by exporting this data to a graph database, Neo4j. Neo4j prioritizes the relationships between entities, and by having a graph view of an issue we can allow better tracking of the relationships between different entities, thus aiding in efficient debugging of problems. Additionally, we utilized a powerful and more human readable query language natively provided by Neo4j, Cypher. The queries in Cypher are expressed more visually, and eliminate the need for a large number of joins required in a traditional query language, leading to reducing time to solution and allowing for faster insights pertaining to the visualizations of syslog data created through our framework. The intent of integrating Apache Hop with Neo4j platforms is to be able to trace the bigger picture related to the: 1) relationships and metadata for the database connection; 2) the systems which are reading and writing to the database; 3) dependencies among database tables used to store the data; 4) the queries used to extract the data; and 5) the scripts/code that transforms the data. As Apache Hop is metadata focused, where everything within the orchestration platform is described as metadata, and native Neo4j perspectives of the lineage for workflow and pipeline executions are provided with minimal configuration changes, we are able to achieve rich traceability of the lifecycle for orchestration tasks within Apache Hop through deeply enriched provenance graphs in Neo4j. With this goal, we additionally sought to extend such traceability within the scope of our HPC environment at NERSC through implementation of a custom Apache Hop orchestration task to integrate Perlmutter syslog and environmental telemetry data into impactful graph visualizations in Neo4j. Thus, employing this provenance framework integrated with OMNI enables automated insight analysis without the need of manually jumping through each stage of a process to make informed decisions about the root cause of the critical system issues. Our design and organization of the framework used to collect and visualize data provenance for monitoring and analyzing HPC environments comprises of four components: 1) Data Collection using GrafanaLoki, 2) Data Preprocessing, 3) Data Orchestration utilizing Apache Hop, and 4) Visualization and Analysis using Neo4j (Shown in Fig. 1).

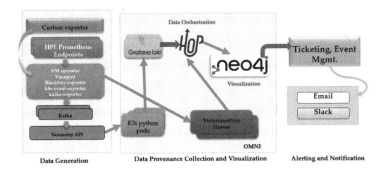

Fig. 1. An Overview of the Data Provenance and Visualization Framework.

3.1   Use Cases

Through prioritization of provenance graphs which seek to highlight the trace-ability of system issues in HPC environments a number of use cases arise from which this framework can be applied. Having a historical perspective of a computational system at any particular moment allows us to understand and piece together a snapshot of how the system operated, the types of data operations and jobs that were performed at such time, relevant network traffic, as well as various software or hardware related failures that occurred within the system. For example, if a compute node unexpectedly enters an emergency power off state as a result of an unspecified hardware failure the need to be able to quickly consolidate and review relevant data pertaining to the root cause of such an event becomes critical. With the introduction of such information, organized in a historical graph perspective, engineers responsible for troubleshooting now can have greater confidence in tracing the contributing factors which led to the event in question while additionally correlating related metadata to determine if the root cause originated from a particular anomalous source. Although the application of this framework is applied to system oriented data, its pattern and approach can be generalized towards user specific data also. Since scientists per-

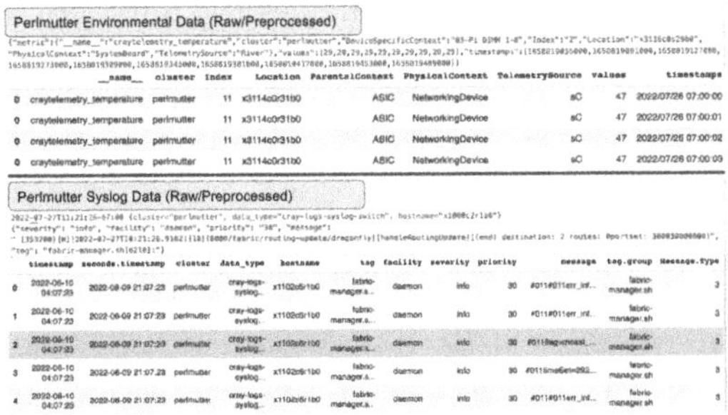

Fig. 2. A sample of the concatenated JSON Perlmutter environmental and syslog data before being expanded as well as the final preprocessed result.

form large-scale workloads and jobs accessing various compute and filesystem related resources, the approach towards tracing the provenance of these actions, their dependencies, inputs as well as parameters follows a similar motivation. Gaining a consolidated view into the provenance of such tasks is not too far distant in motivations compared to our system-oriented approach.

The extensibility of this framework is also not limited to just one particular system. As OMNI acts as a data warehouse in collecting storage, network, cyber and facility data the opportunity to enrich a larger perspective of our provenance graphs is available. Since the data which arrives from Grafana Loki or Victoria-Metrics to OMNI is structured in a similar JSON schema, minimal changes are necessary in order to accomplish a similar task of preprocessing, data orchestration through Apache Hop and eventual Neo4j data provenance graph output. With added data sources which highlight a more inclusive perspective of our particular HPC environment at NERSC we are able to enable a more effective provenance collection and visualization framework towards triaging issues within our computing facility and ensuring the full availability and robustness of our resources.

1. Data Collection:

The Perlmutter Kubernetes (K8s) environment utilizes and executes containers originating from Kafka or Prometheus endpoints, Telemetry API servers, rsyslogd aggregators, and other services for the management and monitoring of NERSC's computational infrastructure. Moreover, VMagent, also a container executing in the same cluster, enables the collection of health and performance metrics for the services executing in high performance environments and directly submits the gathered metrics to VictoriaMetrics, which is an open source time-series database cluster in our OMNI infrastructure. The data pertaining to the temperature, humidity, power, fan speed and more is collected by sensors installed in each cabinet, node, switch, chassis, and cooling unit. Following the data collection, a RESTful interface for infrastructure management, named Redfish endpoint on each controller enables a HMS(hardware management service) collector to receive the metrics and events(e.g. power down). This action is followed by data submission to Kafka by the HMS collector, where the data is stored in different topics by categories and served to possible consumers by Kafka. Later, the telemetry API server enables the authentication and the balancing of the incoming requests by acting as a mediator between Kafka and data

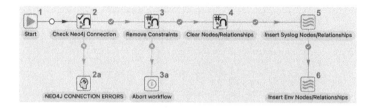

Fig. 3. Apache Hop data orchestration workflow comprising of a series of pipelines.

consumers. As a final step, the telemetry API client creates a subscription to a Kafka topic by sending an API server request, and then data is pushed by Kafka to the client by using the API where the client converts the data format prior to delivering to VictoriaMetrics or Grafana Loki. The Grafana Loki platform encompasses a fully featured logging stack that enables storing and querying of all applications and infrastructure logs.

2. Data Preprocessing:

The data collected from NERSC's HPC systems and infrastructure arrives in a concatenated JSON format, thus data preprocessing is employed to further clean and structure such data to be used as an input for Apache Hop. Syslog messages originating from Perlmutter were first imported using the Pandas library read _json method. Next, we disjoin the concatenated data using the split method and use the Pandas rename method to format the column labels, to remove missing values, and to add a numerical severity column based on our string-type severity column (ex: info, err, emerg, warning, notice). The telemetry data is preprocessed in a similar manner by first being read using the Pandas library read_json method. Next, columns are expanded to show additional concatenated data using Pandas json_normalize method. After checking for null values we explode the values column to present each value in its own unique row. The concatenated JSON environmental and syslog data before being expanded as well as the final preprocessed result is shown in Fig. 2. After preprocessing of both datasets, the data is ingested into our Apache Hop data orchestration step to be harmonized and output into a provenance graph visualization.

Fig. 4. Neo4j Cypher Script queries for removing constraints and clearing Nodes/ Relationships.

3. Apache Hop

Apache Hop is an open source data orchestration platform integrated in our framework for collecting fine grained metadata and aggregating processes which are being investigated. Apache Hop orchestrates importing the Perlmutter syslog and telemetry data into our Neo4j database. The preprocessed syslog and telemetry data is utilized as an input, and transformed through a main workflow comprising of a series of pipelines. The data orchestration workflow is illustrated in Fig. 3. The workflow initializes by ensuring an active Neo4j database connection. Information and credentials for the database are stored and encrypted in

Apache Hop as metadata. Next, we clear the database and ensure there are no overlapping constraints which may prevent the data from being ingested into Neo4j. The queries which accomplish steps 3 and 4 are shown in Fig. 4. After step 4 in our workflow is completed, pipelines (5 - 6) are executed which transform our input data (syslog or telemetry) into node and relationships that are then created in our active Neo4j database. To demonstrate how these pipelines operate, the "Insert Env Nodes/Relationships" (6) pipeline is shown in Fig. 5. Note that the "Insert Syslog Nodes/Relationships" (5) pipeline mimics a similar behavior. In essence, we specify the input data in the first column (labeled 1). In the next column we specify which data we want to keep in our output, and rename column values where necessary. The next column sorts only those columns which are used for creating a specific node (ex: Voltage, Temperature) or relationship (has_voltage, has_temperature). Note that implicit parallelization amongst actions in Apache Hop pipelines allows the specific types of actions in a stage (Write Voltage, Write Temperature, Write Current, Write Energy) to be run in parallel. This greatly improved our resulting execution times. The finalized output after completing the Apache Hop step in workflow is then displayed using Neo4j.

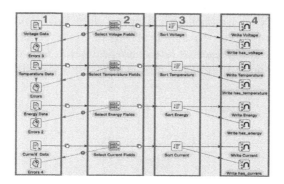

Fig. 5. Pipeline for inserting telemetry data nodes/relationships into Neo4j.

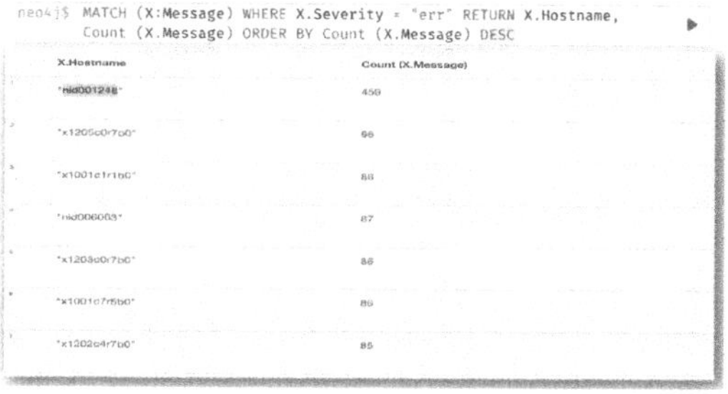

Fig. 6. A sample Neo4j query to discover host (nid001248) with highest count of error messages.

4. Neo4j:
Neo4j is a graph database management system used in our framework for ingesting metadata, lineage, and provenance data to gain an increased visual understanding of changes made within our postgres database or apache hop workflow. Neo4j acts as the final data store for nodes and relationships created using Apache Hop and enables visualization that aids in tracing patterns in our log data by fast and impactful query results, leading to proactive monitoring and alerting in HPC environments.

4   Data Provenance Collection and Visualization Workflow and Results

The data provenance collection and visualization framework employed using Perlmutter syslog and environmental telemetry data integrated OMNI, a primary Apache Hop workflow containing multiple pipelines and Neo4j to aid in root cause analysis for investigating incidents within HPC environments. This section presents some of the cases illustrating the use of our preliminary framework to execute simple operational queries to explore the benefits of the introductory analysis into our data and to aid in investigating high-level issues within a particular component of the Perlmutter system. The code was implemented using Python 3, Apache Hop 1.0.0, Neo4j 1.4.12 on a system with 8 cores and 16 GB of RAM. Moreover, the dependencies required for implementation include: Numpy v1.23, Datetime v4.3, JSON v3.10.5, Sklearn v0.1.1, and Scipy v1.7.0,010statsmodels. Our use case experiments were conducted using 635, 000 syslog and telemetry datasets aggregated by Graphana Loki from all Perlmutter clusters. The preprocessing of 635K syslog data took about 2 s and of 635K environment data took about 8 s. Moreover, the execution time of our workflow detailed in above sections (including all pipeline dependencies) was about 3 s, where Apache Hop created over 7 million nodes/relationships in Neo4j generating 1.5 GB of Neo4j Database after completion of our Apache Hop step in the workflow.

4.1   Discovering Hosts with the Highest Count of Error Messages

This case study illustrates the use of our proposed framework to investigate the host which is generating the most "noise" (highest error count) in the computational environment. These high-level data discovery queries provide beneficial initial insights into our provenance graphs, allowing us to dig deeper into specific system issues. Further example queries which demonstrate this data discovery phase can be applied to discover the types of system modules which generated syslog messages on a host, the types of messages generated by a specific service, as well as a count of which type of hosts (compute, non-compute, login, switch, or filesystem gateway hosts) generated the most noise. Through exploiting a more fine-grained data provenance view, more information is discovered using log messages which can aid in a better understanding about a system fault's or an issue's origination and alerting. Once Apache Hop processed the syslog and telemetry data, a few analysis queries were executed to determine the output of the framework. Neo4j Browser was used to query the database to gain high-level insights into our data and the cypher query language was used to aid in our analysis to inquire into which hosts logged the most errors, sorted in descending order. The query and corresponding output illustrate that the compute node nid001248 returned the highest error count, shown in Fig. 6.

4.2 Visualize Lineage for Host with Highest Count of Error Messages

The framework additionally aided in a fine grained understanding and visualization of the lineage for any particular Perlmutter host, so that traceability of the messages generated by the system can be explored efficiently as shown in Fig. 7. More importantly, as illustrated in Fig. 7, an individual node can be expanded to view additional lineage as well as more metadata about the origin of the data.

4.3 View Lineage for Potential Hardware Faults and Leaks

The log messages originating from redfish-cmmd pertain specifically to hardware related information. With implementation and execution of simple cypher queries returning syslog data collected by redfish-cmmd, a view of high level hardware failures can be provided. Additionally, queries can aid in investigating in detail the reason behind the changing behavior for a particular host over time leading to a better understanding and analysis of the system failure, origin and current state. The log messages are investigated further to discover some root causes such as a coolant leak in a particular cabinet. These messages are critical in identifying and analyzing incidents, and our proposed framework demonstrates how impactful graph visualizations can aid in such use case.Fig. 7 illustrates that the syslog message originated from cray compute node syslog logs, and was a kernel specific log message. As an additional example, the lineage for messages originating from redfish-cmmd (a Redfish tool) is displayed which aids data center hardware management. The query and the results gathering syslog messages which have been generated by the redfish-cmmd service are shown in Fig. 8. Moreover, Fig. 9 illustrates queries to further investigate into log messages which indicate power failure or a leak detected. The first cypher query returns the lineage of messages which originate from the same tag (redfish-cmmd[4278]). Additionally, the operations staff can also view messages (shown in Fig. 10) indicating that there may be coolant detected in a cabinet by executing the query shown in Fig. 10.

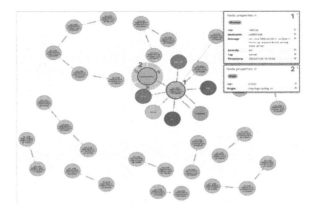

Fig. 7. Discovering metadata and more information about the hosts with the highest count of error messages.

Fig. 8. A sample Neo4j cypher query to return those syslog messages which have been generated by the redfish-cmmd service.

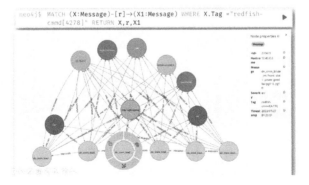

Fig. 9. Neo4j cypher query illustrating the lineage of messages which originate from the same tag (redfish-cmmd[4278]).

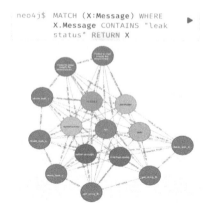

Fig. 10. Neo4j cypher query illustrating the detection of coolant in a cabinet.

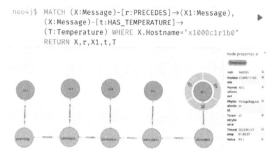

Fig. 11. Neo4j cypher query for telemetry data on a specific Perlmutter rosetta switch (x1000c1r1b0) returning the data lineage for a specific host, as well the temperature values recorded during the same timestamp.

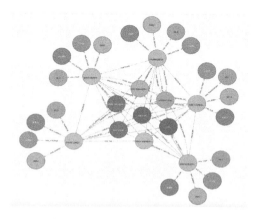

Fig. 12. Visualization of fine-grained metadata context of one node including the temperature, voltage, energy, and current values.

4.4   Visualize Telemetry Data and Lineage for Rosetta Switches

In instances where there is a need to correlate log messages with environmental readings for the system, the framework proposed can utilized to help gain larger-scale visualizations of the system and environmental behavior during a particular time frame, for specific hosts and more. In this use case, an outline of a strategy towards using this framework for identifying the presence of power issues is illustrated using queries based on messages returned by a particular network related rosetta switch (x1000c1r1b0). Traditionally, only lineage for a particular host with limited metadata is revealed when the message is returned. However, our framework enables visualization of the values of the environmental variables when the message was generated. For example, a query for telemetry data on a specific Perlmutter rosetta switch (x1000c1r1b0) will return the data lineage for a specific host, as well the Temperature values which were recorded during the same timestamp (shown in Fig. 11). Moreover, instead of viewing just temperature environmental values an individual message node can be expanded further to gain the context view of the fine-grained metadata, most importantly including the temperature, voltage, energy, and current values (shown in Fig. 12).

5   Conclusion and Future Work

The preliminary framework encompassing the usage of high performance computing resources, the OMNI infrastructure, the HPC system and environment data sets, Apache Hop and Neo4j for automating data provenance collection and visualization in HPC environments is presented in this paper. The framework enhances traditional approaches towards data provenance by employing graph databases, such as, Neo4j to visualize and trace the relationships that log messages share amongst themselves and other related metadata. Additionally, the real-time automated root cause analysis and visualization enabled via provenance collected from logs of various critical components supports operational staff efficiency by reducing time to investigate the facility incidents proficiently. Our immediate future work will be adding an additional layer on top of the framework that will employ machine learning algorithms to enable quicker actions which can be made to remediate a certain issue, and requires less domain knowledge, making troubleshooting more accessible for a wider demographic of technicians/system engineers at NERSC and other computing facilities.

Acknowledgments. This research used resources of NERSC, a U.S. Department of Energy Office of Science User Facility operated under Contract No. DEAC02-05CH11231.

References

1. Apache hop: The hop orchestration platform. https://hop.apache.org/
2. Neo4j: Graph data platform. https://neo4j.com/

3. Perlmutter: Nersc's next supercomputer. https://www.nersc.gov/systems/perlmutter/
4. Prometheus. https://prometheus.io/
5. Servicenow. https://www.servicenow.com/
6. Victoriametrics. https://victoriametrics.com/
7. Bautista, E., Sukhija, N., Deng, S.: Shasta log aggregation, monitoring and alerting in HPC environments with Grafana Loki and ServiceNow. In: 2022 IEEE International Conference on Cluster Computing (CLUSTER), pp. 602–610. IEEE (2022)
8. Bautista, E., Sukhija, N., Romanus, M., Davis, T., Whitney, C.: Omni at the edge. In: Cybersecurity and High-Performance Computing Environments, pp. 63–84. Chapman and Hall/CRC (2022)
9. Chen, P., Plale, B., Cheah, Y.W., Ghoshal, D., Jensen, S., Luo, Y.: Visualization of network data provenance. In: 2012 19th International Conference on High Performance Computing, pp. 1–9. IEEE (2012)
10. Dai, D., Chen, Y., Carns, P., Jenkins, J., Ross, R.: Lightweight provenance service for high-performance computing. In: 2017 26th International Conference on Parallel Architectures and Compilation Techniques (PACT), pp. 117–129. IEEE (2017)
11. Frew, J., Metzger, D., Slaughter, P.: Automatic capture and reconstruction of computational provenance. Concurr. Comput. Pract. Experience **20**(5), 485–496 (2008)
12. Gadelha, L.M.R., Wilde, M., Mattoso, M., Foster, I.: Exploring provenance in high performance scientific computing. In: Proceedings of the First Annual Workshop on High Performance Computing Meets Databases, pp. 17–20 (2011)
13. Heldens, S., Hijma, P., Werkhoven, B.V., Maassen, J., Belloum, A.S., Van Nieuwpoort, R.V.: The landscape of exascale research: a data-driven literature analysis. ACM Comput. Surv. (CSUR) **53**(2), 1–43 (2020)
14. Kothe, D., Lee, S., Qualters, I.: Exascale computing in the united states. Comput. Sci. Eng. **21**(1), 17–29 (2018)
15. Ma, S., Zhang, X., Xu, D., et al.: Protracer: towards practical provenance tracing by alternating between logging and tainting. In: NDSS, vol. 2, p. 4 (2016)
16. Muniswamy-Reddy, K.K., Holland, D.A., Braun, U., Seltzer, M.I.: Provenance-aware storage systems. In: USENIX Annual Technical Conference, General Track, pp. 43–56 (2006)
17. Souza, R., Silva, V., Coutinho, A.L., Valduriez, P., Mattoso, M.: Data reduction in scientific workflows using provenance monitoring and user steering. Futur. Gener. Comput. Syst. **110**, 481–501 (2020)
18. Tan, W.C., et al.: Provenance in databases: past, current, and future. IEEE Data Eng. Bull. **30**(4), 3–12 (2007)

Tables with Nulls and Functional Dependencies: Explanation and Quality of Query Answers

Dominique Laurent[1]($\boxtimes$) and Nicolas Spyratos[2]

[1] ETIS Lab.-ENSEA, CY Cergy Paris Univ., CNRS, 95000 Cergy-Pontoise, France
dominique.laurent@u-cergy.fr
[2] LISN Lab.-University Paris-Saclay, CNRS, 91405 Orsay, France
nicolas.spyratos@lri.fr

Abstract. Several applications today deal with tables that are the result of merging other tables coming from different sources (as when recording the results of collaborative work or when merging tables during data staging in data warehouses). Such tables usually have missing values (also called *nulls*) and/or contain data that do not respect given constraints (such as key constraints). In this paper we study the influence of nulls and/or inconsistent data on the answers to queries to such tables by (a) providing to the user explanations regarding the expected presence (or absence) of certain tuples in the answer and (b) by defining measures for assessing the quality of query answers.

Keywords: Inconsistent data · Query answering · Explanations · Data quality

1 Introduction

In a traditional relational database, each table is assumed to be consistent before users can query it but, in several applications today, tables are the result of merging two or more other tables coming from different sources. Such tables usually have missing values (also called *nulls*) and/or contain data that do not respect given constraints - such as key constraints. This is especially true when a user collects data coming from web sources and merges them in a single table T. In such a setting, it is difficult if not impossible for the user to know the constraints imposed on data in each source. Given a set FD of constraints over T, extracting from T data that are consistent with FD is then achieved using some query tool. In this paper we propose such a tool.

Three main issues (among others) arising when querying such tables are how to extract consistent answers addressed to possibly inconsistent tables; how to help users explain the expected presence or absence of certain tuples in the consistent answer to a query; and how to give users a measure of the quality

Work conducted while the second author was visiting at FORTH Institute of Computer Science, Crete, Greece (https://www.ics.forth.gr/).

of a query answer. We describe below briefly these issues, placing them in the context of related work.

Consistent Query Answering. Consider the table $T = \{es, es'd, e's'\}$ over universe $U = \{Emp, Sal, Dept\}$, and the functional dependency $Emp \rightarrow Sal$ stating that an employee cannot have more than one salary. T is inconsistent as tuples 1 and 2 violate the dependency $Emp \rightarrow Sal$. However, if we ask the SQL query Q : select Emp, Sal from T, it makes sense to return the set $\{e's'\}$ as the answer. Indeed, there is no reason to reject this answer as it is a consistent answer because it satisfies the dependency $Emp \rightarrow Sal$. In other words, an inconsistent table may contain consistent parts (i.e., some useful information) which can be extracted through queries.

This kind of query answering, known as *consistent query answering*, has attracted a lot of attention since the 1990s and continues to be an important subject of research today [2,3,14,20]. It is thus not possible to review all related approaches here, and we refer to [5] for a detailed survey covering the topic. We emphasize that two main approaches to consistent query answering have emerged: the approach by 'table repairs' [2,20], for tables with functional dependencies but without nulls, and more recently a more general approach without table repairs for tables with functional dependencies *and* nulls [12,13].

Explanation of Query Answers. With the growing popularity of big data, many users with a variety of backgrounds seek to extract high level information from data-sets. A major challenge is then to develop tools to assist users in explaining observed query outputs.

In this paper we study explanations related to the presence of inconsistent tuples in the computation of a query answer. For instance, in our previous example of employees, salaries and departments, if we ask the SQL query Q : select Sal from T the answer will be empty. Given that the consistent query answer over employee and salary contains the tuple $e's'$, the user may wonder why the answer over salary is empty. The explanation is that, although $e's'$ is consistent (that is e' is assigned the only salary s'), s' is also involved in an inconsistent tuple (namely es' as e is assigned two salaries).

Related work in this domain was initiated by Halpern and Pearl in [9,10], where basic motivation and formal definitions of causality are presented and discussed in detail. In particular, in [10], an explanation of φ is defined as *a minimal elaboration of events that suffice to cause φ even in the face of uncertainty about the actual situation*. This generic definition corresponds in our work to explaining why a tuple t is or not in the consistent answer to a given query Q, in the simple case where there is no uncertainty about the actual situation. Our way of explaining the answers to queries is also related to *data lineage* [15]. According to this work, 'explaining' query answers is achieved based on the database content and on the expression of the query. However, in this work the authors do not consider inconsistent databases as we do. Dealing with causality and explanation in the presence of inconsistent data has been presented in [6], relying on the notion of database repairs, which we do not use in our work.

We also note that another typical scenario is when a user integrates data sets, computes some statistics, and then seeks an explanation why certain values are or are *not* outliers ([16,17]). Such kind of explanations lies however out of the scope of the present paper.

Quality of Query Answers. The answer to a query addressed to a consistent table in a relational database, comes from tuples that are consistent and that are *assumed* to be true (a basic assumption in relational databases). In contrast, the answer to a query addressed to a possibly inconsistent table may be computed from inconsistent tuples. For instance, in our previous example of employees, salaries and departments, the answer comes from two inconsistent tuples (*es* and *es'd*) and one consistent tuple (*e's'*). In this paper, we introduce various quality measures such as percentages of consistent or inconsistent tuples in the table expressing the 'influence' of inconsistent data on the answers to queries.

Regarding related work, inconsistency measurement has been addressed in [8], based on three-valued propositional logic. In this setting, the authors propose 10 distinct possible measures, and discuss their relevance in the context of databases. Moreover, it is shown in [8] that, contrary to our approach, most quality measures lead to non tractable computations. In [11], the authors address the issue of 'approximate inference of functional dependency', and to do so they define quality measures for assessing the 'quality' of functional dependencies in a given table. Roughly, these measures are based on the number of *conflicting pairs* of tuples of the form (xy, xy'), for a given functional dependency $X \to Y$. Contrary to the more generic case of [8], the authors of [11] argue that computing their measures is in $\mathcal{O}(N.\log(N))$ where N is the number of tuples in T, thus resulting in a tractable complexity. To compare this work with our work, we notice that although the contexts are similar (namely a possibly inconsistent table with functional dependencies), the goals of the two approaches are different since ours considers the problem of consistent query answering and in [11], the authors address the issue of functional dependency inference.

As will be seen later in the paper, relating explanations and data quality in presence of inconsistent data is a relevant issue. This task, first identified in [4], remains to be further investigated.

Summarizing the above discussion, we address the issues of query answer explanation and quality measures for query answers in a table with nulls and functional dependencies. In order to study these issues, we need to know which tuples of the table are consistent or inconsistent, on the one hand, and which tuples are false or true, on the other hand.

The reason why such knowledge is necessary is twofold. First, we want to define the answer to a query to contain only tuples that are true and consistent (as in relational databases); in this way if a user seeks an explanation such as why certain tuples are (or are *not*) in an answer, we will be able to justify the presence or absence of the tuples in question by telling the user that the tuples are false or inconsistent. Second, we want to be able to provide measures for measuring the quality of data in the table and in the query answers. As we saw in the previous example of employees, salaries and departments, a consistent answer to a query may contain tuples computed from inconsistent tuples. Therefore we want to define measures of the 'influence' of such tuples on the data in the table and on the data of a query answer. For example, the higher the ratio of consistent to true tuples in the table, the higher the quality of the data in the table; and similarly, the higher the percentage of tuples in the answer computed from consistent tuples in the table, the higher the 'confidence' in the query answer.

The remainder of this paper is organized as follows: in Sects. 2 and 3, we recall from [13] our definitions of m-Chase and of consistent query answer, respectively; in Sect. 4 we present our approach to explanations of query answers; in Sect. 5 we present our approach to quality measures for tables with nulls and functional dependencies, as well as for consistent query answers. In Sect. 6 we offer some concluding remarks and perspectives of our work.

2   The m-Chase Algorithm

2.1   Notation and Basic Definitions

As in the relational model, we consider a universe $U = \{A_1, \ldots, A_n\}$ in which every attribute A_i is associated with a set of atomic values called the domain of A_i and denoted by $dom(A_i)$. We call *relation schema* (or simply *schema*) any nonempty sub-set of U and we denote it by the concatenation of its elements.

A *tuple t* over U is a partial function from U to $\bigcup_{A \in U} dom(A)$ such that, if t is defined over A then $t(A)$, also denoted $t.A$, belongs to $dom(A)$. The domain of definition of t is called the *schema* of t, denoted by $sch(t)$. Tuples in our approach satisfy the *First Normal Form* [19], in the sense that each tuple component is an atomic value. A tuple t is denoted by the concatenation of its values: $t = a_{i_1} \ldots a_{i_k}$ means that for every $j = 1, \ldots, k$, $t.A_{i_j} = a_{i_j}$, where a_{i_j} is in $dom(A_{i_j})$, and $sch(t) = A_{i_1} \ldots A_{i_k}$. We define a *table* over U to be a *finite* set of tuples over U (therefore duplicates are not allowed), and we note that as tuples are partial functions, tables may contain nulls.

Given a table T, we denote by $\mathcal{T}$ the set of all tuples built up from values in T. Queries are issued against T and consistent answers are obtained from $\mathcal{T}$. For every relation schema X, we denote by $\mathcal{T}(X)$ the set of all tuples in $\mathcal{T}$ with schema X: $\mathcal{T}(X) = \{t \in \mathcal{T} \mid sch(t) = X\}$. For every A in U, the set of all values from $dom(A)$ occurring in T is called the *active domain of A*, denoted by $adom(A)$, and we let $\mathcal{AD} = \bigcup_{A \in U} adom(A)$. In other words, $\mathcal{AD}$ is the set of all values appearing in T.

Given a tuple t, for every nonempty sub-set S of $sch(t)$ the restriction of t to S, is denoted by $t.S$. In this work, tables over universe U are associated with a fixed set of functional dependencies FD. A functional dependency is an expression of the form $X \to A$ where X is a schema and A an attribute not in X. A table T is said to satisfy $X \to A$ if for all t and t' in T such that $t.XA$ and $t'.XA$ contain no nulls, if $t.X = t'.X$ then $t.A = t'.A$.

2.2   The m-Chase Algorithm

In order to characterize a tuple of a given table T as consistent/inconsistent and as true/false, we define a modified version of the classical chase algorithm

[7,19]. We recall that, given a table T with nulls and a set FD of functional dependencies, the chase algorithm constructs an 'extended' table denoted by $chase(T)$ as follows:

for all t and t' such that there exists $X \to A$ in FD and $t.X = t'X$

    if $t.A$ and $t'.A$ are *distinct* domain values, **then** *fail*

    else if $t.A = a$ and $t'.A$ is null **then** assign a to $t'.A$

If the chase algorithm succeeds then all tuples in the resulting table $chase(T)$, are consistent and are *assumed* to be true (a basic assumption in relational databases). However, if the chase algorithm fails then we do not know which tuples are consistent and which are inconsistent.

    To cope with this problem, a modified version of the chase algorithm was introduced in [13], which allows to *always* know which tuples are consistent and which are inconsistent. This algorithm, called *m-Chase* works as follows: distinct values $t.A$ and $t'.A$ of the chase algorithm above do *not* provoke a failure; instead, such values are accumulated in a set thus creating m-tuples (i.e., tuples in which each component can be a set of values instead of a single value).

    In our introductory example where $T = \{es, es'd, e's'\}$, running the usual chase algorithm with the functional dependency $Emp \to Sal$ would result in failure since the tuples $t = es$ and $t' = es'd$ violate the dependency $Emp \to Sal$. In contrast, our algorithm, called *m-Chase* will put the two values $t.Sal$ and $t'.Sal$ in a set to create what we call an *m-tuple* $(e)(ss')(d)$ (to be defined shortly), where concatenation of values between parentheses denotes a set. For example, (e) stands for $\{e\}$, (ss') stands for $\{s, s'\}$ and (d) stands for $\{d\}$. The idea is to accumulate in a set all values of an attribute violating a dependency. As we shall see shortly, based on the set of m-tuples returned by the m-Chase we can compute the sets of true/false and consistent/inconsistent tuples in polynomial time; and based on these sets we can give explanations of query answers and we can also define quality measures as explained earlier.

    We now recall from [13] the basic formalism on which algorithm *m-Chase* relies. First the notion of *multi-valued tuples*, or *m-tuples*, extends that of tuples in the sense that an m-tuple associates every attribute A with a possibly empty *sub-set* of $adom(A)$, instead of a *single* value from $adom(A)$.

Definition 1. *A multi-valued tuple σ over universe U, or m-tuple, is a function from U to the cross product $\times_{A \in U} P(adom(A))$, where $P(adom(A))$ is the power set of $adom(A)$. The set of all attributes A such that $\sigma(A) \neq \emptyset$, is called the schema of σ, denoted by $sch(\sigma)$. Given σ and a sub-set X of $sch(\sigma)$, the restriction of σ to X, denoted $\sigma(X)$, is the m-tuple defined by $(\sigma(X))(A) = \sigma(A)$ for every A in X and $(\sigma(X))(A) = \emptyset$ for any A not in X.*

    Given an m-tuple σ, the set $\mathsf{tuples}(\sigma)$ denotes the set of all tuples t such that $sch(t) = sch(\sigma)$ and for every A in $sch(t)$, $t.A$ belongs to $\sigma(A)$. ☐

Given an m-tuple σ, the set $\sigma(A)$ is denoted by the concatenation of its elements between parentheses, and σ is denoted by the concatenation of all $\sigma(A)$ such that $\sigma(A) \neq \emptyset$. Moreover, $\sigma \sqsubseteq \sigma'$ denotes the 'component-wise inclusion' of σ in σ', that is $\sigma \sqsubseteq \sigma'$ holds if for every $A \in sch(\sigma)$, $\sigma(A) \subseteq \sigma'(A)$.

Algorithm 1. The m-Chase Algorithm

Input: A table T over U and a set FD of functional dependencies over U.
Output: An m-table denoted by Σ^*.
1: $\Sigma^* := \{\sigma_t \mid t \in T\}$ // σ_t is the m-tuple such that $\sigma_t(A) = \{t.A\}$ for $A \in sch(t)$
2: $change := true$
3: **while** $change = true$ **do**
4:    $change := false$
5:    **for all** σ and σ' in Σ^* **do**
6:       **for all** $X \to A$ in FD such that $XA \subseteq sch(\sigma)$ and $XA \subseteq sch(\sigma)$ **do**
7:          **if** tuples$(\sigma(X)) \cap$ tuples$(\sigma'(X)) \neq \emptyset$ **then**
8:             apply the m-Chase rule to σ and σ'
9:             $change := true$
10: **return** Σ^*

We call *m-table* over U any finite set of m-tuples over U. For all σ and σ' in an m-table Σ, and $X \to A$ such that $XA \subseteq sch(\sigma)$ and $XA \subseteq sch(\sigma')$, the following rule called m-Chase rule generalizes the chase rule.

- m-Chase rule: Let $\sigma_1 = \sigma \cup \sigma'(A)$ and $\sigma_1' = \sigma' \cup \sigma(A)$
  Case of $\sigma_1 \sqsubseteq \sigma_1'$: replace σ with σ_1', and remove σ_1
  Case of $\sigma_1' \sqsubseteq \sigma_1$: replace σ' with σ_1, and remove σ_1'
  Otherwise: replace σ and σ' with σ_1 and σ_1', respectively.

As shown in Algorithm 1 our algorithm consists in applying the m-Chase rule whenever tuples$(\sigma(X)) \cap$ tuples$(\sigma'(X)) \neq \emptyset$ until no further transformation is possible. The output is an m-table Σ^*, and it has been shown in [13] that this algorithm always terminates and that the partition semantics of tuples in T (as introduced in [18] and extended in [12,13]), is defined based on Σ^* as follows.

Definition 2. *For every t in T:*

1. *t is true if there exists σ in Σ^* and q in tuples(σ) such that t is a sub-tuple of q. The set of all true tuples is denoted by True(T).*
2. *t is false if t is not true. The set of all false tuples is denoted by False(T).*
3. *t is inconsistent if there exists σ in Σ^* such that tuples$(\sigma(sch(t))) = \{t\}$. The set of all inconsistent tuples is denoted by Inc(T).*
4. *t is consistent if t is true and not inconsistent. The set of all consistent tuples is denoted by Cons(T).* □

As shown in [13], the computation of Σ^* is in $\mathcal{O}(|\Sigma^*|^3.\delta^2)$, where δ is the maximal cardinality of the components of m-tuples in Σ^*, which is precisely the maximum number of A-values associated with X-values when $X \to A$ is a functional dependency in FD. As Algorithm 1 shows that $|\Sigma^*| \leq |T|$, we state that the computation of Σ^* is in $\mathcal{O}(|T|^3.\delta^2)$, i.e., *polynomial in the size of T.*

Example 1. In the context of our introductory example, where $T = \{es, es'd, e's'\}$ is a table defined over $U = \{Emp, Sal, Dept\}$ with the functional dependency $Emp \to Sal$, Σ^* is built up according to the following steps:

Step 1: Σ^* is first set to $\{(e)(s), (e)(s')(d), (e')(s')\}$.

Step 2: Considering $\sigma = (e)(s)$ and $\sigma' = (e)(s')(d)$, the m-tuples $\sigma_1 = (e)(ss')$ and $\sigma_1' = (e)(ss')(d)$ are generated. Since $\sigma_1 \sqsubseteq \sigma_1'$, $\Sigma^* = \{(e)(ss')(d), (e')(s')\}$.

Step 3: As a new execution of the while-loop line 3 does not change Σ^*, the algorithm returns $\Sigma^* = \{(e)(ss')(d), (e')(s')\}$.

Therefore, $\mathsf{True}(\mathcal{T})$ contains esd, $es'd$, $e's'$ and all their sub-tuples. Hence, $\mathsf{False}(\mathcal{T}) = \{e'sd, e's, e'd\}$. Moreover, $\mathsf{Inc}(\mathcal{T}) = \{esd, es'd, es, es', sd, s'd, s, s'\}$, and thus $\mathsf{Cons}(\mathcal{T}) = \{ed, e's', e, e', d\}$. □

It turns out from Definition 2 that a tuple t can be either *true* or *false*, and that true tuples are either *consistent* or *inconsistent*. However, *false* tuples are neither consistent nor inconsistent. Notice that, since we only focus on true tuples, the consistency of false tuples is irrelevant in this work. Membership of t to $\mathsf{True}(\mathcal{T})$ or $\mathsf{False}(\mathcal{T})$ on the one hand, and to $\mathsf{Cons}(\mathcal{T})$ or $\mathsf{Inc}(\mathcal{T})$ on the other hand, is referred to as the *status* of t. Thus a tuple can have one of the following status: true and consistent, true and inconsistent or false. Referring to Example 1, esd is true and inconsistent, $s'd$ is true and inconsistent and $e's$ is false.

3   Consistent Query Answering

3.1   Query Syntax

The queries Q that we consider in this work have the form of a usual SQL query:

$$Q : \texttt{select } X \texttt{ from } T \texttt{ [where } \Gamma\texttt{]}$$

in which the `where` clause specifies an optional selection condition Γ. The set of all attributes occurring in Γ is called the *schema of* Γ, denoted by $sch(\Gamma)$; and the attribute set $X \cup sch(\Gamma)$ is called the *schema of* Q, denoted by $sch(Q)$.

A selection condition Γ is a well-formed formula built up using connectors $\neg$, $\vee$, $\wedge$ and atomic comparisons of the forms: $A\,\theta\,a$ or $A\,\theta\,A'$, where θ is a comparison predicate, A and A' are attributes, and a is in $dom(A)$. Given Γ, we denote by $Sat(\Gamma)$ the set of all tuples in $\mathcal{T}(sch(\Gamma))$ satisfying Γ, where the notion of satisfaction follows the usual rules in FO logics. For example, the tuple $t = abcc$ over scheme $ABCD$ is in $Sat(\Gamma)$ for $\Gamma = ((A = a')\vee(C = D))\wedge(B = b)$.

We emphasize that, contrary to most existing approaches to consistent query answering [3,14,20], our approach is not restricted to deal with conjunctive queries, since disjunctive selection conditions are allowed. The *consistent answer* to a query Q in our approach relies on the notion of *consistency with respect to a selection condition* as defined below.

Definition 3. *Given a table T over U, and Γ a selection condition, a tuple t such that $sch(\Gamma) \subseteq sch(t)$ is said to be* consistent with respect to Γ *if there exists σ in Σ^* such that t is in* $\mathsf{tuples}(\sigma)$ *and* $\mathsf{tuples}(\sigma(sch(\Gamma))) \subseteq Sat(\Gamma)$.

We denote by $\mathsf{Cons}(\Gamma, \mathcal{T})$ *the set of all tuples consistent with respect to Γ.* □

Algorithm 2. Consistent answer

Input: A query Q : select X from T [where Γ] and Σ^*
Output: C_ans(Q)
  1: C_ans(Q) := $\emptyset$; $ToRem\_X$:= $\emptyset$
  2: **for all** σ in Σ^* such that $X \subseteq sch(\sigma)$ **do**
  3:    **if** $|\mathsf{tuples}(\sigma(X))| > 1$ **then**
  4:      $ToRem\_X := ToRem\_X \cup \mathsf{tuples}(\sigma(X))$
  5:    **else**
  6:      Let x denote the unique tuple in $\mathsf{tuples}(\sigma(X))$
  7:      **if** $sch(\Gamma) \subseteq sch(\sigma)$ and $\mathsf{tuples}(\sigma(sch(\Gamma))) \subseteq Sat(\Gamma)$ **then**
  8:        C_ans(Q) := C_ans(Q) $\cup \{x\}$
  9: C_ans(Q) := C_ans(Q) $\setminus ToRem\_X$
10: **return** C_ans(Q)

We illustrate this definition using Example 1. For the condition $\Gamma = (Sal = s')$ we have $Sat(\Gamma) = \{s'\}$. Thus, $es'd$ is not in $\mathsf{Cons}(\Gamma, \mathcal{T})$ because $(e)(ss')(d)$ is in Σ^* and $(ss') \not\subseteq Sat(\Gamma)$. On the other hand, for $\Gamma' = (Sal = s) \vee (Sal = s')$ we have $Sat(\Gamma') = \{s, s'\}$. Since $(ss') \subseteq Sat(\Gamma')$, $es'd$ is in $\mathsf{Cons}(\Gamma', \mathcal{T})$. As $es'd$ has been shown to be in $\mathsf{Inc}(\mathcal{T})$, this means that tuples in $\mathsf{Cons}(\Gamma', \mathcal{T})$ may be inconsistent. As will be seen shortly, this implies that inconsistent tuples may participate in the computation of consistent answers.

3.2 Consistent Answers

In what follows, given a schema X, we denote by $\mathsf{True}(X)$, $\mathsf{Cons}(X)$ and $\mathsf{Inc}(X)$ the set of all true, consistent and inconsistent tuples of $\mathcal{T}(X)$, respectively. The consistent answer to a query Q is defined as follows.

Definition 4. *Let T be a table over universe U and FD the set of associated functional dependencies. Given a query Q : select X from T [where Γ], the consistent answer to Q, denoted $\mathsf{C\_ans}(Q)$, is the set of tuples x such that*

1. x is in $\mathsf{Cons}(X)$, and
2. there exists t such that $sch(t) \subseteq sch(Q)$, $t.X = x$ and t is in $\mathsf{Cons}(\Gamma, \mathcal{T})$. □

We point out that when T is consistent, our m-Chase algorithm coincides with the standard Chase algorithm. Thus, the m-tuples in Σ^* are 'isomorphic' to tuples in the chased table, which implies that $\mathsf{C\_ans}(Q)$ is equal to the standard answer as defined in [19].
Based on Definition 4, it can be shown that Algorithm 2 correctly computes the consistent answer to a query Q. It is also easy to see that this algorithm is linear in the number of m-tuples in Σ^*, that is linear in the number of tuples in T.

Example 2. We illustrate Definition 4 and Algorithm 2 in the context of Example 1 where $\Sigma^* = \{(e)(ss')(d), (e')(s')\}$. Denoting $(e)(ss')(d)$ by σ_1 and $(e')(s')$ by σ_2, we have the following:

- For Q_1 : `select` Sal `from` T, the expected answer is $\emptyset$ because σ_1 implies that s and s' are inconsistent. Algorithm 2 runs as follows:
  - With σ_1, the test line 3 succeeds. Thus, $ToRem\_X$ is set to $\{s, s'\}$ line 4, and so, C_ans(Q) remains empty.
  - With σ_2, the test line 3 fails and the test on line 7 succeeds (since the query involves no selection condition). Thus, $ToRem\_X$ is not changed, and s' is inserted in C_ans(Q) line 8. Then, when processing line 9, C_ans(Q) is set to $(\{s'\} \setminus \{s, s'\})$, that is to $\emptyset$, as expected.
- For Q_2 : `select` Emp, Sal `from` T, C_ans$(Q_2) = \{e's'\}$ as $e's'$ is the only tuple in Cons$(Emp\ Sal)$. Algorithm 2 runs as follows:
  - With σ_1, the test line 3 succeeds, and so es and es' are inserted in $ToRem\_X$ line 4, while C_ans(Q) remains empty.
  - With σ_2, the test line 3 fails and the test line 7 succeeds. Thus, $ToRem\_X$ is not changed, and $e's'$ is inserted in C_ans(Q) line 8. Since $ToRem\_X = \{es, es'\}$, C_ans(Q) is not changed on line 9, and we have: C_ans$(Q_2) = \{e's'\}$.
- For Q_3 : `select` Emp `from` T `where` $Sal = s'$, we have $Sat(\Gamma) = \{s'\}$ and so, es' is not in Cons(Γ, T). Thus, e is not in C_ans(Q_3). Since e' is in Cons(T) and $e's'$ is in Cons(Γ, T), C_ans$(Q_3) = \{e'\}$. Algorithm 2 runs as follows:
  - With σ_1, the tests line 3 and line 7 fail (since $Sat(\Gamma) = \{s'\}$ and $\{s, s'\} \not\subseteq \{s'\}$). Thus, $ToRem\_X$ and C_ans(Q) remain empty.
  - With σ_2, the test line 3 fails and the test on line 7 succeeds. Thus, $ToRem\_X$ is not changed, and e' is inserted in C_ans(Q) line 8. Since C_ans(Q) is not changed line 9, we have: C_ans$(Q_3) = \{e'\}$. $\square$

4   Explanations

Explanations come in response to a user's request either about the status of a given tuple, or about the presence or the absence of a tuple in the consistent answer to a query Q. Typically, these explanations come as a sentence referring to Σ^* possibly followed by tuples or m-tuples. Obviously, such explanations are meaningful to the user, only if she/he has a clear understanding of how the status of a tuple is obtained.

More precisely, we consider two scenarios: In the first, given a tuple t along with its status, the user seeks for explanations about this status. In Example 1, explaining why the tuple es' is true can be done by displaying "es' is true because es' occurs in Σ^*, in m-tuple $(e)(ss')(d)$"; and explaining why es' is inconsistent can be done by displaying "es' is inconsistent because es' occurs in Σ^* but violates $Emp \rightarrow Sal$, as shown in $(e)(ss')(d)$."

In the second scenario, given a query Q, the user seeks for explanations about the presence or absence of a tuple in the answer. In Example 2, explaining why e' is in the answer to Q_3 can be done by displaying: "e' occurs in Σ^* and violates no functional dependencies" (to explain that e' is consistent); and then "e' occurs in the m-tuple $(e')(s')$" of Σ^* that satisfies the selection condition $Sal = s'$.

In order to provide users with intuitive explanations, we propose first the following generic explanations that allow to deal with the first scenario and based on which explanations in the second scenario are generated.

(A) To explain that t is in $\mathsf{True}(\mathcal{T})$, we display "$t$ occurs in Σ^*", followed by an m-tuple σ such that $t \in \mathsf{tuples}(\sigma(sch(t)))$.

(B) To explain that t is in $\mathsf{False}(\mathcal{T})$, we display "$t$ does not occur in Σ^*" meaning that for every σ in Σ^*, $t \notin \mathsf{tuples}(\sigma(sch(t)))$. Providing evidence of this statement is impossible, unless displaying Σ^*, which is not a reasonable option.

(C) To explain that t is in $\mathsf{Inc}(\mathcal{T})$, we display "$t$ occurs in Σ^* but violates functional dependencies", followed by an m-tuple σ such that $t \in \mathsf{tuples}(\sigma(sch(t)))$, $|\mathsf{tuples}(\sigma(sch(t)))| > 1$ and (at least) one functional dependency $X \rightarrow A$ such that $XA \subseteq sch(\sigma)$, $A \in sch(t)$ and $|\mathsf{tuples}(\sigma(A))| > 1$.

(D) To explain that t is in $\mathsf{Cons}(\mathcal{T})$, we display "$t$ occurs in Σ^* and violates no functional dependencies." Providing evidence of this statement is impossible, unless displaying all σ in Σ^* such that t is a sub-tuple of a tuple q in $\mathsf{tuples}(\sigma)$ to show that they all satisfy that $\mathsf{tuples}(\sigma(sch(t))) = \{t\}$. This looks unrealistic as this would generate an important number of m-tuples!

(E) Given a selection condition Γ, explaining that t is in $Sat(\Gamma)$ is straightforwardly done by displaying "t satisfies the selection condition Γ." To explain that t is in $\mathsf{Cons}(\Gamma, \mathcal{T})$ we display "t occurs in an m-tuple in Σ^* that satisfies the selection condition Γ", followed by a σ such that $t \in \mathsf{tuples}(\sigma(sch(t)))$, $sch(\Gamma) \subseteq sch(\sigma)$ and $\sigma(sch(\Gamma))) \subseteq Sat(\Gamma)$.

Now, given Q : `select` X `from` T `[where` Γ`]`, explaining the presence or the absence of a given tuple x in the consistent answer to Q can be done as follows:

- The explanation of the presence of x in the consistent answer is provided by the definition of the query, namely, x is in the answer because x is in $\mathsf{Cons}(\mathcal{T})$ and x has a super-tuple t in $\mathsf{Cons}(\Gamma, \mathcal{T})$. Therefore, if Q involves no selection condition, explanation **(D)** is displayed and, otherwise, explanations **(D)** and **(E)** above are combined and displayed.
- The explanation of the absence of a tuple x from the answer is due to one of the following three reasons:
  - (a) x is in $\mathsf{False}(\mathcal{T})$, in which case explanation **(B)** is displayed,
  - (b) x is in $\mathsf{Inc}(\mathcal{T})$, in which case explanation **(C)** is displayed,
  - (c) x is in $\mathsf{Cons}(\mathcal{T})$ but x has no super-tuple in $\mathsf{Cons}(\Gamma, \mathcal{T})$, in which case explanation **(D)** is displayed followed by: "x has no super-tuple occurring in an m-tuple of T satisfying the selection condition Γ.

Clearly, providing such explanations assumes that the m-Chase table Σ^* has been computed in advance. We also emphasize here that each of the above explanations requires only a single scan of Σ^*.

Indeed, explanations **(B)** and **(D)** only require to know the status of a tuple (which is computed through a scan of Σ^*), whereas explanations **(A)**, **(C)** and **(E)** display an m-tuple from Σ^*, as an evidence of the message. In any case, *all computations necessary for our explanations are polynomial in the size of T.*

We note that explanations as defined above relate to the work of [16,17], in the sense that our explanations consist in displaying, whenever possible, tuples responsible of the fact being explained. We are currently investigating how our approach could be more formally defined as done in [16,17], although their approaches do not address explaining inconsistencies as we do.

5   Quality Measures

When querying a possibly inconsistent table, it is important for users to have an idea of the 'amount' of inconsistency in the table. In this section, we aim to provide users with tools and measures that quantify inconsistencies in the table and we do so based on the set of tuples that are true according to the semantics introduced earlier. We require all measures μ to be such that $0 \leq \mu \leq 1$ and $\mu = 1$ when T is consistent, that is when $\mathsf{Inc}(T) = \emptyset$.

We distinguish two cases here: (a) quality of data in a table and (b) quality of data in a consistent query answer. In either case, in the definitions of our measures, we assume that the m-chased table Σ^* is available.

5.1   Quality of Data in a Table

Given a table T, we first define the *quality of* T, denoted by $Qual(T)$, as the ratio of the number of consistent tuples over the number of true tuples in T:

$$Qual(T) = \frac{|\mathsf{Cons}(T)|}{|\mathsf{True}(T)|} = 1 - \frac{|\mathsf{Inc}(T)|}{|\mathsf{True}(T)|}.$$

Notice that if T is consistent then $Qual(T) = 1$. Moreover, if $\mathsf{True}(T) = \emptyset$, then Σ^* is empty, implying that T and $\mathsf{Inc}(T)$ are empty as well. Thus, we set $Qual(T) = 1$ when $\mathsf{True}(T) = \emptyset$.

However, computing $Qual(T)$ based on Σ^* and Definition 2 is not trivial because each tuple should be counted only *once*. Since every sub-tuple of a true tuple is also true and every sub-tuple of a consistent tuple is consistent, the computation is not easy. To see this, consider the case of true tuples in $\Sigma^* = \{(a)(b), (a)(b'), (a')(b)\}$. Here $\mathsf{True}(T)$ consists of ab, ab', $a'b$, along with all their sub-tuples. As a occurs in ab and in ab', counting the sub-tuples of each tuple occurring in Σ^* may lead to an incorrect result. Indeed, we have $\mathsf{True}(T) = \{ab, ab', a'b, a, a', b, b'\}$ but as a occurs in ab and in ab', the count in this example *should* be 7 (and *not* 12).

Counting the consistent tuples raises an additional difficulty, because in order to conclude that a tuple t is consistent, *every* m-tuple σ in which t occurs must be such that $|tuples(\sigma(sch(t)))| = 1$. This is why, to compute $Qual(T)$, it is better to count the inconsistent tuples, based on the facts that

(a) $\mathsf{Cons}(T) = \mathsf{True}(T) \setminus \mathsf{Inc}(T)$ and
(b) $\mathsf{Cons}(T) \cap \mathsf{Inc}(T) = \emptyset$,

which imply that $\frac{|\mathsf{Cons}(T)|}{|\mathsf{True}(T)|} = 1 - \frac{|\mathsf{Inc}(T)|}{|\mathsf{True}(T)|}$.

Example 3. In Example 1 where $\Sigma^* = \{(e)(ss')(d), (e')(s')\}$, we have seen that $\mathsf{Inc}(T) = \{esd, es'd, es, es', sd, s'd, s, s'\}$ and thus we have $|\mathsf{Inc}(T)| = 8$ and counting the tuples in $\mathsf{True}(T)$ amounts to counting the number of distinct sub-tuples of esd, $es'd$ and $e's'$, which yields 13. Therefore, we have $Qual(T) = 1 - \frac{8}{13}$, that is $Qual(T) = 5/13$.   □

It turns out that the computation of $Qual(T)$ is *polynomial in the number of tuples in T* (in fact a single scan of Σ^* is sufficient in order to identify 'maximal' true tuples, based on which all tuples of interest are processed), but the computation of $Qual(T)$ is *exponential in the number of attributes in U* (as the status of every sub-tuple of a maximal tuple has to be determined and as every tuple must be counted only once).

We are currently investigating how to efficiently compute this measure. It seems that level-wise techniques borrowed from those in the well-known Apriori algorithm [1] should be relevant in our context. Moreover, investigating how to compute an approximate value for $Qual(T)$ based on sampling is also an issue that we are currently considering, inspired by the work in [11].

Another reliable but easier way of assessing the quality of T is to focus on functional dependencies. To express such a measure, for each $X \to A$ in FD, let $\mathsf{Inc}(X \to A)$ be the set of all true tuples not satisfying $X \to A$, i.e.,

$$\mathsf{Inc}(X \to A) = \{x \in \mathsf{True}(X) \mid (\exists \sigma \in \Sigma^*)(XA \subseteq sch(\sigma) \wedge$$
$$x \in \mathsf{tuples}(\sigma(X)) \wedge |\mathsf{tuples}(\sigma(A))| > 1)\}.$$

If $\mathsf{True}(X)$ is nonempty, the associated measure is:

$$Qual_X^A(T) = 1 - \frac{|\mathsf{Inc}(X \to A)|}{|\mathsf{True}(X)|}.$$

Notice that the definition of $Qual_X^A(T)$ satisfies the property that if T satisfies the functional dependency $X \to A$, then $Qual_X^A(T) = 1$, because in this case, $\mathsf{Inc}(X \to A) = \emptyset$. Therefore, if T is consistent then $Qual_X^A(T) = 1$.

We emphasize that $|\mathsf{Inc}(X \to A)|$ and $|\mathsf{True}(X)|$ are computed through a simple scan of Σ^*, which implies that $Qual_X^A(T)$ is computed efficiently. We then define the following measure as the average of all $Qual_X^A(T)$:

$$Qual_{FD}(T) = \frac{\sum_{X \to A \in FD} Qual_X^A(T)}{|FD|}.$$

In Example 3, we have $\mathsf{Inc}(Emp \to Sal) = \{e\}$ and $\mathsf{True}(Emp) = \{e, e'\}$. Hence, $|\mathsf{Inc}(Emp \to Sal)| = 1$ and $|\mathsf{True}(Emp)| = 2$, and so, $Qual_{Emp}^{Sal}(T) = 0.5$. As $|FD| = 1$, we have $Qual_{FD}(T) = 0.5$.

We note that, if T is consistent then $Qual_X^A(T) = 1$, for every $X \to A$ in FD, and therefore $Qual_{FD}(T) = 1$. We also note that the knowledge of $Qual_X^A(T)$ for every $X \to A$ in FD allows for the definition of additional aggregate measures by replacing 'average' by for example 'maximum' or 'minimum'.

Moreover, as in the work in [11] about *approximate* functional dependencies, the use of a threshold ρ such that $0 < \rho \leq 1$, allows to define the measure:

$$Qual^{\rho}_{FD}(T) = \frac{|\{X \rightarrow A \in FD \mid Qual^{A}_{X}(T) \geq \rho\}|}{|FD|}.$$

Intuitively, ρ is a threshold below which a functional dependency is considered *not* satisfied, and $Qual^{\rho}_{FD}$ returns the ratio of functional dependencies in FD that are 'approximately satisfied' with respect to ρ. In Example 3, for $\rho = 0.33$, $Qual^{\rho}_{FD} = 1$, because $Emp \rightarrow Sal$ is considered 'approximately satisfied'.

We point out that the knowledge of $Qual_{FD}(T)$ and of every $Qual^{A}_{X}(T)$ allow to put forward the inconsistencies in T. Indeed, if we use an appropriate graphical interface to display all values of $Qual^{A}_{X}(T)$, for every $X \rightarrow A$, then one can easily identify the values of $Qual^{A}_{X}(T)$ considered too low; and then, for each of the corresponding functional dependencies, one can justify the consistency or inconsistency of tuples in $T(XA)$ using explanations as seen in Sect. 4.

5.2   Quality of Data in a Consistent Answer

Given Q : `select` X `from` T `[where` Γ`]`, we denote by $\mathsf{Ans}(Q)$ the set of all true tuples x over X having a true super-tuple in $Sat(\Gamma)$. Formally,

$$\mathsf{Ans}(Q) = \{x \in \mathsf{True}(X) \mid (\exists q \in \mathsf{True}(sch(Q)))(q.X = x \wedge q.sch(\Gamma) \in Sat(\Gamma))\}.$$

Notice that, if T is consistent, then $\mathsf{Ans}(Q) = \mathsf{C\_ans}(Q)$. However, if T is not consistent, there may be tuples in $\mathsf{Ans}(Q)$ which are *not* in $\mathsf{C\_ans}(Q)$.

In the context of Example 2, for the query Q_3, we have $\mathsf{C\_ans}(Q_3) = \{e'\}$, whereas $\mathsf{Ans}(Q_3) = \{e, e'\}$ (because es' and $e's'$ are true and satisfy the condition $(Sal = s')$). However, in all cases, we have $\mathsf{C\_ans}(Q) \subseteq \mathsf{Ans}(Q)$.

We define the quality of the consistent answer to Q as the ratio between the number of tuples in $\mathsf{C\_ans}(Q)$ over the number of tuples in $\mathsf{Ans}(Q)$. Formally, assuming that $\mathsf{Ans}(Q)$ is nonempty:

$$Qual(Q) = \frac{|\mathsf{C\_ans}(Q)|}{|\mathsf{Ans}(Q)|}.$$

If $\mathsf{Ans}(Q) = \emptyset$ then we set $Qual(Q) = 1$ because in this case $\mathsf{C\_ans}(Q)$ is empty. Clearly, if T is consistent then, as $\mathsf{Ans}(Q) = \mathsf{C\_ans}(Q)$, we have $Qual(Q) = 1$. Notice also that if Q involves no selection condition then $Qual(Q) = \frac{|\mathsf{Cons}(X)|}{|\mathsf{True}(X)|}$.

To illustrate this quality measure, refer to Example 2, where the consistent answers to Q_1 and Q_3 are respectively $\{ed\}$ and $\{e'\}$. As we also have $\mathsf{Ans}(Q_1) = \{ed\}$ and $\mathsf{Ans}(Q_3) = \{e, e'\}$, we obtain $Qual(Q_1) = 1$ and $Qual(Q_3) = 0.5$.

It is important to note that, if the contents of query answers are displayed together with their qualities, the user has the opportunity to ask for explanations as described in the previous section. For instance, in our example above, a user might wonder why the quality of the answer to query Q_3 is 0.5. The explanation to be provided in this case is that there exist tuples in $\mathsf{Ans}(Q_3)$ which are not in $\mathsf{C\_ans}(Q_3)$. The user can then continue the dialogue with the system, for example by asking to see such tuples.

6   Conclusion

In this paper, we have addressed two issues regarding query processing in tables with nulls and functional dependencies, namely explanation of a query answer and quality of data in a query answer. The starting point was our earlier work on defining consistent answers to queries submitted to such tables [13]. Based on that earlier work we have proposed an approach to explaining the content of a consistent query answer and measuring its quality. We have shown that explaining the contents consists mainly in determining why a given tuple is consistent/inconsistent, or why it is or it is not in the consistent answer to a query. We have also proposed measures for assessing the quality of the data in a table and in a query answer, as well as algorithms for their computation. Finally, we have seen how the simultaneous use of explanations and quality measures can help users to better 'understand' inconsistencies in the input table.

We are currently pursuing three lines of research. First, we aim to improve the algorithm for computing $Qual(T)$, because even if the computation is polynomial in the size of T, it is nevertheless exponential in the size of the universe. Second, our approach to explanation needs to be further refined, probably along the lines of [4,6,16,17]; also, investigating interactions between explanations and quality measures is a challenging issue. Third, we are exploring the possible use of sampling techniques for providing approximate measures and further improving performance. Indeed, as our approach is meant to apply to large tables resulting from the integration of data from several sources, even a simple scan of the m-table might prove expensive.

References

1. Agrawal, R., Mannila, H., Srikant, R., Toivonen, H., Verkamo, A.I.: Fast discovery of association rules. In: Advances in Knowledge Discovery and Data Mining, pp. 309–328. AAAI-MIT Press (1996)
2. Arenas, M., Bertossi, L.E., Chomicki, J.: Consistent query answers in inconsistent databases. In: Vianu, V., Papadimitriou, C.H. (eds.) Proceedings of the Eighteenth ACM SIGACT-SIGMOD-SIGART Symposium on Principles of Database Systems, Pennsylvania, USA, pp. 68–79. ACM Press (1999)
3. Bertossi, L.E.: Database Repairing and Consistent Query Answering. Synthesis Lectures on Data Management, Morgan & Claypool Publishers, San Rafael (2011)
4. Bertossi, L.E.: Specifying and computing causes for query answers in databases via database repairs and repair-programs. Knowl. Inf. Syst. **63**(1), 199–231 (2021)
5. Bertossi, L.E., Chomicki, J.: Query answering in inconsistent databases. In: Chomicki, J., van der Meyden, R., Saake, G. (eds.) Logics for Emerging Applications of Databases, pp. 43–83. Springer, Heidelberg (2003). https://doi.org/10.1007/978-3-642-18690-5_2

6. Bertossi, L.E., Salimi, B.: Unifying causality, diagnosis, repairs and view-updates in databases. CoRR, abs/1405.4228 (2014)
7. Fagin, R., Mendelzon, A.O., Ullman, J.D.: A simplified universal relation assumption and its properties. ACM Trans. Database Syst. **7**(3), 343–360 (1982)
8. Grant, J.: Measuring inconsistency in generalized propositional logic. Log. Univers. **14**(3), 331–356 (2020)
9. Halpern, J.Y., Pearl, J.: Causes and explanations: a structural-model approach. Part II: explanations. CoRR, cs.AI/0208034 (2002)
10. Halpern, J.Y., Pearl, J.: Causes and explanations: a structural-model approach – part 1: causes. CoRR, abs/1301.2275 (2013)
11. Kivinen, J., Mannila, H.: Approximate inference of functional dependencies from relations. Theor. Comput. Sci. **149**(1), 129–149 (1995)
12. Laurent, D., Spyratos, N.: Handling inconsistencies in tables with nulls and functional dependencies. J. Intell. Inf. Syst. **59**(2), 285–317 (2022)
13. Laurent, D., Spyratos, N.: Consistent query answering without repairs in tables with nulls and functional dependencies. CoRR, abs/2301.03668 (2023)
14. Livshits, E., Kimelfeld, B., Roy, S.: Computing optimal repairs for functional dependencies. ACM Trans. Database Syst. **45**(1), 4:1–4:46 (2020)
15. Meliou, A., Gatterbauer, W., Halpern, J.Y., Koch, C., Moore, K.F., Suciu, D.: Causality in databases. IEEE Data Eng. Bull. **33**(3), 59–67 (2010)
16. Meliou, A., Roy, S., Suciu, D.: Causality and explanations in databases. Proc. VLDB Endow. **7**(13), 1715–1716 (2014)
17. Roy, S., Suciu, D.: A formal approach to finding explanations for database queries. In: Dyreson, C.E., Li, F., Tamer Özsu, M. (eds.) International Conference on Management of Data, SIGMOD 2014, Snowbird, UT, USA, 22–27 June 2014, pp. 1579–1590. ACM (2014)
18. Spyratos, N.: The partition model: a deductive database model. ACM Trans. Database Syst. **12**(1), 1–37 (1987)
19. Ullman, J.D.: Principles of Databases and Knowledge-Base Systems, vol. 1–2. Computer Science Press (1988)
20. Wijsen, J.: On the consistent rewriting of conjunctive queries under primary key constraints. Inf. Syst. **34**(7), 578–601 (2009)

PyExplore 2.0: Explainable, Approximate and Combined Clustering Based SQL Query Recommendations

Apostolos Glenis[(✉)]

Athena RC, Athens, Greece
`aglenis@athenarc.gr`

Abstract. While the benefit of data exploration becomes increasingly more prominent, factors such as the data volume and complexity and user unfamiliarity with the database contents, make querying data a non-trivial, time-consuming process. The big challenge for users is to find which query to ask at any point. PyExplore is a data exploration framework that aims to help users explore datasets by providing SQL query recommendations. The user provides an initial SQL query and then pyExplore provides new SQL queries with augmented WHERE clause. In this paper, we extend pyExplore with four new workflows one for approximate query recommendations, one for explainable query completions, one for combined explainable and approximate recommendation and finally a sampled decision tree workflow that is similar to pyExplore's original workflow but this time only a small portion of the dataset gets processed. The purpose of the explainable workflows is to provide recommendations that are intuitive to the end user while the purpose of approximate workflows is to significantly reduce execution time compared to the full workflow. We evaluated the four workflows in terms of execution time and speedup compared to the full workflow. We found out that a) the quality of the approximate recommendations is on-par with the full workflow b) the explainable workflow is faster than using a decision tree classifier to produce the queries c) the approximate workflow is significantly faster than the full workflow.

Keywords: query recommendations · Recommender Systems · explainable methods

1 Introduction

Data growth and availability as well as data democratization have radically changed data exploration. Many different data sets, generated by users, systems and sensors, are continuously being collected. These data sets contain information about scientific experiments, health, energy, education etc., and they can potentially benefit many types of users, from analysts exploring data sets for insight, scientists looking for patterns, to dashboard interactors and consumers looking for information.

© The Author(s), under exclusive license to Springer Nature Switzerland AG 2024
R. Chbeir et al. (Eds.): MEDES 2023, CCIS 2022, pp. 88–102, 2024.
https://doi.org/10.1007/978-3-031-51643-6_7

While the benefit of data exploration becomes increasingly more prominent, querying data is often a non-trivial, and time-consuming process primarily due to: (a) data volume and complexity, (b) user unfamiliarity with the database contents, and (c) users' low degree of comfortableness with query languages such as SQL. As a result, as the user interacts with a data set, it is not always clear which query to ask at any point. Helping users query and explore data is a holy grail of the database community.

In this paper, we aim to design an SQL query recommendation system that does not use query logs to provide SQL query recommendations and creates explainable recommendations that are intuitive to the user and approximate recommendations that aim to reduce execution time.

To achieve this goal, we extend pyExplore [6] with four new workflows for explainable or approximate recommendations.

We have chosen to extend pyExplore since it is a state-of-the-art SQL query recommendation framework that doesn't utilize query logs. The user provides pyExplore with an initial SQL query and pyExplore produces new SQL query recommendations with augmented WHERE clause.

The aim of the explainable workflows is to provide the user with intuitive SQL query recommendation while the aim of the approximate recommendations is to reduce execution time compared to the full workflow. One of the four workflows combines explainable and approximate query recommendations to provide the best of both worlds in a single workflow.

To the best of our knowledge pyExplore 2.0 is the first SQL query recommendation framework to provide combined explainable and approximate SQL query recommendations.

We make the following contributions:

- We provide four new workflows based on PyExplore in order to create explainable and approximate query recommendations.
- We perform a thorough evaluation on three open dataset to determine both the quality of the recommendations produced by the four workflows as well as their execution time and speedup compared to the full workflow.

The rest of the paper is organized as follows: Section 2 describes the related work, Sect. 3 describes the original pyExplore algorithm, Sect. 4.1 describes the sampled decision tree workflow, Sect. 4.2 describes the approximate workflow, Sect. 4.3 describes the explainable workflow, Sect. 4.4 describes the combined approximate and explainable workflow, Sect. 5 describes the datasets used for the evaluation and the research questions the paper aims to answer, Sect. 6 describes the evaluation of the quality of the recommendations produced by pyExplore 2.0. Section 7 evaluates the methods for explainable recommendations in terms of accuracy. Section 8 compares all the methods together to provide a unified view of the execution time of the methods proposed in this paper and finally Sect. 9 provides our final conclusions.

2   Related Work

Work in query recommendations can be categorized along the following dimensions: (*a*) type of queries: structured or unstructured, (*b*) type of analysis: using query logs vs data analysis, and (*c*) query setting: cold-start or warm-start, i.e., with no prior user query or given a user query.

With respect to the type of queries, most work in query recommendations lies in the context of unstructured queries in search engines (see [19] for a recent survey). We focus the remaining discussion of related work on structured queries.

With respect to the type of analysis, query logs have been used either to mine frequent patterns and query dependencies to find completions for user queries [12,20] or to apply typical recommendation strategies such as matrix factorization and latent models [5] to find queries that could be related to what the user is currently looking for. For instance, in [20], the authors present a method to automatically create join query recommendations based on input-output specifications. As a user types a query, SnipSuggest recommends possible additions to various clauses in the query using relevant snippets collected from a log of past queries [12].

In the absence of query logs, approaches are based on *data analysis* [7]. The idea of splitting the initial user query or data space in meaningful areas has been explored in [13,16]. In Bleau [16], the users explore the data through data maps. A data map is a set of clusters prodiced using one of three algorithms. The first algorithm works on small and medium datasets with small number of attributes. The second produces views prior and then feeds the projected data into the first algorithm to produce recommendations. Finally, the third focuses on speed and interaction with the end user. Explique is a simpler version of Bleau [13]. More specifically Explique does not perform view selection and does not handle categorical data. Explique uses clustering and a decision tree classifier to produce the query recommendations.

There are several data exploration efforts that follow different approaches. For example, Clustine is a conversational engine for data exploration [17] that uses cluster analysis and text generation to explain query results. AIDE [3] uses active learning to incorporate user feedback while suggesting areas that present interesting patterns. Searchlight [11] leverages Constraint Programming (CP) logic for query refinement.

With respect to the query setting, a few works [7,16] handle cold-start while the rest focus on warm-start (e.g., [12,20]).

Related to query recommendation, although different, is *view recommendation* [14,21], another tool to assist data analysts in exploring and understanding big data. View recommendation is the problem of finding top-k visualizations over a dataset. A view essentially represents an SQL query with a group-by clause over a database that measures attributes (e.g., number of items sold) over some dimensional attributes (e.g., year, size). For example, Ziggy [18] detects characteristic views, that is, small sets of columns on which the tuples in the results are different from those in the rest of the database (i.e., have an "unusual" statistical distribution).

In [6] the authors present pyExplore an SQL query recommendation framework that supports mixed categorical and numerical datasets as well as String datasets. PyExplore also supports tunable projection selection method with choices for correlation,diversity and random projection selection.

Overall, pyExplore solves many of the shortcomings of past SQL query recommendation frameworks that do not use query logs such as Bleau and Explique (such as native handling of mixed categorical and numerical datasets,handling String datasets).

However none of the frameworks for SQL query recommendation without the use of query logs provide explainable recommendations while when it comes to speeding up the algorithms proposed methods in the related work only use sampling.

3   PyExplore Algorithm Description

In order for the paper to be as self-contained as possible we provide a brief overview of the pyExplore algorithm.

The pyExplore algorithm consists of three phases:

1. Projection selection
2. Subspace construction
3. Query Generation

3.1   Projection Selection

The first step is to find 'interesting' subsets of query attributes. This part of the algorithm aims to combat the curse of dimensionality. PyExplore has two options for projection selection: attribute correlation and diversity.

Correlation-Based. Correlation is the measure of how two features are correlated. Correlated features are grouped together in many data science workflows since there is a definite relationship between the attributes.

Diversity-Based. Intuitively, an attribute that has a diverse set of values is interesting because it allows the user to explore a larger part of the initial query results compared to a less diverse attribute.

3.2   Generating Query Recommendations

Subspace Construction. For each subset of attributes identified by the first step, PyExplore clusters the initial query results using the values of the attributes in the subset. It uses two options. The first is K-means with scaling and encoding categorical values as dummy variables, as proposed in [16]. However, encoding categorical values as dummy variables can lead to increased time and space complexity for data sets with high-cardinality categorical values. To overcome this problem, PyExplore uses K-modes [8–10].

Query Generation. For each subset, the resulting cluster labels are fed into a decision tree classifier to produce the split points of the data. The resulting split points are used to create the recommended SQL queries.

For more information on the PyExplore workflow the reader can read [6].

4 Descripition of the New Workflows

4.1 Sampled Decision Tree Workflow

The sampled Decision Tree workflow is the closest to the original PyExplore workflow.

The main intuition behind the sampled decision tree workflow is that we want to avoid having to process the entire dataset. To do so we replace the K-Modes algorithm of the pyExplore workflow with Mini-Batch K-Means [15]. Mini-Batch K-Means is a variation of K-Means that performs online and incremental clustering and uses only a subset of the dataset to converge. This allows the algorithm to run while only processing a fraction of the original dataset.

More concretely, for the sampled decision tree workflow we use the following approach:

1. We run Mini-Batch K-Means and we keep the indexes of the Mini-Batches processed.
2. We run the Decision Tree only on the batches that Mini-Batch K-Means used to converge.

4.2 Approximate Workflow

In the approximate version of the PyExplore workflow, the clustering step is performed by Mini-Batch K-means [15] and the decision tree classifier uses Hoeffding Tree [4].

We used Mini-Batch K-Means as an alternative to K-Modes and a Hoeffding Tree as an alternative to the Decision Tree. Hoeffding Trees are an online and incremental variant of a decision trees that uses Hoeffding bounds to guarantee that their output is asymptotically nearly identical to that of a conventional Decision Tree. Using Hoeffding Trees allows us to build a decision tree incrementally without having to process the entire dataset.

The main intuition behind the algorithm is as follows:

1. We first use Mini-Batch K-Means to obtain the cluster labels for input dataset
2. We use a batch of predetermined size of the input dataset to test the accuracy of the Hoeffding tree.
3. We train the Hoeffding for as many iterations as needed to obtain accuracy higher than a predetermined value.
4. Once we have built the Hoeffding tree we use the split points to generate the query recommendations.

4.3   Explainable Worfklow

One novel workflow of pyExplore is explainable recommendations. While training a decision tree classifier is a nice way of producing recommendation it has the downside that the recommendation it produces are not explainable. We don't know what the split points of the decision tree represent. To overcome this limitation we introduce explainable recommendations using simple statistical analysis. We use percentiles to describe the cluster as a way to prune outliers from the dataset [1].

Simple Algorithm for Producing Explainable Recommendations. Our first implementation of explainable recommendations uses simple statistical measures such as computing percentiles and top-k processing. More specifically we process the dataset in the following way:

1. After we have obtained the views using correlation or diversity we end up with groups of attributes.
2. For each group of attributes we perform clustering similarly to the original pyExplore workflow.
3. Our next step is to describe each cluster. To do this we perform the following algorithm:
   (a) We split the attributes into numerical and categorical.
   (b) For the categorical we simply take the top-k for each attribute.
   (c) For the numerical attributes we take the 10% percentile as the low split point and the 90% percentile as the high split point.
   (d) Finally we concatenate all the attributes together to generate the final query

Explainable Recommendations Using Space Filling Curves. One problem with the method described above is that it completely disregards the spatial relationship of the numerical attributes and instead treats each attribute separately. To overcome this limitation we use Space Filling Curves [2] to perform dimensionality reduction. The workflow of the space filling curve algorithm is similar to the previous algorithm with a few tweaks to use space filling curves. The workflow for the categorical data does not change. More specifically after we have obtained the numerical attributes for each view, we describe the clusters in the following way:

1. We project the data points of the cluster into a specific grid in order to construct the Space Filling Curve (SFC). For our use case we use a grid of 16 cells along each dimension and the Z-order Space Filling Curve. We chose the Z-order SFC because it was faster to compute and the results were similar to the Hilbert SFC. The choice of SFC is orthogonal to the algorithm.
2. After we have projected our dataset to the grid we compute the index of the SFC for each point of the dataset.
3. Then we compute the percentiles on the SFC of the dataset.

4. Finally we add all the points from the low point to the high point in a list and we convert them back to grid points.
5. We then traverse the list and we end up with coordinates in the grid that best describe the cluster.
6. As a final step we convert the coordinates from the grid back to the original metric space of the dataset and to obtain the final split points for the query.

Using PCA for Dimensionality Reduction. One alternative to using Space Filling Curves to perform dimensionality reduction is to use PCA. The workflow is similar to the SFC workflow only now we do not have to project the dataset into a grid. Instead we use PCA to convert from the n-dimensional plane onto a 1-dimensional plane. After we have our data on the 1-dimensional plane we do the following:

1. We compute the percentiles in the 1-dimensional plane.
2. We convert the percentiles back to the original feature plane.
3. We get the maximum and lower value for each attributes from the percentiles.

4.4   Combined Approximate and Explainable Workflow

For the combined explainable and approximate recommendations we use the following approach:

1. We run Mini-Batch K-Means and we keep the indexes of the Mini-Batches processed.
2. We compute the explainable percentiles similarly to the explainable workflow but only for the samples that the Mini-Batch K-Means algorithm used to converge.

Again the rationale here is to not use the entire dataset in order to produce the recommendations. Mini-Batch K-Means allows us to effectively decide which part of the dataset is required to achieve convergence and then use only that to produce the recommendations.

Table 1. Comparison of the methods

Phase of the algorithm	pyExplore	sampled Decision Tree	Explainable	Approximate	Combined
Subspace Construction	K-Modes	Mini-Batch K-Means	K-Modes	Mini-Batch K-Means	Mini-Batch K-Means
Query Generation	Decision Tree	sampled Decision Tree	univariate, SFC, PCA	Hoeffding Tree	sampled (univariate, SFC, PCA)

Table 2. PyExplore examples

Method Name	Query results
Original pyExplore	SELECT * FROM input_df where 'humidity' < 12.815722 and 'voltage' < 2.543906
	SELECT * FROM input_df where 'humidity' >= 12.815722 and 'voltage' < 2.543906
	SELECT * FROM input_df where 'temperature' < 21.2205 and 'voltage' >= 2.543906
	SELECT * FROM input_df where 'temperature' >= 21.2205 and 'voltage' >= 2.54390
Explainable univariate	SELECT * FROM input_df where 'humidity' >= 29.1869 and 'humidity' <= 45.0442 and 'temperature' >= 18.048 and 'temperature' <= 27.1522 and 'voltage' >= 2.57108 and 'voltage' <= 2.69964
	SELECT * FROM input_df where 'humidity' >= −4.0 and 'humidity' <= −3.83804 and 'temperature' >= 122.153 and 'temperature' <= 122.153 and 'voltage' >= 2.0766400000000003 and 'voltage' <= 2.23278
	SELECT * FROM input_df where 'humidity' >= 34.4317 and 'humidity' <= 48.3517 and 'temperature' >= 19.126 and 'temperature' <= 25.8194 and 'voltage' >= 2.33827 and 'voltage' <= 2.51661
	SELECT * FROM input_df where 'humidity' >= 24.8726 and 'humidity' <= 51.9843 and 'temperature' >= 85.521 and 'temperature' <= 122.153 and 'voltage' >= 2.21612 and 'voltage' <= 2.32
Approximate Explainable univariate	SELECT * FROM input_df where 'humidity' >= 28.9731 and 'humidity' <= 44.9121 and 'temperature' >= 18.0186 and 'temperature' <= 27.4854 and 'voltage' >= 2.58226 and 'voltage' <= 2.71196
	SELECT * FROM input_df where 'humidity' >= −4.0 and 'humidity' <= −3.8380399999999995 and 'temperature' >= 122.153 and 'temperature' <= 122.15300000000002 and 'voltage' >= 2.06941 and 'voltage' <= 2.23278
	SELECT * FROM input_df where 'humidity' >= 34.2577 and 'humidity' <= 48.3517 and 'temperature' >= 19.1456 and 'temperature' <= 25.571460000000002 and 'voltage' >= 2.33827 and 'voltage' <= 2.52732
	SELECT * FROM input_df where 'humidity' >= 25.95868 and 'humidity' <= 51.7933 and 'temperature' >= 84.07844 and 'temperature' <= 122.153 and 'voltage' >= 2.21612 and 'voltage' <= 2.32
Explainable SFC	SELECT * FROM input_df where 'humidity' >= −2223.5030581613514 and 'humidity' <= 24.072899999999194 and 'temperature' >= 85.8090018761726 and 'temperature' <= 185.56199624765478 and 'voltage' >= 1.8463093953095684 and 'voltage' <= 2.45421
	SELECT * FROM input_df where 'humidity' >= −4.0 and 'humidity' <= 55.40982238899312 and 'temperature' >= 15.298361475922455 and 'temperature' <= 68.92960000000001 and 'voltage' >= 2.213763602251407 and 'voltage' <= 2.57108
	SELECT * FROM input_df where 'humidity' >= 14.340700000000002 and 'humidity' <= 57.0984 and 'temperature' >= 13.559599999999998 and 'temperature' <= 37.7166 and 'voltage' >= 2.50599 and 'voltage' <= 2.832365759849906
	SELECT * FROM input_df where 'humidity' >= 16.715999999999998 and 'humidity' <= 77.07622764227642 and 'temperature' >= 81.07280725453408 and 'temperature' <= 122.15300000000002 and 'voltage' >= 1.7995242221200753 and 'voltage' <= 2.3948400000000003
Approximate explainable SFC	SELECT * FROM input_df where 'humidity' >= 28.550738592870545 and 'humidity' <= 60.9799 and 'temperature' >= 14.45993746091307 and 'temperature' <= 67.2538 and 'voltage' >= 2.2538315947467167 and 'voltage' <= 2.56
	SELECT * FROM input_df where 'humidity' >= −4.0 and 'humidity' <= 20.920700000000004 and 'temperature' >= 1.731 and 'temperature' <= 122.153 and 'voltage' >= 1.98635 and 'voltage' <= 2.32
	SELECT * FROM input_df where 'humidity' >= 15.2482 and 'humidity' <= 54.387299999999996 and 'temperature' >= 13.736 and 'temperature' <= 37.501 and 'voltage' >= 2.50599 and 'voltage' <= 2.8157461601000624
	SELECT * FROM input_df where 'humidity' >= 17.8019 and 'humidity' <= 66.31758974358974 and 'temperature' >= 86.81691269543465 and 'temperature' <= 122.153 and 'voltage' >= 2.1458420325203256 and 'voltage' <= 2.35683

Table 1 compares the five available workflows of pyExplore.

As we can see in the examples shown in Table 2 the explainable univariate workflow and the approximate explainable univariate produce results that are almost identical which means that the approximate workflow works very well.

Also the split points of the explainable methods can now be easily interpreted. For example in the first example of the explainable univariate case the low split point for humidity is 29.18 which corresponds to the 10% percentile and the high split point for humidity which corresponds to the 90% precentile is 45.04.

5 Datasets

In our evaluation, we used the following datasets:

1. The movies dataset from Kaggle [1] This dataset provides information about the gross earnings of movies. The dataset contains a single table with 45466 rows and 11 attributes that are 3 categorical and 8 numerical.
2. IBM Car sales dataset[2] This data contains data about car sales. The dataset contains a single table with 78025 rows and 19 attributes that are mixed numeric and categorical (6 categorical and 13 numerical).
3. The Intel dataset[3]: This dataset contains information from sensors in the Intel Berkeley lab. The dataset contains a single table with 2219803 rows and 6 attributes that are numerical only.

All the tests were performed on a Mid 2015 Macbook pro.

Our evaluation aims to answer the following questions:a)how does the use of MB-K-Means affect the quality of the recommendations b) how the use of various methods for explainable recommendation perform in terms of accuracy and c) how do the different workflows compare against each other in terms of execution time and speedup compared to the original pyExplore workflow.

6 Qualitative Evaluation

In this part of our evaluation, we perform a qualitative evaluation to understand the quality of the generated query recommendations and how it is affected by the various design choices in PyExplore. The purpose of our evaluation is two-fold a) to see how the various parameters affect the clustering quality and b) to determine if the Mini-Batch K-Means algorithm used in the approximate workflow yields similar density clusters.

We opted to use density as our quality metric for clustering. Density is defined as:

$$density = 1 - \frac{inertia}{totss}$$

---

[1] https://www.kaggle.com/rounakbanik/the-movies-dataset/version/7.
[2] https://raw.githubusercontent.com/vkrit/data-science-class/master/WA_Fn-UseC_-Sales-Win-Loss.csv.
[3] http://db.csail.mit.edu/labdata/labdata.html.

where *inertia* is the sum of squared euclidian distances of the datapoints and their respective cluster center and *totss* is the total sum of the squared datapoints

Higher density score is better, meaning that the respective query describes a very dense area of the data.

More formaly:

$\mathcal{X} = \{x_i \in \mathbb{R}^D\}_{i=1}^{N}$ is the data set,

$X = [x_1, \ldots, x_N]^{\top} \in \mathbb{R}^{N \times D}$ is the data matrix.

$totss = \sum_{i=1}^{N} \sum_{j=1}^{D} X_{ij}^2$

$inertia = \sum_{i=1}^{N} euclidian\_distance(x_i, \theta_j)^2$ where $j = cluster\_label(i)$ and θ is the array holding the cluster centers.

For all the datasets we use the following parameters:

1. projection_size_max: values 3 and 5.
2. max_completions: values 2, 4 and 8
3. clustering algorithm: K-means and Mini-Batch K-means
4. projection selection method: correlation and diversity

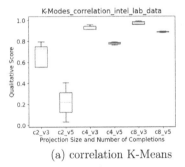
(a) correlation K-Means

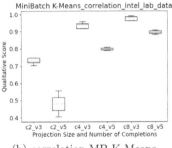
(b) correlation MB-K-Means

Fig. 1. Qualitative scores for the Intel dataset using correlation projection selection

As we can see in Fig. 1 the Mini-Batch K-Means provides similar results in terms of the quality of the recommendations for the correlation projection selection method.

For the diversity projection selection method the results show a larger variance when using Mini-Batch K-Means but the overall trend remains the same as we can see in Fig. 2.

7 Evaluation of Explainable Workflow

We tested the explainable recommendations in terms of accuracy. What we would want from a method for explainable recommendation would be to have perfect

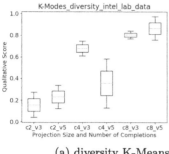 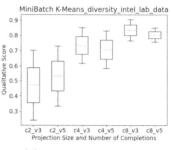

(a) diversity K-Means   (b) diversity MB-K-Means

Fig. 2. Qualitative scores for the Intel dataset using diversity projection selection

accuracy (no point would be assigned to the wrong cluster) and the same number of points as the original dataset (no point gets discarded because of the workflow). Here the perfect score would be to keep 80% of the dataset (since we discard the bottom 10% and the top 10% to prune outliers as part of the method).

7.1 Accuracy Results

Intel Lab Data. As we can see from Fig. 3 PCA and Univariate method achieve perfect accuracy but they filter excessively (especially PCA).

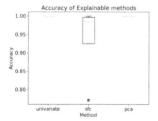 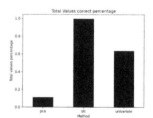

(a) Total accuracy of the methods   (b) Total records identified correctly

Fig. 3. Evaluation of explainable recommendations for the intel dataset

The SFC method on the other hand achieves lower accuracy since it is a more coarse grained method but ends up closer to the ideal number of correct points.

8   Comparing All the Methods Together

Figures 4 and 5 shows a comparison of the execution time and speedup respectively for all the methods and all the datasets without any sampling.

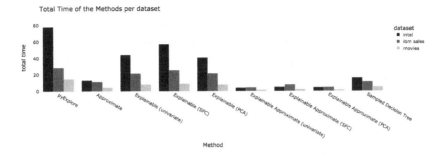

Fig. 4. Total Time in seconds for all the datasets

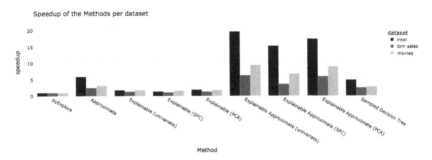

Fig. 5. Speedup for all the datasets

We can see that the Intel dataset takes the most time with 77 s for the full pyExplore workflow.

Using the explainable workflow the execution time drops to 44 s achieving a speedup 1.76×.

Using the combined explainable and approximate and the univariate approach drops the execution time further to 3.96 s achieving a speedup 19.6×.

In comparison the sampled decision tree approach drops the execution time 15.98 s achieving a speedup 4.8×. Finally the approximate workflow drops the execution time to 13.16 s achieving a speedup of 5.9×.

In comparison the sales dataset takes 28.5 s for the full pyExplore workflow.

Using the explainable workflow the execution time drops to 21 s achieving a speedup 1.3×.

Using the combined explainable and approximate and the univariate approach drops the execution time further to 4.5 s achieving a speedup 6.3×.

In comparison the sampled decision tree approach drops the execution time 11.4 s achieving a speedup 2.5. Finally the approximate workflow drops the execution time to 11.4 s achieving a speedup of 2.5×.

Finally the movies dataset takes 14.9 s for the full pyExplore workflow.

Using the explainable workflow the execution time drops to 8.3 s achieving a speedup 1.8×.

Using the combined explainable and approximate and the univariate approach drops the execution time further to 1.5 s achieving a speedup 9.4×.

In comparison the sampled decision tree approach drops the execution time 5.2 s achieving a speedup 2.8×. Finally the approximate workflow drops the execution time to 4.7 s achieving a speedup of 3.16×.

Overall when comparing all the methods together we arrive at the following conclusions:

1. The intel dataset provides more opportunities for speedup since it is the largest dataset but the approximate methods showed promising speedup for smaller datasets too.
2. The combined explainable and approximate methods show the most impressive speedups especially for the larger intel dataset.
3. In most datasets the PCA and univariate explainable methods show the best speedup while the SFC workflow provides adequate speedup.
4. The approximate method also shows significant speedup compared to the original pyExplore workflow.
5. The sampled decision tree approach although not significantly different to the original pyExplore workflow shows significant speedup.
6. The explainable workflow is faster than the original pyExplore workflow.

9   Conclusion

In this paper we have extended pyExplore with four new workflows for explainable and approximate recommendations.

We have evaluated the four workflows both in terms of recommendation quality as well as execution time compared to the original pyExplore workflow.

We also evaluated the quality of the approximate workflows using cluster density as a metric. Our findings is that:

1. The combined explainable and approximate workflow provides the best of both worlds for fast and explainable SQL query recommendations.
2. All the approximate methods provide impressive speedups compared to the original pyExplore workflow.
3. The explainable workflow is faster than the decision tree classifier.
4. The approximate workflow produces recommendations that are of similar quality to the full workflow.
5. The approximate recommendations provide results that are very close to the full workflow.
6. In the explainable workflow PCA filters the dataset excessively while SFC and univariate are closer to the ideal result.

References

1. Aggarwal, C.C.: Outlier analysis. In: Data Mining, pp. 237–263. Springer, Cham (2015). https://doi.org/10.1007/978-3-319-14142-8_8

2. Bader, M.: Space-Filling Curves: An Introduction with Applications in Scientific Computing, vol. 9. Springer, Cham (2012)

3. Dimitriadou, K., Papaemmanouil, O., Diao, Y.: AIDE: an active learning-based approach for interactive data exploration. IEEE Trans. Knowl. Data Eng. **28**(11), 2842–2856 (2016). https://doi.org/10.1109/TKDE.2016.2599168

4. Domingos, P., Hulten, G.: Mining high-speed data streams. In: ACM SIGKDD, pp. 71–80 (2000)

5. Eirinaki, M., Patel, S.: Querie reloaded: using matrix factorization to improve database query recommendations. In: 2015 IEEE International Conference on Big Data, Big Data 2015, Santa Clara, CA, USA, October 29 - November 1, 2015, pp. 1500–1508. IEEE Computer Society (2015). https://doi.org/10.1109/BigData.2015.7363913

6. Glenis, A., Koutrika, G.: Pyexplore: query recommendations for data exploration without query logs. In: Proceedings of the 2021 International Conference on Management of Data, pp. 2731–2735 (2021)

7. Howe, B., Cole, G., Khoussainova, N., Battle, L.: Automatic example queries for ad hoc databases. In: Sellis, T.K., Miller, R.J., Kementsietsidis, A., Velegrakis, Y. (eds.) Proceedings of the ACM SIGMOD International Conference on Management of Data, SIGMOD 2011, Athens, Greece, June 12–16, 2011, pp. 1319–1322. ACM (2011)

8. Huang, Z.: Clustering large data sets with mixed numeric and categorical values. In: Proceedings of the 1st Pacific-Asia conference on knowledge discovery and data mining,(PAKDD), pp. 21–34. Singapore (1997)

9. Huang, Z.: A fast clustering algorithm to cluster very large categorical data sets in data mining. DMKD **3**(8), 34–39 (1997)

10. Huang, Z.: Extensions to the k-means algorithm for clustering large data sets with categorical values. Data Min. Knowl. Disc. **2**(3), 283–304 (1998)

11. Kalinin, A., Çetintemel, U., Zhao, Z., Zdonik, S.B.: Dynamic query refinement for interactive data exploration. In: Bonifati, A., Zhou, Y., Salles, M.A.V., Böhm, A., Olteanu, D., Fletcher, G.H.L., Khan, A., Yang, B. (eds.) Proceedings of the 23rd International Conference on Extending Database Technology, EDBT 2020, Copenhagen, Denmark, March 30 - April 02, 2020, pp. 49–60. OpenProceedings.org (2020). https://doi.org/10.5441/002/edbt.2020.06

12. Khoussainova, N., Kwon, Y., Balazinska, M., Suciu, D.: SnipSuggest: context-aware autocompletion for SQL. Proc. VLDB Endow. **4**(1), 22–33 (2010)

13. Le Guilly, M., Petit, J.M., Scuturici, V.M., Ilyas, I.F.: Explique: interactive databases exploration with SQL. In: Proceedings of the 28th ACM International Conference on Information and Knowledge Management, pp. 2877–2880 (2019)

14. Luo, Y., Qin, X., Tang, N., Li, G.: DeepEye: towards automatic data visualization. In: 34th IEEE International Conference on Data Engineering, ICDE 2018, Paris, France, April 16–19, 2018, pp. 101–112. IEEE Computer Society (2018)

15. Sculley, D.: Web-scale k-means clustering. In: World Wide Web Conference, pp. 1177–1178 (2010)

16. Sellam, T., Kersten, M.: Cluster-driven navigation of the query space. IEEE Trans. Knowl. Data Eng. **28**(5), 1118–1131 (2016)

17. Sellam, T., Kersten, M.: Have a chat with clustine, conversational engine to query large tables. In: Proceedings of the Workshop on Human-In-the-Loop Data Analytics, pp. 1–6 (2016)

18. Sellam, T., Kersten, M.: Ziggy: characterizing query results for data explorers. Proc. VLDB Endowment **9**(13), 1473–1476 (2016)

19. Tahery, S., Farzi, S.: Customized query auto-completion and suggestion - a review. Inf. Syst. **87**, 101415 (2020)
20. Yang, X., Procopiuc, C.M., Srivastava, D.: Recommending join queries via query log analysis. In: Ioannidis, Y.E., Lee, D.L., Ng, R.T. (eds.) Proceedings of the 25th International Conference on Data Engineering, ICDE 2009, March 29 2009 - April 2 2009, Shanghai, China, pp. 964–975. IEEE Computer Society (2009)
21. Zhang, X., Ge, X., Chrysanthis, P.K., Sharaf, M.A.: Viewseeker: an interactive view recommendation tool. In: Papotti, P. (ed.) Proceedings of the Workshops of the EDBT/ICDT 2019 Joint Conference, EDBT/ICDT 2019, Lisbon, Portugal, March 26, 2019. CEUR Workshop Proceedings, vol. 2322. CEUR-WS.org (2019)

Learning Issues

Machine Learning Economy for Next Generation Industrial IoT: A Vision Under Web 3.0

Sourabh Bharti[(✉)], Tharindu Ranathunga, Indika Dhanapala, Susan Rea, and Alan McGibney

Nimbus Research Center, Munster Technological University, Cork, Ireland
`sourabh.bharti@mtu.ie`

Abstract. The centralised nature of the current Internet i.e., Web 2.0, brings data privacy and security issues to the fore as critical barriers to the realisation of the digital economy. Due to such issues, it is difficult for data-driven services such as 'ML-as-a-service' to prosper under the umbrella of Web 2.0. Therefore, it is important to explore the platform utilities Web 3.0 can provide to support such services as they require to be executed and served in a highly distributed manner. This paper envisages an ML model marketplace for Industrial IoT applications exploiting next-generation IIoT components. A theoretical analysis of the ML economy and the technical components required to realize this marketplace are presented in this paper along with the specification of key open research questions.

Keywords: Digital Economy · Web 3.0 · Machine Learning · Trust

1 Introduction

According to the European Commission's Next Generation Internet (NGI) initiative, the current Internet is to be transformed into a 'highly adaptive and resilient', 'trustworthy', and 'sustainably open' human-centric Internet. The motivation for this stems from the disadvantages of centralised control on the current state of the Internet as well as users' private data being held by a few organisations such as Google, Meta, Amazon etc. [29].

In the context of the Internet of Things (IoT) - whose primary motive is to collect data pertaining to connected 'Things' constituting cyber-physical-systems and transform this towards informed decisions and actuation - 75% of such data processing takes place on centralised data centres managed by a few cloud service

This project has received funding from Sustainable Energy Authority of Ireland under the SEAI Research, Development & Demonstration Funding Programme 2021, Grant number 21/RDD/688 and Science Foundation Ireland SFI Research Centres 2017 PhD Awards Program under SFI CONNECT Centre 13/RC/2077 and SFI CONNECT Centre 13/RC/2077 P2.

R. Chbeir et al. (Eds.): MEDES 2023, CCIS 2022, pp. 105–119, 2024.
https://doi.org/10.1007/978-3-031-51643-6_8

providers such as Amazon, Microsoft etc. This brings the perils of compromised data privacy and security as the centralised server can become a single-point-of-attack, moreover, it requires expensive network resources to transmit the Big Data to distant data centres. Next Generation IoT is another initiative towards taking advantage of the new IoT features empowered by Edge Computing - the enabler to shift the paradigm from centralised to real-time data processing. Edge Computing is known to push the data processing/analytics closer to its origin and transmit only the required information to the cloud, to protect data privacy and minimise network expenditures. As Next Generation IoT and Edge Computing Strategy Forum proposed, more than 80% of the data processing will be performed on the Edge by the end of 2025. As data processing is shifting towards the edge, the next generation of IoT is set to move towards a decentralised ecosystem where users/organisations are expected to interact with each other without centralised control.

Industrial IoT (IIoT) is an extension of IoT that connects a number of machines through IoT devices and brings edge/cloud computing, artificial intelligence (AI) and analytics together to create cognitive digital solutions to optimise the industrial processes, minimise manufacturing cost etc. Current IIoT practices involve industrial data siloes utilising centralised storage and processing services provided by external parties to mine the targeted data patterns. However, in order to move towards the Next Generation IIoT (NGIIoT), such data siloes are expected to interact with each other in a trusted and open manner without the need for a third-party control. Such decentralisation is not feasible to realize under the umbrella of Web 2.0 which is dominated by centralised control. However, it is in-line with the envisaged Web 3.0, where web users and/or organisations can buy/sell data-centric services without centralised control - constituting an ML economy. In Web 3.0, applications are not created and deployed on a single cloud service provider, but rather managed and coordinated on a decentralised platform such as Blockchain. As Web 3.0 is expected to utilise AI and machine learning (ML) to create and distribute valuable content as per the user's interests, organisations in NGIIoT can also create and deploy intelligent and open services to be accessed by all.

This paper attempts to highlight how NGIIoT can utilise the foundational structures of Web 3.0 towards realising a trusted, and resilient ML economy of shared data-driven services (Sect. 2). The key enablers and architectures for realising such an ecosystem are also discussed along with their recent research advancements (Sects. 3–6). Finally, this paper presents an ML economy framework and key research challenges to be addressed for making ML economy a reality in NGIIoT (Sect. 7).

2   ML Economy Under Web 3.0: Overview

As discussed in [4], there are three major components of a Web 3.0 ecosystem: (1) Blockchain, (2) Distributed storage, and (3) Privacy computing. Traditionally, Blockchain is considered the backbone of Web 3.0, required to preserve the sovereignty of the use-data. Its major components: Distributed Ledger Technology (DLT), Cryptography, Consensus Mechanisms, and Smart Contracts constitute the technical architecture to support data immutability, trust, consistency, and executable functions, respectively. Distributed storage takes away centralised data control and allows the user application data to be placed at various nodes of the network. Privacy computing methods such as Federated Learning and Secure multi-party communication are the enablers to protect the users' private data. An ML economy solution under Web 3.0 is expected to be built around these essential components to be fully decentralized. This section discusses the fundamentals of Web 3.0 and the key enablers for the ML economy in NGIIoT to take full advantage of the envisaged Web 3.0 architecture.

2.1 Next Generation IIoT and IoT Data Economy

As stated in '*Road-map for IoT Research Innovation and Deployment in Europe*', the forthcoming challenge is to design and develop NGIoT systems which can leverage emerging technologies such as AI and Machine Learning, Edge-cloud computing, 5G/6G, and more. Next generation IIoT (NGIIoT) aims to create a single European market and bring the intelligence closer to the Industry floor, provide an agile response to the time-critical applications, and maintain trust and security/privacy of the shared Industrial data while leveraging these technologies. An integral part of the NGIoT – IoT data market, is emerging as a key enabler, however, it has a limited appeal because of two reasons [7]:

- Limited scale of the available data which is of interest to specific stakeholders, and
- Availability of the raw data which is of limited interest to the buyers.

Both of the above reasons stem from the pitfalls of centralised data control and the limited availability of 'data-driven services' deployed on the data-sharing platform, respectively. In other words, organisations' full control over the access and usage of commercial data can encourage them to participate more in the data-sharing ecosystems and thus increasing the scale and size of available data; on the other hand, sharing the trained models in the form of data-driven services, rather than the raw data can encourage more buyers to explore the shared data-space. To this end, and keeping it in line with the vision of Web 3.0, there is a need for an 'ML economy' which can drive the NGIIoT development.

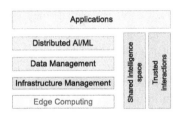

Fig. 1. Elements of a data-driven service in NGIIoT.

ML economies are digital ecosystems where ML models are collected, organised, and exchanged through a trusted network.

The core of the ML economy is an ML model marketplace where organisations develop ML models using their own data and advertise the trained models' (i.e., data-driven services) as services to be monetized. Although ML models are available in marketplaces such as Amazon Web Services (AWS), such are expected to be governed and controlled by big tech giants under the umbrella of Web 2.0. On the contrary, Web 3.0 envisages empowering small and medium-scale organisations towards monetising their resources (data). This can be possible if they are encouraged to put their local data to use (patterns mining) in order to develop and host data-driven services under the ML economy.

However, the challenge lies in maintaining trust to protect commercially sensitive data and, ensure security & privacy during stakeholders' interactions while designing and deployment of data-centric services in an ML model marketplace. Figure 1 shows the key components of data-driven services which mainly includes ML model development, training infrastructure, and trusted, secure sharing of the data-driven services with other parties. While NGIoT is primarily driven by taking advantage of edge computing, this brings distributed infrastructure (edge-cloud) management into play with ML model development/serving. In addition, edge-cloud resource orchestration drives the management of local training data pipelines and overlay distributed AI/ML services. All of these elements in the ML economy depend heavily upon the functionalities of shared intelligence spaces and trusted platforms (i.e., DLTs) in order to take full advantage of the Web 3.0 infrastructure. Subsequent sections discuss Fig. 1 in detail in terms of available enablers, architectures, and further research directions in the context of NGIIoT under Web 3.0.

3   Shared Intelligence Spaces

The shared intelligence space in NGIIoT is the foundation of the ML economy and is in line with the vision of the European digital single market. According to OPENDEI, '*a data space is defined as a decentralised infrastructure for trustworthy data sharing and exchange in data ecosystems based on commonly agreed principles.*'

Along the same lines, an intelligence space can be defined as *a trusted, distributed infrastructure to enable the exchange of data-driven services in the ML economy.* A shared intelligence space takes it one step further to build an ecosystem of multiple organisations developing intelligent data-driven services to monetise their data in an ML model marketplace. For instance, in the context of IIoT, digital manufacturing assets can be exchanged and monetised using such infrastructure provided that it enables trusted and secure interactions.

The development of shared intelligence space can leverage reference architectures such as the international data space (IDS) [3] and data strategies or markets such as Common European data spaces [6]. IDS was created to enable collaboration among organisations where data is treated as a strategic resource. The core of IDS reference architecture is IDS connector which is a generic software component hosting system services ensuring the following design requirements:

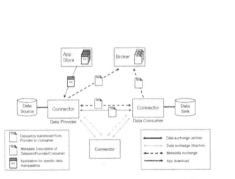

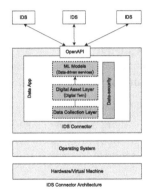

(a) IDS Technical Architecture[3].

(b) IDS Connector Interactions.

Fig. 2. IDS Architecture.

- Interconnection & interoperability: the interconnection of various data spaces by providing the required interoperability mechanisms, such as service exchange APIs, traceability, and ML models and formats;
- Trust: identity and reputation management, user certification, authentication & authorisation, access control policy, secure communication, and security by design;
- Service value: protocols for service discovery, incentivisation, and service usage accounting;
- Governance: common structure to ensure fair, transparent, proportionate, and non-discriminatory access to sharing/use of data;

Data-driven services can be built and integrated into the IDS connector or can be downloaded from the App-Store supported by IDS reference architecture (Fig. 2(a)). Apart from this, IDS reference architecture supports IDS-Broker which can help the consumer to discover the relevant data-driven services in the ecosystem. As described in the EU QUALITY project, Fig. 2(b)) shows a sample application deployment scenario to support data-driven services on top of the IDS connector using the following layers.

1. The bottom-most, **data collection layer** provides a technical interface (using protocols such as REST and MQTT) to access/gather data from physical machines on the production floor.
2. The **digital asset layer** is responsible to process the data received from the data access layer and create a digital version of the physical machines to monitor its behaviour and perform data-processing tasks.
3. The top-most **ML models layer** is responsible to train the ML models by taking process data from the digital asset layer. Apart from this, ML models layer is also responsible to provide other data-driven services such as model quality assessment, model drift, etc.

4. The **OpenAPI** layer offers the gateway to access developed ML models and other data-driven services for other organisations/participants on the IDS ecosystem.
5. The cross-layer functionality of maintaining security and privacy of the data is handled by **data security** layer.

In addition to the design requirements mentioned above, according to [6], shared intelligence spaces should provide *Data/service control*, a set of tools to upload data, change data access rights, give/revoke authorisation to data, and specify new data access/reuse conditions.

4 Trusted Interactions

Trust is a key enabler for NGIIoT ecosystems to operate under the vision of Web 3.0 where decentralised networks and autonomous services collaborate seamlessly to create value for all stakeholders. It is essential for allowing reliable data access, sharing, exchange, and processing to provide quality services with context-aware intelligence within shared intelligence spaces. Trust is a multi-faceted concept [11] that can be defined in many ways. In the context of NGI-IoT, trust refers to the ability of different stakeholders to rely on the security, privacy, resilience, reliability, and safety of the IoT systems, data, and services that are being shared within the ecosystem [21]. This was first characterised by the National Institute of Standards and Technology's (NIST) CPS Framework in May 2016. Complementary to this, the Industry IoT Consortium (IIC) also identifies the same five characteristics as being those that most affect trust decisions for industrial IoT (IIOT) deployments [13].

Trust has emerged as a significant issue in the design frameworks for NGI-IoT, encompassing various areas such as IoT Edge-Cloud, Shared Intelligence Spaces, and Distributed Services [9,12,15]. Trust-enabling mechanisms in these design frameworks mostly overlap in terms of fundamental concepts for ensuring trust in terms of design and operation. The data and service-driven economy in Web 3.0 are enabled by bringing all these pieces together, ensuring end-to-end trusted life cycles for data, infrastructure (software and hardware), services, and stakeholders. There are three main phases from the data generation phase until consumed as processed information or as a data-driven service by the consumer. Trusted interactions needed to be ensured in all these phases:

1. Data Collection - Trust on edge devices needed to be ensured in order to have data veracity and prevent malicious actors from disturbing the ecosystem. It includes securely provisioning IoT devices, ensuring data provenance, maintaining data integrity, preventing unauthorised access, and decommissioning actors with malicious behaviours. The self-sovereign identity mechanisms [33] and decentralised access control mechanism [26] will enable this.
2. Data Exchange - Trusted interactions between the data providers and consumers are essential for shared intelligence spaces. It includes managing the identities of the ecosystem participants and software components (i.e.,

connectors, brokers), assuring compliance with required certifications [16], enabling traceability of transactions. Moreover, privacy-enabling mechanisms like zero-knowledge proofs [35] can facilitate confidential data exchanges without revealing the actual data.

3. Service Composition - Trust in the ML models and other data-driven services on the shared data ecosystem has to be ensured to enhance the overall quality of service. It includes the trusted orchestration of these services on trusted infrastructures and securing the execution (code and data) through mechanisms like isolation on trusted execution environments.

4.1   Role of Distributed Ledger Technology (DLT)

As envisioned by Web 3.0, NGIIoT ecosystems are moving towards a more decentralised, inter-operable, semi-autonomous, self-sovereign and user-centric paradigm where trust needs to be built at its core in the architectural design. In this context, technologies such as DLT can inherently be useful as they provide an extra redundancy layer for distributed processing and computation. DLT continues to gain momentum due to its intrinsic properties of transparency, immutability and the underlying secure-by-design architecture [10]. Moreover, DLT has become more powerful and multipurpose with the introduction of Smart Contracts. They provide a programmable interface that can execute business logic on top of data stored on the ledger. Smart contracts digitally facilitate, verify, or enforce the negotiation or performance of a contract on the distributed ledger.

Due to these capabilities, DLT has the potential to be leveraged as the backbone of trust in the NGIIoT ecosystems. It is already being leveraged in Data Collection, Data Exchange, and Service Composition architectures to enhance traceability, transparency, integrity, and decentralisation. The novel IoT architectures such as TIoTA [14] and FAR-EDGE [15] have emerged to address NGI-IoT concerns by leveraging the potentials of DLT. They are specially designed for industrial automation, leveraging edge computing and the DLT for reliable orchestration of automated IoT networks. Moreover, DLT-based trust models for IoT [17,20,25] can play a major role in ensuring data veracity and trusted interactions in NGIIoT. Specific to shared intelligence spaces DLT can be the underline technology that supports decentralised data brokerage services, clearinghouses, incentives management and self-sovereign identity.

5   Edge Computing and Distributed ML/AI

Edge computing is expected to be at the forefront of the NGIIoT as it significantly reduces the data-sharing cost and brings intelligence to data which fosters data privacy by design. Also, it provides flexibility in solution (analytic/ML-services) deployment near the origin of data which is the key requirement in many time-sensitive IIoT use cases. However, not all data can be processed at the edge devices as more accurate analytic/ML model training requires the variety, veracity, and velocity of the training data which a standalone edge device can not provide. To this end, and in line with the idea of a data-sharing ecosystem, such edge devices can collaboratively execute/train the analytic/ML services while preserving the privacy of their raw data.

The most popular privacy-preserving ML model training method is Federated Learning (FL) which is also known as the decentralised ML model training technique. In addition, edge devices can also execute complex and resource-consuming analytic/ML model inference services in collaboration with each other, known as distributed inference.

5.1   Decentralised ML Model Training

Traditionally, decentralised model training is a method involving independent participants training a common model with their own data for the benefit of all. It is designed to ensure raw data privacy and maximise the robustness of the collectively trained ML model. However, in the ML model economy, decentralised model training techniques such as FL [19] can play a central role in exchanging data-driven services and incentives. A typical FL setup involves multiple clients sharing their locally trained ML models with the centralised server which aggregates the local updates to create a more robust common model to be distributed to the clients for the next round of local training. Usually, clients register their expression of interest in participating in a collaborative model training process. In each round, a fixed number of clients are selected by the centralised server and are provided with the common ML model to train. Organisations willing to participate in a shared intelligence space under the umbrella of NGIIoT need to 'bring intelligence to the data' to foster the privacy and security of commercially sensitive data. FL can be a great enabler in scenarios where even a trusted and secure data space design such as IDS and GAIA-X can not resolve the data privacy concerns of the participant. In such cases, participants may resort to sharing only the intelligence instead of their raw data and train a common model collaboratively. This fosters incentives by design as each of the participants will have access to a more robust common model which can further be customised as per their own private data - an example of transfer learning [28]. Moreover, the core idea of a shared intelligence space is based on exchanging data-driven services rather than the raw data and thus decentralised ML model training and exchange can be supported by FL.

5.2   Distributed ML Model Inference

As the ML models move from training to production, it is important to scale their deployment to fulfil a variety of application requirements. Although most of the deep neural network (DNN) based ML models result in high accuracy, their computational and storage requirements make them unsuitable for resource-constrained edge devices (i.e., mobile phones). To this end, various methods of distributed inference are employed such as hybrid computation and layer-wise fusion & partitioning [24]. The most popular - distributed deep neural networks (DDNNs) in this series propose the trained DNN to be partitioned across the edge-cloud continuum [31]. The lower layers (data ingestion layers) of the DNN at the edge act as a feature extractor which brings data privacy by design as the edge device shares only the features instead of raw data with further devices (i.e., fog nodes) in the edge-cloud continuum. In some instances, edge devices can even make a localised prediction for time-critical applications. Another benefit of using this approach is to minimise the amount of data to be shared by edge devices in the network which further minimises the energy expenditure of the resource-constrained edge devices.

In the context of the ML model marketplace, such distributed ML model inference can support the concept of ML-as-a-service [22], which in its current form is completely dependent upon the centralised cloud infrastructure. Shared intelligence space participants in the NGIIoT can host their ML services deployed over the edge-cloud continuum and offer various subscriptions based on inference time, speed, and other requirements. For instance, a manufacturing organisation with an ample amount of product data can train a vision-based product quality inspection model and offer it to be used by other organisations/sites manufacturing a similar product. The success of ML-as-a-service depends upon the quality of the ML models being exchanged. However, the idea of the ML model marketplace is to re-use the already trained models to learn the patterns already recognized and captured at the model provider's end. The bought models can be utilized for various other applications such as transfer learning, and domain adaptation which do not require the bought model to be 100% accurate on the test data.

6 Data and Infrastructure Management

Development and deployment of data-driven services require computing infrastructure resources. As NGIIoT focuses on exploiting the pervasiveness of edge devices, this opens a plethora of challenges around managing compute infrastructure in the edge-cloud continuum while preparing and/or offering ML models as a service. GAIA-X ecosystem considers infrastructure management with the objective *"to design and implement a data sharing architecture (including standards for data sharing, best practices, tools) and governance mechanism, as well as an EU federation of cloud infrastructure, related infrastructure, and data services."* As shown in Fig. 3, GAIA-X provides support to move data services (in shared data spaces) between different infrastructures in the infrastructure ecosystem. Here, a *node* is a computational resource where data services are hosted. *service* represents a cloud offering whose instances can run on many *nodes* and can even be combined along the same lines as data spaces. Similar to IDS, both data and infrastructure services can be discovered by consumers.

To enable an ML economy, there is a need to expand the infrastructure ecosystem in GAIA-X towards enabling complex model training and deployment rather than limiting its services to raw data storage and management. Although the concept of *node* in GAIA-X ranges from an edge device to a data centre where services can be deployed, the services are limited to cloud services and data assets, whereas, data-driven services are to be built on top of

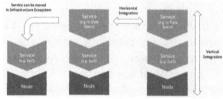

(a) GAIA-X service integration[9].

(b) Compute infrastructure management tasks.

Fig. 3. Design requirements for infrastructure management.

data assets. For instance, if IDS and GAIA-X are to be integrated, IDS containers can be deployed on GAIA-X nodes, and data-driven services can be built and deployed by exploiting the infrastructure ecosystem of GAIA-X which is distributed across the edge-cloud continuum. Thus, sophisticated data-driven service(s) management provisions are required to support the dynamic requirements of the consumers (buyers) of the service.

6.1 Intelligent Service Placement

Unlike the cloud, edge devices are geographically dispersed, resource-constrained, and highly dynamic, making efficient service delivery quite challenging. Applications are decomposed into smaller building blocks called microservices, which are mapped to nodes in the edge-cloud continuum for service provisioning. A crucial component of this is the service placement algorithm that assigns microservices to unique nodes. Such algorithms determine the QoS in terms of communication cost, load balancing, energy consumption, and others [27,32]. Poorly positioned services in the edge-cloud continuum can severely degrade the performance of applications.

Another important aspect of distributed service placement is the discovery of services available in the edge-cloud continuum with minimal user intervention. Nodes advertise the services they offer using a service discovery mechanism, wherein non-disclosure of identities and related attributes to unauthorised recipients and authentic advertisements which are unforgeable are key requirements to ensure the privacy and security of both service providers and users [34]. A popular technique to describe services is by using a semantic-based description method, such as ontology and Resource Description Framework (RDF), wherein the nodes, their services, and their data are given a comprehensible description [1]. OWL, OWL-S, and RDFS are W3C standardised languages used to specify services semantically. The choice of the service discovery mechanism should provide fast service discovery in order to meet stringent QoS requirements, especially for a real-time application deployed in the edge-cloud continuum.

6.2 Service Provisioning

If the organisations are to operate their business under the umbrella of Web 3.0 and NGIIoT, the first step will be to reduce their dependency upon the centralised cloud-based services (mainly data-driven) in order to host the services on the edge-cloud continuum. Current cloud applications are moving away from monolithic architectures [2] towards microservice containers which are managed by Container Orchestration Engines (COEs) such as Kubernetes [18] and Docker Swarm [5]. As shown in Fig. 3, COEs deploy these containers to the suitable compute node based on the application QoS requirement, monitor their performance in terms of application load fluctuations and manage them in case of requirement update. As contemporary applications are deployed as independent microservices - executed as application components on compute nodes, their management is driven by both functional and non-functional requirements [23]. To satisfy the user requirements of the applications, several functional (FR) and non-functional (NFR) requirements can be characterised for edge-cloud architectures.

- FR1: Monitor distributed resource availability;
- FR2: Characterise performance metrics (i.e., latency, reliability, availability, capacity, irregularity, etc.);
- FR3: Characterise data privacy, security and trust metrics;
- FR4: Schedule tasks based on FR1, FR2, FR3, and FR4;
- NFR1: Support system scalability;
- NFR2: Enable infrastructure dynamicity;

7   ML Economy Framework and Open Research Questions

Figure 4 presents an ML economy framework for IIoT applications. Taking a cue from the idea of a data ecosystem presented in [8], the following are the key actors responsible for a minimum viable framework design. The novelty of the proposed framework is the envisaged ML model marketplace where participants can advertise their data-driven services to be exchanged with each other for the benefit of all.

1. Data Provider: Traditionally, it is a plant operator or can also be an independent manufacturing organisation registered with the intelligence space provider via a connector (e.g., IDS connector).
2. Data Consumer: It can be an entity interested to buy the data/services from a provider. Traditionally it can be another organisation or a third party developing data-driven services.
3. Intelligence space provider: Acting as an ML model marketplace, it should provide all functional design requirements listed in Sect. 3. The intelligence space is the key enabler in this ML model-sharing ecosystem.
4. Infrastructure provider: It is responsible to provide both software and hardware infrastructure to enable the design and development of intelligence space providers. It can also be utilised by data consumers/providers to support the development of their data-driven services to be shared with each other.

5. Data analytics provider: An internal entity to the data consumers and providers, responsible for providing the ML-based specific analytic services e.g., model aggregation in FL.

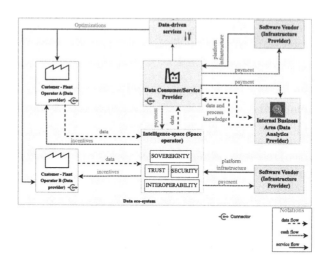

Fig. 4. ML economy framework for IIoT

Every registered data provider advertises its available data (trained ML models) to the space provider which acts as an ML model marketplace with a broker service to facilitate the services exchange with the consumer. There can be two types of benefits/incentives provided for data sharing: monetary and services. For instance, in the context of FL, the services include the optimisations resulting from aggregating the provider's ML model with the consumer's. Data consumers can directly pay brokerage fees to the space provider while the payment to the data providers can be incentivised in form of data-driven services.

Both data providers and consumers can avail of the services of an infrastructure provider to develop their ML models for the market. Whereas, the space provider can avail of these services to develop the soft architecture of the intelligence space/ML model marketplace. The Intelligence space designs novel incentive mechanisms and ensures the privacy, security, and sovereignty of the service by proving full control/access to the provider. Multiple data consumers can get connected with the marketplace through software such as IDS connectors to avail of services. Given the background of an ML economy and its enablers, the following are the key open research questions to be answered:

– *RQ1: How to lay the foundations to identify the emerging business models from both the data provider and consumer perspectives?*
Both providers and consumers of data-driven services should be aware of the potential value and business use cases their participation can bring to the

organisation. This involves identifying the digital maturity of the existing services that can consume other services and/or can be provided to benefit the consumer. Identifying such data maturity can help to shape the potential value that the data can create when shared and/or combined with other data.

– *RQ2*: *How to ensure trust in a such distributed multi-party data-sharing ecosystem?*
Although data-space designs such as IDS and GAIX-X have attempted to standardize and regulate the policies regarding trusted data-sharing and usage, the participants can still be apprehensive about sharing their data/services in a distributed multi-party interaction. Recent advancements around the data-confidence fabric can be handy in infusing trust in data exchange [30].

– *RQ3*: *How to design an efficient intelligence space for a given set of functional and technical requirements?*
There is no one-size-fits-all design for an intelligence space as the technical components are often driven by functional and non-functional requirements of the use-case/domain of the use-case. Existing design attempts such as IDS and GAIA-X provide a broad sketch of the essential data-space components to realize a minimum viable dataspace. However, a proper suitability analysis of the available dataspaces is important before being tailored for the specific use cases.

– *RQ4*: *How to take full advantage of the edge-cloud continuum while maintaining the privacy and security of the data/services?*
Edge computing is central to the NGIIoT architectures and aligns well with the idea of 'bringing the intelligence to data' rather than bringing data to intelligence. The execution at the edge can be linearly scaled over the edge-cloud continuum while maintaining the privacy and security of the data/services. Finding a fine balance between these two ends of the spectrum can be the key to agile and robust NGIIoT applications.

The proposed framework will be validated by developing local and global digital threads leveraging open-source software tools such as IDS Connectors. The local thread will be used to pull local data from different local devices followed by deploying a data-driven service(s) overlay. The global digital thread will be connecting data sources residing on geo-distributed data endpoints. Locally developed ML models will be exchanged through the global digital thread connecting multiple sites/organizations.

8   Conclusion

This paper presented an overview of ML digital economy for next-generation Industrial IoT applications. It is discussed under the purview of the future Internet i.e., Web 3.0 as to utilize the Web 3.0 components for ML service implementation and exchange in a trusted and secure manner. Key elements of ML-based services are explained along with their technological enablers to develop and deploy them in a fully distributed manner. This analysis leads to the proposal of a minimum viable ML economy framework as an enabler of NGIIoT. Although the domain of this paper is Industrial IoT, however, the ML economy framework is applicable to other domains as well such as healthcare, transport, etc. The realisation of this framework requires further exploration of some critical research questions, these have been identified and will be the subject of future research work.

References

1. Achir, M., et al.: Service discovery and selection in IoT: a survey and a taxonomy. J. Netw. Comput. Appl. **200**, 103331 (2022)
2. Ali, S., et al.: Design methodology of microservices to support predictive analytics for IoT applications. Sensors **18**(12), 4226 (2018). https://doi.org/10.3390/s18124226
3. Otto, B., Steinbuß, S., Teuscher, A., Lohmann, S.: Reference Architecture Model - Version 3.0 (2019)
4. Chen, C., et al.: When digital economy meets web3.0: applications and challenges. IEEE Open J. Comput. Soc. **3**, 233–245 (2022)
5. Docker Swarm .https://docs.docker.com/engine/swarm/. Accessed 23 Nov 2022
6. European Commission: COMMISSION STAFF WORKING DOCUMENT on Common European Data Spaces. Technical report SWD(2022) 45 final, European Commission (2022). https://digital-strategy.ec.europa.eu/en/library/staff-working-document-data-spaces
7. Francisco, C., et al.: Roadmap for IoT Research, Innovation and Deployment in Europe 2021–2027. White Paper, NGIoT (2022). https://www.ngiot.eu/ngiot-report-a-roadmap-for-iot-in-europe/
8. Fraunhofer: Data ecosystems: conceptual foundations, constituents and recommendations for action (2019). https://www.isst.fraunhofer.de/content/dam/isst-neu/documents/Publikationen/StudienundWhitePaper/FhG-ISST_DATA-ECOSYSTEMS.pdf
9. Gaia-X: Gaia-X Architecture Document - 21.12 Release (2021)
10. Garamvölgyi, P., et al.: Towards model-driven engineering of smart contracts for cyber-physical systems. In: IEEE/IFIP International Conference on Dependable Systems and Networks Workshops. IEEE (2018)
11. Guo, J., et al.: A survey of trust computation models for service management in internet of things systems. Comput. Commun. **97**, 1–14 (2017)
12. IIC: The industrial internet of things volume g1: Reference architecture (2016). https://www.iiconsortium.org/IIC_PUB_G1_V1.80_2017-01-31.pdf. Accessed 31 Jan 2017
13. IIC: Industrial internet of things volume G4: security framework (2016). https://www.iiconsortium.org/pdf/IIC_PUB_G4_V1.00_PB-3.pdf
14. IIC: The industrial internet consortium and the trusted IoT alliance announce liaison (2019). https://www.iiconsortium.org/press-room/07-10-19.htm. Accessed 10 July 2019
15. Isaja, M., et al.: Combining edge computing and blockchains for flexibility and performance in industrial automation. In: International Conference on Mobile Ubiquitous Computing, Systems, Services and Technologies (UBICOMM) (2017)
16. Karthikeyan, S., Patan, R., Balamurugan, B.: Enhancement of security in the internet of things (IoT) by using X.509 authentication mechanism. In: Khare, A., Tiwary, U.S., Sethi, I.K., Singh, N. (eds.) Recent Trends in Communication, Computing, and Electronics. LNEE, vol. 524, pp. 217–225. Springer, Singapore (2019). https://doi.org/10.1007/978-981-13-2685-1_22

17. Kouicem, D.E., et al.: A decentralized blockchain-based trust management protocol for the internet of things. IEEE Trans. Dependable Secure Comput. **19**, 1292–1306 (2020)
18. Kubernetes. https://kubernetes.io/. Accessed 23 Nov 2022
19. Li, L., Fan, Y., Tse, M., Lin, K.Y.: A review of applications in federated learning. Comput. Ind. Eng. **149**, 106854 (2020). https://doi.org/10.1016/j.cie.2020.106854, https://www.sciencedirect.com/science/article/pii/S0360835220305532
20. Liu, Y., et al.: A survey on blockchain-based trust management for internet of things. IEEE Internet Things J. **10**, 5898–5992 (2023)
21. NIST: CPS PWG Cyber-physical systems (CPS) framework release 1.0 (2016). https://pages.nist.gov/cpspwg/
22. Onose, E.: Machine learning as a service: what it is, when to use it and what are the best tools out there (2023). https://neptune.ai/blog/machine-learning-as-a-service-what-it-is-when-to-use-it-and-what-are-the-best-tools-out-there
23. Orive, A., et al.: Quality of service aware orchestration for cloud-edge continuum applications. Sensors **22**(5), 1755 (2022). https://doi.org/10.3390/s22051755
24. Parthasarathy, A., Krishnamachari, B.: Defer: distributed edge inference for deep neural networks. In: International Conference on Communication Systems & NETworkS (COMSNETS) (2022)
25. Ranathunga, T., et al.: The convergence of blockchain and machine learning for decentralized trust management in IoT ecosystems. In: Proceedings of the ACM Conference on Embedded Networked Sensor Systems (2021)
26. Rouhani, S., et al.: Distributed attribute-based access control system using permissioned blockchain. World Wide Web **24**, 1617–1644 (2021)
27. Salaht, F.A., et al.: An overview of service placement problem in fog and edge computing. ACM Comput. Surv. **53**(3), 1–35 (2020)
28. Tan, C., Sun, F., Kong, T., Zhang, W., Yang, C., Liu, C.: A survey on deep transfer learning. In: Kůrková, V., Manolopoulos, Y., Hammer, B., Iliadis, L., Maglogiannis, I. (eds.) ICANN 2018. LNCS, vol. 11141, pp. 270–279. Springer, Cham (2018). https://doi.org/10.1007/978-3-030-01424-7_27
29. Team, T.I.: Web 3.0 explained, plus the history of web 1.0 and 2.0 (2022). https://www.investopedia.com/web-20-web-30-5208698
30. Technologies, D.: Data confidence fabric and the importance of vetted data (2020). https://www.dell.com/en-us/perspectives/data-confidence-fabric-and-the-importance-of-vetted-data/
31. Teerapittayanon, S., et al.: Distributed deep neural networks over the cloud, the edge and end devices. In: International Conference on Distributed Computing Systems (ICDCS) (2017)
32. Wang, Y., et al.: A reinforcement learning approach for online service tree placement in edge computing. In: IEEE International Conference on Network Protocols (ICNP) (2019)
33. Windley, P.: How sovrin works. Sovrin Foundation (2016)
34. Wu, D.J., Taly, A., Shankar, A., Boneh, D.: Privacy, discovery, and authentication for the internet of things. In: Askoxylakis, I., Ioannidis, S., Katsikas, S., Meadows, C. (eds.) ESORICS 2016. LNCS, vol. 9879, pp. 301–319. Springer, Cham (2016). https://doi.org/10.1007/978-3-319-45741-3_16
35. Wu, W., Liu, E., et al.: Blockchain based zero-knowledge proof of location in IoT. In: ICC 2020–2020 IEEE International Conference on Communications (ICC). IEEE (2020)

Detecting Cyberattacks to Federated Learning on Software-Defined Networks

Himanshi Babbar[1], Shalli Rani[1], Aman Singh[2,3,4],
and Gabriele Gianini[5(✉)]

[1] Chitkara University Institute of Engineering and Technology, Chitkara University,
Rajpura 140401, Punjab, India
{himanshi.babbar,shalli.rani}@chitkara.edu.in
[2] Universidad Europea del Atlantico, 39011 Santander, Spain
[3] Universidad Internacional Iberoamericana, Arecibo, PR 00613, USA
[4] Universidad Internacional Iberoamericana, Campeche 24560, Mexico
[5] Universita degli Studi di Milano, via Celoria 18, 20133 Milano, Italy
gabriele.gianini@unimi.it

Abstract. Federated learning is a distributed machine-learning technique that enables multiple devices to learn a shared model while keeping their local data private. The approach poses security challenges, such as model integrity, that must be addressed to ensure the reliability of the learned models. In this context, software-defined networking (SDN) can play a crucial role in improving the security of federated learning systems; indeed, it can provide centralized control and management of network resources, enforcement of security policies, and detection and mitigation of network-level threats. The integration of SDN with federated learning can help achieve a secure and efficient distributed learning environment. In this paper, an architecture is proposed to detect attacks on Federated Learning using SDN; furthermore, the machine learning model is deployed on a number of devices for training. The simulation results are carried out using the N-BaIoT dataset and training models such as Random Forest achieves 99.6%, Decision Tree achieves 99.8%, and K-Nearest Neighbor achieves 99.3% with 20 features.

Keywords: Software Defined Networks · Federated Learning · RSA · Cyber Security · NBaIoT

1 Introduction

Cybersecurity in federated learning and SDN refers to the measures taken to protect sensitive or confidential data and prevent unauthorized access, theft, or tampering. Federated learning involves sharing model updates between decentralized devices and a central controller, which creates security concerns as sensitive data may be transmitted over the network [14].

Some of those concerns can be addressed through software-defined networks (SDNs). SDN is a type of networking architecture that separates the control plane (which manages network traffic flow) from the data plane (which forwards traffic to its destination). Whereas in traditional networking, network devices, such as switches and routers, perform both control and data plane functions, in SDNs, the control plane is moved to a centralized controller, which can be programmed using software to manage the network traffic flow, allowing for more efficient and flexible network management [19].

SDN can help address some of the cybersecurity challenges in federated learning by providing tools and techniques for securing the network and the data transmitted over it [4]. Some notable resources made available by SDN are the following:

1. **Network Segmentation:** SDN can be used to segment the network and restrict access to sensitive data, helping to prevent unauthorized access or data breaches.
2. **Traffic Monitoring:** The central controller in an SDN-based federated learning architecture can monitor network traffic and detect any malicious activity, such as malware or network attacks [9].
3. **Secure Data Transport:** The central controller can also dynamically configure the network to ensure secure data transport between federated devices and the central controller [12]. This can include using encryption, secure protocols, and firewalls to protect against data tampering or theft.
4. **Access Control:** The central controller can implement access control to ensure that only authorized devices are allowed to participate in the federated learning process. This can include authentication and authorization mechanisms, such as digital certificates or biometric authentication.
5. **Model Integrity:** The central controller can monitor the model updates generated by federated devices and detect any malicious modifications. This can help to ensure the integrity and trustworthiness of the federated learning model.

It is important to note that while SDN can enhance the security of federated learning, it is not a silver bullet [10]. Adequate security measures, including proper network configuration, strong access controls, and secure data storage, must also be in place to ensure the security and privacy of sensitive data in a federated learning system. Rather, it is important to prioritize cybersecurity in federated learning to ensure the integrity and trustworthiness of the models generated and to prevent unauthorized access to or misuse of sensitive data [6].

1.1   Integration of Cybersecurity with Federated Learning in SDN

Federated learning and SDN have the potential to revolutionize the way data is processed and managed. Integrating cybersecurity into these technologies can help secure networks and prevent sensitive data from being compromised. In federated learning [8], multiple decentralized devices collectively contribute to building a shared machine-learning model without sharing the raw data with a central server. Integrating cybersecurity measures into this process can ensure that the data is protected while in transit and at rest. This can be achieved through encryption, secure communication protocols, and access control mechanisms. There are various contributions to integration:

1. **Decentralized Model Training:** Federated learning enables decentralized training of machine learning models, reducing the risk of a single point of failure and increasing the overall robustness of the system.
2. **Enhanced Privacy:** By allowing models to be trained locally on edge devices, federated learning enhances the privacy of the data and reduces the risk of sensitive information being intercepted or leaked during the model training process.
3. **Dynamic Resource Allocation:** By leveraging SDN, federated learning can dynamically allocate network resources based on the needs of the system, improving network efficiency and reducing the risk of network congestion.
4. **Improved Security:** SDN enables the centralized management and control of network security policies, improving the overall security of the system.
5. **Efficient Data Collection:** By using federated learning, data collection can be optimized to reduce data transmission overhead and improve the accuracy of the models.
6. **Improved Performance:** The integration of federated learning and SDN can lead to improved system performance through the efficient use of network resources and the efficient training of models.
7. **Resilience:** Federated learning and SDN can make cybersecurity systems more resilient by enabling the efficient distribution of tasks and resources across the system, reducing the risk of single-point failures.

The main contributions of the paper are:

1. To enhance the security, efficiency, and overall performance of these systems, the potential of combining federated learning and SDN in cybersecurity is discussed.
2. Integrating cybersecurity into Federated Learning and SDN can help secure the network infrastructure, prevent sensitive data from being compromised, and ensure the reliability and availability of the network.
3. The architecture is proposed to detect attacks with federated learning in SDN to build a secure cybersecurity architecture for networks.
4. The N-BaIoT dataset is deployed for IDS in IoT networks and contains benign and malicious traffic generated from real IoT devices.
5. The performance is evaluated on different models (Decision tree, Random forest, and K-nearest neighbor) based on the dataset using metrics such as accuracy, precision, recall, and F1-score.

The rest of the paper is organized as: Sect. 2 describes the related work to secure federated learning from any kind of attack; Sect. 3 describes the methodology of encrypted algorithms and proposed architecture for cybersecurity; Sect. 4 represents the performance analysis and evaluation of the proposed work; Sect. 5 showcase the results; and Sect. 6 concludes the paper.

2   Related Work

The various researchers are focusing on the work to secure federated learning from any kind of attack. Secure federated learning [20] Researchers have proposed various methods for securing the federated learning process, such as homomorphic encryption, secure multiparty computation, and secure aggregation. These methods aim to protect the privacy of sensitive data and ensure the integrity of the federated learning model updates. In Privacy-preserving federated learning [1], there has been a growing interest in developing privacy-preserving methods for federated learning, such as differential privacy and secure aggregation. These methods aim to protect the privacy of sensitive data while still allowing for the training of accurate machine-learning models. In this, the centralized control plane, i.e., SDN, provides a single point of management for the network, which can be leveraged to implement privacy-preserving techniques in Federated Learning. This can include the use of encryption and secure communication protocols to protect data in transit, as well as access control mechanisms to ensure that only authorized devices can access the data. In Federated Learning, privacy preservation can be achieved through the use of differential privacy techniques, such as adding random noise to the data before it is shared, to protect the privacy of individual users. Additionally, privacy-preserving aggregation methods can be used to combine the model updates from multiple devices in a way that protects the privacy of each individual device.

In [7], the authors have used machine learning for IDS to detect malicious activity on networks. However, this requires collecting large amounts of network traffic data, which can be a privacy risk. Federated learning is a new approach that allows IDS to train models without sharing data. This can help protect privacy while still providing effective security. The authors of [13] proposed a new federated deep learning scheme called DeepFed to detect cyber threats against industrial CPSs. First, we design a new deep learning-based intrusion detection model for industrial CPSs using a convolutional neural network and a gated recurrent unit. Second, we develop a federated learning framework that allows multiple industrial CPSs to collectively build a comprehensive intrusion detection model in a privacy-preserving way. Finally, we create a secure communication protocol based on the Paillier cryptosystem to protect the security and privacy of model parameters during the training process.

There have been efforts to develop privacy-preserving methods for software-defined networking, such as secure multiparty computation, homomorphic encryption, and differential privacy. These methods aim to protect the privacy of sensitive data while still allowing for the efficient and secure management of network resources. According to the authors of [5], researchers have proposed various methods for securing software-defined networking, such as using encryption and authentication techniques, network segmentation, and access control. These methods aim to prevent unauthorized access to sensitive data and network attacks, such as malware or hacking.

This is a rapidly growing field, and there is a lot of ongoing research into improving the security and privacy of federated learning and software-defined networking. The goal of this research is to create secure and scalable systems for machine learning that can effectively protect the privacy and security of sensitive data.

3 Methodology

Encryption algorithms are mathematical algorithms that are used to convert plain text into an encrypted, or ciphertext, form that can only be deciphered by someone who has the appropriate decryption key. The purpose of encryption algorithms is to ensure that sensitive data is kept confidential and secure, even if it is intercepted by an unauthorized third party.

There are many different encryption algorithms available, including symmetric and asymmetric algorithms. Very few of the most commonly used algorithms in encryption include **Advanced Encryption Standard (AES):** is defined as the symmetric-based encryption algorithm that is widely used for the encryption of data. It uses 122 bits for fixed block size and assists key sizes of 128, 192, and 256 bits; **RSA** is an asymmetric encryption algorithm that is widely used for transmitting data securely. It uses a public key for the encryption and a private key for decryption, respectively [16]; **Blowfish** is a symmetric encryption algorithm that uses variable-length key sizes and is known for its speed and efficiency; **Twofish** is a symmetric encryption algorithm that is similar to Blowfish but uses a 128-bit block size and supports key sizes up to 256 bits; **Triple DES** is a symmetric encryption algorithm that utilizes three rounds of the DES encryption algorithm to provide increased security.

We chose RSA as the most effective in countering the attacks with federated learning in SDN.

3.1 Federated Learning with RSA

RSA, a public-key cryptography algorithm that is based on the mathematical properties of prime numbers was first described in 1977 by Ron Rivest, Adi Shamir, and Leonard Adleman, whose first letters of their last names form the acronym RSA.

The RSA algorithm utilizes two keys, a public and a private key, for encryption and decryption purposes [17]. The public key is used for encrypting the messages, and the private key is used for decrypting the messages. This means that anyone can encrypt a message employing the recipient's public key, but the message can be decrypted by only the recipient, who holds the private key.

The security of public-key cryptography algorithms, such as RSA, is based on the computational infeasibility of certain mathematical problems, such as factoring large numbers or computing the discrete logarithm. This makes it difficult for an attacker to obtain the private key, even if they have access to the public key.

3.2   Proposed Architecture for Cybersecurity with Federated Learning in SDN

The integration of Federated Learning and SDN can be used to build a secure cybersecurity architecture for networks as shown in Fig. 1. The following steps outline a general architecture for this integration [18]:

1. **Secure Data Collection:** Sensitive data from various sources is collected and securely stored in a centralized data repository. This data can then be used for training machine learning models.
2. **Federated Learning:** The decentralized devices in the network contribute to building a shared machine learning model without sharing the raw data with a central server. The devices only share the model updates with each other, which helps to protect the privacy of the data.
3. **Secure Communication:** Encryption and secure communication protocols, such as SSL/TLS, are used to protect the data in transit between the devices and the central server. This helps to prevent eavesdropping and tampering with the data.
4. **Access Control:** Access control mechanisms are implemented to ensure that only authorized devices have access to the sensitive data. This can be achieved through the use of authentication and authorization protocols.
5. **Intrusion Detection and Prevention:** Intrusion detection and prevention systems are implemented in the network to detect and prevent malicious traffic from spreading through the network. This can be achieved through the use of firewalls, intrusion detection systems, and other security measures.
6. **Network Management:** The centralized control plane in SDN is used to manage the network, including the implementation of security policies and configuration of security-related devices.

In the architecture, there are three IoT clusters which consist of various switches, routers and various IoT devices [11]. The attacks that are included in federated learning can be evaluated by deploying local data of IoT devices or the model parameters that are there on the client or at the side of the server. The question arises "how an attacker may execute the different attacks in federated learning?" By observation, it is said that the cyber attacker may control the IoT devices to compromise the local machine learning model to produce the model. The attacks did not degrade the performance of the machine learning model, but also exposed the user's private information. The machine learning model is applied to the local data of IoT clusters for training, then the data is sent to the SDN controller and local updates are transferred to the aggregation server. The cyber attack happened on the model in IoT cluster 1, if the adversary gains control of the aggregation server, the attacker can get complete knowledge of the history of updated devices' parameters and the structure of the global model during the training process done in a local model with the intention of generating a biased model. With this information, attackers can get the device's privacy through the use of reverse engineering attacks. Federated learning is vulnerable to attacks that are carried out through devices in IoT clusters.

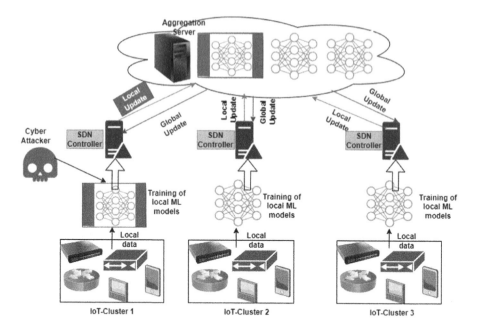

Fig. 1. Proposed architecture for detection of attacks with federated learning in SDN

The proposed architecture offers a number of advantages, such as:

1. Since the data is encrypted before being delivered to the federated learning server, it safeguards the privacy of the data sources.
2. It enables the training of a federated learning model using data from different sources without requiring data sharing.
3. Due to the fact that the attack detection model is trained using data from many sources, it may increase accuracy.

There are other difficulties with the proposed architecture, such as:

1. One must have trust that the federated learning server to properly gather the data and train the model.
2. The output of the federated learning model must be accurately interpreted by the attack detection application.

Therefore, the architecture is a potential strategy for SDN network attack detection. In addition to allowing many data sources to train a federated learning model and preserving the privacy of the data sources, it can increase the precision of the attack detection model. Before the suggested architecture can be widely used, there are a few issues that must be resolved. Overall, the integration of Federated Learning and SDN in a cybersecurity architecture helps to ensure that sensitive data is protected and that the network is secure and reliable. This can help to promote trust in the network and ensure that it is used in a responsible and secure manner.

4   Performance Analysis and Evaluation

4.1   Dataset

The N-BaIoT dataset [15] is a widely used dataset for intrusion detection in IoT networks. It contains benign and malicious traffic generated from real IoT devices such as smart homes, IP cameras, and smart plugs. The dataset was created by the National Institute of Standards and Technology (NIST) and can be used to train machine learning models for intrusion detection in IoT networks. The dataset contains over 140 million network flows and covers a wide range of attack types, including Distributed Denial of Service (DDoS), unauthorized access, and malware infections.

The N-BaIoT dataset is commonly used for detecting attacks in IoT domains for federated learning in SDN. It contains a large number of network-based attacks on IoT devices, including DDoS attacks, unauthorized access, and data manipulation. The dataset is designed to be used in a federated learning scenario, where multiple IoT devices can collaborate to train a shared machine learning model for attack detection.

4.2   Data Preprocessing

Data preprocessing is an important step in using the N-BaIoT dataset for intrusion detection. The following are some common preprocessing steps that can be applied to the N-BaIoT dataset:

Data cleaning: This involves removing any irrelevant, missing, or inconsistent data from the dataset. **Data normalization:** This involves scaling the data to a common range, such as $[0, 1]$, to ensure that the features have equal importance in the analysis. **Data balancing:** This involves ensuring that the dataset has a balanced distribution of benign and malicious samples. An imbalanced dataset can lead to biased results and poor performance of machine learning models. **Feature selection:** This involves choosing a subset of relevant features from the dataset to improve the performance of the machine learning models and reduce the dimensionality of the data [2]. **Data splitting:** This involves splitting the dataset into training and testing sets. The training set is employed for training the machine learning models, the validation set is employed for tuning the model hyperparameters, and the testing set is employed for evaluating the performance of the models.

4.3   Feature Extraction

Extraction of features is defined as the process of transforming raw data into a set of relevant and informative features that can be used to train machine learning models. In the case of the N-BaIoT dataset, the following features can be extracted for intrusion detection:

Flow-based features: These features capture information about the flow of network traffic, including the number of packets, the size of the payload, and the duration of the flow.

Protocol-based features: These features capture information about the protocols used in the network, including the type of the protocol, the source and destination ports, and the flags set in the protocol header.

Content-based features: These features capture information about the content of the network traffic, including the frequency of specific keywords or patterns.

Statistical features: These features capture information about the distribution of network traffic, including the mean and standard deviation of the flow size and duration.

4.4   Models Used for Evaluation

The following are some common models used for intrusion detection on the N-BaIoT dataset:

1. **Decision Trees:** This is a tree-based model that can be used to model the relationships between the features and the target variable. Decision Trees divide the feature space into a series of regions, with each region corresponding to a different class [3]. They're simple to interpret and can be used for both binary and multiclass classification problems.
2. **Random Forest:** This is an ensemble of decision trees that can be used to improve the accuracy of the predictions by combining the outputs of multiple trees. Random Forest creates multiple decision trees on randomly sampled subsets of the training data, and the final prediction is made by combining the predictions of all the trees.
3. **K-Nearest Neighbor (KNN):** The choice of the value of K is an important decision in KNN. A larger value of K means that the prediction is based on a larger number of neighbors, which may improve accuracy but may also introduce more noise. A smaller value of K means that the prediction is based on a smaller number of neighbors, which may be more sensitive to outliers but may also be more accurate in some cases.

5   Results and Discussions

The performance of different models on the N-BaIoT dataset can be compared using various performance metrics, including accuracy, precision, recall, F1 score, and area under the receiver operating characteristic curve (AUC-ROC).

There are two types of attacks: Mirai and Bashlite. The main aim of binary classification is to categorize malicious and normal traffic. The dataset is trained with three classifiers: Random Forest, K-Nearest Neighbor and Decision tree. The number of features changes as the accuracy improves. Random Forest is considered as the most effective because of its performance in comparison with

K-Nearest Neighbor and Decision Tree. The selected number of features are 2, 3, 5, 10 and 20, demonstrating unique results.

The Table 1 focus on the binary classification of Mirai attacks, in which there are 20 features with regard to the various models. The minimum number of attacks in a decision tree with three features achieves 98.8% as compared to the other models. The Fig. 2 shows the comparative analysis in graphical form to highlight the accuracy amongst different models. As depicted, decision tree with green line showing the minimum number of attacks.

Table 1. Binary Classification with Mirai Attack

Number of features	Random Forest	K-Nearest Neighbor	Decision Tree
2	99.1	99.3	98.8
3	99.1	99.3	98.8
5	99.3	99.5	99.0
10	99.5	99.6	99.0
20	99.6	99.8	99.3

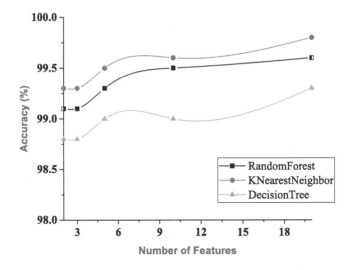

Fig. 2. Binary Classification with Mirai Attack

Table 2 focuses on the binary classification of Bashlite attacks, in which there are 10 features with regard to the various models. The minimum number of attacks in a decision tree with two features achieves 94.6% as compared to the other models. The Fig. 3 shows the comparative analysis in graphical form to highlight the accuracy amongst different models. As depicted, decision tree with green line showing the minimum number of attacks.

Table 2. Binary Classification with Bashlite Attack

Number of features	Random Forest	K-Nearest Neighbor	Decision Tree
2	96.3	96.5	94.6
3	96.5	95.5	95.5
5	96.6	95.5	94.8
10	97.8	97.3	96.3
20	97.6	96.6	96.5

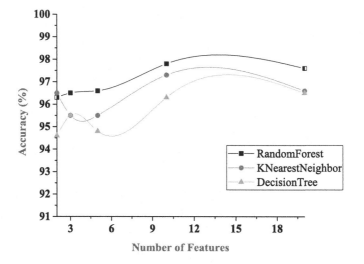

Fig. 3. Binary Classification with Bashlite Attack

6 Conclusions

In conclusion, the use of federated learning in SDN can provide an effective solution for detecting attacks in cyber security. FL allows for the aggregation of data from multiple sources without requiring data to be centralized, thereby maintaining the privacy and security of individual data sources. In the context of SDN, this approach can enable more accurate and efficient detection of attacks, while minimizing the risk of false positives and false negatives. The architecture is proposed for the detection of attacks with FL in SDN for secure data transfer. The performance analysis has been done using the NBaIoT dataset with baseline models of decision tree, random forest, and K-nearest neighbor, in which the proposed model achieved maximum accuracy as compared to the state-of-the-art models. However, further research is essential to evaluate the performance of FL-based solutions in real-world scenarios and address potential challenges such as communication overhead and privacy concerns.

References

1. Abou El Houda, Z., Hafid, A.S., Khoukhi, L.: Mitfed: a privacy preserving collaborative network attack mitigation framework based on federated learning using SDN and blockchain. IEEE Trans. Netw. Sci. Eng. (2023)
2. Alazab, M., RM, S.P., Parimala, M., Maddikunta, P.K.R., Gadekallu, T.R., Pham, Q.V.: Federated learning for cybersecurity: concepts, challenges, and future directions. IEEE Trans. Industr. Inform. **18**(5), 3501–3509 (2021)
3. Ali, M.N., Imran, M., din, M.S.U., Kim, B.S.: Low rate DDoS detection using weighted federated learning in SDN control plane in IoT network. Appl. Sci. **13**(3), 1431 (2023)
4. Anand, A., Rani, S., Anand, D., Aljahdali, H.M., Kerr, D.: An efficient CNN-based deep learning model to detect malware attacks (CNN-DMA) in 5G-IoT healthcare applications. Sensors **21**(19), 6346 (2021)
5. Balasubramanian, V., Aloqaily, M., Reisslein, M., Scaglione, A.: Intelligent resource management at the edge for ubiquitous IoT: an SDN-based federated learning approach. IEEE Network **35**(5), 114–121 (2021)
6. Balyan, A.K., et al.: A hybrid intrusion detection model using EGA-PSO and improved random forest method. Sensors **22**(16), 5986 (2022)
7. Duy, P.T., Hung, T.V., Ha, N.H., Hoang, H.D., Pham, V.H.: Federated learning-based intrusion detection in SDN-enabled IIoT networks. In: 2021 8th NAFOSTED Conference on Information and Computer Science (NICS), pp. 424–429 (2021). https://doi.org/10.1109/NICS54270.2021.9701525
8. Ferrag, M.A., Friha, O., Hamouda, D., Maglaras, L., Janicke, H.: Edge-IIoTset: a new comprehensive realistic cyber security dataset of IoT and IIoT applications for centralized and federated learning. IEEE Access **10**, 40281–40306 (2022)
9. Gebremariam, G.G., Panda, J., Indu, S., et al.: Blockchain-based secure localization against malicious nodes in IoT-based wireless sensor networks using federated learning. Wirel. Commun. Mob. Comput. **2023** (2023)
10. Hbaieb, A., Ayed, S., Chaari, L.: Federated learning-based ids approach for the IoV. In: Proceedings of the 17th International Conference on Availability, Reliability and Security, pp. 1–6 (2022)
11. Huong, T.T., et al.: Detecting cyberattacks using anomaly detection in industrial control systems: a federated learning approach. Comput. Ind. **132**, 103509 (2021)
12. Kapoor, K., Rani, S., Kumar, M., Chopra, V., Brar, G.S.: Hybrid local phase quantization and grey wolf optimization based SVM for finger vein recognition. Multimedia Tools Appl. **80**, 15233–15271 (2021)
13. Li, B., Wu, Y., Song, J., Lu, R., Li, T., Zhao, L.: Deepfed: federated deep learning for intrusion detection in industrial cyber-physical systems. IEEE Trans. Industr. Inf. **17**(8), 5615–5624 (2021). https://doi.org/10.1109/TII.2020.3023430
14. Ma, X., Liao, L., Li, Z., Lai, R.X., Zhang, M.: Applying federated learning in software-defined networks: a survey. Symmetry **14**(2), 195 (2022)
15. Meidan, Y., et al.: N-BaIoT-network-based detection of IoT botnet attacks using deep autoencoders. IEEE Pervasive Comput. **17**(3), 12–22 (2018)
16. Mothukuri, V., Khare, P., Parizi, R.M., Pouriyeh, S., Dehghantanha, A., Srivastava, G.: Federated-learning-based anomaly detection for IoT security attacks. IEEE Internet Things J. **9**(4), 2545–2554 (2021)
17. Preuveneers, D., Rimmer, V., Tsingenopoulos, I., Spooren, J., Joosen, W., Ilie-Zudor, E.: Chained anomaly detection models for federated learning: an intrusion detection case study. Appl. Sci. **8**(12), 2663 (2018)

18. Rahman, S.A., Tout, H., Talhi, C., Mourad, A.: Internet of things intrusion detection: centralized, on-device, or federated learning? IEEE Network **34**(6), 310–317 (2020)
19. Ramesh, T., Lilhore, U.K., Poongodi, M., Simaiya, S., Kaur, A., Hamdi, M.: Predictive analysis of heart diseases with machine learning approaches. Malays. J. Comput. Sci. 132–148 (2022)
20. Zhang, L., Xu, J., Vijayakumar, P., Sharma, P.K., Ghosh, U.: Homomorphic encryption-based privacy-preserving federated learning in IoT-enabled healthcare system. IEEE Trans. Netw. Sci. Eng. (2022)

Heterogeneous Transfer Learning from a Partial Information Decomposition Perspective

Gabriele Gianini[1]([✉]) [iD], Annalisa Barsotti[2] [iD], Corrado Mio[3] [iD],
and Jianyi Lin[4] [iD]

[1] Dipartimento di Informatica, Sistemistica e Comunicazione, Università degli Studi di Milano-Bicocca, U14, viale Sarca 336, 20126 Milano, MI, Italy
gabriele.gianini@unimi.it

[2] Università degli Studi di Milano, via Celoria 18, 20133 Milano, MI, Italy
annalisa.barsotti@unimi.it

[3] EBTIC, Khalifa University of Science and Technology, Abu Dhabi, UAE
corrado.mio@ku.ac.ae

[4] Università Cattolica del Sacro Cuore, Milano, Italy
jianyi.lin@unicatt.it

Abstract. Transfer Learning (TL) encompasses a number of Machine Learning Techniques that take a pre-trained model aimed at solving a task in a Source Domain and try to reuse it to improve the performance of a related task in a Target Domain An important issue in TL is that the effectiveness of those techniques is strongly dataset-dependent. In this work, we investigate the possible structural causes of the varying performance of Heterogeneous Transfer Learning (HTL) across domains characterized by different, but overlapping feature sets (this naturally determine a partition of the features into Source Domain specific subset, Target Domain specific subset, and shared subset). To this purpose, we use the Partial Information Decomposition (PID) framework, which breaks down the multivariate information that input variables hold about an output variable into three kinds of components: Unique, Synergistic, and Redundant. We consider that each domain can hold the PID components in implicit form: this restricts the information directly accessible to each domain. Based on the relative PID structure of the above mentioned feature subsets, the framework is able to tell, in principle: 1) which kind of information components are lost in passing from one domain to the other, 2) which kind of information components are at least implicitly available to a domain, and 3) what kind information components could be recovered through the bridge of the shared features. We show an example of a bridging scenario based on synthetic data.

Keywords: Heterogeneous Transfer Learning · Partial Information Decomposition · Transferable Information Components

1 Introduction

The expression Transfer Learning (TL) covers a wide collection of Machine Learning (ML) methods aimed at reusing knowledge across domains. In machine

R. Chbeir et al. (Eds.): MEDES 2023, CCIS 2022, pp. 133–146, 2024.
https://doi.org/10.1007/978-3-031-51643-6_10

learning, most often it refers to the reuse of a pre-trained model aimed at solving a task in a Source Domain to improve the performance of a related task in a Target Domain [7].

For instance, one can learn to classify instances from a low cardinality dataset of the target domain by leveraging the knowledge gained from the instances from a large dataset in a similar domain: this first case is an example of homogeneous Transfer Learning. Furthermore, new and potentially useful knowledge can be imported into a target domain from a source domain characterized by different variables when the two sets of variables do not completely overlap: this case is an example of Heterogeneous Transfer Learning (HTL) [1].

The landscape of specific problems and approaches in TL is varied. A significant number of techniques have been proposed for HTL, including Heterogeneous Feature Augmentation [2] and Heterogeneous Max-Margin Classifier Adaptation [4]), and Sparse Heterogeneous Feature Representation (SHFR) for multiclass Heterogeneous Domain Adaptation (HDA) [6], however, it has been reported that their effectiveness is strongly dataset dependent. In this work, we are interested in understanding the prerequisites necessary for a successful transfer and the related challenges in the case of HTL with partial feature set superposition.

To this end, we propose an approach based on the Partial Information Decomposition (PID) framework, proposed by Williams and Beer in 2010 [5]. The framework decomposes the multivariate information that a set of input variables holds about an output variable into Unique, Synergistic, and Redundant components. In addition, we consider the degree of accessibility to information components (such degree can depend upon representational issues and noise).

We point to a naming-related issue in discussing TL and PID together in a ML context: the terms "source" and "target" can take two different meanings. In the TL context one speaks of *Source Domain* and *Target Domain*: they refer to the spaces *from* which and *to* which, respectively, information has to be moved (the information is typically about joint distributions of predictor and predicted variables). In the PID context one speaks of *information source* to refer to a predictor variable or a set of predictor variables. In ML the term *target* refers to predicted variables (e.g. class labels). To avoid confusion, along this work, we always add a specification to the terms "source" and "target" and use capitalization to mark the distinction. For example: we mention Source Domain variables and Target Domain variables; the Source Domain variables include input features and target/output variables; furthermore, within each Domain it can be useful to distinguish among a number of information sources, i.e. subsets of input variables providing information about a target variable.

In HTL with partial feature set superposition it is useful to distinguish the following three subsets of features: Source-Domain-specific features (we identify this set of features, available only to the Source Domain, with information source α), target-domain-specific features (we identify this set of features, available only to the Target Domain, with information source γ) and shared features (we identify this non-empty set with information source β). In other words the Source Domain holds the information sources α and β, whereas the Target Domain holds the information sources β and γ.

The functional dependence relationships among these three information sources and with the target/output variable determine the potential usefulness or irrelevance of the transfer schemes. Based on the correlation structure of the three feature sets our framework is able to tell in principle:

- what PID components could be readily *available* in the Source Domain to transfer to the Target Domain and what could be *accessible* in practice
- which part of that information is it actually needed in the Target Domain to improving the classification/regression task performance
- and, for the information that would be needed, but is not accessible, whether a surrogate/proxy could be transferred exploiting the shared features.

In this way, one can analyze the different transfer learning schemes and tell if they have the potential to exploit the synergistic information when present. We study in particular the most relevant transfer scheme, based on *bridging* through the shared features and show an example of this approach using synthetic data.

Notice that for the sake of illustration we limit our examples to the case of a single-bit output variable (which could represent a dichotomous label classifier): the two domains (Source Domain and Target Domain) can hold shares of information about this output. Similarly, for the sake of clarity in the theoretical discussion of the framework, we consider only feature sets consisting of a single one-bit variable (α, β and γ each consisting of one bit): the Source Domain holds the two bits α and β, and the target domain holds the two bits β and γ. This structure can, in principle, be extrapolated to any number of bits in the input domain variables and any number of bits in the output variable.

The paper is structured as follows. After recalling in Sect. 2, definitions and concepts related to Transfer Learning in general and to Heterogeneous Transfer Learning in particular, we outline, in Sect. 3 the theory of Partial Information Decomposition. Then in Sect. 4 we present our framework for the application of PID to HTL. Finally, in Sect. 5 we demonstrate the result of some experimentation using synthetic data. A summary of the findings and an outlook for future work conclude the paper in Sect. 6.

2   Transfer Learning

Sometimes, the knowledge acquired from solving a task on a dataset can be reused to solve the same or a related task on a different dataset: this is called Transfer Learning.

Domain. A Domain $\mathcal{D} = \{\mathcal{X}, P\}$ is defined by a space and a probability distribution on its samples. The space is denoted by $\mathcal{X}$ (for example, it could be $\mathbb{R}^n$) and called *feature space*. A Source and a Target Domain are different when they have different feature spaces ($\mathcal{X}^S \neq \mathcal{X}^T$) or different probability distributions ($P^S(X) \neq P^T(X)$).

Task. In supervised learning, a task $\mathcal{T} = \{\mathcal{Y}, f\}$ consists of a label space $\mathcal{Y}$ (e.g. $\{0, 1\}$) and a predictive function f, which is expected to be learned from the training data. Two tasks are different if they have two different label spaces $\mathcal{Y}^S \neq \mathcal{Y}^T$ or different or different conditional probability distributions $P^S(y|X) \neq P^T(y|X)$.

Transfer Learning. The Transfer Learning problem consists of finding approaches to exploit the knowledge *implemented* in a Source Domain and a task $(\mathcal{D}^S, \mathcal{T}^S)$ to improve the performance of the learned decision function f^T for a task $\mathcal{T}^T$ in a target domain and task $(\mathcal{D}^T, \mathcal{T}^T)$.

Homogeneous vs. Heterogeneous Transfer Learning. There are several categorizations of transfer learning problems. One of them is based on the consistency between Source Domain and Target Domain feature spaces and label spaces. If $\mathcal{X}^S = \mathcal{X}^T$ and $\mathcal{Y}^S = \mathcal{Y}^T$ – that is, if the feature spaces in the Source and Target Domains use the same attributes and labels – the scenario is called *homogeneous transfer learning*. Otherwise, if $\mathcal{X}^S \neq \mathcal{X}^T$ and/or $\mathcal{Y}^S \neq \mathcal{Y}^T$, the scenario is called *heterogeneous transfer learning*.

Setup of the Present Work. In this work we assume that $\mathcal{Y}^S = \mathcal{Y}^T$ but $\mathcal{X}^S \neq \mathcal{X}^T$ and that the two different set of features partially overlap: $\mathcal{X}_\cap \equiv (\mathcal{X}^S \cap \mathcal{X}^T) \neq \emptyset$.

3 Partial Information Decomposition (PID)

The goal of Partial Information Decomposition (PID), first proposed by Williams and Beer in 2010 [5], is to break down the multivariate mutual information that a set of source variables provides about a target output variable, into its simplest components – non-negative terms called sometimes *information atoms*. For example, in a two-source setting, some information about the output variable might only be found in a certain source, while other information might be shared by the two sources, and still other information might be made synergistically accessible only by combining both sources. This framework can be used in our setting since also in classification and regression it is crucial to understand how information about the target variable is distributed among the different sources, which are given by the feature variables.

3.1 PID for Two Information Sources

Assume we have two variables, called X_1 and X_2, and assume that to each item described by combination of their values (x_1, x_2) a function f (that we want to learn) assigns a Boolean label $y \in Y = \{0, 1\}$. We can break down the information about the target into redundant, unique and synergistic

- *Redundant information* ($Rdn_{12} \equiv Rdn(Y : X_1, X_2)$: the same information is present both in source 1 and source 2, each source holds one bit of information about the label),

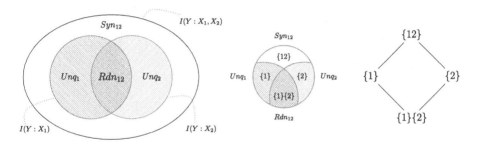

Fig. 1. Partial Information diagrams for two information sources 1 and 2. Left: the Venn diagram. Center: its compact representation. Right: the corresponding lattice of coalitions. In the center and right diagrams {1} and {2} are singletons and represent the unique information held by the sources about the target variable; whereas {1}{2} (the shorthand for {{1}{2}}) represents the two singleton sources that can provide the same information, i.e. redundant information; finally, {12} represents the *coalition* of both information sources.

- *Unique information* ($Unq_1 \equiv Unq(Y : X_1)$): information present in 1 only (not available to 2), i.e. 1 holds a bit of information; $Unq_2 \equiv Unq(Y : X_2)$: information present in 2 only (not available to 1), i.e. 2 holds a bit of information),
- *Synergistic information* ($Syn_{12} \equiv Syn(Y : X_1, X_2)$): the information can only be provided by source 1 and source 2 jointly, they cannot provide that information individually, i.e. individually they hold zero bits of information, jointly they hold one). A prototypical example of this is the XOR function.

In other words, the information that source 1 alone holds about the target is composed by the unique part and the redundant part, similarly for source 2:

$$I(Y : X_1) = Rdn_{12} + Unq_1 \qquad I(Y : X_2) = Rdn_{12} + Unq_2 \qquad (1)$$

The information that the two sources hold together contains all the four terms

$$I(Y : X_1, X_2) = Rdn_{12} + Unq_1 + Unq_2 + Syn_{12} \qquad (2)$$

Figure 1 illustrates this decomposition. The above equations form an underdetermined system of three equations with four unknowns: the PI decomposition alone does not provide a method to work out the PI terms. To the latter purpose one needs to specify one of the four variables in the system, e.g. by postulating a formula to compute either Rdn or Syn. A number of proposals for defining the PID terms have been advanced (see Kolchinsky [3] for a list of pointers). This problem, however, is out of the scope of the present work: we use the PID framework to assess the transfer learning schemas and do not take a quantitative approach, thus we do not need to measure the precise size of PID components.

3.2   The PID for Three Information Sources

Whereas the PID lattice for two information sources consists of 4 nodes, the PID lattice for three sources consists of 18 nodes (see Fig. 2). The singletons nodes

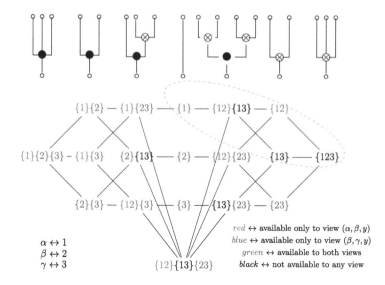

Fig. 2. The 18 node three-variate redundancy lattice. Above the lattice are represented for illustrative purposes, the Boolean circuit prototypes for the components for the setting where each input source provides a single bit and the output consists of a single bit: the solid circle • represents redundancy, and the symbol ⊗ represents synergy. The sources 1, 2, and 3, in the discussion of Sect. 4 correspond, respectively, to the variables α, β and γ, whereas in the example of Sect. 5 they correspond, respectively, to the variables κ^α, κ^β and κ^γ. To the benefit of the discussion in Sect. 4, the colors denote the availability of the Partial Information components to the different views (Source Domain view, Target Domain view, and all-encompassing view). The dashed ellipse indicates the Partial Information components not available to the Target Domain view.

$\{1\}$, $\{2\}$, and $\{3\}$ represent the unique information held by the sources about the target; the nodes $\{12\}$, $\{13\}$, $\{23\}$, and $\{123\}$ that represent synergistic information; the remainder are nodes that represent redundant information shared by two singletons, such as with $\{1\}\{2\}$ – by a singleton and a coalition, such as in $\{1\}\{23\}$ – by two coalitions, such as in $\{12\}\{13\}$ – or by three coalitions, such as in $\{12\}\{13\}\{23\}$.

One can look at the three information source diagram as a breakdown of the two information source PID components according to their relationship with an extra source. Notice that in the two-source lattice and in the three-source lattice the same symbol denotes two different kinds of information. For example, in the two-source diagram the term $\{12\}$ denotes the *whole* synergistic information of source 1 and 2, whereas in the three-source diagram the term $\{12\}$ denotes the part of synergistic information of 1 and 2 that has no redundancies, i.e. that cannot be found elsewhere. To avoid confusion from now on we denote the two-source cprime, for example

$$\{12\}' = \{12\} + \{12\}\{3\} + \{12\}\{13\} + \{12\}\{23\} + \{12\}\{13\}\{23\} \tag{3}$$

4   Heterogeneous Transfer Learning Meets PID

In HTL with overlapping feature sets we can regard the sets

$$\alpha = \left(\mathcal{X}^S \setminus \mathcal{X}^T\right) \qquad \beta = \left(\mathcal{X}^S \cap \mathcal{X}^T\right) \qquad \gamma = \left(\mathcal{X}^T \setminus \mathcal{X}^S\right)$$

as three sources of information about the target variable Y:

- the Source Domain view (X^S, Y) includes the information sources α and β,
- the Target Domain view (X^T, Y) includes the information sources β and γ.

We denote the Source Domain view by (α, β, y), the Target Domain view by (β, γ, y), and for the sake of comparison the all-encompassing view by $(\alpha, \beta, \gamma, y)$.
    If we map the information sources α, β and γ respectively to 1, 2, and 3, i.e.

$$1 \leftrightarrow \alpha \qquad 2 \leftrightarrow \beta \qquad 3 \leftrightarrow \gamma \tag{4}$$

we have that

- the Source Domain view holds the components $\{1\}'$, $\{2\}'$, $(\{1\}\{2\})'$, $\{12\}'$;
- the Target Domain view holds the components $\{2\}'$, $\{3\}'$, $(\{2\}\{3\})'$, $\{23\}'$;
- the all-encompassing view holds all the 18 components shown in Fig. 2.

Notice the following key points

- the sole fact that the information is held by a source, does not grant that it can be readily used for the prediction: the information has obviously to be learned from the data before being used for prediction, and the process of learning can fail for several reasons: this happens for instance when the model chosen for learning is not suitable for the task.[1]
- *when an information component is not held by a two-source view – or when is held by the view, but is hard to learn – it still can, in principle, be at least partially recovered by that view from the redundant components* (redundant with the missing information): this can be considered a sort of *bridging*.

In this capability lies the specificity of Heterogeneous Transfer Learning: the process of HTL can involve at the same time domain adaptation (as in Homogeneous TL) over the shared features, and bridging of information through exploitation of PID redundancies. A bridging example is given in the next Section.[2]
    For example, by construction the Target Domain view (β, γ, y) does not directly hold the synergistic information of the two sources 1 and 2 (i.e. $\{12\}'$); nonetheless $\{12\}'$ can be broken into parts (see Eq. (3)), some of which are redundant with components actually held by the Target Domain view:

---

[1] For example, if a full dataset defining the XOR function in a Cartesian plane is available to an information source, say β, the attempt to learn the corresponding classifier using a straight line as class separation boundary is bound to fail.

[2] In that example we will bridge from α to β information that is synergistic to γ for the prediction of the target/output variable, so that the Target Domain view can exploit the synergy between the available γ and the non-available α.

– the part $\{12\}\{3\}$ can in principle be recovered from $\{3\}'$
– the part $\{12\}\{23\}$ can in principle be recovered from $\{23\}'$
– the part $\{12\}\{13\}\{23\}$ can also in principle be recovered from $\{23\}'$
– the part $\{12\}\{13\}$ is not accessible to the Target view
– the part $\{12\}$ is equally not accessible to the Target view

The first three components can act as *bridges* between views.

Overall, looking at Fig. 2 one can see that with respect to bridging, from the stand point of the Target Domain view, there are only three kinds of component: those potentially available in full (i.e. $\{2\}'$, $\{3\}'$, and $\{23\}'$, those not available and not recoverable, due to lack of redundancy (within the ellipse), and those not available but potentially recoverable, thanks to redundancy.

Recoverable Information. The components that by construction are not immediately available to the Target Domain view are

$\{1\}'$ that can be partially recovered from $\{1\}\{2\}$, $\{1\}\{23\}$, $\{1\}\{2\}\{3\}$, $\{1\}\{3\}$;
$\{12\}'$ that can be partially recovered from $\{12\}\{23\}$, $\{12\}\{3\}$, $\{12\}\{13\}\{23\}$;
$\{13\}'$ that can be partially recovered from $\{2\}\{13\}$, $\{13\}\{23\}$, $\{12\}\{13\}\{23\}$.

On the contrary, $\{123\}$, i.e. the synergistic information in the coalition of the three sources is completely lost from the point of view of the Target Domain.

5   An Illustrative Example of Bridging

We provide an illustrative example of the bridging discussed above.

Notice that, in the example, the mapping between the sources α, β, γ, and the elements of Fig. 2 (where each source was represented as a single bit) is not direct: to allow a pictorial representation in the Cartesian plane, each source consists of two variables, i.e. two coordinates, each defined by several bits; however each point in the Cartesian plane (each coordinate pair) is associated with a Boolean class κ^σ with $\sigma \in \{\alpha, \beta, \gamma\}$: thus the relationship with the elements of the diagram in Fig. 2 is defined by

$$1 \leftrightarrow \kappa^\alpha \qquad 2 \leftrightarrow \kappa^\beta \qquad 3 \leftrightarrow \kappa^\gamma \tag{5}$$

Also notice that in the following for notation convenience the target/output variable about which the domains hold some information is denoted by z. The reason for the choice will be apparent from the data description.

5.1   A Source-View and Target-View Model

We generate the data according to the following stylized scenario graphically illustrated in Fig. 3:

– the Cartesian plain points of α and γ are generated independently from one another (they also form two tables with an equal number of rows);

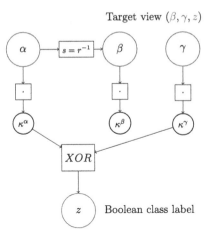

Source view (α, β, z)

Target view (β, γ, z)

Fig. 3. Schematic view of the feature dependencies: α and γ are independent, so are their Boolean labels (unavailable to the observers), which are combined by a XOR to yield the labels z. Thus α and β can synergistically predict z. However, neither the source view nor the target view can observe the two feature sets at the same time. The Source Domain observer can only see α, β and the label z, while the Target Domain observer can only see β, γ, and the label z.

- generation of the label z:
  - the Boolean labels κ^α, κ^β, and κ^γ are assigned to the points of the α, β and γ datasets respectively based on their geometrical position (further details later);
  - the labels κ^α, κ^β, and κ^γ are not included in the source or target views, but are combined by an XOR function to yield the Boolean label $z \in \mathcal{Y}$, i.e.
  $$z = XOR(\kappa^\alpha, \kappa^\gamma)$$
  (κ^β is not used): this makes α and γ *synergetic* for the prediction of z: the source-specific features alone cannot predict the target better than a static dummy classifier issuing always the majority class label, the same holds for the target-specific features;[3]
- then each point of β is generated from a point of α through a deterministic transform – consisting in a non-linear deformation – and some added noise;
- finally we prepared a single, all-encompassing dataset, from which we later extracted the Source view and the Target view, as illustrated in Fig. 4.

---

[3] It is apparent that in this scenario α and γ can, together, predict the target variable z. However, neither the Source Domain nor the Target Domain encompass both feature sets. However, since α can in principle be partially recovered from β, there is room for improving the target domain prediction, with respect to those of a model learned solely on the basis of view (β, γ, z).

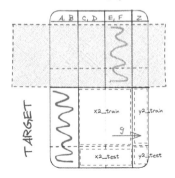

Fig. 4. Schematic view of the construction of the Source Domain side dataset (left) and Target Domain side dataset (right): the wiggles in the upper and the lower part of the table indicate columns that are not available to the Source side or to the Target side respectively. From the Target-side dataset one can learn a classifier g, that does not have optimal performance, since it misses some synergistic features, available only at the Source side.

- the Source Domain dataset (α, β, z) is built by the columns of the variable sets α and β, plus the target z, and using the first half of the rows;
- similarly the Target Domain dataset (β, γ, z) is built by the columns of the variable sets β and γ, and the target z and with the reminder rows.

The feature sets α, β and γ are defined by two variables each: $\alpha = \{A, B\}$, $\beta = \{C, D\}$, $\gamma = \{E, F\}$, and the class label variable is the Boolean variable Z.

Generation of the Dataset with the Desired Features. We generated the features as follows (hereafter n_0 and n_1 indicate, respectively, the size of the class 0 and class 1 portions of the dataset, and $n = n_0 + n_1$ while $\mathcal{U}(a, b)$ denotes a random uniform over the interval $[a, b]$.

$$r_i \sim \mathcal{U}(0, a), \quad i = 1, \ldots, n_0 \qquad r_i \sim \mathcal{U}(b, c), \quad i = n_S + 1, \ldots, n_S + n_T$$
$$\kappa_i^\alpha = 0, \quad i = 1, \ldots, n_0 \qquad \kappa_i^\alpha = 1, \quad i = n_0 + 1, \ldots, n_0 + n_1$$

and $\theta_i = \mathcal{U}(0, 2\pi)$, for $i = 1, \ldots, n$. With $a = 4^2, b = 6^2, c = 8^2$ this generates the radial coordinates of random points within, respectively, an inner disc (class 0) and an outer annulus (class 1). Then we put them in polar coordinates and add some Gaussian noise

$$x_i = r_i \cos(\theta_i) + \varepsilon_x \qquad \text{where } \varepsilon_x \sim \mathcal{N}(0, (x_{max} - x_{min})/d)$$
$$y_i = r_i \sin(\theta_i) + \varepsilon_y \qquad \text{where } \varepsilon_y \sim \mathcal{N}(0, (y_{max} - y_{min})/d)$$

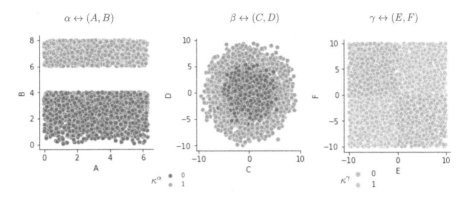

Fig. 5. Scatter-plots of the synthetic dataset. The colors correspond to the Boolean values of the class κ^α and κ^γ (see legend) of the 2D points; the class label for the 6D points are obtained by $Z = XOR(\kappa^\alpha, \kappa^\gamma)$.

with $d = 15$. Then we set two other Cartesian coordinate variables $u_i \sim \mathcal{U}(-\ell, +\ell)$, and $v_i \sim \mathcal{U}(-\ell, +\ell)$ for $i = 1, \ldots, n$ (with $\ell = 10$), and set the class of the corresponding points to the Boolean value $\kappa_i^\gamma = (1 + \text{sgn}(u_i)\,\text{sgn}(v_i))/2$.

The class for the point $(r_i, \theta_i, x_i, y_i, u_i, v_i)$ was set to $z = XOR(\kappa^\alpha, \kappa^\gamma)$

Finally, we set $A = r$, $B = \theta$, $C = x$, $D = y$, $E = u$, $F = v$ and $Z = z$. The result is graphically illustrated in Fig. 5.

5.2 Outcomes

Notation. Let $a_c(w)$ indicate the accuracy of a classifier c based on a given view w: for example, $a_{SVM}((\alpha, \beta))$ denotes the accuracy of an SVM classifier trained on view (α, β); we are going to use the Support Vector Machine classifiers $(c = SVM)$, and Random Forest $(c = RF)$.

In the following we are going to demonstrate that using either $c = SVM$ or $c = RF$, without transfer learning we have

$$a_c(\alpha, \gamma) > a_c(\alpha, \beta, \gamma) > a_c(\beta, \gamma) > a_c(\alpha, \beta) \tag{6}$$

This happens because (α, γ) holds the synergistic information without the noise that β contributes to (α, β, γ); furthermore (β, γ) contains the synergistic information but only in noisy form, while (α, β), does not hold that information and cannot predict the output variable.

The performance of the prediction using the Target Domain data set (β, γ, z), i.e., with columns (C, D, E, F), is far from optimal. The SVM classifier obtained optimizing the model parameters (through random search) yields a test accuracy of 0.770 and a test precision of 0.726, against a dummy classifier accuracy and precision of 0.580 (reflecting the proportion of the classes: the dummy classifier always bets on the same class). Thus, the improvement over the Dummy classifier is of only 0.190 for the accuracy and 0.164 for the precision. From now on we

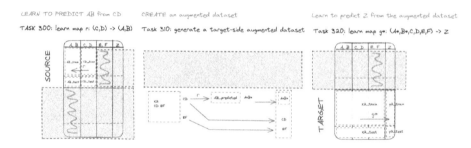

Fig. 6. Schematic view of the transfer learning approach. The shaded areas refer to rows or parts of the columns that are not involved in the specific phase of the procedure.

quote the results in terms of improvement with respect to the dummy classifier, which in this dataset has by construction $accuracy = precision = 0.580$ and $recall = 1$.

However, there is room for increasing the performance. For the sake of comparison we trained an SVM (again optimizing the hyperparameters by random search) on the whole feature set $(\alpha, \beta, \gamma) \leftrightarrow (A, B, C, D, E, F)$ and obtained an improvement over the dummy dataset of 0.453 in accuracy and of 0.422 in precision. The performance gets even better if we remove the redundant (in principle) but (in practice) skewed and noisy columns $\beta \leftrightarrow (CD)$: In fact, the feature set $(\alpha, \gamma) \leftrightarrow (A, B, E, F)$ fares an increase of 0.463 and 0.439 respectively in accuracy and precision w.r.t. the dummy classifier.

The Transfer Learning Approach. To transfer synergetic information from the source data set to the Target Domain side, we use the procedure shown in Fig. 6.

- First, using the Source Domain dataset, we learn an SVM regressor r mapping (C, D) onto (A, B) (i.e., we learn the *bridge*).
- Then, using the Target Domain dataset we run the regressor r and map the features (C, D) onto estimates of (A, B), which we denote by (A^*, B^*).
- At this point we augment the target dataset with the new predicted features, obtaining the dataset with features (A^*, B^*, C, D, E, F)
- and finally use the augmented dataset to train the new SVM classifier g^*

The SVM regressor r (obtained by optimizing the hyper-parameters by random search), is set to play the role of an effective bridge between the domains: evaluating the effectiveness of r in predicting (A, B) based on (C, D), one finds that the regressor is able to explain a considerable part of the variance. If we predict the feature $B*$ and the feature A^* separately, the proportion of explained variance (defined as $1 - $ (variance of residuals/(total variance)) for the feature B^* is 0.81, while for the feature A^* it is 0.60.

Table 1. Results of SVM and RF classifiers on different feature sets. The Extra Accuracy and the Extra Precision, with respect to the ones of the dummy classifier (always issuing the same label) are reported. The comparison between the performances of the feature sets CDEF and A*B*CDEF, highlighted in boldface, shows that the transfer learning process has been effective.

Feature Sets		Features	Dummy Classifier Accuracy == Precision	SVM Classifier Extra Accuracy	SVM Classifier Extra Precision	RF Classifier Extra Accuracy	RF Classifier Extra Precision
ALL rows	(α, β, γ)	ABCDEF	0.498	0.453	0.422	0.495	0.498
	(α, γ)	AB EF		0.463	0.439	0.498	0.498
Source rows	(α, β)	ABCD	0.544	−0.055	0.243	−0.050	−0.014
Target rows	(β, γ)	**CDEF**		**0.190**	**0.146**	**0.275**	**0.253**
		B*CDEF	0.580	0.250	0.254	0.320	0.337
	$(\alpha^*, \beta, \gamma)$	**A*B*CDEF**		**0.410**	**0.408**	**0.420**	**0.420**

Performance Outcomes with Transfer Learning. The outcomes of the process in the synthetic data set support the possibility of transferring some information from source-only features to the target side classifier. In fact, the SVM classifier g^* has an improvement over the dummy classifier of 0.410 for accuracy and of 0.408 for precision. A more comprehensive account is reported in Table 1. One can observe that in terms of accuracy a_c and in terms of precision p_c, for both the SVM classifier and the RF classifier we have

$$a_c(\alpha^*, \beta, \gamma) > a_c(\beta, \gamma)$$

$$p_c(\alpha^*, \beta, \gamma) > p_c(\beta, \gamma)$$

In other words the transfer learning process, when using SVMs or RFs is effective.

In addition, the analysis of feature importance confirms the effectiveness of this TL scheme on this data set. Using the Shapley Value of the features and their permutation importance (results not reported here), we find that the reconstructed features, in particular $B*$ are among the most impacting on precision.

On the other hand, trying the same transfer learning schema with Logistic Regressor classifiers fails completely. This model is not able to predict the correct class better than the Dummy classifier, no matter which set of features is provided for training.

6 Discussion and Conclusion

In Transfer Learning, not only the various sources may refer to differently distributed populations, but also the corresponding feature sets can overlap only partially. Each source will have a number of unique features: leaving them out of the analysis means missing the opportunity to exploit their synergistic effects.

In this work, we provided a framework based on Partial Information Decomposition to analyze the kinds of information that can be transferred from the

Source Domain to the Target Domain, when their feature sets overlap. Some information component from the source is irremediably lost to the Target Domain, some is implicitly available, some can be recovered using a bridging approach based on the shared features. We demonstrate the latter case with a numerical example based on synthetic data. We outline a pattern where heterogeneous transfer learning can be useful and where a specific heterogeneous transfer learning schema can be effective.

This HTL approach contrasts with other approaches that focus on domain adaptation over shared features, such as that in [2], which works by using a symmetric transformation that maps the feature spaces of the source and target data to a common subspace using projection matrices. Such a method to incorporate the original features of the data into the transformed data in the common subspace uses two feature mapping functions that involve plugging zeros for the nonshared features (that is, the Source Domain specific features and the Target Domain specific features) to match the domain dimensions. This operation does not preserve domain-specific information and hinders the exploitation of bridging and possible synergies.

We plan to extend the present work by experimenting with different dependency patterns and extending the analysis to real-world datasets.

Acknowledgements. The work was partially supported by the project MUSA - Multilayered Urban Sustainability Action - project, funded by the European Union - NextGenerationEU, (CUP G43C22001370007, Code ECS00000037). The work was also partially supported by the project SERICS (PE00000014) under the NRRP MUR program funded by the EU - NextGenerationEU.

References

1. Day, O., Khoshgoftaar, T.M.: A survey on heterogeneous transfer learning. J. Big Data **4**, 1–42 (2017)
2. Duan, L., Xu, D., Tsang, I.: Learning with augmented features for heterogeneous domain adaptation. arXiv preprint arXiv:1206.4660 (2012)
3. Kolchinsky, A.: A novel approach to the partial information decomposition. Entropy **24**(3) (2022). https://doi.org/10.3390/e24030403. https://www.mdpi.com/1099-4300/24/3/403
4. Mozafari, A.S., Jamzad, M.: A SVM-based model-transferring method for heterogeneous domain adaptation. Pattern Recogn. **56**, 142–158 (2016). https://doi.org/10.1016/j.patcog.2016.03.009
5. Williams, P.L., Beer, R.D.: Nonnegative decomposition of multivariate information. arXiv Information Theory (2010)
6. Zhou, J.T., Tsang, I.W., Pan, S.J., Tan, M.: Multi-class heterogeneous domain adaptation. J. Mach. Learn. Res. **20**(57), 1–31 (2019). http://jmlr.org/papers/v20/13-580.html
7. Zhuang, F., et al.: A comprehensive survey on transfer learning. Proc. IEEE **109**(1), 43–76 (2020)

Impact of Feature Normalization on Machine Learning-Based Human Fall Detection

Moustafa Fayad[1]([✉]), Mohamed-Yacine Hachani[1], Ahmed Mostefaoui[2],
Mohammed Amine Merzoug[1], Isabelle Lajoie[1], and Réda Yahiaoui[1]

[1] Nanomedicine, Imagery, and Therapeutics Laboratory, Univ. of Franche-Comté,
25030 Besançon, France
{moustafa.fayad,mohamed-yacine.hachani,mohammed.merzoug,isabelle.lajoie,
reda.yahiaoui}@univ-fcomte.fr, moustafa.fayad@hotmail.fr
[2] DISC Department, FEMTO-ST Institute, Univ. of Franche-Comté, 90000 Belfort,
France
ahmed.mostefaoui@univ-fcomte.fr

Abstract. This paper investigates the impact of normalizing data acquired from different multimedia sensor devices on the performance of machine-learning-based human fall detection. Specifically, we consider two fall detection datasets (URFD and UP-Fall) and study the impact of eight normalization techniques (min-max, z-score, decimal, sigmoid, tanh, softmax, maximum absolute, and statistical column) on the accuracy and training time of four machine learning classifiers optimized using Grid-Search (namely, support vector machine with radial basis function, k-nearest neighbors, Gaussian Naive Bayes, and decision tree). The conducted experiments confirm that data normalization leads to a significant speed-up in the training of machine learning models and demonstrate which data normalization techniques are the most efficient in terms of accuracy in the context of elderly fall detection.

Keywords: Human fall detection · elderly fall detection · machine learning · data normalization impact

1 Introduction

According to the World Health Organization [31], the number of older vulnerable people is increasing sharply compared to other age groups, increasing thus the risk of falls, chronic diseases, and household accidents with severe consequences. Recent reports and statistics [28,31] also show that falling is the second most significant cause of unintentional injury mortality, especially among the elderly: 684,000 people die every year from falls, and those over 60 years old experience the highest number of fatal falls [31].

To address this public health problem, the scientific community has prioritized developing fall detection solutions that are both fast and reliable (with zero

R. Chbeir et al. (Eds.): MEDES 2023, CCIS 2022, pp. 147–161, 2024.
https://doi.org/10.1007/978-3-031-51643-6_11

false alarms) to reduce risks and consequences. Because in a critical situation, a delay or an error in the elderly monitoring system could cost a person's life. For instance, a long period of lying on the ground after a fall influences both physical and psychological health and increases mortality [6,12].

Particular attention has been given to the development of machine learning-based fall detection models [13,29], which have shown promising results in terms of minimizing decision-making errors without human intervention and are more favorable over classical processing techniques based on thresholds [24].

The efficiency of AI models depends heavily on the investment in the data pre-processing stage. In this regard, numerous works in the literature have examined different techniques that can be deployed at the different stages of fall detection models. However, to the extent of our knowledge, no studies have investigated the impact of feature normalization (scaling) on classification performance in the case of elderly fall detection. The existing research works focus mainly on feature preprocessing such as segmentation and representation domain.

In this paper, we investigate this path by studying the impact of eight normalization techniques (min-max, z-score, decimal, sigmoid, tanh, softmax, maximum absolute, and statistical column) on the performance (accuracy and training time) of four classifiers: SVM-RBG (support vector machine with radial basis function), KNN (k-nearest neighbors), GNB (Gaussian Naive Bayes), and DT (decision tree). Indeed, these 2 performance metrics are essential considerations when developing and deploying a model. The conducted experimentation has been structured as follows: i) dataset selection, ii) data preprocessing, iii) hyper-parameters tuning, and iv) evaluation of each optimized model with both normalized and unnormalized data. To have a fair analysis and comparison, we i) selected two public fall datasets of different sizes but with the same imbalance ratio: URFD (University of Rzeszow Fall Detection) [15] and UP-Fall [17], and ii) tuned the hyperparameters of each considered model using Grid-Search.

The obtained results presented in the paper confirm that data normalization has a significant impact on speeding up the training of machine learning models and also demonstrate which normalization techniques are the best and which are the worst in terms of accuracy in the context of elderly fall detection.

The remaining of this paper is organized into four sections. Section 2 presents previous studies related to our research work in the field of human fall detection. Section 3 provides the background of this study. Section 4 details the conducted experimentation and then presents and analyzes the obtained results. Finally, Sect. 5 concludes the paper with future work.

2   Related Work

The topic of fall detection has attracted much attention from researchers. Several works in the literature examine the techniques that can be deployed at different stages of the fall detection approach's life cycle. Nevertheless, there are no studies on the impact of feature Normalization. Indeed, the research community has fundamentally focused on feature preprocessing (segmentation, representation domain, etc.). In this part, we will not compare the performance of existing works but rather present an exhaustive picture to position our new work.

(1) Data segmentation aims to carry out processing according to criteria making it possible to define the relevant information. It also aims to estimate the decision of the model correctly. Aziz et al. [1] evaluate the impact of window size and lead time on the sensitivity and specificity of a pre-impact fall detector. Kinematic data is acquired using an Opal model containing a triaxial accelerometer and a gyroscope at 128 Hz for 15 s for each trial. 18 features related to triaxial acceleration, velocity, and angular velocity are evaluated by deploying the SVM-RBF model and 10 cross-validations. In the experiment, window sizes and lead time vary between 0.125–1.125 s and 0.0625–1.125 s with an increment step of 0.0625 s. Therefore, system performance is high (>95% sensitivity and >90% specificity) for combinations of window size 0.0625–0.1875 s and lead time of 0.125–1 s.

(2) The data representation allows us to evaluate the impact of the domains (temporal, frequencies, differential, etc.) and the relationships between the variables on the performance. Wagner et al. [30] investigated the impact of 5 regularized numerical differentiation methods on the performance of a Naïve Bayes-based fall detector. The methods used are central difference, regularized central difference, Kalman filter, Tikhonov regularization, and smoothing approximation followed by analytical differentiation. Three features related to the person's center of mass (maximum downward vertical velocity, maximum horizontal velocity, and maximum total velocity) were processed using the leave one out cross-validation procedure. For the UR Fall Detection Dataset, using a regularized version of the central difference method provided superior performance (increased the true positive rate and reduced the false positive rate) compared to the other methods.

The authors in [26] explored the performance of 4 classifiers (Naïve Bayes, KNN, J48, and random Forest) separately and in an ensemble based on the stacking of classifiers. They calculated 8 features from each segment of accelerometer data provided by central one-second values around the peak. These characteristics include (resultant, variance, standard deviation, Euclidean norm, Root mean square, Kurtosis, Skewness, and the geometric mean). They demonstrated that the stacking-based ensemble had superior performance, SE 89%, and SP 95%, compared to the other classifiers.

The above studies in the literature show that different techniques strongly impact the performance of a fall detection approach. However, no research has analyzed the influence of feature scaling techniques on classification performance. Therefore, we deployed 8 normalization methods and 4 types of classifiers in our study to conduct a fair comparison against non-normalized features.

3   Background

This section presents the considered data normalization techniques and introduces the Grid-Search method utilized to optimize the considered fall detection classifiers.

3.1   Data Preprocessing and Normalization

The main critical step in fall detection approaches is measuring the relevant parameters during the target's movement. The different smart devices that allow the acquisition of such essential data can be classified into i) body sensors (accelerometers, gyroscopes, magnetometers, RFID) and ii) external sensors (piezoelectric, passive infrared, microphones, cameras) [18,21].

These devices generate data that machine-learning models cannot directly use. The raw format causes difficulties in extracting relevant information and has a significant impact on performance. Several factors could cause the quality decrease, for instance: aberrant measurements, error in the distribution of variables, absence of variables, and presence of duplicate or redundant data [8,19].

To remedy this problem and have an optimal data interpretation, data preprocessing is the first mandatory step for machine learning-based approaches. This transformation step resolves the dominance of large-scale features over the decision of which model to deploy. Specifically, it generates new values in new scales while preserving the distribution and ratios of original data.

In the following, we introduce the considered normalization techniques.

– Min-max [9] is one of the most popular data normalization techniques. As the name implies, the new measurements are calculated according to the minimum and maximum data values (Eq. 1), and the distribution of original data is kept in the new scale of [0, 1].

$$x_{scaled} = \frac{x - x_{min}}{x_{max} - x_{min}} \tag{1}$$

– Z-Score [9] expresses directly the distance of each measurement from the mean value in standard deviation (σ). The sign of a normalized value gives an idea about the observation position to the mean value (μ).

$$x_{scaled} = \frac{x - \mu}{\sigma} \tag{2}$$

– In decimal normalization [9], values are transformed by moving the decimal point. In other words, this scaler divides each value by the maximum absolute value of data.

$$x_{scaled} = \frac{x}{10^j} \tag{3}$$

where j is the smallest integer such that $max(|x_{scaled}|) < 1$.

- The idea of sigmoid normalization [3,32] is to bring all feature values into a range between 0 and 1. More specifically, input variables that are greater than 1 are transformed into 1 and those that are less than 0 are transformed into 0. The form of normalized values corresponds to an S-form from 0 to 1 passing through 0.5.

$$x_{scaled} = \frac{1}{1 + e^{-x}} \tag{4}$$

- Tanh [32] maps feature values into probabilistic values between 0 and 1. The tanh function has the following formula:

$$x_{scaled} = \frac{1 - e^{-2x}}{1 + e^{-2x}} \tag{5}$$

- Softmax [32] converts the input vector of n real numbers into a probability distribution of n possible outcomes. The new observations are calculated according to the following equation.

$$x_{scaled} = \frac{e^x}{\sum_{j=1}^{n} e^{x_j}} \tag{6}$$

- Maximum absolute scaling technique [7] re-scales each feature between -1 and 1 by dividing each value by the absolute maximum of each feature.

$$x_{scaled} = \frac{x}{max(|x|)} \tag{7}$$

- Statistical column [14] calculates the new observations according to Eq. 8. The sum of transformed values of each characteristic is equal to 1.

$$x_{scaled} = 0.1 \frac{x - \frac{\sum_1^n x}{10+n}}{\frac{\sum_1^n x}{10+n}} \tag{8}$$

3.2   Grid-Search

The proper functioning of machine learning models depends strongly on the adjustment of their hyper-parameters which control the learning process. One way to achieve this is that hyper-parameters can be manually adjusted by experimenting and then choosing the optimal values with minimum error and high performance. However, such manual configuration is time-consuming and does not guarantee the selection of optimal values (at least during the first attempts).

In the literature, several methods (such as Grid-Search, Random-Search, and Genetic Algorithm) facilitate this crucial task of model building [16]. In the present study, we deployed Grid-Search, which is one of the most used techniques for the optimization of hyper-parameters [2]. As the name implies, Grid-Search treats hyper-parameter tuning as a search in a grid (Fig. 1). It checks all the combinations of hyper-parameters and compares performance to deduce the best values. In other terms, for each combination of values, the algorithm will be

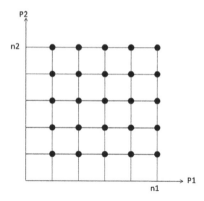

Fig. 1. A search grid presenting each possible combination of two hyper-parameters P1 and P2.

Table 1. Utilized URFD and UP-Fall datasets.

Dataset	Year	Activities	Sensors	Actors	IMU position	Camera position	IR
URFD	2014	70 (30 falls and 40 ADLs)	- 2 Kinect cameras - 1 PS Move - 1 x-IMU	5	Near the pelvis (waist)	Parallel to the floor (1 m) and ceiling configuration (2.5 m)	$\frac{9741}{1803} \approx 5$
UP-Fall	2019	11 (5 falls and 6 ADLs)	- 2 Microsoft Life-Cam - 5 IMU - 1 ECG NeuroSky MindWave - 6 infrared	17	Ankle, pocket, waist, neck and wrist	Frontal view (1.82 m) Lateral view (1.82 m)	$\frac{248727}{45951} \approx 5$

trained and a score calculated. Then, the combination with the highest score will be selected. For instance, if we use Grid-Search with a model that has two parameters $(1 \leq P1 \leq n1, 1 \leq P2 \leq n2)$ and k-fold cross-validation, we have $n1 \times n2 \times k$ attempts. Therefore, one should not overdo this method when defining hyper-parameter scales to avoid reaching limits regarding computational capacity and model training time.

4   Experimentations

To study the impact of data normalization on the accuracy and training time of fall detection models, we proceeded according to the following four steps (Fig. 2): *i*) dataset selection, *ii*) data preprocessing, *iii*) hyper-parameters tuning, and *iv*) evaluation of optimized models with both normalized and unnormalized data.

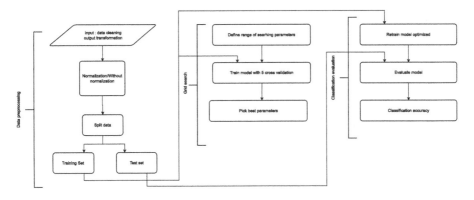

Fig. 2. Experimental approach.

4.1 Dataset Selection

We considered the publicly available URFD [15] and UP-Fall [17] datasets because *i*) they are rich in vision and movement information, and *ii*) they share the same imbalance ratio of 5. We recall that the imbalance ratio (denoted IR) is defined as follows [11,25]:

$$IR = \frac{N_-}{N_+} \tag{9}$$

where N_- is the number of majority (or negative) observations in the dataset and N_+ is the number of minority (or positive) observations [11]. Specifically, in our case, N_- is the number of both ADLs (activities of daily living) and fall-like, and N_+ is the number of fall instances. Table 1 summarizes the details of the considered datasets.

The URFD dataset was constructed using 2 Microsoft Kinect cameras and 2 accelerometers (PS Move (60 Hz) and x-IMU (256 Hz) devices). All RGB and depth images were synchronized with the corresponding motion data based on timestamp values. Camera 0 was positioned parallel to the floor at an approximate height of 1 m, while camera 1 was configured for ceiling placement 2.5 m above the floor. In addition, accelerometers were strategically mounted on the waist or near the pectoral muscles. URFD contains data from 70 activities (30 falls and 40 daily and fall-like activities) performed by 5 volunteers (actors). The activities (falling while standing and sitting on a chair, walking, sitting, lying on the floor, picking, lifting or placing objects on the floor, tying shoelaces, bending to the left, squatting) took place in conventional indoor spaces such as offices and classrooms). Our study uses features extracted from depth data captured by the cam-0. In total, 11544 samples have been used in our experiments.

The UP-Fall dataset includes 11 activities where measurements were acquired using different sensors (namely, 2 Microsoft LifeCam Cinema cameras, 5 IMUs (inertial measurement units), 1 NeuroSky electroencephalograph (EEG) headset MindWave, and 6 infrared). UP-Fall was collected with the collaboration of

17 volunteers (young healthy men and women) aged between 18 and 24, with an average height of 1.66 m and an average weight of 66.8kg. These volunteers simulated 5 falls and 6 ADLs, with 3 attempts each. UP-Fall combines over 850 GB of body, ambient, and visual sensor data. It encompasses various activities (falling forward with hands, falling forward with knees, falling backward, falling to the side, falling while sitting on a chair, walking, standing, sitting, picking up an object, jumping, and lying down). We used the 294678 available motion samples acquired from the sensors (3-axis accelerometer and 3-axis gyroscope) positioned at the waist. This choice is motivated by the fact that the waist is one of the most appropriate optimal places on the human body to detect falls [22,23].

4.2 Data Preprocessing

We preprocessed data (features and output) as follows (to make it better suited for the used fall detection classifiers): data cleaning, output transformation, and normalization.

- Data cleaning: the correct structuring of data has been validated by ensuring the absence of duplicate, outlying, and missing values.
- Output transformation: fall detection is a binary classification problem (1: fall, 0: ADL/fall-like) [20]. However, in the URFD dataset, the position/status of subjects is labeled into three groups for each measurement: (-1) the person is not lying on the ground, (0) when the person begins to fall, and (1) for post-fall (i.e., the person is lying on the ground). In our study, we replaced the output (-1) with (0) and $(0, 1)$ with (1).
  For the UP-Fall dataset, the output is labeled from 1 to 10. The first five correspond to the different types of simulated falls by the volunteers and the last five correspond to ADLs. We replaced the (1, 2, 3, 4, 5) output with 1 and (6, 7, 8, 9, 10) with 0, where 1 represents falls and 0 represents ADLs and fall-like observations.
- Normalization: we scaled the numerical values of attributes by applying the eight considered data normalization techniques presented in Sect. 3.1. This step aims to improve the quality of features by avoiding the domination of those at a large scale on the model's performance. We have also considered an additional experimental process without data normalization to compare it to the above techniques and hence better study the impact of normalization.

After data preprocessing, we divided each dataset into two subsets, 70% for training and 30% for evaluation (Fig. 2). Thus, we maintained approximately the proportion of output values in the two subsets.

4.3 Hyper-parameters Tuning

Rather than using default (random) values, we adjusted the parameters of each model to achieve high performance. To do so, we defined the range of each hyper-parameter and used an exhaustive search on the grid proposed by scikit-learn [4].

We have also chosen a 5-fold cross-validation in the training data to make the model robust and more general. Table 2 summarizes the configuration of hyper-parameters (range of values, step, number, and type of scale). At the end of this tuning phase, we obtained the optimal parameters for each classifier.

Table 2. Hyper-parameters configuration.

Model	Tuning	Interval	Step	#elements	Scale
SVM-RBF	C	$[2^{-5} : 2^{15}]$	2^2	11	Logarithmic
	gamma	$[2^{-13} : 2^3]$		10	
KNN	N_neighbors	$[1{:}40]$	1	40	Linear
GNB	Var_smoothing	$[10^{-9} : 10^2]$	$10^{0.11}$	100	Logarithmic
DT	Max_depth	$[2{:}19]$	1	18	Linear
	Min_samples_split	$[2{:}19]$		18	
	Min_samples_leaf	$[1{:}9]$		9	

4.4   Performance Evaluation

To assess the performance of each model, we considered two metrics: *training time* and *accuracy*. The latter is the primary evaluation criterion used in classification problems [5]. It expresses the number of correctly detected examples. For instance, in the fall detection context, it shows the success rate by calculating the fraction of positive (fall) and negative (ADL/fall-like) observations that have been correctly predicted compared to the total number of observations.

$$Accuracy = \frac{TP + TN}{TP + TN + FP + FN} \qquad (10)$$

Each classifier has been evaluated using the optimal parameters from Grid-Search with the test set. This evaluation has been performed after re-training the optimized model with the training set without cross-validation. Because in practice the parameters resulting from cross-validation are already appropriate for the training dataset [10].

Before presenting the obtained results, we point out that the SVM-RBF model has been excluded from the experiments with the UP-Fall dataset because it requires a massive training time when dealing with large datasets [27].

Accuracy. The obtained results presented in Table 3 and Figs. 3 and 4 show the accuracy of the (SVM-RBF, KNN, GNB, and DT) classifiers (with and without normalization) using the URFD and UP-Fall datasets. When analyzing these results, we notice that the considered data normalization techniques impact the accuracy of classifiers as follows when compared to the non-normalization approach:

Table 3. Accuracy of (SVM-RBF, KNN, GNB, and DT) classifiers (with and without normalization) using the URFD and UP-Fall datasets.

Algorithm / Technique	SVM-RBF URFD Params	Acc	Delta	SVM-RBF UP-Fall Params	Acc	Delta	KNN URFD Params	Acc	Delta	KNN UP-Fall Params	Acc	Delta	GNB URFD Params	Acc	Delta	GNB UP-Fall Params	Acc	Delta	DT URFD Params	Acc	Delta	DT UP-Fall Params	Acc	Delta
Without normalization	2^{15}, 2^{-15}	93.8	-	-	-	-	7	92.1	-	10	88.7	-	0.46	86.4	-	4.64e-5	86.8	-	14, 2, 2	94.1	-	19, 6, 2	94.9	-
Min-max	2^{15}, 8	96.8	3	-	-	-	1	96.8	4.7	4	96.7	8	2.15	87.3	0.9	0.02	86.9	0.1	14, 2, 2	94.1	0	19, 6, 2	94.9	0
Z-score	2^{5}, 2	97.3	3.5	-	-	-	1	96.5	4.4	4	96.4	7.7	3.59	87.3	0.9	0.17	86.8	0	14, 2, 2	94.1	0	19, 6, 2	94.9	0
Decimal	2^{15}, 2^{3}	87.1	-6.7	-	-	-	21	90.4	-1.7	3	96.7	8	0.36	87.3	0.9	0.003	86.9	0.1	15, 2, 11	91.9	-2.2	16, 13, 2	94.3	-0.6
Sigmoid	2^{15}, 2^{3}	93.4	-0.4	-	-	-	4	95.4	3.3	6	91.5	2.8	0.6	87.1	0.7	1e-9	84.5	-2.3	14, 1, 7	92.6	-1.5	19, 4, 2	94.9	0
Tanh	2^{13}, 2^{3}	94.5	0.7	-	-	-	4	95.4	3.3	4	92.6	3.9	2.15	86.7	0.3	1e-9	84.4	-2.4	14, 1, 7	92.6	-1.5	19, 2, 2	94.8	-0.1
Softmax	2^{-5}, 2^{-15}	84.4	-9.4	-	-	-	5	94.6	2.5	14	97	8.3	0.1	84.4	-2	7.74	84.4	-2.4	19, 2, 5	92.7	-1.4	8, 4, 1	84.5	-10.4
Maximum absolute	2^{15}, 2^{3}	96.7	2.9	-	-	-	1	96.8	4.7	4	96.7	8	1.67	87.2	0.8	0.03	86.9	0.1	14, 2, 2	94.1	0	19, 6, 2	94.9	0
Statistical column	2^{15}, 2^{3}	94.5	0.7	-	-	-	1	97	4.9	8	93.1	4.4	1	87.2	0.8	4.64e-5	86.7	0.1	14, 2, 2	94.1	0	19, 2, 2	94.9	0

(Columns per algorithm: Optimized parameters | Accuracy | Delta)

- SVM-RBF: accuracy difference from -9.4% to 3.5% in URFD.
- KNN: accuracy difference from -1.7% to 4.9% in URFD and from 2.8% to 8.3% in UP-Fall.
- GNB: accuracy difference from -2% to 0.9% in URFD and from -2.4% to 0.1% in UP-Fall.
- DT: accuracy difference from -2.2% to 0% in URFD and -10.4% to 0% in UP-Fall.

For instance, for the SVM-RBF model, the above percentages mean that data normalization improves its accuracy by 3.5% when compared to that without normalization, which is a significant increase in the healthcare sector. Specifically, the accuracy difference (increase or decrease) when considering each normalization technique for the SVM-RBF model is as follows: (softmax, -9.4%), (decimal, -6.70%), (sigmoid, -0.4%), (statistical column, 0.7%), (tanh, 0.7%), (maximum absolute, 2.9%), (min-max, 3%), and (z-score, 3.5%). The detailed results (optimized parameters, accuracy, and accuracy difference) of each considered normalization technique for the (SVM-RBF, KNN, GNB, and DT) classifiers with both URFD and UP-Fall datasets are depicted in Table 3.

As shown in Table 3 and Figs. 3 and 4, data normalization allows achieving a considerable accuracy improvement for SVM-RBF (3.5% in URFD) and KNN (4.9% in URFD and 8.3% in UP-Fall). In contrast, for GNB, we notice a slight improvement (0.9% in URFD and 0.1% in UP-Fall) and no improvement for DT.

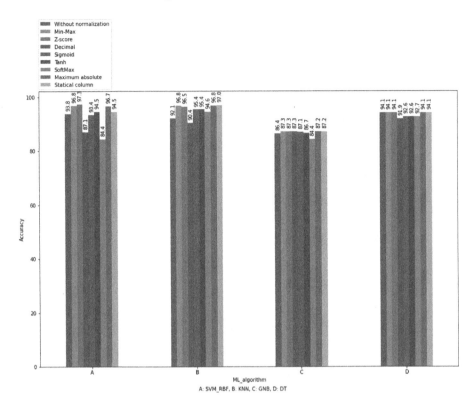

Fig. 3. Accuracy of (SVM-RBF, KNN, GNB, and DT) classifiers (with and without normalization) using the URFD dataset.

Also, note that the accuracy of models with unnormalized data is not always the lowest when compared to that with normalized data. For example, for SVM-RBF in URFD, the accuracy without normalization is 93.8%, and with softmax normalization is 84.4% (i.e., an accuracy decrease of 9.4%). As a second example, for DT in UP-Fall, the accuracy without normalization is 94.9% versus 84.5% for softmax (i.e., a decrease of 10.4%).

Overall, the conducted experiments show that min-max and z-score provide the best accuracy results and that softmax has in most cases the worst performance. This finding can be explained as follows. Data normalization techniques that keep the relationships of original data improve the performance, whereas processes that cause complications in the features (for instance, losing some properties by making values very low) decrease the performance and accuracy of classifiers.

Training Time. To analyze the impact of data normalization on training time, we applied the hard voting algorithm of ensemble learning. We stacked the optimized models with the hyper-parameters shown in Table 3 for each dataset.

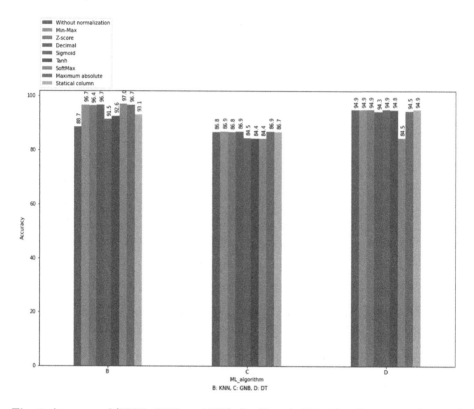

Fig. 4. Accuracy of (KNN, GNB, and DT) classifiers (with and without normalization) using the UP-Fall dataset.

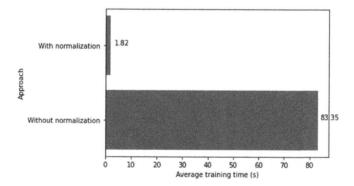

Fig. 5. Average training time of considered models.

Figure 5 shows the average training time on the two considered datasets. Indeed, changing the scale of a model's characteristics improves its training time. The obtained results demonstrate that we need 1.82 s with normalization against 83.35 s without it.

5   Conclusions and Future Work

A model with high accuracy and reasonable training time is more likely to be reliable and efficient in real-world applications. In this paper, we studied the impact of eight data normalization techniques (min-max, z-score, decimal, sigmoid, tanh, softmax, maximum absolute, and statistical column) on the performance (accuracy and training time) of four classifiers (SVM-RBG, KNN, GNB, and DT) of elderly fall detection while considering two datasets of different sizes (URFD and UP-Fall). To have a fair comparison and analysis, we tuned the hyper-parameters of each model using Grid-Search. The obtained experimental results show that data normalization improves the performance of machine learning classifiers that depend on the relationships between data (i.e., SVM-RBF and KNN) compared to those based on probability (i.e., GNB and DT) by increasing the accuracy and decreasing the training time. In particular, the conducted experiments show that min-max and z-score outperform the other normalization techniques in the context of fall detection and that softmax has the worst performance.

In future work, we aim to consider both min-max and z-score normalization to study the impact of different hyper-parameter tuning techniques on the performance of activity classifiers.

Acknowledgements. This work was supported by: The FEDER "European regional development fund" project "Reper@ge" (https://www.europe-bfc.eu/beneficiaire/reperge/).

References

1. Aziz, O., Russell, C.M., Park, E.J., Robinovitch, S.N.: The effect of window size and lead time on pre-impact fall detection accuracy using support vector machine analysis of waist mounted inertial sensor data. In: 2014 36th Annual International Conference of the IEEE Engineering in Medicine and Biology Society, pp. 30–33. IEEE (2014)
2. Bergstra, J., Bengio, Y.: Random search for hyper-parameter optimization. J. Mach. Learn. Res. **13**(2) (2012)
3. Brownlee, J.: Develop deep learning models on theano and tensorflow using keras. Deep Learning with Python. Jason Brownlee, Melbourne (2018)
4. Buitinck, L., et al.: API design for machine learning software: experiences from the scikit-learn project. arXiv preprint arXiv:1309.0238 (2013)
5. Delahoz, Y.S., Labrador, M.A.: Survey on fall detection and fall prevention using wearable and external sensors. Sensors **14**(10), 19806–19842 (2014)
6. Fayad, M., Mostefaoui, A., Chouali, S., Benbernou, S.: Toward a design model-oriented methodology to ensure QoS of a cyber-physical healthcare system. Computing 1–27 (2022)
7. Galli, S.: Python Feature Engineering Cookbook: Over 70 Recipes for Creating, Engineering, and Transforming Features to Build Machine Learning Models. Packt Publishing Ltd, Birmingham (2020)

8. Gudivada, V., Apon, A., Ding, J.: Data quality considerations for big data and machine learning: going beyond data cleaning and transformations. Int. J. Adv. Softw. **10**(1), 1–20 (2017)
9. Han, J., Kamber, M., Pei, J.: Data Mining: Concepts and Techniques, 3rd edn. The Morgan Kaufmann Series in Data Management Systems, vol. 5, no. 4, pp. 83–124 (2011)
10. Hsu, C.W., Chang, C.C., Lin, C.J., et al.: A practical guide to support vector classification (2003)
11. Huang, L., Zhao, J., Zhu, B., Chen, H., Broucke, S.V.: An experimental investigation of calibration techniques for imbalanced data. IEEE Access **8**, 127343–127352 (2020)
12. Igual, R., Medrano, C., Plaza, I.: Challenges, issues and trends in fall detection systems. Biomed. Eng. Online **12**(1), 1–24 (2013)
13. Islam, M.M., et al.: Deep learning based systems developed for fall detection: a review. IEEE Access **8**, 166117–166137 (2020)
14. Jayalakshmi, T., Santhakumaran, A.: Statistical normalization and back propagation for classification. Int. J. Comput. Theory Eng. **3**(1), 1793–8201 (2011)
15. Kwolek, B., Kepski, M.: Human fall detection on embedded platform using depth maps and wireless accelerometer. Comput. Methods Programs Biomed. **117**(3), 489–501 (2014)
16. Liashchynskyi, P., Liashchynskyi, P.: Grid search, random search, genetic algorithm: a big comparison for NAS. arXiv preprint arXiv:1912.06059 (2019)
17. Martínez-Villaseñor, L., Ponce, H., Brieva, J., Moya-Albor, E., Núñez-Martínez, J., Peñafort-Asturiano, C.: UP-fall detection dataset: a multimodal approach. Sensors **19**(9), 1988 (2019)
18. Merzoug, M.A., Mostefaoui, A., Kechout, M.H., Tamraoui, S.: Deep learning for resource-limited devices. In: Proceedings of the 16th ACM Symposium on QoS and Security for Wireless and Mobile Networks, pp. 81–87 (2020)
19. Munappy, A., Bosch, J., Olsson, H.H., Arpteg, A., Brinne, B.: Data management challenges for deep learning. In: 2019 45th Euromicro Conference on Software Engineering and Advanced Applications (SEAA), pp. 140–147. IEEE (2019)
20. Nahar, N., Hossain, M.S., Andersson, K.: A machine learning based fall detection for elderly people with neurodegenerative disorders. In: Mahmud, M., Vassanelli, S., Kaiser, M.S., Zhong, N. (eds.) BI 2020. LNCS (LNAI), vol. 12241, pp. 194–203. Springer, Cham (2020). https://doi.org/10.1007/978-3-030-59277-6_18
21. Nooruddin, S., Islam, M., Sharna, F.A., Alhetari, H., Kabir, M.N., et al.: Sensor-based fall detection systems: a review. J. Ambient Intell. Humaniz. Comput. 1–17 (2021)
22. Ntanasis, P., Pippa, E., Özdemir, A.T., Barshan, B., Megalooikonomou, V.: Investigation of sensor placement for accurate fall detection. In: Perego, P., Andreoni, G., Rizzo, G. (eds.) MobiHealth 2016. LNICST, vol. 192, pp. 225–232. Springer, Cham (2017). https://doi.org/10.1007/978-3-319-58877-3_30
23. Özdemir, A.T.: An analysis on sensor locations of the human body for wearable fall detection devices: principles and practice. Sensors **16**(8), 1161 (2016)
24. Rastogi, S., Singh, J.: A systematic review on machine learning for fall detection system. Comput. Intell. **37**(2), 951–974 (2021)
25. Rout, N., Mishra, D., Mallick, M.K.: Handling imbalanced data: a survey. In: Reddy, M.S., Viswanath, K., K.M., S.P. (eds.) International Proceedings on Advances in Soft Computing, Intelligent Systems and Applications. AISC, vol. 628, pp. 431–443. Springer, Singapore (2018). https://doi.org/10.1007/978-981-10-5272-9_39

26. Shrivastava, R., Pandey, M.: Ensemble of multiple classifiers for accelerometer based human fall detection. In: Smys, S., Palanisamy, R., Rocha, Á., Beligiannis, G.N. (eds.) Computer Networks and Inventive Communication Technologies. LNDECT, vol. 58, pp. 865–874. Springer, Singapore (2021). https://doi.org/10.1007/978-981-15-9647-6_67

27. Syarif, I., Prugel-Bennett, A., Wills, G.: SVM parameter optimization using grid search and genetic algorithm to improve classification performance. TELKOMNIKA (Telecommun. Comput. Electron. Control) 14(4), 1502–1509 (2016)

28. Turner, S., Kisser, R., Rogmans, W.: Falls among older adults in the EU-28: key facts from the available statistics. EuroSafe, Amsterdam (2015)

29. Usmani, S., Saboor, A., Haris, M., Khan, M.A., Park, H.: Latest research trends in fall detection and prevention using machine learning: a systematic review. Sensors 21(15), 5134 (2021)

30. Wagner, J., Mazurek, P., Morawski, R.Z.: Regularized numerical differentiation of depth-sensor data in a fall detection system. In: 2017 IEEE International Conference on Computational Intelligence and Virtual Environments for Measurement Systems and Applications (CIVEMSA), pp. 234–236. IEEE (2017)

31. WHO: Falls (2021). https://www.who.int/news-room/fact-sheets/detail/falls. Accessed 28 Feb 2023

32. Zheng, A., Casari, A.: Feature Engineering for Machine Learning: Principles and Techniques for Data Scientists. O'Reilly Media Inc., Sebastopol (2018)

Services and Systems

Association Rule Mining for Multifactorial Diseases: Survey and Opportunities

Hend Amraoui[1,2] and Faouzi Mhamdi[1,3(✉)]

[1] Laboratory of Technologies of Information and Communication and Electrical Engineering (LaTICE), National Higher School of Engineers of Tunis (ENSIT), University of Tunis, Tunis, Tunisia
faouzi.mhamdi@ensi.rnu.tn
[2] Faculty of Mathematical, Physical and Natural Sciences of Tunis, University of Tunis El Manar, Tunis, Tunisia
hend.amraoui@fst.utm.tn
[3] Higher Institute of Applied Languages and Computer Science of Beja, University of Jendouba, Jendouba, Tunisia

Abstract. Association Rule Mining is an efficient Data Mining task that has been largely used in health informatics research since its emergence. As health informatics and in particular multifactorial diseases have received a lot of attention from researchers in the last decade, and have shown its great importance, it is therefore worth considering the state of the art of multifactorial diseases research. Since researchers and knowledge discovery experts have implemented a set of Data Mining techniques for knowledge extraction from health data, the application of Association Rule Mining techniques for multifactorial diseases has been condensed and investigated in detail in this study. The limitations related to the applications of Association Rule Mining for the discovery of factors responsible for multifactorial diseases were highlighted and recommendations were given to address these limitations. In addition, algorithms and tools employed for the application of Association Rule Mining were also specified, conclusions were learned from the reviewed literature, and future research guidelines were provided.

Keywords: Association Rule Mining · Multifactorial Disease · Big Data

1 Introduction

In the last two decades the need to manage large-scale databases efficiently has become an integral task for the scientific and academic community. Data mining is one of the most important and challenging field of research, whose aim is to find useful information from huge datasets. In particular, Association Rule Mining task is very useful in analyzing datasets in order to find interesting associations and relationships among large databases. Association Rule Mining can

R. Chbeir et al. (Eds.): MEDES 2023, CCIS 2022, pp. 165–178, 2024.
https://doi.org/10.1007/978-3-031-51643-6_12

be handled the ability to effectively process massive datasets to a wide range of disciplines such as health care and for many applications, such as extraction of rare and useful Association Rules, fast extraction of useful Association Rules, Parallel extraction of useful Association Rules, disease diagnosis and process digitisation. Since researchers and practitioners of Knowledge Discovery have employed a wide variety of data for knowledge extraction from health datasets, the application of Association Rule Mining techniques to the health informatics domain has been condensed and investigated in detail in this study. Our article demonstrates the links between Association Rule Mining and multifactorial diseases for predicting the probability of common diseases. Multifactorial diseases are the result of multiple risk factors that are both genetically and environmentally determined [1].

2   Big Data Context

The term "Big Data" has been used to refer to such large datasets that it becomes difficult to process them using traditional database management systems. These datasets' size goes beyond the capacities of commonly used software tools and storage systems to capture, store, manage, and process the data in a reasonable amount of time. The concept of Big Data was initially associated with so-called "Vs" dimensions of challenge in data management. The most commonly used are based on the three (or five) "Vs" definitions: Volume, Variety, Velocity, as well as Veracity and Value [2] which were subsequently suggested by further developments [3, 4].

- Volume, refers to the amount of data to be managed;
- Variety, refers to types of data that should be taken into consideration;
- Velocity, refers to the speed at which data is managed at the generation, procurement and processing stage;
- Veracity, refers to the reliability features of the data;
- Value, refers to the real value for the data, whether it is business value, useful knowledge, etc.

The term Big Data has spread as recently as 2011. Figure 1 shows how executives differed in their understanding of big data, where some definitions focused on what it is, while others tried to answer what it does [5].

Analyzing large sets of historical data is crucial while creating decision support systems [6]. Knowledge Discovery in Databases (KDD) was first defined by Frawley et al. [7] in 1992 as *the nontrivial extraction of implicit, previously unknown, and potentially useful information from data*. Then it was redefined by Fayyad et al. [8] in 1996 as *the non-trivial process of identifying valid, novel, potentially useful, and ultimately understandable structure in data*.

Data Mining, is the essential phase in the whole KDD process. It is defined by Fayyad et al. [8] as *a step in the KDD process consisting of applying computational techniques that, under acceptable computational efficiency limitations, produce a particular enumeration of patterns (or models) over the data*.

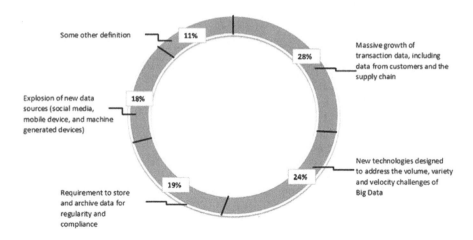

Fig. 1. Definitions of Big Data based on an online survey of 154 global executives in April 2012 [5].

Nowadays, it is getting quite difficult to analyze Big Data with classical data analysis techniques and the term *Big Data Mining* was brought in [9]. Technological adjustments have been established to deal with Big Data such as Big Data Optimization which refers to optimization problems and have to manage very large amounts of data [10], the Hadoop framework, which offers an efficient model for performing parallel processing. It uses a so-called "Map Reduce" technique which is implemented to solve the problems that come on the way of implementation of Big Data technology and is considered as an effective way of analyzing huge datasets [11].

3 Main Data Mining Tasks

As previously stated, in Data Mining, intelligent methods are applied in order to extract hidden knowledge from databases. Relevant patterns in a particular representational form, or a set of such representations are searched for. Data mining entails many tasks that can be classified into two categories:

- Predictive or supervised Data Mining like Classification, Regression, Time Series Analysis and Prediction; is used if some observations can already be labeled according to a known target concept and a rule or function (also called model) for this assignment should be learned from the data [12].
- Descriptive or unsupervised Data Mining like Association Rules, Sequence Discovery, Clustering and Summarization, where the system is only directed to search the data for interesting associations, and attempts to group elements by postulating class descriptions for sufficiently many classes to cover all items in the database [13].

The four basic tasks of the Data Mining are: Classification, Regression, Clustering and Association Rule Mining (See Fig. 2).

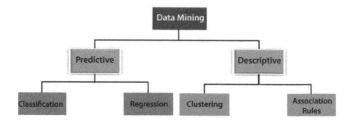

Fig. 2. Main Data Mining Tasks.

- Classification, also called supervised classification, consists in assigning a new element to one of the predefined classes.
- Regression, consists in examining the dependence between attributes and provides some qualitative knowledge of the relationship between inputs and outputs from an equation.
- Clustering, also called unsupervised classification, consists in building classes from a dataset. The classes are formed in such a way that two elements of the same class are much more similar than two elements of two different classes.
- Association Rule Mining, finds frequent patterns, associations, correlations for informal structures among sets of items or objects in transactional databases and other information repositories [14].

4   Association Rule Mining

Association Rule Mining, one of the most valuable tasks in Data Mining, was introduced by Agrawal *et al.* [15] in the early 1990s. It is the most famous and precise approach which spots the potential hidden patterns from the massive transaction database [16]. Association Rule is used to identify interesting relationships between items in massive databases. It is a relationship between two non-empty itemsets which make an implication of the form *Antecedent* → *Consequence*, where both *Antecedent* and *Consequence* have no common items. Since the database is large and users are only looking for relevant ARs, users predefined rule quality measures in order to drop rules that are not so interesting or useful. The two significant main measures of Association Rules are *support*(s) and *confidence*(c).

The two thresholds are named *minimalsupport* and *minimalconfidence* [17]. The generation of Association Rules is mostly performed in two steps:

- The first one is designed to obtain the sets of frequent items or frequent patterns in the database.
- The second one is designed to generate Association Rules using the frequent items extracted in the first step.

Association Rule Mining task has gained the attention of scientists and has been used in a wide range of important areas over the last decade, such as medical diagnostics, biomedical literature, protein sequences, census data, logistic regression and web fraud detection, etc. [18]. In our work, we are interested in medical diagnosis issues specifically the use of Association Rule Mining for the discovery of multifactorial diseases.

5   Multifactorial Diseases

In the medical field, we can distinguish between monogenic and multifactorial diseases also known as complex/polygenic diseases. Monogenic diseases, are those where one genetic factor is involved and considered as the main risk factor, however, the influence of the environment is often minimal. Multifactorial diseases, unlike monogenic ones, are by definition the result of multiple risk factors that are both genetically and environmentally determined [1] (See Fig. 3). It is the common presence of these genetic factors in the same patient that leads to the onset of the disease. The susceptibility to these diseases results from the combined action (additive effects, multiplicative effects) of a large number of genes. The environment has to be taken in the broad sense: what surrounds or has surrounded the patient as well as certain aspects of the patient's lifestyle. With the availability of environmental factors and the human genome sequence, a multifactorial polygenic disease, can be considered as a realistic challenge to the scientific community. Therefore, the rest of this paper will present, how the task of Association Rules presented above was used for the identification of factors responsible for multifactorial diseases with a special focus on big data.

Fig. 3. Multifactorial disease.

6   Association Rule Mining for Multifactorial Diseases

In this section, we discuss in detail the applications of Association Rule Mining in the health informatics domain. The research articles were discussed in ascending chronological order. For each of the selected papers we have focused our discussion on presenting the abstract topic of the paper, describing the dataset(s), explaining the proposed algorithm or approach, providing tools and technologies, experimental parameters, results, conclusion and future work.

In **Development of a New Metric to Identify Rare Patterns in Association Analysis: The Case of Analyzing Diabetes Complications**, Piri *et al.* [19] carried out an association analysis on electronic medical records of patients with diabetic complications and suggested a new evaluation metric to generate rare items and patterns without over-generating Association Rules. They also carried out an association analysis among various demographic groups at more granular levels. In parallel to the association analysis, Piri *et al.* investigated comorbidity status within the different diabetic demographic groups, examined and compared the prevalence of diabetes complications in each patient demographic group. In order to evaluate the suggested metric, authors mined data from a large, feature-rich electronic medical record data warehouse and executed an association analysis on the resulting dataset, which contained 492 025 unique patients diagnosed with diabetes and related complications. By applying the new metric, authors revealed interesting associations among the complications of diabetes. As future work, authors will take into account other diseases that may have been diagnosed in patients not included in this study. Potentially, the involvement of these existing potential complications would lead to even more informative results.

In **Identifying Risk Factors for Adverse Diseases using Dynamic Rare Association Rule Mining**, Borah and Nath [20] identified the symptoms and risk factors for three adverse diseases: cardiovascular disease, hepatitis and breast cancer, in terms of rare Association Rules. The suggested algorithm was able to produce the new set of rare Association Rules from updated medical databases in a single scan of the database without re-running the entire mining process and it could successfully deal with transaction insertions and deletions and also offered the user the ability to generate a new set of rare Association Rules when the threshold is updated. The proposed approach involves two steps: building the tree where a compressed prefix tree representation of the original database is built in a one-time scan of the database and exploring the patterns where significant frequent and rare patterns are produced from the tree data structure without having to check back to the original database. The experimental analysis highlighted the importance of the proposed approach compared to traditional approaches.

In **A MapReduce-Based Association Rule Mining Using Hadoop Cluster—An Application of Disease Analysis**, Bhattacharya *et al.* [21] implemented the apriori algorithm in the Hadoop MapReduce framework. They used medical data to generate rules that could be applied to get the relationship between diseases and their symptoms and eliminate incoherent information. Authors used a MapReduce job which partitions the input transaction database into multiple blocks, and a mapper is induced once for each transaction entered as an argument. The map task scans one transaction at a time and extracts each element contained in the transaction it got as input. After treatment, the mapper transfers the set of items to the partitioner by sending the set of items and the associated frequency as <key, value> pair, where 'key'is a candidate itemset and "value" is 1. The partition task picks up all intermediate <key,value> pairs emitted by the map task as input and operates as a hash function. Given the size of each key, the partitioner indicates that all the values of each item are gathered and that all the values of the same key move to the same reducer. The output pairs of all partitioners are mixed and swapped to get the list of values assigned to the same key as <key,list(value)> pairs. The reduce task picks up each key by handing over all the values given out for the same key. Next, it sums the values of the corresponding keys and discards candidate itemset whose sum of values is less than the minimum support. The global dataset used includes different types of diseases with their symptoms and contained five datasets with varying numbers of transactions for analysis. The total number of transactions in each dataset are 25,000, 50,000, 100,000, 150,000, and 200,000 and each transaction contains an average of 10 items. The proposed algorithm proved to be a marked improvement in performance. As future work, authors want to implement this algorithm in the cloud computing system for better access and real time execution.

In **Parallel extraction of Association Rules from genomics data**, Agapito *et al.* [22] utilized a Parallel Association Rules Extractor from SNPs (PARES). The novel method aims to correlate the presence of several allelic variants with the clinical status of patients, i.e., the most likely set of alleles responsible for the occurrence of adverse drug reactions. PARES is a multi-thread version which uses the optimized version of the Frequent Pattern Growth (FP-Growth) algorithm. It includes a personalized approach to preprocess SNP datasets using a Fisher test filter to prune trivial transactions. The algorithm succeeded in reducing the search space as well as the size of the FP tree, which leads to a better use of the main memory. PARES is developed in Java and has a simple and intuitive graphical user interface, where particular skills in parallel computing are not required to extract the multiple relationships between genomic factors embedded in the datasets. PARES can process input files in text or xls format. The results can be exported to a txt or rtf (rich text format) file. It is supported by Windows, Linux/UNIX and Mac OS operating systems. It is released under a Creative Commons license and is provided as a free download to academic and non-profit institutions. In order to evaluate the performance of the software, Agapito *et al.* analyzed synthetic SNP datasets ranging in size from less than 1 MB to 20 MB. They generated five synthetic datasets holding 1936 rows which are fixed, and varying the number of columns from 400 to 4000. Authors concluded that the software can efficiently perform the extraction of frequent items and therefore improve the overall performance of the sequential FP-Growth algorithm.

In **Fast Exhaustive Search Algorithm for Discovering Relevant Association Rules**, Amraoui *et al.* [23] presented a Fast Exhaustive Search algorithm FES-ARM for discovering efficient Association Rules to predict the chance of occurring the Diabetes Mellitus. They used an objective function called fitness which is a function for evaluating rules, it shows if an Association Rule is a good solution or not. FES-ARM Algorithm relies on three enhancements: The first one consists of using a setRulesDone which held all the already analyzed rules, to avoid analyzing the same rule several times. The second one consists of computing the fitness of each transaction by pre-computing the mapping transactions by items while parsing rules from the database file and the third one, consists of keeping track for all computed fitnesses for all analyzed rules, which takes a costly part of the treatment and this was efficient since fitness was likely to be computed many times for the same rule. Authors used a dataset of PIMA Indian population near Phoenix, Arizona, which is known to be one of the communities with the highest percentage of diabetes in the world. Experimental results proved the improvements of the proposed algorithm in terms of complexity, CPU time and quality of the generated Association Rules.

In **Parallel and distributed Association Rule Mining in life science: A novel parallel algorithm to mine genomics data**, Agapito *et al.* [24] developed BPARES a novel balanced parallel algorithm for learning Association Rules from biological data, focusing on SNP microarrays data produced by Drug Metabolism Enzymes and Transporters (DMET) technology. The algorithm is used for mining frequent itemsets without candidate generation. BPARES leverages an automatic workload balancing algorithm to optimize performance, and two new data structures labeled TDB and FLIST to assist in the construction of the FP tree to rapidly count the support of the elements and to prune the search space. Experimental studies using synthetic SNP datasets demonstrate that BPARES can reach the similar performance as its predecessor PARES in terms of frequent extracted sets by utilizing lower computational power thanks to the automatic workload balancing strategy. Automatic workload balancing also enables BPARES to have good scalability and to restrict memory requirements to a fixed size proportional to the size of the SNP dataset being processed. As future work, authors will include the design of methodologies to make BPARES operational with the new high-resolution genomic data generated by high-throughput technologies which are marked by a huge volume of data. They will also put BPARES on a cloud infrastructure, and implement it as a peer-to-peer (P2P) distributed model, which would make it even more extensible.

In **Discovering symptom patterns of COVID-19 patients using Association Rule Mining**, Tandan *et al.* [25] discovered symptom patterns in COVID-19 patients and explored the patterns which are disaggregated by age, gender, chronic condition and mortality using Association Rules. Authors considered each patient as a unique transaction. They first induced Association Rule Mining on the symptom data and discovered symptom rules. They then filtered out redundant rules and extracted significant rules by applying the "fisher exact" test for pattern discovery. As well, they included the sex variable in the symptom data and applied a similar approach to discover the symptom rules between male and female patients. In parallel, they added data on age categories (<20 years/ 20–45 years/45–65 years$\geq$65 years), chronic disease (yes/no), and death (survived/deceased) independently and found symptom rules among the categories. They used a minimum support threshold greater than 0.001 and a "lift" threshold greater than 1 for positively correlated rules. Information was extracted from the online platform of the Wolfram Data Repository. They then proceeded to analyze the data after discarding those with "missing" and "unavailable" values.

The weakness of this method lies on the fact that rules can be inferred by other rules and caused time consuming.As future work, Tandan *et al.* want to apply the same idea to dynamic datasets.

In **A novel framework for prognostic factors identification of malignant mesothelioma through Association Rule Mining**, Alam *et al.* [26] proposed a machine learning framework study to extract knowledge of factors associated with malignant mesothelioma disease (a rare type of cancer). Specifically, they used algorithms based on Association Rule Mining and feature selection techniques to extract significant features. In the first step, they used an unbalanced dataset to build a model to identify prognostic factors. Next, they pre-processed the dataset by cleaning it in order to eliminate data redundancy and inconsistency. While data are subject to a class imbalance problem. An oversampling based on the borderline-SMOTE (synthetic minority over-sampling technique) model is applied to avoid the class imbalance. Later, they converted the dataset from numerical values to nominal values and finally they introduced the various association feature selection techniques in order to identify prognostic factors and validate the results. A health record of patients with mesothelioma from the Diyarbakir region of southeast Turkey has been analysed. Experiments have proven that the results are valid and that the extracted factors may be handled at the early stage of the disease before becoming a danger to human life. As future work, authors will expand the dataset for better training and validation and test the proposed model on other benchmarks.

In **Research on Frequent Itemset Mining of Imaging Genetics GWAS in Alzheimer's Disease**, Liang *et al.* [27] used two Frequent Pattern Mining (FPM) frameworks, the FP-Growth and Eclat algorithms, to analyze GWAS results of functional Magnetic Resonance Imaging (fMRI) phenotypes. They also provided the definition of confidence to FP Growth and Eclat to enhance the FPM framework. By computing the conditional probability of the identified SNPs, they have got the related Association Rules to generate confidence support between these significant SNPs. Authors used imaging and genotyping data from ADNI (Alzheimer's Disease Neuroimaging Initiative accessed on 4 December 2021), it was composed of 1515 non-Hispanic white individuals. There are both genotype data and high-quality MRI image data in the ANDI database simultaneously, so they were incorporated into the study after quality control. Next, MRI images of these samples were preprocessed with T1-weighted data and normalized by the Montreal Neurological Institute (MNI) space. The experimental results showed that the novel framework is powerful in both identifying SNPs and yielding candidate SNPs for later research. As future work, authors will sample the MRI image after performing the GWAS analysis in order not to ignore some important information.

In **Human Depression Prediction Using Association Rule Mining Technique**, Biilah *et al.* [28] identified the most critical depressive factors. In order to build the dataset, authors employed depression questionnaires from various psychiatrists and collected responses from students. Next, they cleaned the data through procedures such as filling in missing values or removing missing data rows, smoothing noisy data, or resolving data inconsistencies for each particular feature. Then they extracted the relevant patterns. For each function, they calculated the chi-square value in order to find the correlation between the different variables and finally, they used Apriori algorithm to extract significant rules. The dataset for this study includes 23 characteristics. In this study, the 18 most significant characteristics were identified. Of these, 9 features are identified as highly correlated, 4 as moderately correlated, and 5 as weakly correlated. As future work, authors will use other algorithms for the detection of factors responsible for depression such as artificial neural network, random forest and different boosting techniques and fuzzification. A summary table of the analyzed work is presented below (Table 1).

Table 1. Summary table of essential and characteristic contributions to the works analysed

References	Multifactorial Diseases	**Applications**	Proposed Approaches
Piri *et al.* [19]	Diabetes	Extraction of useful rare Association Rules	- Piri *et al.* proposed a new assessment metric for rare items detection called adjusted_support to discover rare Association Rules for diabetes complications. - They applied adjusted_support instead of considering the entirety of patients' records. - They focused on a subset of records in order to capture the rare Association Rules.
Borah and Nath [20]	Cardiovascular disease, hepatitis and breast cancer	Extraction of useful rare Association Rules	- Borah and Nath proposed an algorithm capable of generating a new set of rare Association Rules from updated medical databases in a single database scan without re-executing the entire mining process. - They devised a tree structure for efficient generation of complete set of patterns. - The proposed approach consists of two phases: * Tree construction: A compressed prefix-tree representation of the original database is constructed in a single database scan in the initial phase. * Pattern mining: Significant frequent and rare patterns are generated from the tree data structure without referring the original database.
Bhattacharya *et al.* [21]	Various types of disease	Fast extraction of useful Association Rules	- Bhattacharya *et al.* provided an efficient implementation of the apriori algorithm in Hadoop MapReduce framework. - A MapReduce job splits the input transaction database into various blocks, and a mapper is invoked once for each transaction passed as arguments for parallel and distributed computing.

(continued)

Table 1. (*continued*)

References	Multifactorial Diseases	Applications	Proposed Approaches
Amraoui *et al.* [23]	Diabetes Mellitus	Fast extraction of useful Association Rules	- Amraoui *et al.* proposed Fast Exhaustive Search Algorithm (FES-ARM) to mine data in less time and less complexity without losing information. - They treated the problem of Association Rule Mining as a multi-objective optimization problem using an objective function called fitness. FES-ARM Algorithm relied on three enhancements: * They used a *setRulesDone* which held all the already analyzed rules, to avoid analyzing the same rule several times. * They computed the fitness of each transaction by pre-computing the mapping *transactions_by_items* while parsing rules from the database file. * They kept track for all computed fitnesses for all analyzed rules, which takes a costly part of the treatment and this was efficient since fitness was likely to be computed many times for the same rule.
Agapito *et al.* [22]	Various types of disease	Parallel extraction of useful Association Rules	- Agapito *et al.* proposed a Parallel Association Rules Extractor from Single Nucleotide Polymorphisms SNPs (PARES). - PARES is a multi-thread software tool based on the optimized version of the Frequent Pattern Growth (FP-Growth) developed in Java for the parallel extraction of Association Rules by which to correlate the presence of a multiple allelic variants with the patients' clinical condition. - PARES encompasses a customized SNP dataset preprocessing approach based on a Fisher's Test Filter. * To prune trivial transactions allowing to shrink the search space. * To reduce the FP-Tree size enabling a better management of the main memory.
Agapito *et al.* [24]	Various types of disease	Parallel extraction of useful Association Rules	- Agapito *et al.* proposed a Balanced Parallel Association Rule Extractor from SNPs (BPARES). - BPARES employed parallel computing and a novel balancing strategy to improve response time. - The dataset is split horizontally among the available threads. - Each thread received its chunk of data and it started the computation independently. - The end of this step produced the calculation of the frequency of every single item stored in FrequentList (FLIST). - FLIST contains the items whose frequency is greater than the minimum support provided by the user. - At the end of the dataset pre-processing, the algorithm produced a Transaction database (TSD) from which it is possible to mine Association Rules.

(*continued*)

Table 1. (*continued*)

References	Multifactorial Diseases	**Applications**	Proposed Approaches
Tandan *et al.* [25]	COVID-19	Disease diagnosis	- Tandan *et al.* aimed to discover symptom patterns and overall symptom rules, including rules disaggregated by age, sex, chronic condition, and mortality status, among COVID-19 patients. - They considered each patient as a unique transaction. - They induced Association Rule Mining on the symptom data and discovered symptom rules. - They filtered out redundant rules and extracted significant rules by applying the "fisher exact" test for pattern discovery. - They used a minimum support threshold greater than 0.001 and a "lift" threshold greater than 1 for positively correlated rules.
Alam *et al.* [26]	malignant mesothelioma	Process Digitisation	- Alam *et al.* suggested a novel framework for identifying prognostic indicators utilizing non-invasive and cost-efective methods based on various techniques. - They used Apriori method, recursive feature elimination method to extract significant features. - In the first step, they used an unbalanced dataset to build a model to identify prognostic factors. - Next, they pre-processed the dataset by cleaning it in order to eliminate data redundancy and inconsistency. - They fixed the oversampling problem to avoid the class imbalance. Later, they converted the dataset from numerical values to nominal values. - Finally they introduced the various association feature selection techniques in order to identify prognostic factors and validate the results.

Biilah *et al.* [28]	mpsychiatric illnesses	Disease diagnosis	- Biilah *et al.* cleaned the data through procedures:
			  * filling in missing values.
			  * removing missing data rows.
			  * smoothing noisy data.
			  * resolving data inconsistencies for each particular feature.
			- They extracted the relevant patterns.
			- For each function, they calculated the chi-square value in order to find the correlation between the different variables.
			- They used Apriori algorithm to extract significant rules.

Liang *et al.* [27]	Alzheimer's Disease	Disease diagnosis	- Liang *et al.* used two Frequent Pattern Mining (FPM) framework, the FP-Growth and Eclat algorithms, to analyze the Genome-Wide Association Study (GWAS) results of functional Magnetic Resonance Imaging (fMRI) phenotypes. - To obtain the significance of voxel and SNP, they applied voxel based GWAS (vGWAS) to the genotyping data and imaging data of 1515 participants. - They, applied FP-Growth and Eclat - They used the Association Rules of hidden patterns sequentially to mine closely connected frequent SNPs. - They analyzed the correlation between identified SNP frequent itemsets and hippocampus, memory, and Alzheimer's Disease.

7   Conclusion

Analytical Data Mining for multifactorial diseases is an emerging area, and Association Rule Mining can be essential in shaping its future. It was observed that older approaches for frequent set exploration, such as Apriori and its variants, are often still employed by researchers when the datasets involved are of very limited size. When it comes to big data, researchers have resorted to new and more sophisticated methods. It was also observed that Association Rule Mining techniques have progressed significantly over the years. As future work, we propose to adapt metaheuristics for Association Rule Mining in the context of big data especially since metaheuristics have several important advantages that do not only take into account the potentially large size of the datasets. However, they are flexible methods, the representation they use can be adjusted to take into account the variety of data, and they have the great advantage of being able to handle different types of features simultaneously.

References

1. Stolk, R.P., et al.: Universal risk factors for multifactorial diseases. Eur. J. Epidemiol. **23**(1), 67–74 (2008)
2. Dhaenens, C., Jourdan, L.: Metaheuristics for data mining: survey and opportunities for big data. Ann. Oper. Res. **314**, 1–24 (2022)
3. Terzo, O., Ruiu, P., Bucci, E., Xhafa, F.: Data as a service (DaaS) for sharing and processing of large data collections in the cloud. In: 2013 Seventh International Conference on Complex, Intelligent, and Software Intensive Systems, pp. 475–480. IEEE (2013)
4. Laney, D., et al.: 3D data management: controlling data volume, velocity and variety. META Group Res. Note **6**(70), 1 (2001)
5. Gandomi, A., Haider, M.: Beyond the hype: big data concepts, methods, and analytics. Int. J. Inf. Manag. **35**(2), 137–144 (2015)
6. Renu, R.S., Mocko, G., Koneru, A.: Use of big data and knowledge discovery to create data backbones for decision support systems. Procedia Comput. Sci. **20**, 446–453 (2013)
7. Frawley, W.J., Piatetsky-Shapiro, G., Matheus, C.J.: Knowledge discovery in databases: an overview. AI Mag. **13**(3), 57–57 (1992)
8. Fayyad, U., Piatetsky-Shapiro, G., Smyth, P.: From data mining to knowledge discovery in databases. AI Mag. **17**(3), 37 (1996)
9. Che, D., Safran, M., Peng, Z.: From big data to big data mining: challenges, issues, and opportunities. In: Hong, B., Meng, X., Chen, L., Winiwarter, W., Song, W. (eds.) DASFAA 2013. LNCS, vol. 7827, pp. 1–15. Springer, Heidelberg (2013). https://doi.org/10.1007/978-3-642-40270-8_1
10. Barba-Gonzaléz, C., García-Nieto, J., Nebro, A.J., Aldana-Montes, J.F.: Multiobjective big data optimization with jMetal and spark. In: Trautmann, H., et al. (eds.) EMO 2017. LNCS, vol. 10173, pp. 16–30. Springer, Cham (2017). https://doi.org/10.1007/978-3-319-54157-0_2
11. Bhat, P., Hegde, P.: Big data analytics: knowledge discovery from map reduce. Harbin Gongye Daxue Xuebao/J. Harbin Inst. Technol. **54**(2), 208–212 (2022)

12. Lieber, D., Stolpe, M., Konrad, B., Deuse, J., Morik, K.: Quality prediction in interlinked manufacturing processes based on supervised & unsupervised machine learning. Procedia Cirp **7**, 193–198 (2013)

13. Cattral, R., Oppacher, F., Deugo, D.: Supervised and unsupervised data mining with an evolutionary algorithm. In: Proceedings of the 2001 Congress on Evolutionary Computation (IEEE Cat. No. 01TH8546), vol. 2, pp. 767–774. IEEE (2001)

14. Srikant, R., Agrawal, R.: Mining quantitative association rules in large relational tables. In: Proceedings of the 1996 ACM SIGMOD International Conference on Management of Data, pp. 1–12 (1996)

15. Agrawal, R., Imieliński, T., Swami, A.: Mining association rules between sets of items in large databases. In: Proceedings of the 1993 ACM SIGMOD International Conference on Management of Data, pp. 207–216 (1993)

16. Qi, X., Zong, M.: An overview of privacy preserving data mining. Procedia Environ. Sci. **12**, 1341–1347 (2012)

17. Zhao, Q., Bhowmick, S.S.: Association rule mining: A survey, p. 135. Nanyang Technological University, Singapore (2003)

18. Heraguemi, K.E.: Approche bio-inspirée pour l'extraction des règles d'association, Ph.D. thesis (2018)

19. Piri, S., Delen, D., Liu, T., Paiva, W.: Development of a new metric to identify rare patterns in association analysis: the case of analyzing diabetes complications. Expert Syst. Appl. **94**, 112–125 (2018)

20. Borah, A., Nath, B.: Identifying risk factors for adverse diseases using dynamic rare association rule mining. Expert Syst. Appl. **113**, 233–263 (2018)

21. Bhattacharya, N., Mondal, S., Khatua, S.: A MapReduce-based association rule mining using hadoop cluster—an application of disease analysis. In: Saini, H.S., Sayal, R., Govardhan, A., Buyya, R. (eds.) Innovations in Computer Science and Engineering. LNNS, vol. 74, pp. 533–541. Springer, Singapore (2019). https://doi.org/10.1007/978-981-13-7082-3_61

22. Agapito, G., Guzzi, P.H., Cannataro, M.: Parallel extraction of association rules from genomics data. Appl. Math. Comput. **350**, 434–446 (2019)

23. Amraoui, H., Mhamdi, F., Elloumi, M.: Fast exhaustive search algorithm for discovering relevant association rules. In: SEKE, pp. 681–727 (2019)

24. Agapito, G., Guzzi, P.H., Cannataro, M.: Parallel and distributed association rule mining in life science: a novel parallel algorithm to mine genomics data. Inf. Sci. **575**, 747–761 (2021)

25. Tandan, M., Acharya, Y., Pokharel, S., Timilsina, M.: Discovering symptom patterns of COVID-19 patients using association rule mining. Comput. Biol. Med. **131**, 104249 (2021)

26. Alam, T.M., et al.: A novel framework for prognostic factors identification of malignant mesothelioma through association rule mining. Biomed. Signal Process. Control **68**, 102726 (2021)

27. Liang, H., et al.: Research on frequent itemset mining of imaging genetics GWAS in Alzheimer's disease. Genes **13**(2), 176 (2022)

28. Biilah, M.A.-M., Raihan, M., Akter, T., Alvi, N., Bristy, N.J., Rehana, H.: Human depression prediction using association rule mining technique. In: Khanna, A., Gupta, D., Bhattacharyya, S., Hassanien, A.E., Anand, S., Jaiswal, A. (eds.) International Conference on Innovative Computing and Communications. AISC, vol. 1388, pp. 223–237. Springer, Singapore (2022). https://doi.org/10.1007/978-981-16-2597-8_19

A Service Infrastructure for the Italian Digital Justice

Valerio Bellandi$^{(\boxtimes)}$ iD, Silvana Castano iD, Stefano Montanelli iD,
Davide Riva iD, and Stefano Siccardi iD

Università degli Studi di Milano, DI - Via Celoria, 18, 20135 Milan, Italy
{valerio.bellandi,silvana.castano,stefano.montanelli,davide.riva,
stefano.siccardi}@unimi.it

Abstract. The management of legal documents, especially court judgments, can be a daunting task due to the vast amounts of data involved. Traditional methods of managing legal documents are no longer sufficient, as the volume of data continues to increase, leading to the need for more advanced and efficient systems. The proposed infrastructure seeks to address this challenge by organizing a repository of textual documents and annotating them in a way that facilitates various downstream tasks. The framework is designed to be developed and maintained in a sustainable way, ensuring multiple services and uses of the annotated document repository while considering the limited availability of annotated data. This approach ensures that the output of the annotation algorithms aligns with the organizational processes used in Italian courts. The experiments conducted to demonstrate the feasibility of the solution employed different low-resource methods and solutions designed to combine these approaches in a meaningful way.

Keywords: Legal Document Annotation · Named Entity Recognition · Concept Extraction · Zero-Shot Learning

1 Introduction

In this paper, we present an infrastructure designed to facilitate the management of legal documents such as court rulings and orders. The primary objective of this infrastructure is to allow for flexible use, meaning that it can accommodate any service that may be required throughout the project's lifetime, without prescribing specific types of information management in advance. Legal documents are valuable sources of information for various purposes and stakeholders. For instance, judges may need to find court decisions in similar cases or lawsuits involving the same individuals or entities. The legal community may require statistics on general trends in areas such as maintenance granted and the economic conditions of partners in divorces. Justice department officials may need to assess court performance in terms of the time taken to complete lawsuits, the number of sentences confirmed or changed in appellate judgments, and other

R. Chbeir et al. (Eds.): MEDES 2023, CCIS 2022, pp. 179–192, 2024.
https://doi.org/10.1007/978-3-031-51643-6_13

metrics [23]. The infrastructure we propose aims to provide solutions to these various needs by allowing for the integration of additional services as required. This flexibility enables the infrastructure to accommodate different stakeholders and their varying needs. The ability to integrate additional services ensures that the infrastructure can evolve over time and continue to meet the needs of its users. The infrastructure design achieves several goals, such as storing text documents and relevant metadata, conducting standard searches on text and metadata by utilizing logical operators to locate occurrences of strings or numbers. The infrastructure includes modules and services to recognize entities occurring within documents and to classify them by using reference entity types. It has the capability to disambiguate the recognized entities and to search for their occurrences in the documents, locate document sections, cluster documents, and perform advanced statistical analyses. Furthermore, it can enforce knowledge extraction based on a combination of *context-aware embedding* models and *zero-shot classification* techniques. The goal is to mine a concept network extracted from documents without relying on any external knowledge base. The network can be exploited to provide concept-driven services to users, like citizens and legal actors (e.g., layers, practitioners), interested in searching, exploring, and analyzing the underlying corpus of legal documents ingested by the system. The design must also prioritize stability and scalability, which are essential for ensuring that the system can handle large volumes of data and continue to deliver high-quality services [19]. By incorporating these features into the infrastructure design, we can ensure that it meets the diverse needs of its users and can evolve over time to keep up with changing requirements. The paper also provides two application examples of the proposed architecture to concrete case-studies in the framework of the Italian digital justice. Evaluation results are finally discussed to show the feasibility of the proposed solution in real situations. In conclusion, the main contribution of this work is the description of a semantically enriched document management system, to support daily operations of multiple users. Judges, clerks of the courts and of the central Justice offices, statisticians, to mention a few, can access the system to search for information suited to their specific needs.

2   Related Work

Several infrastructure have been described, to support document management in the legal domain, focusing on one or more associated tasks. For instance, a software architecture with a specific pipeline to extract knowledge from documents is described in [1]. The systems aims at assisting lawyers in resolving legal cases by automatically extracting key information and suggesting potential arguments. It uses a combination of rule based and statistical NLP techniques. [2] describes a document management system that combines NLP and ontologies in the legal domain. An architecture that analyzes and extracts a set of specific data from texts in natural language has been described in [3] and later improved in [4], implementing an architecture based on microservices and message brokers.

It is based on an ontology containing information about the types of documents, their properties and sections, entities from each section and how their relations. From the point of view of the semantic text analisys several approaches propose NLP techniques to support knowledge extraction and integration in the broad legal domain [9]. An overview can be found in [5], which emphasizes the roles of Named Entity Recognition (NER) techniques and Relation Extraction (RE). Several papers are related to the legal case retrieval task that consists in reading a new case Q, and extracting supporting cases S_1, S_2, ... S_n for the decision of Q. See for instance the Competition on Legal Information Extraction/Entailment (COLIEE) organized since 2017 [6] and the Artificial Intelligence for Legal Assistance (AILA) shared task [18]. For the present work, the Relation Extraction (RE) task is particularly relevant. In general, it is considered quite challenging, especially when arbitrary relations are of interest, see [7], sometimes, joint entity and relation extraction has been proposed. For instance [8] uses a pre-trained BERT model to find and classify text spans and relations given a set of predefined relation classes. For concept extraction, the lack of annotated data poses an additional issue to consider for the application of supervised techniques. Zero-shot classification (ZSC) techniques have been proposed as a solution to such an issue (e.g., [12]). The use of fine-tuned embedding models has been also proposed for legal documents in the English language [15], as well as in the Italian language [17]. Our proposed solution to knowledge extraction exploits ZSC techniques to enforce classification on unlabeled data instances without annotation. The proposed solution is also characterized by the use of a pre-trained model without any fine-tuning for a semantically-meaningful document representation rather than a token representation, by relying on a contextual, transformer-based embedding models (i.e., Sentence-BERT [13]).

3   Architecture

In this section the main features of the proposed infrastructure will be described in detail. In particular, Fig. 1 illustrates the layers and their components. The layer deputed to storage and elaborate the data are composed by the **Ingested documents** and their metadata stored in a document database. It is the repository of the raw data coming from the legacy system [11]. Furthermore, the storage layer is composed of i) a repository for storing the **annotations** created by the system and ii) an **index** system for full text, metadata, and annotation search. A graph database is also maintained to manage the **Entity Registry** (ER), which is deputed to store a unique entry for each entity found in the ingested documents. The ER exposes APIs to manage both the entity types (the ER metamodel) and the entity instances as described in [22]. A module for **System logs** is also defined to monitor the system.

As back-end components, our service architecture provides a set of **NLP Services**, each one performing a specific text-driven operations such as Named Entity Recognition, Linking, and Concept Extraction. A **Service Catalog** is also provided to manage the available services, both for data analysis and to

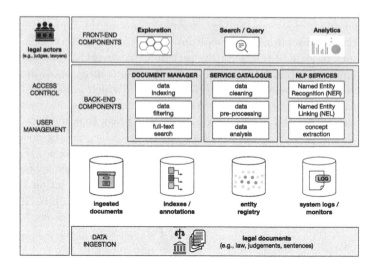

Fig. 1. Main Modules System Infrastructure.

create manipulated versions of the texts (e.g. data cleaning, data pre-processing, summarization). The component is in charge to perform some service orchestration functions to manage workflows of services. The **Document Manager** components, with their APIs, can be considered proxies for client programs to index, filter, and fetch data stored in the system as well as to update them. Regarding the interaction with the users we extended our previous work [16] and we propose front-end components that permit i) to *explore* documents: after reading a document the user wants to move to other documents sharing the same entities or concepts. ii) to *query* documents: the user wants to find documents containing specific entities or concepts, like in a search engine and iii) to *analyse* the document set, for instance number of entities or concepts in a document, and averages, or number of document for an entity or concept and averages; shortest path (through documents) between concepts or entities; entities and concepts centrality, and so on. In our architecture, texts and metadata are stored in an ElasticSearch [10] instance, while annotations are stored in a SQL database as described in our previous work [16]. Moreover a communication queue is created when a NLP service must be invoked, with information needed to get the data. All services must expose standard APIs to be called by the system; they must read the queue and use the parameters found in it to obtain the input texts. At the end, they pass back their output to the Document Manager components, in order to store it. We stress that the system is equipped with configurable pre-processing services, to be used at ingestion time. The user may choose to store both the raw data (i.e., the incoming legal documents) as well as the pre-processed version, or just the latter. The pipeline and the involved services are defined using the Service Catalog components. As an example, a typical ingestion pipeline would consider: storage of the document *as is*, the raw data;

creation and storage of a cleaned copy, where for instance extra blank lines or page breaks, dirty characters inserted by OCR, page headings and so on, are stripped away; pre-processing of the cleaned text to find document sections and store their positions; full text and metadata indexing. Another important point is that the input of any services is a subset of documents, filtered by the user through the functions of the Front-End components.

4   Statistical Data Generation Pipeline Using Entity Extraction

Entity extraction is a critical step in NLP pipelines, and it involves identifying and extracting relevant entities from text, such as names of people, organizations, locations and so on. There are several motivations for applying entity extraction algorithms in NLP pipelines in the context of legal documents: i) in the *Information Retrieval* area Entity extraction can be used to improve information retrieval by enabling better search results. For instance, if a user searches for a company name, entity extraction can help identify all the mentions of that company in a corpus of text, ii) *Named Entity Recognition (NER)* is a subtask of entity extraction that involves identifying specific types of entities, such as names of people, organizations, and locations. NER can be useful in various applications, such as text classification, statistical report generation from text etc., iii) *Information Extraction*: Entity extraction can also be used to extract structured information from unstructured text. For instance, extracting entities and their relationships from court sentences can be used to create knowledge graphs that capture the underlying structure and meaning of the text. In its simplest form, a pipeline to extract entities from a set of documents may consist of running a single service that annotate some portion of text containing the entity. In our proposal, one of the main objectives is to provide a methodology that allows to define a pipeline for identifying entities from texts to generate statistical information. Usually the statistical reports released by the institutions are based on information contained in structured data or metadata, on the contrary, our infrastructure allows the users to extract the entities present in the documents and generate statistical data from them. This is an innovative tool in the context of legal documents.

The pipeline adopted in our infrastructure can be described as: 1. **Data selection**, that permits create a set to process using a query filters on metadata and/or the words in the text. 2. **Text partitioning**, this step identifies the three main part of Italian court decision: preamble, description of the case and decision, 3. **Named Entities Recognition**: this step receives as input the preambles of the documents and performs a Named Entity Recognition task. It permits to annotate persons, companies, fiscal codes and other information. 4. **Internal Linking**, that consists in relating to each other entities found in the previous step. For example it relates namely persons and companies to their fiscal codes, addresses, birth places and dates and role in the trial (plaintiff, defendant or lawyer). This is a complex task and it is the core of pipeline. 5. **Entity Registry**

Building the entities, enriched with attributes deduced through the linking step, are added to the ER, avoiding duplicates and disambiguating homonyms when possible. Text annotations are updated with identifiers to the entities 6. **Statistical Data Generation**, Once the Entity Registry is populated and the annotations are referred to the entities, it is possible to query the documents using entities instead of text strings; accordingly, any entity related statistics can be computed.

Referring to the infrastructure proposed above we can consider that the data selection step involves the Front-End exploration and search components to enter query parameters and to present results, then Data Filtering component of the Document Manager subsystem to fetch the data. When the user executes the statistical data generation pipeline, the Service Catalog composes the tasks pipeline and for that reasons it checks the analysis services that must be run: text partitioning (from the data pre-processing set services), then Named Entity Recognition service to search in the preambles for the required entity types, and Named Entity Linking. The Entity Registry is updated in the final step. Parameters needed by each service are stored, then services are run in the proper sequence. Each service receives parameters to fetch the documents, and calls the proper document manager components to retrieve the data. Depending on the users' choice, the services may check if their tasks have been already performed and results are not obsolete on a document, to avoid unnecessary processing. For instance, if document segmentation has already been done at ingestion time, it may be skipped. All involved services call again the document manager functions to store the annotations they compute. The last service in the pipeline calls the Entity Registry interface to store the entities (persons and companies) with their identifying attributes; moreover, it calls the document manager to update the annotations.

5   The Knowledge Extraction Pipeline

The knowledge extraction pipeline exploits the ingested documents to mine a set of featuring concepts that provide a topic-oriented description of their textual contents. The concepts extracted from the documents are organized in a graph, where a pair of similar concepts is linked by an edge. Each concept is also connected to the document portions from which the concept emerged, meaning that we can explore the pertinent document segments where a certain concept somehow occurs. Our solution exploits Natural Language Processing (NLP) techniques based on zero-shot learning and context-aware embedding models to enforce concept extraction. A detailed description of the proposed zero-shot learning approach to classification of legal documents is provided in [21]. In the following, we discuss how such an approach to knowledge extraction has been integrated as a pipeline in the infrastructure of Fig. 1.

5.1 Data Pre-processing

For knowledge extraction, the data pre-processing stage is based on a tokenization step, where the text of each ingested document d is split into a set of chunks. A *document chunk* k represents the text unit to consider for classification and it determines the granularity of the document that can be associated with a concept. We stress that the size of the document chunk should be large enough, so that the context can be captured, but not too much extended to avoid segments that are long to read and potentially noisy due to the presence of multiple concepts. In this paper, we choose to tokenize documents by defining a chunk for few sentence/phrase detected in a document, up to a maximum size of 512 words. This is particularly appropriate for legal actors (e.g., lawyers, practitioners) that are typically interested in retrieving precise document excerpts in which a given concept of interest appears and can be rapidly read/assimilated.

As a further pre-processing step, the terms appearing in document chunks are lemmatized and a vector-based representation of each document chunk is finally built. The use of embedding techniques to represent chunks allows to map the document contents on a semantic vector space where the similarity of two chunks can be measured by comparing the corresponding vector representations through a similarity metric (e.g., cosine similarity). For embedding construction, Sentence-BERT [13], a modification of the original BERT model based on siamese and triplets networks, is employed to derive a semantically meaningful embedding for a given sentence/phrase. As such, a document chunk is associated with a set of terms W_k therein contained. Any term is described as $w = (w_l, w_d, \bar{w})$, where w_l is the label of the term (i.e., the lemma), w_d is a description of the term meaning taken from a reference dictionary/vocabulary (e.g., WordNet), and $\bar{w}$ is the corresponding vector-based representation according to Sentence-BERT, respectively. A document chunk k has the form $k = (k_d, \bar{k})$, where k_d is the original textual content of the chunk and $\bar{k}$ is the corresponding vector-based representation calculated as the mean of term vectors $\bar{w}$ with $w \in W_k$. Embedding models have the capability to represent and compare the meaning of entire text blocks like document chunks. On such a target, context-aware embedding models fine-tuned on document similarity tasks, like Sentence-BERT, are appropriate. In the legal field, the phrase structure can be highly articulated, and some common terms can have a precise technical meaning when used in a court (e.g., citation, clemency, designation). Sentence-BERT can handle such a kind of situations, which may strongly deviate with respect to everyday conversations.

5.2 Concept Extraction

The document chunks are exploited by zero-shot learning techniques to enforce a multi-label classification process with the aim at detecting a set of featuring concepts. Zero-shot learning is an unsupervised classification technique, characterized by the capability to enforce classification without requiring any pre-existing annotation of the considered documents.

Initially, a *seed knowledge* is defined as a set of textual descriptions, each one featuring a concept of interest, namely a *seed concept*, to consider for classification. Typically, for a seed concept, a basic, gross-grained description is provided as a short text (e.g., one or two phrases) or a list of keywords. As an example, for a seed concept about banking contract, a corresponding textual description used for embedding is bank deposit, safe deposit box, bank credit opening, bank advance, bank account, bank discount. Further concepts are derived from seed ones during the extraction process, and they usually provide a more fine-grained description of the concept instances occurring in the document chunks. A concept c, either seed or derived, is defined as a pair $c = (c_l, \bar{c})$, where c_l is a label featuring the meaning of the concept expressed in a synthetic and human-understandable way, and $\bar{c}$ is a vector-based concept representation. Each concept c is initially associated with the set of terms W_c extracted from the textual description of c. The vector concept $\bar{c}$ is built as the mean of the vectors of all the terms in W_c. Finally, the label c_l corresponds to the label w_l of the term $w \in W_c$, whose vector representation $\bar{w}$ is closest to the concept vector $\bar{c}$. Concept extraction is defined as a progressive, iterative process articulated in the following three steps:

Zero-Shot Classification. Given a set of concepts (i.e., the seed concepts at the beginning of the process), the document chunks are classified through zero-shot learning. A similarity measure σ, e.g. cosine similarity, is calculated over any pair of embeddings between chunks and concepts. A document chunk k is classified with the concept c when the similarity value satisfies $\sigma(\mathbf{k}, \mathbf{c}) \geq \alpha$, with α defined as a similarity threshold configured in the system. The value of α is empirically determined according to experimental results. In this paper, the value $\alpha = 0.3$ is employed in the proposed case-studies and experiments.

Terminology Enrichment. Given a document chunk k classified with the concept c, the terms in W_k are exploited for enriching the term set W_c. The idea is that the initial description of the concept c can become more detailed if we add terminology taken from chunks that are pertinent (i.e., classified) with c. This is done by calculating the similarity between any pair of embeddings $\bar{w}$ and $\bar{c}$ in W_k and W_c. The most similar terms of W_k are inserted in W_c according to a system-defined β similarity threshold.

Concept Derivation. By enriching the term set W_c, it is possible that more fine-grained concepts emerge from c, and they can be generated as new concepts. The discovery of possible new concepts emerging from c is enforced by clustering the embedding vectors $\bar{w}$ of terms in W_c. The Affinity Propagation (AP) algorithm is adopted to this end, since it allows to detect the emergence of sub-groups of similar terms within W_c, without requiring to "a-priori define" the number of clusters to generate. A new concept c' is created for each cluster returned by AP on the terms W_c of a concept c. A link is defined between a concept c' and c to denote that c' is derived from c and they are somehow similar/related in content. The concept c is then updated since the terms in W_c can be changed due to enrichment. As a consequence, c_l and $\bar{c}$ are re-calculated.

The set of concepts obtained after derivation can trigger the execution of a new cycle based on the above three steps. New derived concepts can contribute to improve the classification of chunks in more fine-grained concepts. Further new concepts can be also discovered through a new execution of enrichment and derivation on the basis of a refined classification result. As such, concept extraction is characterized by a predefined endpoint condition based on a *termination threshold*. When the number of new concepts created in the derivation step is lower than the threshold, the concept extraction process is concluded. A final concept graph providing a topic-based description of the underlying document corpus is stored in the entity registry for subsequent exploitation by the front-end services. An example of concept graph extracted from a case-study of Italian legal documents will be discussed in Sect. 6.

6   Application to the Italian Context and Evaluation

In the following, we discuss some application examples and evaluation results about entity and knowledge extraction. To this end, we consider a corpus of Italian court decisions collected in the framework of the *Next Generation UPP* (*NGUPP*) project, funded by the Italian Ministry of Justice. We will propose our results in the main areas of analysis exposed in the previous sections.

6.1   Statistical Data Generation Using Entity Extraction

Performance of NER algorithms with their attributes has been manually checked on a subset of 50 documents issued by 4 courts on 3 kinds of debates. the results are summarized in Table 1, regarding the main entities annotation we consider True Positive (T.P.) only the value correctly found, False Positive (F.P.) correspond to text strings not related to any entities and False Negative (F.N.) are the entities not found by the algorithm. The percentages are considered with respect to total entities found of each type. True Negative do not make sense in this context. We also consider *Inaccurate* entities when either the string denoting the entity was not completely detected, or the entity was not assigned the correct meaning in the document (e.g. a lawyer was considered as a plaintiff). For example: 7.4 % of entity person was not be linked as a lawyers etc. Regarding the *Linked entities* are considered correctly found (True Positive) only when they are correct and linked to the proper main entity.

After the steps of NER pipeline have been performed, we report some statistics about people involved in trials. As an example, we computed the percentage of male and female plaintiff in divorce trials, in three districts (Milan, Rome and Palermo). The meaning of the statistics is of course which of the partners started the divorce. Results are shown in Table 2. We considered only cases where parties have been identified with their gender.

Table 1. Estimated performances of NER and linking: percentages of instances identified

Main entities:	T.P	F.P	F.N	Linked entities	T.P	F.P	F.N
Plaintiffs (persons)	76.8	7.6	23.2	Gender	88.5	1.3	10.2
Plaintiffs (companies)	100.0	7.1	0.0	Fiscal code	81.8	0.0	18.2
Defendants (persons)	84.8	7.6	15.2	Birth date	78.0	0.0	22.0
Defendants (companies)	78.6	7.1	21.4	Birth place	65.9	7.3	26.8
Lawyers	81.9	7.0	10.7	Postal address	77.8	0.0	22.2

Table 2. Percentages of divorces started by males and females

District	Trial n	Male %	Female %
Milan	3195	55.9	44.1
Rome	4583	62.3	37.7
Palermo	1726	53.3	46.7

6.2 Concept-Driven Data Exploration

We consider a case-study about "unfair competition" as subject matter and we invoke our knowledge extraction pipeline with the aim to explore the concepts extracted from the corpus on such a subject. The user can enforce a preliminary filtering step over the document metadata to select the set of court decisions to consider for concept exploration. The example is based on a dataset of 34 documents resulting from the following filtering operations: first level of judgment, judicial district in North-Western Italy, year of decision from 2008 onwards, subject matter corresponding to 172011 or 172012, that are subject codes related to unfair competition in the Italian law. In Fig. 2, we show the concept graph returned by the knowledge extraction pipeline for describing the filtered dataset on unfair competition. We note that most of the graph concepts pertain to the domain of trade justice (e.g., "consortium", "partnership", "transaction"), by also describing specific aspects concerned with unfair competition. Through links, it is possible to move from specific concepts (e.g., "sponsorship") to more general ones (e.g., "business"), and vice-versa. In the example, general concepts are usually associated with more chunks than specific concepts. We also note that some concept labels appear many times (e.g., "business", "sponsorship"), meaning that they refer to different senses of the concept label.

For evaluation of our concept extraction process, we consider EurLex57k [14], that is a dataset of 57,000 EU legislative documents annotated with labels representing entities, concepts, and topics from the EuroVoc thesaurus[1]. The goal of the evaluation is to assess whether our extracted concepts correspond with the labels of EuroVoc used for annotating the EurLex57k dataset. As a baseline, we

---

[1] https://eur-lex.europa.eu/browse/eurovoc.html?locale=en.

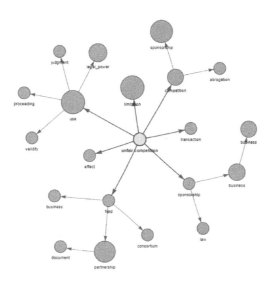

Fig. 2. Example of concept graph returned by the knowledge extraction pipeline for the case-study on "unfair competition". The size of a concept node is proportional to the number of document chunks classified with the concept. The original Italian labels of concepts have been translated into English for the sake of readability.

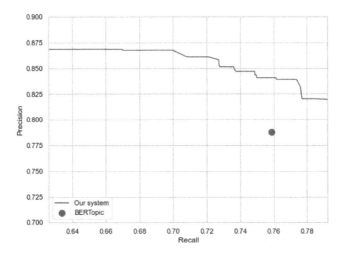

Fig. 3. Precision-Recall curve for concept extraction on the EurLex57k dataset.

consider BERTopic [20] since it is a topic modeling approach based on BERT and the mined topics can be straightforwardly compared to our extracted concepts. In Fig. 3, we show the precision-recall curve obtained by our concept extraction pipeline when various values of α and β thresholds are employed.We note that our solution outperforms the BERTopic baseline: despite a 0.05 decrease, precision remains higher than the baseline even when recall increases (i.e., when more concepts are extracted).

As a further experiment, we consider the results of the zero-shot classification and we evaluate the correspondence of our extracted concepts assigned to chunks w.r.t. the EuroVoc label assigned to documents. Results in terms of precision and recall are shown in Table 3 by providing mean and standard deviation at the document level. In the experiment, the following thresholds are set: $\alpha = \beta = 0.3$.

Table 3. Mean (standard deviation) results for document classification.

Model	Precision	Recall
Our system	**0.593 (0.061)**	**0.681 (0.078)**
BERTopic	0.455 (0.306)	0.422 (0.287)

We note that precision and recall of our concept extraction pipeline are not only higher, but also significantly less variable than the ones obtained by BERTopic according to the standard deviation.

7   Concluding Remarks

In this paper, an infrastructure for managing legal documents and related metadata has been proposed. In particular, a service architecture was presented that provides the functionalities of ingestion, archiving and analysis of legal sentences. Some specific processing pipelines based on NLP and machine learning were described and tested. As far as the evaluation of the proposal is concerned, the experiments illustrated above have demonstrated how the proposed infrastructure and services make it possible to provide a new set of semantic functions which allow for the semi-automation of some needs of the Italian Ministry of Justice. In particular, both the excellent quality of the results of the single processing services and the sustainability of the infrastructural proposal were demonstrated. Since the proposed solution is part of a process of continuous development and evolution, various future activities have been planned. Specifically, the expansion of the set of knowledge extraction services and the introduction of a complex workflow management system are planned.

Acknowledgements. This work is partially supported by i) the Next Generation UPP project within the PON programme of the Italian Ministry of Justice, ii) the Università degli Studi di Milano within the program "Piano di sostegno alla ricerca",

iii) the MUSA - Multilayered Urban Sustainability Action - project, funded by the European Union - NextGenerationEU, under the National Recovery and Resilience Plan (NRRP) Mission 4 Component 2 Investment Line 1.5: Strenghtening of research structures and creation of R&D "innovation ecosystems", set up of "territorial leaders in R&D, and iv) the project SERICS (PE00000014) under the MUR NRRP funded by the EU - NextGenerationEU.

References

1. Breit, A., Waltersdorfer, L., Ekaputra, F.J., Sabou, M.: An architecture for extracting key elements from legal permits. In: 2020 IEEE International Conference on Big Data (Big Data), pp. 2105–2110 (2020). https://doi.org/10.1109/BigData50022.2020.9378375
2. Amato, F., Mazzeo, A., Penta, A., Picariello, A.: Using NLP and ontologies for notary document management systems. In: Database and Expert Systems Application, DEXA 2008, pp. 67–71 (2008). https://doi.org/10.1109/DEXA.2008.86
3. Buey, M.G., Garrido, A.L., Bobed, C., Ilarri, S.: The AIS project: boosting information extraction from legal documents by using ontologies. In: Proceedings of the 8th International Conference on Agents and Artificial Intelligence (ICAART 2016), pp. 438–445 (2016). https://doi.org/10.5220/0005757204380445
4. Ruiz, M., Roman, C., Garrido, A.L., Mena, E.: uAIS: an experience of increasing performance of NLP information extraction tasks from legal documents in an electronic document management system. In: Proceedings of the 22nd International Conference on Enterprise Information Systems (ICEIS 2020), pp. 189–196 (2020). https://doi.org/10.5220/0009421201890196
5. Zhong, H., Xiao, C., Tu, C., Zhang, T., Liu, Z., Sun, M.: How Does NLP Benefit Legal System: A Summary of Legal Artificial Intelligence, arXiv, cs.2004.12158 (2020)
6. Rabelo, J., Goebel, R., Kim, M. Y., Kano, Y., Yoshioka, M., Satoh, K.: Overview and discussion of the competition on legal information extraction/entailment (COLIEE) 2021. Review Socionetwork Strategies 16, 111–133 (2022). https://doi.org/10.1007/s12626-022-00105-z
7. Yu, D., Huang, L., Ji, H.: Open relation extraction and grounding. In: Proceedings of the Eighth International Joint Conference on Natural Language Processing (Volume 1: Long Papers), pp. 854–864 (2017). https://aclanthology.org/I17-1086
8. Eberts, M., Ulges, A.: Span-based joint entity and relation extraction with transformer pre-training. Front. Artif. Intell. Appl. **325**, 2006–2013 (2020). ECAI 2020
9. Dragoni, Mauro, Villata, Serena, Rizzi, Williams, Governatori, Guido: Combining natural language processing approaches for rule extraction from legal documents. In: Pagallo, Ugo, Palmirani, Monica, Casanovas, Pompeu, Sartor, Giovanni, Villata, Serena (eds.) AICOL 2015-2017. LNCS (LNAI), vol. 10791, pp. 287–300. Springer, Cham (2018). https://doi.org/10.1007/978-3-030-00178-0_19
10. Gormley, C., Tong, Z.: Elasticsearch: The Definitive Guide: A Distributed Real-Time Search and Analytics Engine. O'Reilly Media Inc, Sebastopol (2015)
11. Anisetti, M., Ardagna, C.A., Braghin, C., Damiani, E., Polimeno, A., Balestrucci, A.: Dynamic and scalable enforcement of access control policies for big data. In: Proceedings of the 13th International Conference on Management of Digital EcoSystems (MEDES 2021), pp. 71–78. Association for Computing Machinery, New York (2021). https://doi.org/10.1145/3444757.3485107

12. Chang, M.-W., Ratinov, L.-A., Roth, D., Srikumar, V.: Importance of semantic representation: dataless classification. In: AAAI, vol. 2, pp. 830–835 (2008)
13. Reimers, N., Gurevych, I.: Sentence-bert: sentence embeddings using siamese bert-networks. arXiv preprint arXiv:1908.10084 (2019)
14. Chalkidis, I., Fergadiotis, M., Malakasiotis, P., Androutsopoulos, I.: Large-scale multi-label text classification on EU legislation. arXiv preprint arXiv:1906.02192 (2019)
15. Chalkidis, I., et al.: LEGAL-BERT: the muppets straight out of law school. arXiv preprint arXiv:2010.02559 (2020)
16. Batini, C., Bellandi, V., Ceravolo, P., Moiraghi, F., Palmonari, M., Siccardi, S.: Semantic data integration for investigations: lessons learned and open challenges. In: 2021 IEEE International Conference on Smart Data Services (SMDS), Chicago, IL, USA, pp. 173–183 (2021). https://doi.org/10.1109/SMDS53860.2021.00031
17. Licari, D., Comandè, G.: ITALIAN-LEGAL-BERT: a pre-trained transformer language model for Italian law. In: CEUR Workshop Proceedings, vol. 3256. CEUR-WS (2022)
18. Bhattacharya, P., et al.: FIRE 2019 AILA track: artificial intelligence for legal assistance. In: Proceedings of the 11th Annual Meeting of the Forum for Information Retrieval Evaluation (2019)
19. Ardagna, C.A., Bellandi, V., Bezzi, M., Ceravolo, P., Damiani, E., Hebert, C.: Model-based big data analytics-as-a-service: take big data to the next level. IEEE Transactions Services Computing 14(2), 516–529 (2021). https://doi.org/10.1109/TSC.2018.2816941
20. Grootendorst, M.: BERTopic: neural topic modeling with a class-based TF-IDF procedure. arXiv preprint arXiv:2203.05794 (2022)
21. Bellandi, V., et al.: Knowledge-based legal document retrieval: a case study on Italian civil court decisions. In: Proceedings of the 1st International Knowledge Management for Law Workshop (KM4LAW), Bozen-Bolzano, Italy. CEUR-WS (2022)
22. Bellandi, V., Siccardi, S.: An Entity Registry: A Model for a Repository of Entities Found in a Document Set, pp. 1–12 (2023). https://doi.org/10.5121/csit.2023.130301
23. Carmignani, A., Giacomelli, S.: Too many lawyers? Litigation in Italian civil courts. Bank of Italy, Economic Research and International Relations Area (2010). https://ideas.repec.org/s/bdi/wptemi.html

Open-Source Software Development Communities: An Analysis Approach as a Social Network

Georgios C. Makris[1]([email]) [ID], Alexandros Z. Spyropoulos[2] [ID], and Ioannis Stamelos[1] [ID]

[1] School of Informatics, Aristotle University of Thessaloniki (AUTH), 54124 Thessaloniki, Greece
{geormakr,stamelos}@csd.auth.gr
[2] Department of Physics, School of Science, International Hellenic University (IHU), Kavala's Campus, 57001 Thessaloniki, Greece
daspyro@physics.ihu.gr

Abstract. Open-source software plays a very important role in today's technological world. Developer communities are sharing solutions and exposing their work through large organizations like GitHub. Based on the above, an interesting question arises: "Do the developer communities behave in a similar way regardless of the language they work with?" and following "which programming languages favor forking the most?". In an effort to answer questions, data from twenty different communities of programming languages were collected, as they emerged through GitHub. From the data (43,704,340 nodes and 39,038,833 connections) twenty different social networks were formed which were studied with simple tools of statistics and network theory. The results showed that all communities behaved in a similar way to the exclusion of the R programming language community.

Keywords: Open-source Software · Developer Communities · Social Networks · Network Theory · Density · Degree Centralization · GitHub

1 Introduction

Software development is one of the main activities of the computer science community [1–8]. From the first steps of this new activity, ways were developed through which the members of the community of open-source software developers were able to exchange information and solutions to emerging problems [1, 2]. Nowadays there are huge organizations that aim to share open source software and improve cooperation between people from different social, economic, political, academic backgrounds from all over the world [9]. The globalism of the open source software community demonstrates the human need for cooperation and solving common problems [2].

Supplementary Information. The online version contains supplementary material available at https://doi.org/10.1007/978-3-031-51643-6_14.

The dynamics of this community show exponential growth [10–12]. This has been reinforced by: the existence and development of new programming languages, the specialized use of different programming languages, as well as the operation of open source software sharing organizations [7, 9, 11]. The above is also a basis for creating confusion and problems. That is, plagiarism phenomena are observed, as well as the development of a kind of competition between users of older and newer programming languages [11].

Members of the community of open-source software developers work together through the above organizations as follows: Someone publishes a piece of code, offering a solution to a problem. This piece is then used as part of someone else's code and so on. This process in the language of open-source developers is called *"forking"*. Forking is controversial as it contains elements of plagiarism, but it is noted that the developer community argues that this is necessary and is the multiplier of open-source software. Forking saves time developing new code and proposes new uses for codes that have already been developed [13–15]. Thus, the creation of a network of cooperation is observed [5, 9, 10, 16]. As is well known, a network is any system that can be presented as a set of nodes (or vertexes) and connections (or edges) that constitute the visual representation of the interdependence - interaction relationships between the nodes [17–25]. The network theory is an interdisciplinary tool for analyzing structures with many variables. Its interdisciplinary character of network theory is based on the fact that it examines the nodes of the network not on the basis of their individual characteristics, but on their topological position in relation to the other nodes of the network [17, 18, 21].

The tools of network theory can have local use, analysis of the characteristics – properties of each node of the network (local indicators), or even total use, analysis of the overall picture of the network (global indicators) [18, 21, 25]. Global indicators when giving normalized values can be used to compare different similar networks [25, 26].

This can be made more complex - and give clearer interpretations - if we take into account the direction. That is, each link of the network represents an asymmetrical interdependence relationship between the nodes of the network. More simply A $\rightarrow$ B $\neq$ B $\rightarrow$ A, where A there B are nodes of the network and $\rightarrow$ the link that denotes the relationship between them [18, 24, 26, 27].

The above as tools can help analyze the community of open-source developers as a social network. The present study addresses the following research questions:

Q1 "Do the developer communities behave in a similar way regardless of the language they work with?".
Q2 "which programming languages favor forking the most?".

The research methodology (selected indicators) and the datasets are presented in Sect. 2. The results and discussion are presented in Sect. 3. In the conclusions, the usefulness of this study in the analysis of the community of open-source developers is presented.

2 Methodology and Datasets

To answer the research questions Q1 and Q2, real data derived from GitHub are used [9]. The number of nodes and connections from twenty programming languages is examined. The ratio of nodes and connections shows the density of the network. The *density* will be assessed independently as a separate indicator for each programming language. In addition, the degree centralization index for each network is examined.

2.1 Global Indices

The global indices of a network result from the network geometry of interconnections, and reveal the overall features and qualities of the network [25, 28–30].

2.1.1 Density

The density of a network is the ratio of the size (number of edges the network) over the maximal possible number of edges, with range (0,1). The density of an undirected network with N nodes of size E is: $\frac{2E}{N(N-1)}$ [25, 31, 32].

2.1.2 Degree Centralization

The degree of node i in a network of order N, is the number of connections of the node i and takes values from 0 to $N - 1$. The value 0 indicates the absence of links and there are no self-loops. The normalized degree is the degree centrality [18, 24, 33]: $DEG_\kappa = \frac{\sum_{\lambda=1}^{N} a_{\kappa\lambda}}{N-1}$, where: $a_{\kappa\lambda}$ is the $\kappa\lambda$ – element of the adjacency matrix [18, 24, 28, 29, 34] of the network.

Centralization was introduced by Freeman [18] as the degree to which the centrality of the most central node exceeds the centrality of all other nodes [18, 21, 25, 35, 36].

Degree centralization is defined as $\text{DEG} = \frac{\sum_{\kappa=1}^{N}\left(\max\limits_{\nu=1,2,\dots,N}\{DEG_\nu\}-DEG_\kappa\right)}{N-2}$ [25, 37], where DEG_ν is the degree centrality of the node ν, $\nu = 1, 2,\dots, N$.

2.2 Datasets

To retrieve the data, a script written in the javascript programming language was used that communicated with github's REST API. Specifically, the URI GET/repositories were used to find the IDs of all public repositories and then for each one identifier retrieved, a request was made to the URI GET/repositories/:id to provide more data. All public repositories present on github were collected on 28/2/2020. The procedure was repeated on 20/9/2020. In the end, only repositories that were active in both data collections were selected. The total number of repositories is 126,354,366 (Table 1). The data obtained due to the gigantic volume presented in this work have been produced using the Aristotle University of Thessaloniki (AUTh) High Performance Computing Infrastructure and Resources.

Table 1. Table with sets of nodes and edges for the developer communities for the twenty programming languages selected.

Language	Number of nodes	Number of edges
C	1968302	1761589
C#	1491459	1296269
C++	2478449	2217777
CSS	1347686	1173563
Go	1219690	1129116
HTML	2546007	2189899
Java	6125345	5497776
Javascript	9611513	8661112
Jupyter Notebook	1292104	1157935
Kotlin	159326	139640
Objective_C	1093452	1008481
PHP	2166524	1875008
Python	5845366	5213290
R	438974	386396
Ruby	2910551	2668884
Scala	263993	236928
Shell	1278893	1113339
Swift	539924	485218
TypeScript	686991	608148
Vue	239791	218465

2.3   The Interpretation of Indicators in the Networks Under Consideration

The indicators in Sect. 2.1 have a separate interpretation depending on the type of network being studied. In social networks, such as those presented in this paper, each of the aforementioned indicators is meaningful as follows.

The multitudes of nodes and connections highlight the popularity of the language and, byextension, its usefulness.Density signals the willingness of users (nodes) to collaborate, exchange information and take advantage of the previous creation.The degree centralization is indicating how central the most central nodes are, in relation to how central all the other nodes are.

3   Results and Dictation

The following results were obtained from the analysis of the above data (Sect. 2.2) in terms of the three global network indicators, namely, number of nodes and edges, density, degree centralization.

The results of the calculations are presented in Sect. 3.1 and visual representation graphs of the results are presented in Sect. 3.2.

3.1 Results of the Calculations

The results of the calculations of the number of nodes, number of edges, density, forks, degree centralization is presented in the Supplementary Materials S1 due to their large size. The calculations of the relevant local indicators (degree centrality) for each node are also included in the Supplementary Materials S2.

Supplementary Material S1: The results of the calculations for the global indicators.
Supplementary Material S2: The results of the calculations for the local indicators.

3.2 Number of Nodes, Number of Edges, Density, Degree Centralization and Forks

The following graphical representations visualize the results for the number of nodes, number of edges (Fig. 1) and density indicators (Fig. 2) for the twenty programming languages under consideration.

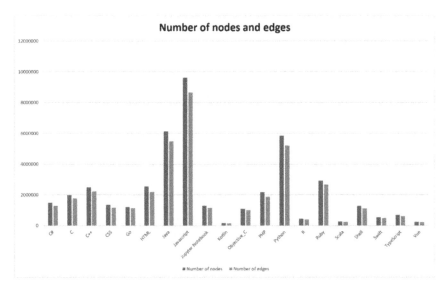

Fig. 1. This graph shows the multitudes of nodes and connections for the networks of the twenty programming languages communities, as collected from the page https://github.com/ the March of 2020. In it appears a clear superiority of the Java script while in the second and third places we have the java and python languages.

3.3 Discussion

In the light of the results of the calculations as they appear in Supplementary Materials S1 and S2 but also in the diagrams of Sect. 3.2 it is concluded that the networks of the

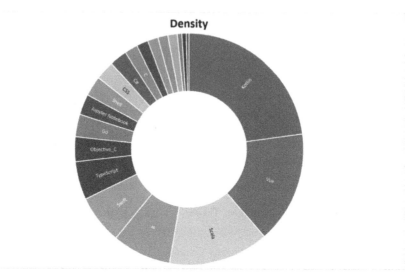

Fig. 2. This graph shows the densities of the networks of the twenty programming languages communities, as collected from the page https://github.com/ the March of 2020. This shows a clear predominance of the Kotlin, Vue, Scala and R languages.

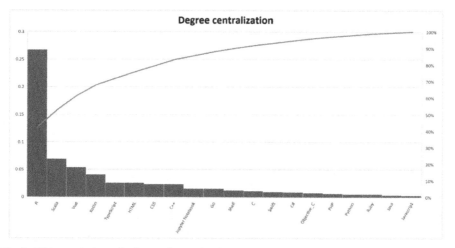

Fig. 3. This graph shows in descending order the values of the degree centralization index of the twenty programming languages, as collected from the page https://github.com/ the March of 2020. This shows a clear superiority of the programming language R.

developer communities are extremely sparse. In other words, we have many nodes and few connections. This shows that most teams create standalone work based on basic packages of ready-made solutions and less look for pieces of code from other creators. The Javascript, Java, Python, and HTML, C++, C, and C# communities are very strongly aware of the fact that the nodes are multiples of the connections. While the Kotlin, Vue,

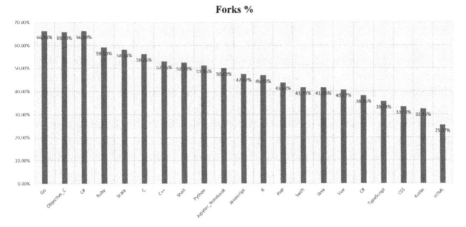

Fig. 4. This graph shows in descending order the values of forks in % of nodes index of the twenty programming languages, as collected from the page https://github.com/ the March of 2020. Here it seems that all languages are quite high in percentage Forks.

Swiftm, and R language communities seem to have an approximate equal number of nodes and connections (see Fig. 1).

The above, as expected, is strongly reflected by the density index. Here it is observed that the communities of programming languages are the protagonists, which although they have few nodes, nevertheless show a similar number of connections (Fig. 2). As expressed in Sect. 3.4, Density signals the willingness of users (nodes) to collaborate, exchange information and take advantage of the previous creation. Therefore, it can be said that language communities with few users are doing better in collaborating and making the most of previous tasks than programming languages with many developers (see Fig. 2).

The analysis of Fig. 3 is quite interesting. Here it is observed that the community of users of the R language has an extremely higher (almost 4 times higher) value in the degree centralization index than the second Scala. The degree centralization index is interesting as it certifies that in the R language community there are some users with a clear leading and pioneering role in the utilization of material by and/or for other users.

As mentioned in Sect. 1 forking is very important for the open-source developer community. In essence, it is the way in which the analyzed networks in this paper were built. Figure 4 clearly shows that all programming languages favor forking. The percentages range from 25% to 66%, with the average being quite high at 52% with a relatively small standard deviation. It is observed that forking as a process is presented to all developer communities. Forking is as much about programming languages that were developed in the past years, and those that are now current are in great bloom [38]. Finally, we see that programming languages related to page creation, the most characteristic example being HTML, have the least tendency for the forking process. The behavior of HTML users can also be explained by the fact that HTML is a markup language and not a pure programming language. So, perhaps, not many forks are observed because HTML does not lend itself to reuse.

4   Conclusion

This paper attempted to investigate whether communities of open-source software developers behave in a similar way regardless of the programming language in which they work. The answer to this question seems to be of particular importance for understanding both the evolution of software, but also in general the behavior of developers in terms of sharing information and/or creating original code.

To answer the query, public data was collected from GitHub, the largest code software sharing page. Thus, 20 networks were created, one for each programming language under consideration, nodes of the networks were users-programmers, while connections between the nodes were considered the use of stand-alone pieces of code from one code to another. Based on this methodology, 20 directed social networks emerged which were analyzed with simple tools of statistics and network theory.

Although the networks that emerged were sparse, it is concluded that the programmers of the examined programming languages follow a similar behavior. Most choose to create self-contained works, without using pieces of code of previous works as such. This conclusion emerges from the study of the density of networks as a result of the fact that all networks have more users than connections between users. Finally, it was observed that no programming language has prominent nodes. An exception to this behavior is the community of the R language which has four times greater degree centralization than the second and thus it is concluded that some nodes seem to play a leading role.

In addition, it was observed that forking as a process occurs in all examined programming languages. But it's less about programming languages related to web development.

In the future it is planned to study the communities of developers of the programming languages with the highest values in the considered indicators. Then, the tools used in the development of these programming languages with the method of forking will be presented.

Acknowledgments. The authors would like to acknowledge the support provided by the IT Center of the Aristotle University of Thessaloniki (AUTh) throughout the progress of this research work.

Conflicts of Interest. The authors declare no conflict of interest.

References

1. Feller, J., Fitzgerald, B.: Understanding Open Source Software Development. Addison-Wesley Longman Publishing Co., Inc., Boston (2002). ISBN 0-201-73496-6
2. O'Reilly, T.: Lessons from open-source software development. Commun. ACM **42**, 32–37 (1999)
3. Crowston, K., Wei, K., Howison, J., Wiggins, A.: Free/libre open-source software development: what we know and what we do not know. ACM Comput. Surv. CSUR **44**, 1–35 (2008)
4. Osterloh, M., Rota, S.: Open source software development—just another case of collective invention? Res. Policy **36**, 157–171 (2007)

5. Wu, M.-W., Lin, Y.-D.: Open source software development: an overview. Computer **34**, 33–38 (2001)
6. Nuvolari, A.: Open source software development: some historical perspectives. First Monday **10**, 3 (2005)
7. Von Krogh, G.: Open-source software development. MIT Sloan Manag. Rev. **44**, 14 (2003)
8. Stewart, K.J., Gosain, S.: The impact of ideology on effectiveness in open source software development teams. MIS Q. 291–314 (2006)
9. GitHub. https://en.wikipedia.org/w/index.php?title=GitHub&oldid=1096425256. Accessed 10 July 2022
10. Ye, Y., Nakakoji, K., Yamamoto, Y., Kishida, K.: The co-evolution of systems and communities in free and open source software development. In: Global Information Technologies: Concepts, Methodologies, Tools, and Applications, pp. 3765–3776. IGI Global (2008)
11. Tang, T.Y., Fang, E.E., Qualls, W.J.: More is not necessarily better: an absorptive capacity perspective on network effects in open source software development communities. MIS Q. **44** (2020)
12. Guimarães, A.L., Korn, H.J., Shin, N., Eisner, A.B.: The life cycle of open source software development communities. J. Electron. Commer. Res. **14**, 167 (2013)
13. Havelund, K., Larsen, K.G.: The fork calculus. In: Lingas, A., Karlsson, R., Carlsson, S. (eds.) ICALP 1993. LNCS, vol. 700, pp. 544–557. Springer, Heidelberg (1993). https://doi.org/10.1007/3-540-56939-1_101
14. Chua, B.: Detecting sustainable programming languages through forking on open source projects for survivability. In: Proceedings of the 2015 IEEE International Symposium on Software Reliability Engineering Workshops (ISSREW); August 2015, pp. 120–124 (2015)
15. Badashian, A.S., Stroulia, E.: Measuring user influence in GitHub: the million follower fallacy. In: Proceedings of the Proceedings of the 3rd International Workshop on CrowdSourcing in Software Engineering; Association for Computing Machinery, New York, NY, USA, 14 2016 February, pp. 15–21 (2016)
16. Open Source Guides. https://opensource.guide/. Accessed 10 July 2022
17. Kolaczyk, E.D., Csárdi, G.: Network topology inference. In: Kolaczyk, E.D., Csárdi, G. (eds.) Statistical Analysis of Network Data with R, pp. 115–140. Springer, Cham (2020). https://doi.org/10.1007/978-3-030-44129-6_7
18. Freeman, L.C.: Centrality in social networks conceptual clarification. Soc. Netw. **1**, 215–239 (1978). https://doi.org/10.1016/0378-8733(78)90021-7
19. Rodríguez, J.A., Estrada, E., Gutiérrez, A.: Functional centrality in graphs. Linear Multilinear Algebra **55**, 293–302 (2007). https://doi.org/10.1080/03081080601002221
20. Klein, D.J.: Centrality measure in graphs. J. Math. Chem. **47**, 1209–1223 (2010). https://doi.org/10.1007/s10910-009-9635-0
21. Boldi, P., Vigna, S.: Sebastiano axioms for centrality. Internet Math.**10**, 3–4, 222–262
22. Kolaczyk, E.D., Csárdi, G.: Modeling and prediction for processes on network graphs. In: Kolaczyk, E.D., Csárdi, G. (eds.) Statistical Analysis of Network Data with R, pp. 141–167. Springer, Cham (2020). https://doi.org/10.1007/978-3-030-44129-6_8
23. Kolaczyk, E.D., Csárdi, G.: Descriptive analysis of network graph characteristics. In: Kolaczyk, E.D., Csárdi, G. (eds.) Statistical Analysis of Network Data with R, pp. 43–68. Springer, Cham (2020). https://doi.org/10.1007/978-1-4939-0983-4_4
24. Spyropoulos, A.Z., Bratsas, C., Makris, G.C., Ioannidis, E., Tsiantos, V., Antoniou, I.: Entropy and network centralities as intelligent tools for the investigation of terrorist organizations. Entropy **23**, 1334 (2021). https://doi.org/10.3390/e23101334
25. Spyropoulos, A.Z., Bratsas, C., Makris, G.C., Ioannidis, E., Tsiantos, V., Antoniou, I.: Investigation of terrorist organizations using intelligent tools: a dynamic network analysis with weighted links. Mathematics **10** (2022). https://doi.org/10.3390/math10071092

26. Farquhar, I.E., Seeger, R.J.: Ergodic theory in statistical mechanics. Am. J. Phys. **33**(11), 973–973 (1965)

27. Kolaczyk, E.D., Csárdi, G.: Dynamic networks. In: Kolaczyk, E.D., Csárdi, G. (eds.) Statistical Analysis of Network Data with R, pp. 207–223. Springer, Cham (2020). https://doi.org/10. 1007/978-3-030-44129-6_11

28. Vespignani, A., Caldarelli, G.: Large Scale Structure And Dynamics of Complex Networks: From Information Technology to Finance and Natural Science. World Scientific, Singapore (2007). ISBN 978-981-4475-41-9

29. Estrada, E.: The Structure of Complex Networks: Theory and Applications. OUP Oxford, Oxford (2012). ISBN 978-0-19-959175-6

30. Newman, M.: Networks. Oxford University Press, Oxford (2018). ISBN 978-0-19-252749-3

31. Wang, J., Mo, H., Wang, F.: Evolution of air transport network of China 1930–2012. J. Transp. Geogr. **40**, 145–158 (2014). https://doi.org/10.1016/j.jtrangeo.2014.02.002

32. Humphries, M.D., Gurney, K.: Network 'small-world-ness': a quantitative method for determining canonical network equivalence. PLoS ONE **3**, e0002051 (2008). https://doi.org/10. 1371/journal.pone.0002051

33. Wasserman, S., Faust, K.: Social Network Analysis: Methods and Applications. Cambridge University Press, Cambridge (1994). ISBN 978-0-521-38707-1

34. Barrat, A., Barthélemy, M., Vespignani, A.: Dynamical Processes on Complex Networks. Cambridge University Press, Cambridge (2008). ISBN 978-1-107-37742-4

35. Opsahl, T., Agneessens, F., Skvoretz, J.: Node centrality in weighted networks: generalizing degree and shortest paths. Soc. Netw. **32**, 245–251 (2010). https://doi.org/10.1016/j.socnet. 2010.03.006

36. Das, K., Samanta, S., Pal, M.: Study on centrality measures in social networks: a survey. Soc. Netw. Anal. Min. **8**, 13 (2018). https://doi.org/10.1007/s13278-018-0493-2

37. Kang, S.M.: Equicentrality and network centralization: a micro-macro linkage. Soc. Netw. **29**, 585–601 (2007). https://doi.org/10.1016/j.socnet.2007.07.004

38. TIOBE Index. https://www.tiobe.com/tiobe-index/. Accessed 20 Feb 2023

Business and Communication Technologies

Don't "Just Do It": On Strategically Creating Digital Ecosystems for Commodity Functionality

Helena H. Olsson[1](✉) and Jan Bosch[2]

[1] Malmö University, Malmö, Sweden
helena.holmstrom.olsson@mau.se
[2] Chalmers University of Technology, Gothenburg, Sweden
jan.bosch@chalmers.se

Abstract. For years, research on software ecosystems has focused on the many opportunities for stakeholders to engage in collaborative innovation and creation of new customer value. With a common platform as the basis, companies co-evolve capabilities around a shared set of technologies, knowledge, and skills, to develop new products and services that would have been difficult for the involved parties to realize internally. Previous studies present key elements for successful innovation ecosystems and strategies for when and how to align with external partners to accelerate innovation while maintaining competitive advantage. However, while research on innovation ecosystems is important for future value creation, research on ecosystems for managing commodity functionality is limited. Although commodity functionality constitutes a large part of existing systems, strategies for how to maintain, manage and evolve this type of functionality are often neglected and not paid as much attention. In this paper, and based on multi- case study research, we present a strategic framework that allows companies to systematically create a fully developed digital ecosystem around commodity functionality. The framework outlines a sequence of strategies starting from outsourcing and moving on to preferred supplier, supplier network and with the final stage being a fully developed ecosystem.

Keywords: Digitalization · digital transformation · software ecosystems · commodity functionality · strategic framework

1 Introduction

Digitalization and digital transformation are transforming businesses and ways-of-working across all industry domains. With enabling technologies such as software, data, and artificial intelligence, products and systems are rapidly being complemented with services and digital offerings that support, extend, and enhance existing functionality [1–4]. While this trend has an enormous impact on the technology and development side of companies, it has a potentially even bigger impact on the business side as it opens for entirely new models in which companies engage with each other and with customers. For more than a decade, research on software and business ecosystems has received increasing attention as what used to be viewed as relatively stable partnerships within an industry domain is now becoming increasingly dynamic. In the embedded systems domain, companies are experiencing a situation in which their well-established brands are being challenged, and disrupted, due to new entrants that fundamentally change conventional businesses. As an example, incumbents in the automotive industry are facing tremendous challenges with new entrants such as e.g., Tesla, as these organize around novel customer behaviors rather than the traditional notion of what constitutes a car. To keep up and stay on-par with new competitors, incumbent companies focus a lot of attention on innovation of new functionality. Similarly, research focuses its attention on the innovation ecosystem and the strategies that companies employ to engage in collaboration and innovation with external partners.

However, even if often neglected in research, commodity functionality constitutes the main part of an embedded system, and it keeps receiving most development resources. Typically, commodity is known as functionality that is critical for a system, but that is interchangeable with other goods. In telecom, an example would be the ability to make a call with your mobile phone. The functionality that allows the user to make a call is critical, but it is not the functionality that makes a user pick a certain mobile phone brand over another brand. There exist well-established strategies that companies use to reduce the cost of ownership for commodity functionality, e.g., [5–7]. The primary ones are to outsource development or to replace bespoke functionality developed in-house with externally developed commercial off-the-shelf (COTS) or open-source solutions. In situations where there is no external solution available, most companies resort to in-sourcing strategies to keep the functionality in-house, but transition development and maintenance of this functionality to more cost-efficient locations. Additional strategies exist and companies are using them, but in situations when the functionality doesn't need to be kept in-house and when there are no external commercial or open-source solutions available we still see companies that continue in-house development of functionality that would benefit from being transitioned to ecosystem partners. In our collaboration with industry partners, we note that there is the potential to create a digital ecosystem around commoditizing functionality, but that the companies lack strategic guidance for how to pursue this opportunity. In this paper, we present a systematic strategy framework that addresses this situation. Our intention is to add to the existing, and limited, research on commodity ecosystems and provide practitioners with support and guidance for how to reason about functionality that consumes significant development efforts but little return on investment.

The contribution of this paper is two-fold. First, we focus our research on the commodity ecosystem and we highlight the importance of strategically managing commodity functionality. Second, we provide a strategic framework that allows companies to systematically create a fully developed digital ecosystem around commodity functionality. The remainder of this paper is organized as follows. In the next section, we present background and related work. Section 3 discusses our research method and the case study companies. We present our findings in Sect. 4. In Sect. 5, we present a strategy framework for how to create a fully developed digital ecosystem. Finally, we discuss threats to validity in Sect. 6 and we share our conclusions and plans for future research in Sect. 7.

2 Background and Related Work

2.1 Software and Business Ecosystems

Digitalization is often viewed as the most impactful enabler for new business opportunities and for innovation. At the same time, it is causing disruption in industry after industry and companies struggle to survive and succeed in the digital transformation we experience. As described in [8], the competitive battleground for companies is rapidly shifting from focusing on internal scale, efficiency, quality, and serving customers in a one – to– one relationship, to orchestrating and contributing to an ecosystem of multiple players. Across industry domains, engaging with external partners is critical to scale, extend offerings, and increase value delivery to customers. In this transformation, companies engage in multiple ecosystems as their systems tend to involve functionality of different types, i.e., commodity functionality, differentiating functionality, and innovative functionality [9, 10]. Depending on the type of functionality, the engagement models and strategies companies use when engaging with ecosystem partners vary [11–14]. Although ecosystem engagements allow for more than collaborative innovation initiatives, this has so far been the primary focus of research and over the years, significant attention has been directed towards orchestration of innovation, strategies for collaboration, and open innovation. In particular, and as studied in [15], innovation requires an approach that extends beyond the traditional focus on internal value capture to instead focus on challenges that different actors, collaborators as well as competitors, need to overcome for open innovation initiatives to happen. In [11], ecosystem innovation is elaborated upon from an orchestration perspective. Also, there is rigorous research on engagement models for open innovation [15], use of open communities and customers for innovation purposes [16], and how innovation goes beyond the boundaries of the firm [17]. However, while innovation ecosystems are increasingly important for new value creation, commodity functionality often constitutes the main part of an embedded system. The typical definition of commodity is that it is a basic good that is interchangeable with other goods of the same type and hence, not what customers perceive as differentiating in terms of value. In our experience, the ability to decrease costs and efforts invested in commodity functionality by sourcing this functionality to external partners is critical. To achieve this, utilizing existing partners, or even creating an entirely new ecosystem around commodity functionality, are key for companies that seek to increase return on investment and shift resources from commodity to more value-adding activities. Still, research on commodity ecosystems is limited and there is little strategic guidance for how to strategically engage with external partners. In [18], the authors conclude that further research is needed concerning the strategic choices made by firms to engage with their ecosystems. Similarly, recent research recognizes the importance of strategic choices when existing technologies are commoditizing, and new technologies are introduced [19].

2.2 Management of Commodity Functionality

Although software ecosystems are continuously evolving, digitalization accelerates the pace of change with orders of magnitude. To respond to this, companies need to continuously engage with their ecosystem [20]. This involves managing the ambidexterity between maintaining the existing ecosystems and the current relationships to partners, while at the same time exploring and creating new ecosystems and new partner relationships. In [21], the authors recognize how "commodity eats innovation for breakfast" meaning that companies often fail in identifying what features are differentiating and what features are commodity and hence, non-value adding to customers. Consequently, many companies invest in development activities that do not deliver value and innovation initiatives are suppressed by commodity. Similarly, [22], highlight the risk of maintaining investment into what customers consider commodity. As a conceptual model for how to distinguish between commodity, differentiating and innovative functionality, [10] presents the 'Three Layer product Model' (3LPM). While this model was originally developed to help companies reduce architectural complexity and for distinguishing between different functionality layers, it is equally useful for distinguishing between the different ecosystems that companies operate in. The model outlines how functionality transitions from being innovative to becoming differentiating to, in the end, commoditize. In particular, the model recognizes a fundamental problem in that companies tend to treat the different layers of functionality as if they are equal and ignore the fact that each layer has its specific characteristics and hence, require different strategies. As a result, several problems occur, e.g., proprietary solutions are not replaced with other available solutions, commoditized functionality receives more development resources than it warrants, the percentage of development investment in differentiating functionality shrinks, and fewer development resources can be devoted to enhancing system competitiveness. In this paper, our intention is to add to the existing, and limited, research on commodity ecosystems and provide practitioners with support and guidance for how to reason about functionality that consumes significant development efforts but little return on investment.

3   Research Method

3.1   Case Study Research

The findings reported in this paper is part of a research collaboration between 17 companies in the embedded systems domain and five Swedish universities (www.software-cen ter.se). For more than a decade, we have had the privilege to engage with these companies in case study research [23] within the field of software engineering. The companies represent different domains, and they share the similar experiences of how digitalization and digital transformation is challenging their current practices and ways-of-working. Currently, all companies are exploring different strategies for how to engage with ecosystem partners as they face a situation in which their existing ecosystems, focusing on the physical products, are rapidly being complemented with new ecosystems focusing on digital technologies such as software, data, and artificial intelligence. As a common challenge, the companies experience difficulties in how to strategically manage commodity functionality to avoid investing in non-value adding development activities with limited, if any, return on investment. In this paper, we report on on-going research that was initiated in January 2022 in which we explore ecosystem engagement models in a selected set of the companies. The case companies were selected based on their on-going initiatives that were considered highly relevant, and representative, for the topic explored in this research. Also, the case companies showed a deep interest and willingness to engage in this research as they are eager to advance their skills and improve their understanding of how to strategically manage commodity and develop their ecosystem engagements. As can be seen in our previous work, we studied innovation ecosystem strategies [24], ecosystem challenges and strategies for mitigating these [9], ecosystem repositioning [20], and digital transformation and the effects on software-intensive embedded systems ecosystems [4, 19]. In this paper, we build on our previous experiences and complement these with recent empirical work. In alignment with our research interests, we adopted a qualitative research approach with multi-case study research as our method. Case study research is well-suited for research concerned with identifying patterns of action and for studying organizational contexts in which emphasis is put on stakeholder's perceptions and experiences [23].

3.2 Case Companies

As our empirical basis, we present a selected set of examples from the following case companies:

Case Company A: A company manufacturing trucks, buses, and construction equipment as well as a supplier of marine systems. The company has a broad network of Tier 1, Tier 2 and Tier 3 suppliers and are actively exploring new collaborations and partnerships also outside these ecosystems. Due to the disruptive forces of digital technologies, the automotive industry is experiencing rapid transformation of its core business and companies such as company A are facing a situation in which new entrants are forcing them to reinvent themselves and their ecosystem engagements.

Case Company B: A company manufacturing network cameras, access control, and network audio devices for the security and surveillance industries. The company has a broad network of distributors, resellers, system integrators, and customers and a partnership program that involves thousands of partners around the world. As part of the digital transformation, the company is expanding its business to increasingly include systems, solutions, and services offerings and with new technologies being a basis for these.

Case company C: A company developing pump units, circulator pumps, submersible pumps, and centrifugal pumps. With increasingly connected solutions, the company utilizes intelligence, cloud connectivity, and digital services to enable real-time monitoring, remote control, fault prediction, and system optimization of pumps and water technology. The current business ecosystem involves hundreds of partners who are carefully selected to support the digital transformation.

Case Company D: A manufacturing company focusing on technology and engineering within areas such as industry, infrastructure, transport, and healthcare. The company engages in multiple ecosystems due to its broad portfolio of products and has a large network of suppliers. The company has a set of platforms to which 3rd parties contribute and that allow for collaborative as well as competitive ecosystem engagement models.

Case Company E: A vehicle company manufacturing a broad variety of sports and utility vehicles. The company is one of many subsidiaries of its owner and operates within a large network of equipment manufacturers and suppliers at different levels. Due to the rapid changes in the industry, the company is facing a situation in which strategies for ecosystem engagements are critical. With regards to the suppliers to the company, these typically represent two very different worlds with hardware and mechanics being the focus of the traditional players while the new players are increasingly focused on software.

Case Company F: An engineering and technology company developing cutting edge software components and solutions in the areas of connectivity, security, mobility solutions and artificial intelligence. The company is one of the Tier 1 suppliers within the automotive industry with products such as e.g., powertrain solutions electrical drive, connected mobility, safety systems, and aftermarket products.

Case Company G: A networking and telecommunications company with a multi-national network of partners such as, e.g., operators, suppliers, vendors, and customers. Due to digitalization, the company is experiencing a big shift in the interactions with customers. While the operators are the strongest players in the business ecosystem, company G has a strong reputation in solving problems and the company is world-class when it comes to development, adoption, and diffusion of new technologies.

3.3   Data Collection and Analysis

Throughout this research, we engaged with company representatives from all case companies in workshop sessions and meetings. These were held either on-site at the companies or on-line and gave us the opportunity to meet, discuss, and learn from a variety of key stakeholders in teams involved in, and responsible for, product development, product maintenance, architecture, product sales and product management. In addition, we met with people in roles closely related to business strategy and development for whom ecosystem management is one of the key topics. Since January 2022, we organized a total of 10 on-site workshops (at company A, B, C, D and E), and 12 on-line workshops (with company A, B, C, D, E and F). Typically, the on-site workshop sessions lasted for 2–4 h and involved 4–8 people. The online workshop sessions were often shorter (30 min–1-h sessions) and an effective way to follow-up, share ideas and results and for monitoring progress. All workshop discussions were documented and, when possible, pictures were taken of whiteboard illustrations. In addition to the on-site and online workshops, we met with the case companies at two larger cross-company full-day events that were organized to report our preliminary findings and get company feedback. For data analysis, we adopted an interpretive approach [23, 25, 26]. As suggested by [26], we perceive the generalizations we make based on our case study findings as valuable for organizations that experience similar situations and challenges as the case companies involved in our research.

4   Empirical Findings

The companies involved in our research apply several different strategies for decreasing cost and reducing efforts spent on commodity functionality. Below, we present selected examples from the case companies involved in our study.

4.1 Case Examples: Telecom

In case company G, there is a well-established tradition of transitioning commoditizing functionality, or activities, to lower cost development sites. The company refers to this as 'rationalized in-sourcing' as the functionality is handed over to another location but still within the boundaries of the organization. For the company, this implies keeping control over functionality that is unique for them, and for which high quality is key, but for which they still need to reduce costs. In addition, it enables higher cost resources to be allocated to development of more differentiating and innovative functionality. However, and as mentioned by several key contacts at the company, in-sourcing is not always as cost-efficient as outsourcing which is another approach that the company frequently applies. As in many other companies, company G uses outsourcing for smaller and repetitive jobs in situations where quality control is considered legitimate to hand over to a carefully selected external part. For example, test activities that can be efficiently de-coupled from related development activities are a common subject for outsourcing as they are considered "commodity" in that they are often repetitive and relatively easy to hand over in situations where test cases are well-defined and limited in scope. Moreover, functions outside software development are often outsourced to gain competitive advantage by utilizing local competence in a certain geographical location. Yet another example, and a very common one, is outsourcing of all manufacturing of hardware to have internal resources focus on software and digital technologies as these are where opportunities for differentiation exist. By outsourcing manufacturing, company G can focus their efforts on novel and value-adding functionality, and this was mentioned as one of the key reasons and benefits in our interactions with the company. As outsourcing has become a frequently used strategy, it is supported by a sourcing organization that helps in establishing a one-to-one relationship with an external part.

4.2 Case Examples: Manufacturing

Case company C is an example of why suppliers seek to maximize their differentiation by becoming a preferred supplier, or the only supplier, of subsystems and components to their customers. As an example, company C engages as a preferred supplier relationship with company D in the areas of water and wastewater applications, industrial automation and building technology. In this relationship, company C provides domain expertise and know-how and as a customer, company D enjoys the opportunity to have someone else provide functionality that would be perceived as a cost internally and with little ROI even if critical for the system. For company D, the preferred supplier approach allows for a carefully selected, and limited, set of suppliers that provide functionality for e.g., optimization and integration of products and that ensure reliable deliveries that adhere to domain standards and the quality required for the system at hand. As an example, company C provide pumps in large-scale wastewater solutions developed by company D and in which the pump itself is only one of many components. In a preferred supplier model, it is interesting to note that the incentives and drivers are very different for the involved parties. For the customer side, i.e., company D in our example, a preferred supplier model lays the foundation for a supplier network and potentially even creation of an entirely new ecosystem. For the preferred supplier however, i.e., company C in our example, the desired state is to become exclusive in this relationship, i.e., become the only supplier.

4.3   Case Examples: Automotive

Supplier networks consisting of Tier 1, Tier 2 and Tier 3 suppliers are the typical engagement model in the automotive industry and if looking at case company A in our study this is indeed how it operates. The company is a strong player with ecosystems of partners for the different products and brands. Typically, there is a high involvement of system and module suppliers, and the company collaborates with a relatively stable set of suppliers for basic functionality. In most situations, there is a long-term agreement and a collaborative model where company A provides the functional interface that allow for partners to provide and integrate their components to the systems. For company A, the supplier know-how is critical for development and manufacturing of systems that include a large portion of commodity functionality but also an increasing amount of innovative functionality based on digital technologies. However, there are situations in which even strong and well-established companies fail in utilizing their suppliers in ways they wish for. In a workshop with a larger group of participants, one of the technology specialists described a situation in which they wished to transition the responsibility for development of one of their commodity components but where they failed in establishing an interest from suppliers in taking this on. The use case involved wind screen wipers as these are considered commodity functionality and something that company A wanted to let go of. The intention was to create a network of suppliers but when presenting this opportunity to potential suppliers there was nobody out there who was willing to provide the desired functionality. Hence, company A had no other solution than continue in-house development. In hindsight, the failure in creating a supplier network was because company A jumped a step too far when going for this strategy without first establishing a preferred partner relationship. Based on our experiences, a company looking to transition functionality has better chances to succeed if it starts by engaging with one or a few selected partners. In aiming for creating a supplier network as the first step company A could not build on, and benefit from, an already existing partnership for development of the wind screen wiper component. In addition to the case in company A, we have experiences from other companies in the automotive domain where we see similar supplier models. For example, company E is a manufacturer of a broad variety of sports and utility vehicles and one of many subsidiaries of its owner. The company operates within a large network of equipment manufacturers and suppliers providing the company with hardware and electronics as well as software components. In this network, suppliers such as company F engage by providing e.g., sensor technology and software, and there are numerous examples of software functionality where company F seeks to have many suppliers providing similar functionality as it brings the opportunity for the company to select the optimal solution and minimize total cost of ownership.

4.4   Case Examples: Security & Surveillance and Manufacturing

Case company B is an example of a company that has managed to position itself and create a new ecosystem within the larger Linux open-source community. The company started out using the sourcing approach to get their commoditizing functionality integrated into the Linux kernel and has, since many years, engaged very actively to build a reputation and strengthen its relationships within the Linux community. As one of the use cases, the company has managed to create an ecosystem around image processing functionality as this functionality is considered commodity and no longer the differentiator it used to be.

In company D, the creation of new ecosystems is currently a strategy primarily for engaging partners in offering new and innovative functionality. However, the company is actively looking into the opportunity to make use of existing platform infrastructures to create entirely new ecosystems with the intent to engage partners in development and maintenance of commodity functionality. As one example, the company have subsystems, e.g., in the areas of transportation and logistics, that are certified and where certification requirements are strict as well as very costly. Because of the high costs and strict requirements associated with certification, the available supplier network is highly limited and with low competition among suppliers. From the perspective of company D, the desired state would be to have a fully developed ecosystem, i.e., rich set of suppliers, to choose from to increase competition and reduce costs. As one of the tactics for achieving this, company D is exploring an approach where the company takes ownership of the certification of the functionality currently provided by suppliers. During our research, and when engaging with key stakeholders responsible for what is internally referred to as 'ecosystem marketplaces', we learnt that this strategy viewed as critical to reduce investments in commodity and that would yield higher return elsewhere.

5   Discussion

Below, we provide a strategic framework that allows companies to systematically create a fully developed digital ecosystem around commodity functionality. The framework outlines a sequence of strategies starting from outsourcing and moving on to preferred supplier, supplier network and with the final stage being a fully developed ecosystem. The framework is inductively derived from the case company examples with the intention to provide researchers and practitioners with support for how to reason about functionality that has stopped providing differentiation to customers but that is still critical for system performance and operation.

5.1   Ecosystem Strategy Framework

All case study companies experience the same pattern in that functionality that initially starts of as innovative and then becomes differentiating over time commoditizes. While this pattern was recognized already in our previous research [9], we notice that the time it takes for functionality to commoditize is rapidly decreasing. Commodity functionality is critical in that the product doesn't work without it, but as it doesn't provide a reason for customers to select the company's offering over those offered by competitors, it needs to be optimized for minimal total cost of ownership. To accomplish this, companies use several different approaches to engage with ecosystem partners in development and maintenance of this functionality. Based on our experiences in the case companies, we identify four strategies that companies engage in when developing an ecosystem for commodity functionality. These strategies are *outsourcing, preferred supplier, supplier network and a fully developed digital ecosystem*. Before detailing these strategies, it should be kept in mind that in situations where there is no external solution available, most companies resort to in-sourcing strategies to keep the functionality in-house, but transition development and maintenance of this functionality to more cost-efficient locations. When the functionality is so unique that there is no incentive for external parties to provide it, this may be the best solution. As another well-known strategy, companies often replace bespoke functionality developed internally with externally developed commercial off-the-shelf (COTS) functionality. Also, a common strategy is to leverage open-source communities and the solutions these provide. What we note in situations like this, i.e., when using COTS or open-source solutions, is that the component offered by external parties is seldom a perfect match and therefore, the company looking to replace bespoke functionality needs to engage and nudge the external provider or the open-source community towards the preferred solution. Additional strategies might exist, but in situations when the functionality doesn't need to be kept in-house and when there are no external commercial or open-source solutions available we still see companies that continue in-house development of functionality that would benefit from being transitioned to ecosystem partners. In such cases, we believe that the sequence of strategies we identify provide valuable insights in how to move towards a fully developed digital ecosystem in which suppliers compete to offer the optimal solution. It should be noted that the strategies build on each other as we see that companies need to move sequentially through these to successfully create a fully developed digital ecosystem around commodity.

- **Outsourcing:** As a first strategy, and based on the cases we studied, we see that a company looking to create a new ecosystem starts by engaging with one external partner in an outsourcing model. In such a model, you let go of functionality to have an ecosystem partner take full responsibility for it and the model is often used as a first step towards building a preferred supplier network. In an outsourcing model there is one selected partner, and as the company outsourcing functionality you keep a high level of control.
- **Preferred supplier:** As a second strategy, companies look to engage with more than one external partner to have a couple, or a few, preferred suppliers that offer the desired functionality. The preferred supplier strategy is a collaborative model in which there are multiple suppliers and even if the company creating the network sets the rules, the outcomes cannot be controlled in the same way as in a one-to-one outsourcing relationship. In the case examples we provide, we see that this is a commonly used strategy as it allows for companies to collaborate with a relatively stable set of suppliers for basic functionality.
- **Supplier network:** When having a preferred supplier model in place, the third step is to grow this into a supplier network in which there are multiple suppliers available and that a company can use. As in the preferred supplier model, this model offers less control of the outcomes but with the main advantage being that a network of carefully selected suppliers gives the company creating the network numerous options from which it can select the supplier and the functionality that best matches its preferences.

- **Fully developed digital ecosystem:** As the fourth and final stage, the fully developed digital ecosystem is a model in which external partners compete to offer something for the company creating the ecosystem, i.e., a model that is competitive between suppliers. While marketplace models and platforms are well-known as mechanisms for innovation, we see that they can be equally beneficial for reducing cost and ownership in commodity functionality by having external partners compete in offering the optimal and most cost-efficient solution for you. A fully developed digital ecosystem can be created based on the large supplier network that has been built and in which suppliers already engage to provide what is perceived as commodity by the customer side.

Our empirical data shows that the transition from the first to the final stage in the sequence is a transition that few companies accomplish but that if, and when, successful, provides a strong and solid basis for cost-effective management of commodity. It should also be noted that while certain functionality is perceived as commodity for one stakeholder it might constitute a business opportunity for someone else.

5.2 Ecosystem Forces

The continuous delivery of value that is nowadays expected by customers, is forcing a shift towards fully developed digital ecosystems as no company can afford in-house development and maintenance of commodity functionality. However, depending on the forces and the relative strengths of the different stakeholders in the ecosystem, there is not always the opportunity to successfully get to a fully developed digital ecosystem. In general, and as a reflection on the insights we got during this study, we see that there is a set of forces that will pull either towards the outsourcing stage or towards the fully developed digital ecosystem. As illustrated in the cases we present, the customer (buyer) side pulls towards the fully developed ecosystem stage as it looks to maximize choices, increase competition, and reduce total cost of ownership. The supplier (seller) side, however, pulls towards the outsourcing and supplier stages as it seeks to maintain exclusivity and the possibility of being "the only one". In our view, and based on the case company experiences, the more a company can change the balance of differentiation versus commodity in favor of itself, the better off it is. It should also be noted that although all companies aspire to be the "king of their own hill", most are operating as complementors in another company's ecosystem. Without having explored this in detail in this study, we believe that for any company, understanding the dynamics of the ecosystem will allow for a proactive approach and the opportunity to act before becoming a victim of external forces that are very difficult, if not impossible, to control. As discussed in this paper, reaching the ignition point in a fully developed digital ecosystem requires significant investment, a well-defined strategy and effective execution of that strategy. Succeeding in this involves additional dimensions than those described in this paper, but we believe that reducing investment in commodity is a prerequisite for any company interested in freeing up internal resources by effectively engaging with external partners.

6 Threats to Validity

As recognized by [27], the validity of a study implies the trustworthiness of the results, which is divided into four parts: construct, internal, external, and reliability. To address *construct validity*, we made sure to define and explain key concepts and terminology in the introduction of each workshop. To address *internal validity,* we made sure to examine the complexity of the studied phenomena and to engage with key stakeholders and experts who could provide a holistic understanding of interdependencies and relationships between actors, technologies, and businesses. To address *external validity*, we used our empirical cases to derive a conceptual framework with the intention to enable analytical generalization and value for cases that have common characteristics as the cases we studied. Finally, *reliability* is concerned with to what extent the data and the analysis are dependent on the specific researchers. To address this aspect, we applied established practices for data collection, analysis, and triangulation, we documented all discussions, and our results were reviewed by company representatives.

7 Conclusions and Future Work

Digitalization and digital transformation are transforming businesses and ways-of-working across all industry domains. To keep up and stay on-par with competitors, incumbent companies focus a lot of attention on innovation of new functionality and on engagement models that allow for innovation with existing and new partners in the ecosystem. Previous research focuses on the innovation ecosystem and the many strategies that companies employ to engage in collaboration with external partners. However, even if often neglected in research, commodity functionality constitutes the main part of an embedded system, and it keeps receiving most development resources. Our collaboration with industry partners shows that there are many situations where there is significant potential to create a digital ecosystem around commoditizing functionality, but companies lack strategic guidance for how to pursue this opportunity. In this paper, we present a systematic strategy framework that addresses this situation. Our intention is to add to the existing, and limited, research on commodity ecosystems and provide practitioners with support and guidance for how to reason about functionality that consumes significant development efforts but little return on investment. The framework outlines a sequence of strategies starting from outsourcing and moving on to preferred supplier, supplier network and with the final stage being a fully developed ecosystem. In future work, we aim to work with additional cases based on this framework with the intent of increasing its validity. In addition, our cases are concerned with companies that seek to outsource functionality and we aim to complement that with companies that act as suppliers to better understand their incentives.

Acknowledgements. This work was funded by Software Center, and we would like to thank all case companies involved in this research.

References

1. Matt, C., Hess, T.B.A.: Digital transformation strategies. Bus. Inf. Syst. Eng. **57**(5), 339–343 (2015)
2. Berman, S., Marshall, A.: The next digital transformation: from an individual-centered to an everyone-to-everyone economy. In: Strategic Leadership, pp. 9–17 (2014)
3. Sahu, N., Deng, H., Mollah, A.: Investigating the critical success factors of digital transformation for improving customer experience. In International Conference on Information Resources Management (CONF-IRM). Association for Information Systems (2018)
4. Bosch, J., Olsson, H.H.: Digital for real: a multi-case study on the digital transformation of companies in the embedded systems domain. J. Softw. Evol. Process. **33**(5), e2333 (2021)
5. Van der Linden, F., Lundell, B., Marttiin, P.: Commodification of industrial software: a case for open source. IEEE Softw. **26**(4), 77–83 (2009)
6. Di Giacomo, P.: COTS and open-source software components: are they really different on the battlefield? In: Proceedings of the 4th International Conference COTS Based Software Systems (ICCBSS), vol. 5, pp. 301–310 (2005)
7. Stol, K.J., Ali Babar, M.: Challenges in using open-source software in product development: a review of the literature. In: Proceedings of the 3rd International Workshop on Emerging Trends in Free/Libre/Open-Source Software Research and Development, pp. 17–22 (2010)
8. Bosch, J.: Speed, data, and ecosystems: the future of software engineering. IEEE Softw. **33**(1), 82–88 (2015)
9. Olsson, H.H., Bosch, J.: From ad hoc to strategic ecosystem management: the Three-Layer Ecosystem Strategy Model (TeLESM). J. Softw. Evol. Process. **29**(7), e1876 (2017)
10. Bosch, J.: Achieving simplicity with the three-layer product model. IEEE Comput. **46**(11), 34–39 (2013)
11. Still, K., Huhtamäki, J., Russell, M.G., Rubens, N.: Insights for orchestrating innovation ecosystems: the case of EIT ICT Labs and data-driven network visualizations. Int. J. Technol. Manag. **66**(2/3), 243–265 (2014)
12. Hanssen, G.K.: A longitudinal case study of an emerging software ecosystem: implications for practice and theory. J. Syst. Softw. **85**(7), 1455–1466 (2012)
13. Manikas, K., Hansen, K.M.: Software ecosystems: a systematic literature review. J. Syst. Softw. **86**, 1294–1306 (2013)
14. Ritala, P., Huizingh, E.: Business and network models for innovation: strategic logic and the role of network position. Int. J. Technol. Manag. **66**(2/3), 109–119 (2014)
15. Adner, R., Kapoor, R.: Value creation in innovation ecosystems: how the structure of technological interdependence affects firm performance in new technology generations. Strateg. Manag. J. **31**(3), 306–333 (2010)
16. Von Hippel, E.A.: Sources of innovation (1988)
17. Powell, W.W., Koput, K.W., Smith-Doerr, L.: Interorganizational collaboration and the locus of innovation: Networks of learning in biotechnology. Adm. Sci. Q. 116–145 (1996)
18. Bosch-Sijtsema, P.M., Bosch, J.: Plays nice with others? multiple ecosystems, various roles and divergent engagement models. Technol. Anal. Strateg. Manag. **27**(8), 960–974 (2015)
19. Olsson, H.H., Bosch, J.: Going digital: disruption and transformation in software-intensive embedded systems ecosystems. J. Softw. Evol. Process. **32**(6), e2249 (2020)
20. Bosch, J., Olsson, H.H.: Ecosystem traps and where to find them. J. Softw. Evol. Process. **30**(11), e1961 (2018)
21. Fabijan, A., Olsson, H.H., Bosch, J.: Commodity eats innovation for breakfast: a model for differentiating feature realization. In: Product-Focused Software Process Improvement: 17th International Conference, PROFES 2016, Trondheim, Norway, 22–24 November 2016, pp. 517–525 (2016)

22. Soltani, M., Knauss, E.: Challenges of requirements engineering in autosar ecosystems. In: The 23rd International Requirements Engineering Conference (RE), pp. 294–295 (2015)
23. Easterbrook, S., Singer, J., Storey, M-A., Damian, D.: Selecting empirical methods for software engineering research. In: Guide to Advanced Empirical Software Engineering, pp. 285–311. Springer, Heidelberg (2008). https://doi.org/10.1007/978-1-84800-044-5_11
24. Olsson, H.H., Bosch, J.: Collaborative innovation: a model for selecting the optimal ecosystem innovation strategy. In: Proceedings of the 42nd Euromicro Conference on Software Engineering and Advanced Applications (SEAA), pp. 206–213 (2016)
25. Maxwell, J.A.: Qualitative Research Design: An Interactive Approach. Sage publications, Thousands Oaks (2012)
26. Walsham, G.: Interpretive case studies in is research: nature and method. Eur. J. Inf. Syst. **4**(2), 74–81 (1995)
27. Runeson, P., Höst, M.: Guidelines for conducting and reporting case study research in software engineering. Empir. Softw. Eng. **14**(2), 131 (2009)

Enterprise Architecture as an Enabler for a Government Business Ecosystem: Experiences from Finland

Reetta Ghezzi[1(✉)], Taija Kolehmainen[1], Manu Setälä[2], and Tommi Mikkonen[1]

[1] University of Jyväskylä, Jyväskylä, Finland
{reetta.k.ghezzi,taija.s.kolehmainen,tommi.j.mikkonen}@jyu.fi
[2] Solita, Tampere, Finland
manu.setala@solita.fi

Abstract. Public sector procurement units in the field of ICT suffer from siloed, application-specific architectures, where each system operates in isolation from others. As a consequence, similar or even identical data is maintained in several different databases, hosted by different organizations. Such problems are caused by the lack of standard guidelines and practices that would result in interoperable systems, instead of overlapping ones. In the Finnish public sector, an enterprise architecture (EA) is a mandatory requirement, so that an ecosystem can be formed to overcome the above problems. However, the adoption rates are low, and the focus is often on technology rather than processes and practices. This study investigates the use of EA and its potential in Finnish procurement units through semi-structured interviews. Five procurement units and four vendors participated in the study, and altogether 12 interviews took place. As a result of the study, a practical implication is establishing decentralized project management practices in procurement units and enhancing leadership to establish a holistic EA. Furthermore, EA maturity evolution increases agility in the procurement unit.

Keywords: Public sector software · enterprise architecture · software procurement · business ecosystem · digital ecosystem · government business ecosystem

1 Introduction

Public organizations follow procurement directives when procuring goods and services, including software. The implementation of procurement directives can vary nationally, and there are no international standards for purchasing software for the public sector. However, most procurement directives aim at ensuring transparency, fairness, and cost-effectiveness in the procurement process. Procurement directive generally includes vendor selection requirements, contract negotiations, and software management. For the latter, enterprise architecture (EA) is a commonly used tool that defines guidelines for how the public organization in question

ⓒ The Author(s), under exclusive license to Springer Nature Switzerland AG 2024
R. Chbeir et al. (Eds.): MEDES 2023, CCIS 2022, pp. 219–233, 2024.
https://doi.org/10.1007/978-3-031-51643-6_16

operates and uses IT and data. These guidelines then form the basis for a business ecosystem that delivers services to the public organization.

Ecosystem development is one of the cross-cutting priorities for developing strategic and responsible procurement practices in Finland [19]. By establishing ecosystem thinking, public procurers can pool their resources, relate to innovations taking place in businesses, and maximize their market power and impact. A business ecosystem is a network of interdependent, loosely interconnected organizations, individuals, and other entities that co-create value [1,11], by, for example, distributing goods and services [23]. The business ecosystem concept encompasses the entities that make up a business environment, including suppliers, customers, competitors, regulators, and other stakeholders [11]. These ecosystem actors have a specific position in the ecosystem; they are linked to each other and undertake activities to create and capture value in the ecosystem [1]. Each component of a business ecosystem affects and is affected by the others, creating a complex web of dependencies [23]. For example, changes in one ecosystem component, such as introducing new software, may cause ripples throughout the entire ecosystem and lead to changes in other components. Hence, a business ecosystem can be seen as a symbiotic, living organism constantly evolving and adapting to changes in its environment in a robust manner [11,23]. By examining the relationships and interdependence within the ecosystem, organizations can identify opportunities to respond to challenges and boost their performance.

In this paper, we identify the existence of different ecosystems such as digital ecosystems [5], software ecosystems [12] and digital platform ecosystems [8]. We generally concentrate on government business ecosystems where actors interact and transact to co-create value in the context of public procurement. As a concrete contribution, we present a study that examines the state of EA in the Finnish public sector, and its ability to facilitate a government business ecosystem. In this study, twelve semi-structured interviews are performed with actors that participate in building public sector EA and have a holistic understanding of what could be done to evolve further.

The rest of this paper is structured as follows. In Sect. 2, we present the benefits of mature EA compared to what business ecosystem creation demands. In Sect. 3, the research approach is given, and the research method is described. In Sect. 4, we present our results. In Sect. 5, we discuss the results, and in Sect. 6, we draw some final conclusions.

2   Background and Motivation

Characteristics commonly associated with the software include ease of deployment, modifiability, and scalability. The same code can be used in different organizations and different applications. A well-designed approach allows data sharing between other software systems, for instance. Hence, there is no need to re-produce similar software as long as the software components used are generic and reusable instead of monolithic applications.

In Finland, a certain level of national EA is mandatory, but practical implementations by different actors vary. Fundamentally, with roots in the Open

Group Architecture (TOGAF) [6], recommendation JHS-179 [13] guides how to describe an organization's EA. Unfortunately, while TOGAF is the most widely used EA framework, it has not been thoroughly adopted. In addition, the seminal Zachman framework for enterprise architecture [36] is recognized as the foundation of all EA frameworks. This study understands that the Zachman framework is well suited to describe the enterprise architecture of complex and large organizations [36]. However, in the public sector context, the Zachman framework is unsuitable for procurement units with little or no IT skills, whereas IT procurement in Finland is commonly carried out by employees whose daily job does not include IT. To this end, we prefer an approach that is intuitively accessible and presents all the interconnections between different roles effortlessly.

Unfortunately, outside the IT domain, procurement unit stakeholder groups fail to adopt EA artifacts in practice [22,30]. Public sector software sustainability issues can be overcome with EA, where different services and vendors can quickly deploy and integrate into the ecosystem environment [31]. Moreover, research performed with 26 practitioners in public agencies reveals that ecosystem thinking in EA software is still missing in practice, even though it is necessary [22]. Furthermore, Nurmi et al. [22] state that public sector EA should utilize the capabilities of the organizations which participate in the ecosystem, develop solutions in co-creation, hold a holistic view over EA, and have need-based EA modeling to enhance ecosystem formation.

Unfortunately, these viewpoints do not reveal how the public sector and vendors position themselves in the public sector digital ecosystem. An ecosystem, where every piece gives something, may be achieved with services that interact via well-defined APIs but with no direct access to other services [31]. Techniques in the system need to support systematic and fast development and deployment [31]. Moreover, public sector software suffers from vendor lock-in, high maintenance costs, and time-consuming and error-prone public tendering. In addition, need-based user utilization, co-creation, holistic view, and organizational capabilities are essential building blocks for public EA [22]. Modular business units [31] [28] attached to the organization's core infrastructure help in this regard.

Improvements in IT efficiencies, such as standardized technology and technology management, lead to increased centralization in management [28]. The aim is to look forward to shared practices and infrastructure, reduce platforms, and raise cost-effectiveness. The organization's key benefits may require sacrificing some business unit needs [25,26,28]. Similar findings have been detected among Finnish municipalities. The comparison between the six largest cities in Finland showed that once IT governance becomes centralized and practices somewhat controlled, IT costs and personnel diminish by thirty percent [18].

As a part of digitization, fundamental organizational attitudes need reconsideration, in contrast to traditional processes. When a unit searches for new systems, the negotiating happens among accepted systems and platforms rather than defining a tailored solution and aiming for the best in the markets. Standardization brings new risks to management; the IT department must be on the nerve to monitor and upgrade the standards. Hence, the complexity of investment decisions rises. The top-management issues haunt hidden behind the problems mentioned above. If the EA lacks top-management sponsorship [9, 29, 30], it is demanding to receive the EA benefits such as cost reduction, IT standardization, process enhancement, and strategic differentiation [34]. The lacking leadership hinders EA process adoption. Furthermore, [30] recognize that EA practice demands specialized skills and capabilities to manage vast entities. The leader must have leadership and management skills and an understanding of the technical side of the entity. The following list summarises the benefits mature and well-managed EA for an organization:

- EA effectively manages IT assets and aligns IT investments and requirements in business [4, 15, 24, 25, 28].
- High maturity in EA is a prerequisite for agility in an organization [4, 28].
- Ea maturity development enhances the formation of modular business units, where unit managers regain their power by giving them a greater choice to design front-end interfaces [27].
- Modular business units enable selective standardization by module [27], and cost-effective IS replacements [31].
- IT [18, 27] and personnel costs diminish [18].
- Agility increases through EA, which builds on modular business unit information systems [31].

However, EA modeling seems insufficient in terms of digital ecosystem creation. Anwar and Gill [2] thoroughly analyzed the seven most common EA frameworks and discovered that the existing frameworks, such as TOGAF, provide tools to support the business and information layers, but not social and professional layers. In this research, we consider these layers to be of utmost significance. Moreover, it seems that existing frameworks could be combined to create a framework to offer a holistic view of EA in digital ecosystem creation [2].

Maneuvering complex ecosystem interdependencies demands organizations to move towards a more holistic and dynamic mindset, instead of concentrating on controlling the current resources [7]. The ecosystem approach introduces new requirements for structure and functions in value creation, in comparison to, e.g., networks, clusters, and innovation systems. However, understanding the complex ecosystem dynamics and system behavior is challenging [3, 7]. In this research, we concentrated on evaluating the following characterization of ecosystems:

- Scalability via, e.g., greater integrability and standardization [32].
- Adaptivity via, e.g., open and adaptive resource integration [32].
- Shared alignment via, e.g., mutual agreement and compatible incentives [1].
- Dynamic nature via, e.g., improved agility [7].
- Higher interoperability in terms of multilateral connections [1].
- Partnership via, e.g., fostering collaboration and flexibility in control over the ecosystem [11].
- Value co-creation via, e.g., innovation [11].
- Service digitization as it is indispensable for ecosystem creation [32].

Table 1. Interview participants.

Organization	Abreviation	Position	Field	Duration
Vendor 1	V1	Senior Principal	ICT	49
Vendor 2	V2A	Head of department	ICT	49
Vendor 2	V2B	Specialist	ICT/Procurement	49
Vendor 3	V3	Chief position	ICT	45
Vendor 4	V4	Vice President	ICT/Sales	56
Procurement unit 1	PU1	Chief position	ICT	47
Procurement unit 2	PU2A	Manager position	ICT	48
Procurement unit 2	PU2B	Senior Specialist	ICT	62
Procurement unit 3	PU3A	Head of procurement	Procurement	63
Procurement unit 3	PU3B	Manager position	ICT	49
Procurement unit 4	PU4	Chief position	ICT	58
Procurement unit 5	PU5	Manager position	ICT	56

We realize that the above-mentioned characterization is not comprehensive, and that it is collected to observe public sector EA and ecosystem initiatives. In this research, we aim at recognizing how the ecosystem-creation inhibitors such as silo structure and rigidness [32], lack of robustness [7], low need for central control [11], high control over ecosystem [11], and high dominance in value [32] present themselves in public sector EA and ecosystem initiatives.

3 Research Approach

Research Setup and Data Collection. The participants selected for the study all have experience in public procurement practices and enterprise architecture development in the public sector. The goal was to find which kinds of relationships exist in ICT procurement between procurement units and vendors and how public sector EA guides this process. In some cases, the chosen organizations cooperated with each other or had collaborated previously. The upcoming changes in Finnish public sector infrastructure guide us to examine the state of Finnish public sector EA. The research question we seek to answer is:

How does enterprise architecture support digital ecosystem development in the public sector?

Semi-structured interviews were performed between November 2021 and May 2022. The initial literature search and media attention on the Finnish public sector IS project failures [16,35] presented points to be considered themes in the interviews. These themes were ICT vision, public procurement, financials, IS life cycle, know-how, and commitment. The themes guided the discussions, but the participants were encouraged to contribute what they felt was important. The interview duration varied from 45 min to 63 min. Sometimes intriguing topics need to be discussed more thoroughly. The average time was 55 min. Table 1 presents the participant info.

Data Analysis. All the interviews were recorded and transcribed. The identification data and the repetitions or when the interviewee or interviewer searched for the words were removed. Coding took place in Atlas.ti software's cloud version. The approach was inductive, and the phenomena in the data had a guiding role. Hence, the initial coding and theme formation was data-driven, as well as intuitive and reactive [21], producing 99 initial codes, and 21 themes. Comparing the themes with literature, Ross et al. [28] four-stage EA maturity model began to make sense. This resulted in five themes; 1) information system procurement objectives, 2) procurement processes, 3) responsibilities and control, 4) perceptions of the legislative environment, and 5) EA solutions. These themes formulated bundles between the initial themes and codes, and Ross' [27] stages helped to understand the differences between the organizations.

However, some phenomena did not directly link to the Ross' [27] model. For these cases, the ecosystem literature revealed the next steps. To gain a more systematic and structured understanding of the public sector and vendors' position in ecosystems that take place in the context of public procurement, we used a domain-specific modeling language called Ecosystem Governance Compass [33] to model the ecosystem components, interactions, and dependencies. The language concepts were derived from literature and based on a holistic, dynamic system-based view of collaborative ecosystems [17]. The language objects were divided into four categories representing different aspects of ecosystem governance: governance, business, technology, and legal and regulatory context. Ecosystem Governance Compass announced places where the EA approach failed to interpret the results, which led to the creation of five additional themes: 6) higher sustainability components, 7) value co-creation, 8) shared objectives, 9) dynamic nature, and 10) holistic view. These ten themes revealed this research's key findings, where the EA and public sector procedures inhibit or facilitate sustainable ecosystem formation.

4   Results

Participants are presented with acronyms to introduce our results, where procurement units are PU1, PU2, PU3, PU4, and PU5. Vendors are V1, V2, V3, and V4. To make a difference between multiple participants from one organization, they are presented with letters A and B, for example, V2A and PU2A.

4.1   Government Business Ecosystem Inhibitors

Most Commonly Used Opportunities in Public Procurement Guide Towards a Stiff Waterfall-Like Development Model. In this study, public agencies use open, restricted, and competitive negotiated procedures in ICT procurement. Open and restricted procedures are the most common ICT procurement procedures in Finland [10]. The competitive negotiated procedure leads to better IS procurement outcomes. In other public procurement procedures, the procurement unit must know precisely what they want and need before the tendering. Furthermore, negotiated procedures without tender hand-in-hand in-house procurement are considered emergency solutions (Table 2).

Table 2. Government business ecosystem formation inhibitors.

Characteristic	Ecosystem Related Characteristic
Most commonly used opportunities in public procurement guide towards a rigid waterfall-like development model.	Inhibitor for dynamic nature
Actors have no shared alignment	Inhibitor for shared goal and objectives creation
Immature EA and lack of control dynamic control	Missing collaboration and
Silo structure	Inhibitor for dynamic, adaptive nature
Vendor lock-in	Inhibitor for dynamic, adaptive nature
Budgeting IT expenses to the procurement units, the IT department	Inhibitor for holistic view

Actors have No Shared Alignment. Sometimes the actors miss mutual agreement on goals, or their incentives are incompatible. The procurement unit is searching for solutions to fulfill legislative tasks. Vendors are looking for new business opportunities, sales, and good word-of-mouth. PU1 and PU2 understand that interviewing the vendors is essential to know whether the common ground exists, whether the vendor is ambitious to engage in the development process, and whether the view over the issues is holistic. Besides monetary motives to engage in an ecosystem, the incentives should be something else too. However, these incentives are not easily detected in public organizations. Ideally, suppose the consortium of vendors builds the product (identification from one, databases from the other, operational control from the third). In that case, genuine cooperation is created to solve the problem of the procurement unit. Procurement units agree that the procurement act sets challenges to forming the above-mentioned coalitions. Tendering is error-prone, time-consuming, and difficult to predict outcomes. Therefore developing a genuine ecosystem-like and sustainable consortium is demanding, if not nearly impossible. Finally, tailored versus ready-made systems seems to divide opinions among vendors and procurement units. PU1, PU2, and PU3 recon that evaluating the purposefulness of the old processes and ways to work is vital when acquiring new systems to determine if something can be done more efficiently.

Immature EA and Lack of Control, Silo Structure and Vendor Lock-in. The governance of the public organization has a significant role in committing to the EA decisions. However, some of the interviews reveal that, in many cases, public organizations have immature enterprise architectures and inadequate leadership behind them. Public organizations that lack firm leadership to support EA initiatives tend to have a silo structure, where the procurement unit has lots of freedom to tailor solutions that fit one procurement unit. In these cases, the IT department remains in the dark about decision-making and purchasing. Furthermore, these organizations do not have EA units to cross-check the information system's interoperability and compatibility with the existing EA. PU3 has developed its practices and has an EA unit to cross-check the projects, IS, and budget. However, the leadership to put holistic EA thinking into practice is missing. PU3A depicts that every procurement unit leader needs to consider EA in mind, which is troublesome, and the actors are not coordinated optimally. Hence, when the procurement unit purchases a system where compatibility with existing EA is not investigated, problems arise, such as silo architecture [32], vendor lock-in, data integrity, data management, and additional development hours leading to exceeding original budgets, to name a few common ones.

To overcome the data integrity problem, PU3 has determined master systems where the data can be edited. PU3 and PU4 have introduced an incentive to get rid of the solutions that are tailored to one unit, but only those information system purchases that exceed the national thresholds proceed to the EA unit's or project portfolio management's evaluation. In PU5, those information system projects that exceed national thresholds also demand upper-level decision-making. However, no one evaluates the new demand against the existing EA, which has caused a challenging situation in PU5. To this end, PU5 depicts in the interview that:

"We have 1400 information systems."

Without established coherent EA practices, procurement units seem to create disposable EA for IS procurement. In PU5, even that failed. The acquired system in PU5 enables structured documentation and is used throughout the organization and in similar organizations in the area. However, PU5 has encountered difficulties in it:

"Two things where it fails; in the tendering phase, the organization's EA and the system's architecture were not evaluated, how they would fit. The second thing is leadership. In large entities, such as this system, the discipline should be in place to guide the development."

PU4 describes that sometimes the IT department receives the information from the purchase afterward, even if the organization has set processes to inform the IT department on all IS-related purchases. PU4 does not have decentralized project management practices. Before the purchase, necessarily no-one maps out the budget and personnel resources. Even if the chain of command is not explicitly drafted, the actual purchasing is standardized in all public organizations. In this research, all public organizations have procurement teams or units, where experts help to prepare the procurement and are responsible for the tendering phase. The procurement units provide well-prepared procurement practices and tenders. The incentives are to avoid legal issues – especially the market court – and to offer vendors equal, non-discriminating tendering processes.

Vendors depict that resources in public organizations may limit which kind of systems are acquired. Smaller public organizations may not have the resources to go through the heavy public procurement in personnel, competence, and funding. The technology seems to be very flexible, and public organizations can get anything they wish for. V1 expresses concerns when the procurement unit outsources requirement analysis solely to the consultant. The vendor may help the procurement unit with technical requirement analysis, but the needs should emerge from procurement unit functions and objectives. Therefore, V1 is concerned when the procurement unit starts the procurement process with requirement definition before the public procurement. It seems to waste resources, especially in cases when the system itself already exists in the market, but the public sector is not aware of it. In this situation, vendors would only need public organization guidance to understand what exists in their technical field already to avoid going to the path of tailored systems. Hence lack of knowledge of the existing technical field, in terms of compatibility and interoperability, guides vendors to produce tailored solutions if the EA is drafted only for the acquisition in hand. These characteristics describe the inefficient scalability adaptivity in an organization [22,30,32]. In addition, the environment is rigid and lacks robustness.

Budgeting IT Expenses to the Procurement Units Rather than to the IT Department. Budgeting practices may inhibit coherent EA formation and enhance silo structure. Some public organizations distribute the expenses when the procurement unit administers the funds between its functions. It appears that this is not a viable solution and results in overlapping tasks and IS systems in the organization. There is a low need for interdependent relationships and centralization, which inhibit ecosystem creation [11]. Furthermore, it seems unthinkable that units which do not hold the competence to evaluate IS-related needs are responsible for IS budget and have the freedom to acquire whatever is wanted under the national threshold. This is the situation in PU3, PU4, and PU5; procurement units control the budget. These units suffer from vendor lock-in and have excessively locally tailored systems.

All procurement units have legislative tasks that guide service production in society. In Finland, norms such as the public procurement act and procurement directive obligate seeking the most advantageous offer through public procurement. Evaluating the most advantageous offer appear to cause issues for the procurement units. The narrative is apparent between the "old" way of evaluating the most advantageous offer and the "new" way.

PU3 is incentivized to evaluate the cost and quality of the business operations against the receivable benefits. However, the solutions are not assessed holistically against the EA, and EA is not managed top-down. In addition, different unit leaders are supposed to have a clear understanding of the EA. PU3A sees this as a problem. Some units have a clear picture, others do not, and the top management does not rule or guide them to acquire solutions that serve the whole organization. In PU4 and PU5, the current business objectives are towards reduced IT costs.

4.2   Government Business Ecosystem Facilitators

Mature EA and Sufficient Control. Sufficient control enables EA practices throughout the organization. Moreover, research by Nurmi et al. [22] states that EA modeling should be need-based. In this research, PU1 and PU2 have

Table 3. Government business ecosystem formation facilitators.

Characteristic	Ecosystem Related Characteristic
Mature EA and sufficient control	Facilitator for dynamic and adaptive nature
Shared ambition to improve practices between the public organization and vendor	Facilitator for shared goals and objectives
Budgeting IS expenses to IT department	Facilitator for holistic view
Cooperation with universities	Interdependencies between stakeholders, Value co-creation and innovation creation

top-down support for EA endeavors, which allows a coherent EA landscape. In PU1 and PU2, procurement units cannot purchase anything that suits only one unit's purposes. Hence, these two viewpoints, need-based EA modeling and top-down support, seem to coexist nicely in PU1 and PU2. In these units, operations guide the needs, and the best practices to execute the solutions are holistically evaluated against EA. PU1 and PU2 seek efficient, predictable, and interoperable systems for their EAs. In addition, the procurement units that have top-down determined EA seem to have more uniform purchasing practices. PU1 aims to purchase systems as a service solution (SaaS) to the cloud rather than tailored software. PU1 depicts that they do not have even one developer in the agency and purchase all the software. PU1 has diminished the number of vendors significantly. At first, PU1 had nearly 100 vendors executing the information systems. Furthermore, many of the solutions had a price tag of just under 60 000€, which is the threshold that demands procurement. PU1 representative thinks these solutions were the result of unplanned spending and panic. In recent history, PU1 has then overcome technology standardization which diminished the number of vendors. PU1 has customized software besides the ready-made solutions, aiming to purchase reusable platforms with modifiable user interfaces. It enables PU1 to have standardized technology and keep the core optimized. PU1 shows minimal data and software duplicity, and the systems interoperate. PU4 depicts that the old ridged systems are replaced gradually with new systems, which creates the grounds for developing data management practices. Here, technology-enabled change is a stepping stone toward standardized technology.

Shared Ambition to Improve Practices and Make the Change Between the Public Organization and Vendor. V4 has plans to scale the most popular product to the markets in a plug-and-play sort of system because market research shows that it is what procurement units want. V1 is interested in producing better systems that interoperate with local systems, enable standardized working environment units across Finland, and improve working habits. V1 depicts that it is not always easy to measure quality-related improvements, which may not manifest immediately but with time.

Budgeting IS Expenses to the IT Department. As mentioned earlier, budgeting practices may inhibit or facilitate ecosystem creation. PU1 and PU2 have centralized IS finance management. The procurement units do not control the IS budget. PU3 is transitioning to centralized IS budget management and revising IS budget management responsibilities as the old IS contracts change to new ones. In PU1 and PU2, the IT department is the financial gatekeeper and the buyer. If the system wished for is suitable with EA and otherwise advantageous, it proceeds to public procurement. This applies similarly to the IS under the national threshold, even if public procurement is unnecessary. This means, for example, hardware or services under €60k. Public organizations which realize the benefits of centralizing some functions selectively, also understand that the cost at procurement may be an insufficient metric to evaluate the value generated with EA compatibility, planned lifespan expectancy, improved workflows, and knowledge management. PU1 depicts that sometimes the legislative tasks are mandatory but lack business cases. Here, the benefits cannot be measured directly with a cost-benefit analysis. Therefore, during ICT procurement, efficiency might seem ostensible, and the benefits may generate over time indirect ways. PU1 and PU2 determined that whatever is purchased needs to be evaluated and considered throughout. For example, PU2 depicts that a potential vendor lock-in does not matter, if it fits EA and is the best option available to solve the problem organization-wide. In these units, the benefit evaluation reaches from monetary evaluation to non-monetary assessment of the functions.

Cooperation with Universities . Procurement units work with universities in research and development projects. PU3 depicts that the procurement unit may receive something that does not exist yet through these projects. For universities, cooperation offers real-world situations and problems to solve for students. PU3 depicts that:

> *"It was calculated that if one person does the recording work, it will take 5 years. Now we are collaborating with the university to develop a robot and artificial intelligence that can read, interpret and retrieve the right things from the drawings of the built environment and convert them into electronic form."*

Furthermore, collaboration with universities seems to enhance innovation. This facilitates co-evolving capabilities with actors [20] and hence, contribute interdependencies and enhance value co-creation in the ecosystem [22].

5 Discussion

In this work, we used Ecosystem Governance Compass to detect the government business ecosystem facilitators and inhibitors. As the result, we found out that ecosystem thinking is mostly missing from public sector EA and purchasing practices. In general, public sector software sustainability seems questionable, since the actors do not have compatible incentives for building up collaboration. In contrast, some public organizations have high-expertise units that form a genuine collaborative web, where every unit works towards similar goals, for example, coherent and efficient EA. However, in some public organizations, the shared goals are not identified [1], and working toward them systematically is missing. Public organizations that have identified the goals can develop solutions in co-creation with different units and vendors, which Nurmi et al. [22] have recognized as vital for public organizations to enable the formation of the digital ecosystem.

Holistic EA, controlled purchasing, and developing systems iteratively with vendors are signs of adaptivity in this research [32]. To consider government business ecosystem formation, we realized that when the procurement units consider the procurement act to offer possibilities in the competitive dialogue and innovation partnership opportunities, these organizations could also selectively standardize [27] and scale solutions from across the organization [32].

The government business ecosystem helps to form a holistic view of EA for purchasing and budgeting, creating possibilities to scale solutions, and aiding co-creation and innovation within the ecosystem. Satisfaction towards management increases as the EA maturity evolves. Risk management, IT development time, and strategic business impacts improve, similar to the EA maturity benefits found by Ross [27]. The organization becomes dynamic. Furthermore, procurement units that have created precise and disciplined EA practices do not waste resources in information system procurement by creating disposable EA.

In contrast, procurement units that struggle to establish EA also struggle to form a government business ecosystem. These organizations have silo structures [32], where different procurement units can determine which solutions to acquire, and the control is insufficient. Vendor lock-in exists in many places, and public procurement is often seen as a risk of receiving a solution that does not comply with the needs. Furthermore, units with silo structures are missing holistic comprehension of the IT landscape in the organization. The budgeting supports this. The procurement units control the budget, including IS-related purchases, which leads to a situation where the shared incentive to build holistic EA is missing. In this case, the procurement unit purchases and solves problems that concern only one unit.

Exploring EAs in procurement units reveal that the EA initiatives exist in all participating procurement units, even if they might not be visible in practice. In theory, they exist. Some of the results are similar to Seppänen et al. [30], and Nurmi et al. [22], who discovered low EA adoption rates in Finnish public sector EA. In this study, procurement units with disciplined decision-making practices are higher in EA maturity. The leadership shows throughout the organization, and the strategy exploits the EA practices and purchases.

The changes are slow in public sector. Hence, to overcome and dissolve the challenges such as silo structure and vendor lock-in, we trust that the EA approach combined with the ecosystem mindset could help the public organizations to gain a more holistic view of their functions. In particular, modeling tools such as Ecosystem Governance Compass provide an excellent way of describing the formation of a holistic relationship-based ecosystem. Furthermore, Nurmi et al.

[22] suggest a centralized EA repository that would update in real-time. This could help national efforts to create a single, interoperable EA.

Threats to Validity. The research method, semi-structured interviews, allowed the interviewees to depict what was relevant to them. However, this might be a weakness as well [21], as the data set was large. Luckily, we had expertise from the University of Jyväskylä to contribute to Ecosystem Governance Compass, which helped us to combine complex phenomena in EA and government business ecosystem creation. The data collection and analysis follow Myers [21] semi-structured interviews and thematic analysis guidelines. Data is collected and analyzed iterative way and rigorously, which makes the study's reliability high. However, the researcher's interpretation may have affected the results because the initial coding was intuitive and interpretive. Myers [21] depicts that inner validity could be improved with triangulation or multiple researcher evaluation. In this research, the authors collaborated to analyze and discuss the categorizations of the codes. The results describe facilitators and inhibitors for the government business ecosystem. Interestingly, the results suggest that EA development in public organizations is at very different stages, which may affect the generalisability of the results. In this study, we do not distinguish EA maturity levels in public organizations.

6 Conclusion

In this study, we have analyzed if EA acts as an enabler for a government business system in Finland. As a tool for analysis, we used Ecosystem Governance Compass to recognize factors that either facilitate or inhibit government business ecosystem creation. As a result, the facilitators are mature EA and sufficient control, shared ambitions, centralized IS budgeting, and cooperation with universities. The inhibitors are the insufficient choice of procurement opportunity, not sharing goals and understanding, immature EA and lack of control, and lack of selective centralization in IS budgeting. The leadership and top-down support for EA practices are highlighted – the more mature the EA, the firmer leadership and top-down support. Furthermore, all procurement units in this study have adopted one EA section, standardized purchasing, and use a multi-talented procurement unit or team which prepares the call for tender. However, a hinder to agility lies in the practice before the procurement proposal reaches procurement personnel. Higher EA maturity procurement units have decentralized project management, which is missing from the lower EA maturity procurement units.

In conclusion, future EA frameworks and practices seem to lean on modular business units in an ecosystemic environment. However, the changes are difficult to implement nationally because each organization acquires services only for itself. However, modeling can imitate the chosen standards, and, with approaches such as openEHR [14], may be practical to combine accurate modeling and serving user needs in detail. However, more research is needed, because such modeling has scarce scientific literature and empirical results.

References

1. Adner, R.: Ecosystem as structure: an actionable construct for strategy. J. Manag. **43**(1), 39–58 (2017)
2. Anwar, M.J., Gill, A.Q.: A review of the seven modelling approaches for digital ecosystem architecture. 2019 IEEE 21st Conference on Business Informatics (CBI) (2019). https://doi.org/10.1109/cbi.2019.00018
3. Basole, R.C., Russell, M.G., Huhtamäki, J., Rubens, N., Still, K., Park, H.: Understanding business ecosystem dynamics: a data-driven approach. ACM Trans. Manag. Inf. Syst. (TMIS) **6**(2), 1–32 (2015)
4. Bradley, R., Pratt, R., Byrd, T., Simmons, L.: The role of enterprise architecture in the quest for it value. MIS Q. Execut. **10**(2), 73–80 (2011). https://aisel.aisnet.org/misqe/vol10/iss2/5/
5. Briscoe, G., De Wilde, P.: Digital ecosystems: evolving service-orientated architectures. In: Proceedings of the 1st International Conference on Bio Inspired Models of Network, Information and Computing Systems, pp. 17-es (2006)
6. Cameron, B., McMillan, E.: Analyzing the current trends in enterprise architecture frameworks. J. Enterp. Arch. **9**(1), 60–71 (2013). https://eapad.dk/wp-content/uploads/2014/11/2012-4.pdfpage=60
7. Dattée, B., Alexy, O., Autio, E.: Maneuvering in poor visibility: how firms play the ecosystem game when uncertainty is high. Acad. Manag. J. **61**(2), 466–498 (2018)
8. Hein, A., et al.: Digital platform ecosystems. Electron. Mark. **30**, 87–98 (2020)
9. Hjort-Madsen, K.: Enterprise architecture implementation and management: a case study on interoperability (2006). https://doi.org/10.1109/HICSS.2006.154
10. Holma, A.M., Vesalainen, J., Söderman, A., Sammalmaa, J.: Service specification in pre-tender phase of public procurement - a triadic model of meaningful involvement. J. Purchasing Supply Manag. **26**(1), 100580 (2020). https://doi.org/10.1016/j.pursup.2019.100580
11. Iansiti, M., Levien, R.: Strategy as ecology. Harv. Bus. Rev. **82**(3), 68–78 (2004)
12. Jansen, S., Cusumano, M.: Defining software ecosystems: a survey of software platforms and business network governance (2013). https://ceur-ws.org/Vol-879/paper4.pdf
13. JHS179: JHS 179 Kokonaisarkkitehtuurin suunnittelu ja kehittäminen. In Finnish. (2017). https://www.suomidigi.fi/ohjeet-ja-tuki/jhs-suositukset/jhs-179-kokonaisarkkitehtuurin-suunnittelu-ja-kehittaminen
14. Kalra, D., Beale, T., Heard, S.: The openehr foundation. Stud. Health Technol. Inf. **115**, 153–173 (2005)
15. Kearns, G., Lederer, A.: A resource-based view of strategic it alignment: how knowledge sharing creates competitive advantage. Decis. Sci. **34**(1), 1–29 (2003). https://doi.org/10.1111/1540-5915.02289
16. Kolehmainen, A.: CSC kilpailutti IT-konsultit – tässä ovat 35 miljoonan diilin neljä voittajaa. In Finnish (2022). https://www.tivi.fi/uutiset/csc-kilpailutti-it-konsultit-tassa-ovat-35-miljoonan-diilin-nelja-voittajaa/80c48dd6-d874-4e93-ae50-f0e4712974b0
17. Laatikainen, G., Li, M., Abrahamsson, P.: Blockchain governance: a dynamic view. In: Wang, X., Martini, A., Nguyen-Duc, A., Stray, V. (eds.) ICSOB 2021. LNBIP, vol. 434, pp. 66–80. Springer, Cham (2021). https://doi.org/10.1007/978-3-030-91983-2_6
18. Louhelainen, K.: Espoon tietohallinto mietittävä uusiksi - mistä sinä säästäisit 25 miljoonaa? In Finnish (2013). https://kirsilouhelainen.fi/2013/12/04/espoon-tietohallinto-mietittava-uusiksi/

19. Ministry of Economic Affairs and Employment: Network-based competence centre for sustainable and innovative public procurement (KEINO). Ministry of Economic Affairs and Employment, Finland. https://tem.fi/en/keino-en
20. Moore, J.F.: Predators and prey: a new ecology of competition. Harv. Bus. Rev. **71**(3), 75–86 (1993)
21. Myers, M.: Qualitative research in business and management (2020)
22. Nurmi, J., Penttinen, K., Seppänen, V.: Towards ecosystemic stance in finnish public sector enterprise architecture. In: Pańkowska, M., Sandkuhl, K. (eds.) BIR 2019. LNBIP, vol. 365, pp. 89–103. Springer, Cham (2019). https://doi.org/10.1007/978-3-030-31143-8_7
23. Peltoniemi, M., Vuori, E.: Business ecosystem as the new approach to complex adaptive business environments (2004)
24. Pour, M., Fallah, M.: How enterprise architecture influences strategic alignment maturity: structural equation modelling. Int. J. Bus. Excell. **17**(2), 189–209 (2019). https://doi.org/10.1504/IJBEX.2019.097543
25. Rakgoale, M., Mentz, J.: Proposing a measurement model to determine enterprise architecture success as a feasible mechanism to align business and IT (2016). https://doi.org/10.1109/ES.2015.29
26. Ross, J.W.: Creating a strategic it architecture competency: learning in stages (2003). https://doi.org/10.2139/ssrn.416180
27. Ross, J.W.: Enterprise architecture: driving business benefits from IT. SSRN Electron. J. (2006). https://doi.org/10.2139/ssrn.920666
28. Ross, J.W., Weill, P., Robertson, D.C.: Enterprise architecture as strategy - creating a foundation for business execution (2006). https://doi.org/10.4018/978-1-4666-0146-8.ch038
29. Seppänen, V., Heikkilä, J., Liimatainen, K.: Key issues in EA-implementation: case study of two Finnish government agencies (2009). https://doi.org/10.1109/CEC.2009.70
30. Seppänen, V., Penttinen, K., Pulkkinen, M.: Key issues in enterprise architecture adoption in the public sector. Electron. J. e-gov. **16**(1), 46–58 (2018). https://academic-publishing.org/index.php/ejeg/article/view/650/613
31. Setälä, M., Abrahamsson, P., Mikkonen, T.: Elements of sustainability for public sector software – mosaic enterprise architecture, macroservices, and low-code. In: Wang, X., Martini, A., Nguyen-Duc, A., Stray, V. (eds.) ICSOB 2021. LNBIP, vol. 434, pp. 3–9. Springer, Cham (2021). https://doi.org/10.1007/978-3-030-91983-2_1
32. Sklyar, A., Kowalkowski, C., Tronvoll, B., Sörhammar, D.: Organizing for digital servitization: a service ecosystem perspective. J. Bus. Res. **104**, 450–460 (2019)
33. Sroor, M., Hickman, N., Kolehmainen, T., Laatikainen, G., Abrahamsson, P.: How modeling helps in developing self-sovereign identity governance framework: An experience report. Procedia Comput. Sci. **204**, 267–277 (2022)
34. Syynimaa, N.: Method and practical guidelines for overcoming enterprise architecture adoption challenges. In: Hammoudi, S., Maciaszek, L.A., Missikoff, M.M., Camp, O., Cordeiro, J. (eds.) ICEIS 2016. LNBIP, vol. 291, pp. 488–514. Springer, Cham (2017). https://doi.org/10.1007/978-3-319-62386-3_22
35. Tivi: Poliisi kilpailuttaa IT-järjestelmän hankinnan jo kolmannen kerran - mitä projektille kuuluu nyt? In Finnish (2020). https://www.tivi.fi/uutiset/poliisi-kilpailuttaa-it-jarjestelman-hankinnan-jo-kolmannen-kerran-mita-projektille-kuuluu-nyt/9f32837e-25e2-42aa-b559-f9a038a90db5
36. Zachman, J.A.: A framework for information systems architecture. IBM Syst. J. **26**(3), 276–292 (1987). https://doi.org/10.1147/sj.263.0276

Digital Twin and Security

Lightweight Behavior-Based Malware Detection

Marco Anisetti(iD), Claudio A. Ardagna(iD), Nicola Bena(iD),
Vincenzo Giandomenico(iD), and Gabriele Gianini(✉)(iD)

Department of Computer Science, Universita degli Studi di Milano, Milan, Italy
{marco.anisetti,claudio.ardagna,nicola.bena,gabriele.gianini}@unimi.it,
vincenzo.giandomenico@studenti.unimi.it

Abstract. Modern malware detection tools rely on special permissions to collect data that can reveal the presence of suspicious software within a machine. Typical data that they collect for this task are the set of system calls, the content of network traffic, file system changes, and API calls. However, giving access to these data to an externally created program means granting the company that created that software complete control over the host machine. This is undesirable for many reasons. In this work, we propose an alternative approach for this task, which relies on easily accessible data, information about system performances (CPU, RAM, disk, and network usage), and does not need high-level permissions to be collected. To investigate the effectiveness of this approach, we collected these data in the form of a multivalued time series and ran a number of malware programs in a suitably devised sandbox. Then – to address the fact that deep learning models need large training sets – we augmented the dataset using a deep learning generative model (a Generative Adversarial Network). Finally, we trained an LSTM (Long Short Term Memory) network to capture the malware behavioral patterns. Our investigation found that this approach, based on easy-to-collect information, is very effective (we achieved 0.99 accuracy), despite the fact that the data used for training the detector are substantially different from the ones specifically targeted for this purpose. The real and synthetic datasets, as well as corresponding source code, are publicly available.

Keywords: Malware detection · behavior analysis · LSTM · GAN

1 Introduction

Malware, that is, malicious software, is nowadays one of the most common vectors of cyberattacks. It was traditionally considered a problem only for companies; however, in 2017 the situation changed when the ransomware *Wanna-Cry* diffused and infected even hospitals and simple users. Today, malware still represents the main threat [9], with ransoms skyrocketing to 50 M$ and single malware infections costing up to 1M$ per incident [20]. Consequently, the fight between researchers, who try to implement new approaches for detecting malware in the

R. Chbeir et al. (Eds.): MEDES 2023, CCIS 2022, pp. 237–250, 2024.
https://doi.org/10.1007/978-3-031-51643-6_17

fastest way possible, and malware developers, who create increasingly complex malware using evasive strategies to avoid detection, is going on a day-to-day basis and with alternating fates.

The malware detection approaches typically fall into one of two typologies: static analysis and dynamic analysis. The former is focused on features that can be extracted from the malware code itself without executing it. Usually, these features are the hash signature computed on the compiled file, the strings that can be found in such file, and the Assembly operations that can be extracted from the compiled file using a disassembler (e.g., [6,13,27]). Unfortunately, static analysis is gradually becoming less effective because it can be easily sidestepped using techniques such as encryption, encoding, and polymorphism. Dynamic analysis relies instead on the fact that malware behavior cannot be easily changed. To perform dynamic analysis, malware is usually executed in a safe environment, a sandbox, to prevent self–infection, while its behavior is observed and analyzed. The features that can be extracted are many; however, the most common are the API calls (i.e., system calls) that the malware executes to interact and eventually control/damage the machine which is installed on (e.g., [17,31]). Nowadays, advanced anti-malware tools combine static and dynamic analysis with machine learning (ML) to improve detection, giving better results than a simple antivirus limited to signature analysis [7,14,21,23].

Malware behavior can typically be detected by how it interacts with the environment. For example, suspicious behavior includes attempts to modify system files or connections, calls to known malware functions or functions that are typically not used by legitimate software, and system information requests. The crucial drawback is that anti-malware tools need to obtain high-level permissions on the machine they are installed on to detect such a behavior. However, grant permission to anti-malware tools to access this kind of information is equivalent to providing complete control of the machine to the company that produces the anti-malware tool. Users might be reluctant to grant such a high level of privileges to third parties, even just for compliance with the company's internal policies. There were even examples of software with the ability to inspect a machine for good purposes that has been used as a vector for malware[1]

The goal of the present work is to address this issue by developing an alternative approach for malware detection that relies on easily accessible behavioral data, so as not to require high-level permissions, fed to a deep learning model that learns to detect malware behavior. We considered that the information related to the system performances (CPU, RAM, disk, and network usage) does not require high-level permissions to be collected: we set out to find whether this information would be sufficient to train a behavioral model able to distinguish between malware and legit software.

To carry on this investigation, we executed a plethora of well-known malware, and a number of commonly used legit software within a suitably designed sandbox and collected the performance data at system level (i.e., related to the

---

[1] https://www.ccleaner.com/knowledge/security-notification-ccleaner-v5336162-ccleaner-cloud-v1073191.

overall system rather than to individual processes) under the form of a multivalued time series. Then, to address the fact that deep learning models need large training sets, we augmented the data set using a generative adversarial network (GAN); finally, we trained an LSTM network to capture malware patterns. Our investigation found that this approach based on easy-to-collect information is very effective (0.99% accuracy), despite the fact that the data used for training are very different from those typically used for this purpose. Furthermore, the real and synthetic data sets, as well as the corresponding code, are publicly available at https://doi.org/10.13130/RD_UNIMI/LJ6Z8V.

The remainder of the paper is structured as follows. Section 2 points to the state of the art; Sect. 3 outlines the methodology; Sect. 4 discusses the results, and Sect. 5 draws conclusions.

2 Related Works

Machine learning and deep learning have gained ground in many disparate domains [1–4,24,29], including the area of malware detection.

Static analysis is based on data that can be extracted from malicious/legitimate code such as Windows API calls (e.g., [12]) and Assembly instructions (e.g., [13]). These approaches display an excellent classification performance: using a variety of classifier algorithms (e.g., decision tree, random forest, AdaBoost, Gradient Boosting, SVM, kNN) they almost always achieve accuracy, precision, recall well above 0.9. However, as we observed, they are highly invasive. The analysis of Windows PE (Portable Executable) constitutes a large part of the research. For example, Patri et al. [27] modeled PE files in terms of their entropy to be then classified using ML; Naz et al. [26] considered the headers of such files only for feature extraction. Ling et al. [16] focused on the robustness against adversarial attacks of ML-based PE malware detectors; Demetrio et al. [7] conducted a similar evaluation.

Dynamic analysis improves over the inability of static analysis to deal with encryption, obfuscation and polymorphism. Hybrid analysis further improves it by combining static and behavioral information. For example, Miller et al. [22] combined static and dynamic features retrieved from the *VirusTotal* dataset. Dai et al. [6] combined two types of static features: API calls and low-level information retrieved from the hardware of the device, such as performance counters. Their detector consists of an ensemble of ML models.

Android malware received significant attention. For example, Li et al. [15] focused on static analysis, by extracting features from app files containing information such as the required permissions and the API calls. Feng et al. [10] proposed a similar approach taking into account the limited resources of a typical Android device. Ma et al. [19] extracted three types of data related to API calls from the control flow of the app and trained a set of ML models therein. Sihang in el. [31] executed malware inside an Android emulator; application logs are stored, transformed into a feature vector, and fed to a deep learning model.

Hybrid approaches have also been proposed. For example, Lu et al. [17] considered static information by de-/compiling the app's APK file and dynamic information by executing the apps in a safe environment.

Lightweight malware detection is based on dynamic analysis performed on *simple* features that are overlooked in traditional detectors, and is in its infancy. For example, Milosevic et al. [23] collected system- and device-level information on Android devices mostly related to memory. A logistic regression model trained on a reduced set of these characteristics achieved ≈ 0.84 precision and recall. McDole et al. [21] considered two-dimensional samples: the first represents individual processes, while the second features at the process level, such as CPU usage. Multiple deep learning models achieved ≈ 0.93 accuracy and ≈ 0.9 recall in the best cases. Instead, our approach considers system-level information.

Data scarcity is an important issue in the development of malware detectors. Companies that develop malware detectors do not publish their datasets, as competitors could steal information, while attackers could study the dataset to make new malware that are not detected. This problem can be addressed using synthetic data. Among the ways to create synthetic data, we considered a GAN (Generative Adversarial Network) [11]. A GAN is an ML model composed of two networks that are trained against each other. One network (Generator) generates new data preserving the same distribution of real data, and the other network (Discriminator) evaluates the synthetic data by computing the probability that the evaluated data are real or synthetic. Augmentation has already been evaluated in the context of malware detection. For example, Lu et al. [18] used a deep convolutional GAN to increase the *Malimg* dataset representing malware as images [25]. Malimg has been created by converting the malware executable code into 8-bit vectors then transformed into a grayscale image. Interestingly, malware of the same family have a similar image representation. Wang et al. [33] proposed a similar approach to represent malware as black-white images. Another model that can be used to generate synthetic data is Variational Autoencoders. Burks et al. [5] used this approach to augment Malimg showing that the GAN-based approach of Lu et al. [18] yields better results.

Time series have already been used in some of the works mentioned above (e.g., [17,19,27]). A general discussion on time series classification can be found in [8].

LSTM is the model of choice in many time-series analyses. For example, Čeponis et al. [32] compared two deep learning approaches for the classification of malware in time series, showing that the simpler approach gives the same or better results than the other. Sayadi et al. [30] focused on malware hidden inside legit software, whose data set is a set of time series representing branch instructions collected at run time.

In summary, the research community is focusing a lot of attention on ML-based malware detection, and lightweight detection promises the low overhead of static analysis with the quality of static analysis. Our approach puts forward this idea, considering a reduced set of 6 system-level features whose collection does not require any high-level permissions.

3 Methodology

We present an overview of our approach for lightweight behavior-based malware detection (Sect. 3.1) and detail the data collection process (Sect. 3.2), the creation of the dataset (Sect. 3.3), and the classification method (Sect. 3.4).

3.1 Our Approach at a Glance

Figure 1 shows an overview of our approach. Our sandbox implementation considers a Linux machine requesting the execution of malware/legit software in a Windows virtual machine, to collect the initial dataset in a safe environment. This data set was then fed to a GAN network, which was responsible for learning its peculiarities and generating similar synthetic data. The generated data were visually inspected together with real data in lower-dimensional spaces, using *Principal Component Analysis* (PCA) and *t-Distributed Stochastic Neighbor Embedding* (t-SNE). The real and synthetic data sets were merged into the final data set, divided into training, validation, and test sets, to train and evaluate an LSTM model. Section 4 describes the results of this procedure. The real and synthetic data sets, the corresponding code and a detailed description of the complete process are publicly available at https://doi.org/10.13130/RD_UNIMI/LJ6Z8V.

3.2 Sandbox Implementation

Running malware to analyze its behavior introduces the risk of self-infection. The use of a sandbox can mitigate or eliminate this risk. A sandbox is an isolated environment where malware can be executed safely. This approach is not always feasible because some malware are capable of understanding whether they are running inside a sandbox. When this happens, some malware may change their behavior or interrupt their execution; some advanced malware are even capable of escaping the sandbox, causing the infection of the system where the sandbox is installed. For this reason, we used a combination of Linux and Windows machines. Figure 2 shows their interaction. Specifically, we tested Windows malware and legitimate software on a Windows 7 virtual machine (VM) hosted by a Linux machine. The Windows VM is isolated from the Internet through a *host-only connection*. This way, the VM does not have access to the physical network card of the host machine, preventing any malware connections to the Internet.

Executing malware on a machine that cannot communicate on the Internet, however, has some limitations: Some malware needs to connect to remote hosts to carry out their activities (e.g., Wanna-Cry). To allow the malware to still create connections without going to the Internet, we set up a second Linux VM.

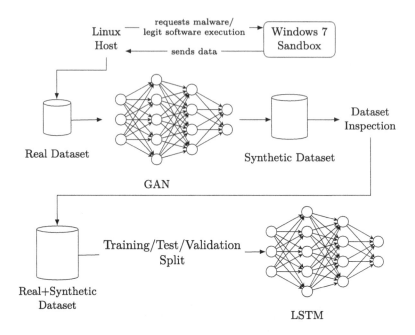

Fig. 1. Overview of our approach

Fig. 2. The sandbox

This VM runs software *iNetSim*[2] to simulate Internet connections. With this configuration, the malware executed on the Windows VM can still make requests and obtain responses without resorting to external connections.

To allow an effective execution of the malware inside the Windows VM, all protection controls like firewalls, Windows update, and Windows defender have been disabled, and certain group policies have been changed to give the malware the capability to act as an administrator. The need to modify these policies motivates the use of an old Windows version, namely Windows 7.

3.3 Dataset

Malware and Legit Software. We retrieved real-world malware from *VirusShare*.[3] The website hosts nearly 55 million malware samples, among which we considered ≈5,000 PE Windows files. For what concerns legit software, we

---

[2] https://www.inetsim.org/.
[3] https://virusshare.com.

installed commonly used software on the Windows VM, to make the environment as realistic as possible. Legit software includes Internet Explorer, Firefox, Mozilla Thunderbird, Spotify, WinRaR.

Dataset Creation. We execute malware and legitimate software for a fixed amount of time while collecting performance metrics. The choice of this time period was critical. On the one hand, a short time span allows to immediately detect malware, and hence preventing system infection. On the other hand, if the time span is too short, the amount of data will not be enough for detection. To identify a suitable time span, we first generated several datasets, comparing the time span and accuracy of the subsequent classification phase. An acceptable trade-off was given by a span of 60 s.

We performed 10,000 executions varying between malware and legitimate software. At each execution, the Windows VM was restored from a clean snapshot (following the state of the art [23]) and the chosen software was run for the given time span. During each execution, we collected the multi-valued time series consisting of 6 features: *i)* CPU usage percentage, *ii)* RAM usage percentage, *iii)* bytes written out and *iv)* bytes read from the disk, *v)* bytes received and *vi)* sent to the network. The collected data are sent back to the Linux host where they are saved.

The usage of the LSTM model requires all time series to have the same length. For this purpose, we pre-processed the collected data normalizing the time series to a fixed length by padding the shorter time series and pruning the longer ones. Each resulting time series contains 10 items each associated with the six aforementioned features. Given the time span of 60 s, the sampling time was 6 s. We note that this time is slightly lower than similar approaches [21].

Dataset Augmentation. Deep learning models require a large number of training samples. Our dataset of ≈10,000 samples is not large enough, but real data collection is very expensive. Consequently, we opt for the generation of synthetic data endowed with the same statistical properties as real-world data. To this purpose, we used one of the most effective methods currently available. GAN. More specifically, *TimeGAN* [34].[4] The code to instantiate TimeGAN is as follows.

```
arg = ModelParameters(batch_size=128, lr=5e-4, noise_dim=32,
    layers_dim=128)
gan = TimeGAN(model_parameters=arg, hidden_dim=10, seq_len=10, n_seq=6,
    gamma=1)
```

We fed our normalized, real data set to the GAN so that the model could learn its statistical characteristics and replicate them in the synthetic data. First, we separated the real data set into malware and legit software. We then fed

---

[4] https://pypi.org/project/ydata-synthetic/.

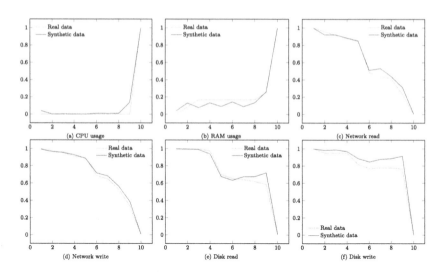

Fig. 3. Comparison of features value of real and synthetic malware samples.

each individual dataset to a separate instance of TimeGAN, generating a synthetic dataset of 50,000 samples. We merged the two synthetic datasets and obtained 100,000 samples in total (10-fold increase). The training of each GAN took approximately 5 h. We then validated the quality of the synthetic dataset according to several comparisons as follows.

– *visual feature comparison:* we randomly selected samples from real and synthetic datasets. For each feature and extracted sample, we plotted their value to visually compare the differences between the real and synthetic samples. Figures 3 and 4 show the similarity of two random samples of malware and legit software, respectively.
– *comparison with reduced dimensionality (PCA):* we perform PCA reduction to a 2-dimensional space on real and synthetic datasets (limited to 500 samples), and plotted the results for visual comparisons. Figures 5(a)–(b) show that the synthetic data match the real data.
– *comparison with reduced dimensionality (t-SNE):* we performed the reduction of t-SNE to a two-dimensional space on real and synthetic datasets (limited to 500 samples). Compared to PCA, t-SNE performs a non-linear transformation. We plotted and visually compared the results. Figures 6(a)–(b) show that the synthetic data match the real data.

We finally created the overall data set by merging the real and synthetic data sets.

3.4 LSTM Model

Table 1(a) describes the structure of the LSTM model we trained, composed of 4 layers (3 LSTM layers and 1 dense layer) interleaved with 3 batch normalization

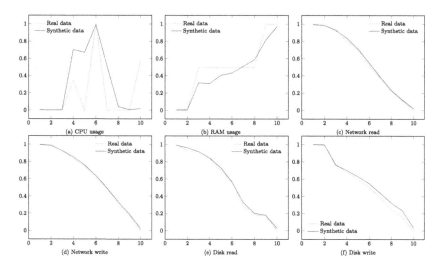

Fig. 4. Comparison of features value of real and synthetic legit software samples.

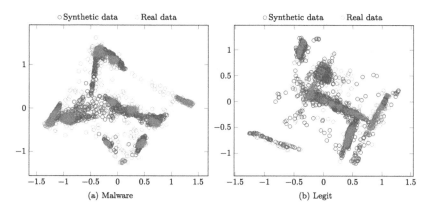

Fig. 5. Scatter plots of malware (a) and legit (b) real and synthetic data in a two-dimensional space according to PCA.

layers. Table 1(b) describes the parameters of the training process. We used 64,871 samples for the training set and 21,624 samples for the validation and test sets over 200 epochs with optimizer *Adam*, loss function *binary cross-entropy*, and initial learning rate of 0.05. In addition, training is based on early stopping (stop if loss function value retrieved from the validation set does not improve in 30 epochs) and on dynamic reduction of the initial learning rate (of a factor of 0.5 if loss function value retrieved from the validation set does not improve in one epoch). More details can be found in our public code at https://doi.org/10.13130/RD_UNIMI/LJ6Z8V.

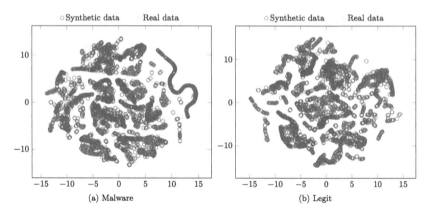

Fig. 6. Scatter plots of malware (a) and legit (b) real and synthetic data in a two-dimensional space according to t-SNE.

Table 1. Details of LSTM training process.

Layer Type	Output Shape	# Params
LSTM	(None, 10, 8)	480
Batch normalization	(None, 10, 8)	32
LSTM	(None, 10, 8)	544
Batch normalization	(None, 10, 8)	32
LSTM	(None, 8)	544
Batch normalization	(None, 8)	32
Dense	(None, 1)	9

(a) LSTM model structure

Parameter	Value
Epochs	200
Batch size	32
Optimizer	Adam
Learning rate	0.05, halved if loss does not improve in 1 epoch, down to $1 \cdot 10^{-8}$
Early stopping	Loss does not improve in 30 epochs
Loss function	Binary crossentropy

(b) Training parameters

4   Analysis Outcome

Starting from the collected real dataset, we executed our experiments on a virtual machine equipped with 16 vCPU Intel Xeon CPUs E5-2620 v4 @ 2.10 GHz and 48 GB of RAM. The VM features Ubuntu 22.02.4 × 64, Python v3.10.6, and ML libraries *scikit-learn* v1.2.2 [28] and *Keras* v2.11.0.

4.1   Results

Training took ≈ 40 min and was completed in 40 epochs out of 200 due to early stopping (see Table 1(b)).

Tables 2(a)–(b) show the results retrieved from the test set. Table 2(a) shows our confusion matrix. Our approach achieves remarkable results, correctly identifying virtually all malware and legit samples. Table 2(b) shows other classification metrics. Our approach can distinguish an infected machine from an

Table 2. Confusion matrix (a), where TP = True Positive count, FN = False Negative count, FP = False Positive count, TN = True Negative count; and classification metrics (b).

	Predicted Positive	Predicted Negative
Actual Positive	TP = 10,869	FN = 29
Actual Negative	FP = 10	TN = 10,701

(a) Confusion matrix

Metric	Definition	Value
Precision	$\frac{TP}{TP+FP}$	0.9977
Recall	$\frac{TP}{TP+FN}$	0.9973
Specificity	$\frac{TN}{TN+FP}$	0.9976
F1-Score	$2 \cdot \frac{Precision \cdot Recall}{Precision+Recall}$	0.9975
Accuracy	$\frac{TP+TN}{TP+TN+FP+FN}$	0.8566
AUC	Area under ROC curve	0.9975

(b) Classification metrics

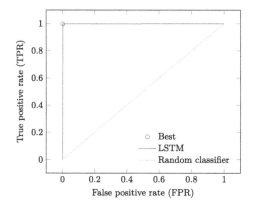

Fig. 7. ROC curve

uninfected machine with an accuracy of 0.99. The same value is achieved in any other metrics, meaning that the detected malware is virtually always malware (precision) and the number of false negatives is negligible (recall). Figure 7 shows the ROC curve (Receiver Operating Characteristics), which represents the true positive rate (TPR, retrieved as TPR=$\frac{TP}{TP+FN}$) vs. the false positiveate (FPR, retrieved as FPR=$\frac{FN}{FP+TN}$) varying the decision threshold of the LSTM classifier. The closeness to both axes once again shows the quality of our approach.

4.2 Discussion

The approach in this paper relies on information related to the system performances (i.e., CPU, RAM, disk, and network usage) that does not require high-level permissions to be collected, and it represents an alternative to the heavily invasive approaches in the state of the art.

The achieved accuracy matches the accuracy retrieved in state-of-the-art hybrid approaches, clearly suggesting that, under the conditions of our settings, malware can be easily distinguished and hence possibly blocked in one minute at most considering system-level performances only. To our knowledge, there exist few comparable works in literature (see Sect. 2). Milosevic et al. [23] considered a larger set of system-level features related to the global behavior of Android apps (e.g., total CPU usage) as individual samples rather than as time series. A logistic regression model achieves 0.86 accuracy at most. McDole et al. [21] considered virtually the same set of features of this work but at the process level rather than system level again as individual samples rather than as time series. A convolutional neural network achieves ≈ 0.93 precision in the best case. Overall, our approach is far superior to its competitors, mainly due to the usage of a large synthetic data set retrieved from a real data set modeled using time series rather than individual disconnected samples. The release of our complete data set could pave the way for further tuning of ML models, on the one hand, and for retrieving additional insights from malware behavior characteristics.

## 5	Conclusion

Malware detection represents an urgent problem that is continuously being investigated by the research community. The approach in this paper sheds new light on the use of data that can be collected with ease and that can distinguish between legit and malicious behavior. The paper leaves room for future work. First, we plan to extend the set of features to other system-level and easily accessible information. Second, we plan to specifically focus on obfuscating malware. Third, we plan to strengthen the classifier from evasion attacks using dedicated techniques, such as adversarial training.

Acknowledgments. The work was partially supported by the projects *i)* MUSA - Multilayered Urban Sustainability Action - project, funded by the European Union - NextGenerationEU, under the National Recovery and Resilience Plan (NRRP) Mission 4 Component 2 Investment Line 1.5: Strengthening of research structures and creation of R&D "innovation ecosystems", set up of "territorial leaders in R&D" (CUP G43C22001370007, Code ECS00000037); *ii)* SERICS (PE00000014) under the NRRP MUR program funded by the EU - NextGenerationEU.

References

1. Alhashmi, N., Almoosa, N., Gianini, G.: Path asymmetry reconstruction via deep learning. In: Proceedings of IEEE MELECON 2022, Palermo, Italy (2022)
2. Almazrouei, E., Gianini, G., Almoosa, N., Damiani, E.: What can machine learning do for radio spectrum management? In: Proceedings of ACM Q2SWinet 2020, Alicante, Spain (2020)
3. Almazrouei, E., Gianini, G., Almoosa, N., Damiani, E.: Robust computationally-efficient wireless emitter classification using autoencoders and convolutional neural networks. Sensors **21**(7), 2414 (2021)

4. Almazrouei, E., Gianini, G., Mio, C., Almoosa, N., Damiani, E.: Using autoencoders for radio signal denoising. In: Proceedings of ACM Q2SWinet 2019, Miami Beach, FL, USA (2019)
5. Burks, R., Islam, K.A., Lu, Y., Li, J.: Data augmentation with generative models for improved malware detection: a comparative study. In: Proceedings of IEEE UEMCON 2019, New York, NY, USA (2019)
6. Dai, Y., Li, H., Qian, Y., Yang, R., Zheng, M.: Smash: a malware detection method based on multi-feature ensemble learning. IEEE Access **7**, 112588–112597 (2019)
7. Demetrio, L., Coull, S.E., Biggio, B., Lagorio, G., Armando, A., Roli, F.: Adversarial EXEmples: a survey and experimental evaluation of practical attacks on machine learning for windows malware detection. ACM TPS **24**(4), 1–31 (2021)
8. Dinger, T.R., Chang, Y.C., Pavuluri, R., Subramanian, S.: What is time series classification? (2022). https://developer.ibm.com/learningpaths/get-started-time-series-classification-api/what-is-time-series-classification/
9. Eurpean Union Agency for Cybersecurity: ENISA Threat Landscape 2022. Technical report, Eurpean Union Agency for Cybersecurity (2022)
10. Feng, R., et al.: Mobidroid: a performance-sensitive malware detection system on mobile platform. In: Proceedings of ICECCS 2019, Guangzhou, China (2019)
11. Goodfellow, I., et al.: Generative adversarial networks. Commun. ACM **63**(11), 139–144 (2020)
12. Hardy, W., Chen, L., Hou, S., Ye, Y., Li, X.: DL4MD: a deep learning framework for intelligent malware detection. In: Proceedings of DMIN 2016, Las Nevas, NV, USA (2016)
13. Kan, Z., Wang, H., Xu, G., Guo, Y., Chen, X.: Towards light-weight deep learning based malware detection. In: Proceedings of IEEE COMPSAC 2018, Tokyo, Japan (2018)
14. Li, D., Li, Q., Ye, Y.F., Xu, S.: Arms race in adversarial malware detection: a survey. ACM CSUR **55**(1), 1–35 (2021)
15. Li, D., Wang, Z., Xue, Y.: Fine-grained android malware detection based on deep learning. In: Proceedings of IEEE CNS 2018, Beijing, China (2018)
16. Ling, X., et al.: Adversarial attacks against Windows PE malware detection: a survey of the state-of-the-art. Comput. Secur. **128**, 103134 (2023)
17. Lu, T., Du, Y., Ouyang, L., Chen, Q., Wang, X.: Android malware detection based on a hybrid deep learning model. Secur. Commun. Netw. **2020**, 1–11 (2020)
18. Lu, Y., Li, J.: Generative adversarial network for improving deep learning based malware classification. In: Proceedings of WSC 2019, National Harbor, MD, USA (2019)
19. Ma, Z., Ge, H., Liu, Y., Zhao, M., Ma, J.: A combination method for android malware detection based on control flow graphs and machine learning algorithms. IEEE Access **7**, 21235–21245 (2019)
20. Malwarebytes: 2023 state of malware. Technical report, Malwarebytes (2023)
21. McDole, A., Abdelsalam, M., Gupta, M., Mittal, S.: Analyzing CNN based behavioural malware detection techniques on cloud IaaS. In: Proceedings of CLOUD 2020, Honolulu, HI, USA (2020)
22. Miller, B., et al.: Reviewer integration and performance measurement for malware detection. In: Proceedings of DIMVA 2016, San Sebastián, Spain (2016)
23. Milosevic, J., Malek, M., Ferrante, A., Malek, M.: A friend or a foe? detecting malware using memory and cpu features. In: Proceedings of SECRYPT 2016, Lisbon, Portugal (2016)

24. Mio, C., Gianini, G.: Signal reconstruction by means of Embedding, Clustering and AutoEncoder Ensembles. In: Proceedings of IEEE ISCC 2019, Barcelona, Spain (2019)
25. Nataraj, L., Karthikeyan, S., Jacob, G., Manjunath, B.S.: Malware images: visualization and automatic classification. In: Proceedings of VizSec 2011, Pittsburgh, PA, USA (2011)
26. Naz, S., Singh, D.K.: Review of machine learning methods for windows malware detection. In: Proceedings of ICCCNT 2019, Kanpur, India (2019)
27. Patri, O., Wojnowicz, M., Wolff, M.: Discovering malware with time series shapelets. In: Proceedings of HICSS 2017, Waikoloa, HI, USA (2017)
28. Pedregosa, F., et al.: Scikit-learn: machine learning in python. J. Mach. Learn. Res. **12**, 2825–2830 (2011)
29. Ramos, I.F.F., Gianini, G., Damiani, E.: Neuro-symbolic AI for sensor-based human performance prediction: system architectures and applications. In: Proceedings of ESREL 2022, Dublin, Ireland (2022)
30. Sayadi, H., et al.: Towards accurate run-time hardware-assisted stealthy malware detection: a lightweight, yet effective time series CNN-based approach. Cryptography **5**(4), 28 (2021)
31. Sihag, V., Vardhan, M., Singh, P., Choudhary, G., Son, S.: De-LADY: deep learning based android malware detection using dynamic features. JISIS **11**, 34–45 (2021)
32. Čeponis, D., Goranin, N.: Investigation of dual-flow deep learning models LSTM-FCN and GRU-FCN efficiency against single-flow CNN models for the host-based intrusion and malware detection task on univariate times series data. Appl. Sci. **10**(7), 2373 (2020)
33. Wang, F., Al Hamadi, H., Damiani, E.: A visualized malware detection framework with CNN and conditional GAN. In: Proceedings of IEEE Big Data 2022, Osaka, Japan (2022)
34. Yoon, J., Jarrett, D., van der Schaar, M.: Time-series generative adversarial networks. In: Proceedings of NeurIPS 2019, Vancouver, Canada (2019)

A Digital Ecosystem for Improving Product Design

Sylvain Lefebvre[1]([envelope]) [ORCID], Michaël Lecointre[3], Benoit Lardeux[1],
Jean-Marie Guyader[2], Olivier Aubrun[3], Birane Touré[3], and Maher Jridi[1]

[1] L@bIsen, Isen Nantes, 33 Quater Avenue du Champs de Manoeuvre,
44470 Carquefou, France
{sylvain.lefebvre,benoit.lardeux,maher.jridi}@isen-ouest.yncrea.fr
[2] L@bIsen, ISEN Brest, 20 Rue Cuirassé Bretagne, 29200 Brest, France
jean-marie.guyader@isen-ouest.yncrea.fr
[3] ACOME, 50140 Romagny-Fontenay, France
{michael.lecointre,olivier.aubrun,birane.toure}@acome.fr

Abstract. Digitization is reaching to every corner of the industry. The
industry 4.0 (I4.0) movement initiated a move towards a stronger reliance
on data in the manufacturing domain in order to improve processes and
product quality. Multiple works highlight the potential benefits of deploying artificial intelligence or big data management platforms for industrial
companies to improve their processes and provide a better understanding
of their production tools. Many I4.0 work often assume the existence of
interconnected machinery, sensors, and Manufacturing Execution System
(MES) in the company and assume that most data is already available
from these interconnected systems on the production line. Unfortunately,
this does not reflect the state of many companies whose production systems are not interconnected due to historical reasons or security and
normative issues. This report describes a big data architecture for the
collection, storage and analysis of industrial prototype data. We provide
details on how such an architecture can be structured and how it supports the engineering cycle in a partner company through a case study.

Keywords: Big Data · Industry 4.0 · Analytics

1 Introduction

Digitization is reaching to every corner of the industry. The industry 4.0 (I4.0) [8]
movement initiated a move towards a stronger reliance on data in the manufacturing domain in order to improve processes and product quality. Multiple works
highlight the potential benefits of deploying artificial intelligence [3,20] or big
data management platforms [12,22] for industrial companies to improve their
processes and provide a better understanding of their production tools. The
extensive use of data collection and data management tools in the I4.0 paradigm
allows companies to implement data-based approaches to manage their production. A data-based approach, per opposition to a model-based approach, is

a methodology where decision making is based on observations on the studied phenomenon rather than on theoretical models. For example, the product engineering cycle can be significantly improved by the usage of advanced data analytics [19].

However, several obstacles hinder the adoption of those approaches in smaller companies across Europe. For example, several studies [6, 15] highlight the difficulties to collect data, as well as a lack of clear return on investment from the deployment of data-based approaches.

Indeed, many I4.0 works assume the existence of a high connectivity of the various components of the shop floor in the company and assume that most data is already available from these interconnected systems on the production line. Unfortunately, this does not reflect the state of many companies whose production systems are not interconnected due to historical reasons or security and normative issues. We argue in this paper that the later type of companies can benefit from data-based I4.0 processes through the use of historical data already present in their IT systems. These historical data sources include, for example, design documents, spreadsheets, normative documents, or specification documents. For example, spreadsheets [4] are often stored in a shared file system over the organization. It is an easily accessible source of information. These represent a significant amount of data available in a large variety of low-structured format which poses a data integration challenge. At the same time, collecting these data has a lower impact on IT infrastructure and production lines, compared to the deployment of new sensors and data collection systems on the manufacturing shop floor. Therefore, the collection of such historical data may be useful to bootstrap data-based processes at a lower cost.

In this report, we describe through a case study in the cable making industry how a big data infrastructure based on I4.0 can be deployed to improve the engineering process. To achieve this goal, multiple obstacles must be overcome:

1. Collect historical data in multiple heterogeneous semi structured format
2. Gather collected data in a central Datalake with an appropriate data model
3. Provide useful data visualization for production engineers.

This work lies at the intersection of several approaches to enhance manufacturing companies processes by using data (See Sect. 2). Our approach was deployed in a case study described in Sect. 3. The main operating principle of the data platform relies on the design of a virtuous cycle of automated importation and user-based update of data sources (See Sect. 4). Finally, we discuss the impact of the platform in Sect. 5 and provide conclusions and future research areas are highlighted in Sect. 6.

2   Background and Related Works

2.1   Big Data Analytics

The usage of big data analytics approaches [2, 11, 12, 22] enable manufacturing organizations to overcome the 5V challenges (Volume, Velocity, Variety, Veracity,

Value) posed by large amounts of data. For example Sun et al. in [19] designed a platform combining Product Life-cycle Management (PLM) software and data analytics processes to generate optimized planning and task assignment to engineers in the Engineer To Order industry. They rely on the CRoss Industry Standard for Data Mining (CRISP-DM) [21] to extract relevant information from collected data.

Datalakes are frequently applied in industry 4.0 related platforms. Commercial offerings from major cloud computing providers such as Amazon[1] or Microsoft[2] include a Datalake for storage and data analytics. In [11] Kebisek et al. describe a platform for quality level prediction of paint on a production chain. The proposed system aggregates data from different production batches in a data lake and allows for historical data analysis. The work focuses on a single production phase and not on the product design stage. The data only include structured data from shop floor equipment.

Multiple approaches coexist to integrate heterogeneous data sources in such platforms. In [2], Bonnard et al. designed a proxy Application Programming Interface to ensure a common data format for ingestion from various shop-floor level sources and provide a generic industry 4.0 Big Data platform. The platform provides services for data analytics and a set of standard dashboard for helping shop floor workers to assess the state of the production system. The BiDRAC model [16] developed by Sanz et al. provides several uses cases related to fault detection and analysis in car paint coating process. Their platform integrates both unstructured data sources and structured data coming from industrial equipment. However, the data extraction process from the unstructured sources is not detailed in the paper. In [9] Kahveci et al. detail the building of a big data infrastructure to collect data in a manufacturing plant. As their approach focuses on real-time process monitoring, they require the deployment of multiple additional equipment in the factory. The proposed architecture relies on standard layers for data integration visualization and dashboards. The collected data is structured in nature as it comes from various industrial equipments. They do not collect or integrate this data with document-based sources.

2.2   Semantic Approaches

Semantic approaches use the tools provided by knowledge modeling and ontologies to facilitate data integration and retrieval. In [14], Patel et al. propose a semantic web-based platform for industrial data sources integration and data based application development. More recently, Semantic Graphs [18] emerged as another approach to solve data integration challenges posed by the multiplicity of data sources in industrial companies. Prominent manufacturers such as Bosch [10], or Siemens [5] implement multiple data integration and analytics

---

[1] https://aws.amazon.com/fr/solutions/case-studies/innovators/volkswagen-group/, last seen December 5, 2023.

[2] https://www.microsoft.com/fr-fr/industry/manufacturing/microsoft-cloud-for-man ufacturing, last seen December 5, 2023.

on top of Knowledge graph based platforms. Graph-based approaches provide a flexible schema which facilitates data integration across multiple sources. However, these systems often rely on specific databases with less standard querying languages, which hinders the empowerment of users to extract their data for analysis. Moreover these reports tend to focus on semi-structured input data (JSON, XML), coming from shop floor machines and sensors. Analytics performed on these data focus on the detection of quality issues during fabrication, and not to improve the product engineering phase.

2.3   Machine Learning in Manufacturing Industry

Data-based approaches to decision making often involve the use of predictive models. Therefore the use of machine learning ecosystems is also rising in the manufacturing industry. These platforms share some common infrastructure with big data platforms. In their reviews of machine learning usage in industry 4.0 [20], Tercan et al. demonstrate the usefulness of predictive approaches for quality prediction in manufacturing. However, they also denote the lack of systematic integration and deployment of these technologies in real production settings. They also note that a large fraction of the complexity of such projects lies in the data acquisition process as well as the connectivity of shop-floor machines. They also do not consider the impact of machine learning techniques on the product design cycle. In industrial process monitoring the development of Soft Sensors extensively use big data and machine learning approaches. Soft Sensors are software components which allow to monitor difficult to estimate process outputs or metrics through predictive models. For example, in [7], Kabugo et al. use a big data analytics and machine learning platform based on cloud technologies to model and develop soft sensors for the monitoring of gas emissions in a Waste To Energy Plant. Their approach collects data from various sensors on the machines and evaluate different machine learning models for the studied phenomenon. In this approach, data used for modeling comes from various industrial sensors which are costly to interconnect to data processing facilities in the cloud. They do not integrate unstructured data and documents in their process.

3   Case Study: Product Prototyping

Product design and prototyping phase is an essential part of the industrial production cycle. This phase happens before the mass production of the product. In our approach we model this phase as an iterative cycle with four steps:

1. *The design step:* Engineers receive desired specifications from the R&D department or from clients. They proceed, based on their experience of the industry or some accumulated data on past designs and simulation tools to propose a product design that should follow the specifications,

2. *The build step:* Based on the target design from the previous step, the study
   engineers send a prototype fabrication order (FO) to the manufacturing floor
   and provide machine parameters for each of the building or processing phases
   of the target product,
3. *Test step:* Once the prototype product is built, qualification engineers proceed to some tests on the built product to check the conformity to the specification,
4. *Analysis step:* If the prototype product does not conform to the tests, study
   engineers gather data from the production phase and test phase and proceed
   to various analysis in order to improve the design of the product.

Engineers iterate over this process to come up with a design that can full-fill
all target specifications.

Iterations which do not come up with the proper design result in wasted raw
materials and machine time that could otherwise be used for more productive
fabrication. It is therefore of great importance to be able to record all attempts
at fabrication to avoid repeating previous mistakes and anticipate possible interactions of various design decisions.

This design data analysis capability is of great importance for many manufacturing organizations. However, as shown by [12] this data is often gathered in
multiple silos across the organization and it remains difficult to provide engineers
with a common entry point for their access and analysis.

4 Solution Architecture

Therefore the building of this data platform focused on the ingestion of various
documents and required the development of three layers as presented in Fig. 1.

The first layer is the *data ingestion and extraction layer.* This layer, described
further in Sect. 4.1 processes raw input files and data sources to map them on the
schema of the Datalake. The *Data Integration Layer* maps and consolidates the
various entities resulting from the data extraction layer into a common Datalake
schema. Finally, the *Access Layer* enables product designers to retrieve data as
well as discover and model relationships between different collected data sources.

4.1 Data Extraction

The Ingestion Layer in Fig. 1 is composed of three sub-components to achieve
data collection as well as extraction, transformation and loading (ETL). The
first part is the Data Exchange Zone (DEZ). This DEZ is a temporary storage
area where the source data coming from the manufacturing company IT system
or Shop Floor data sources can be stored before processing. This space provides
a set of standardized APIs for data transfers. The data exchange zone stores
the data temporarily until its ingestion in the Datalake is confirmed. Once the
ingestion is successful the data in that staging area can be deleted.

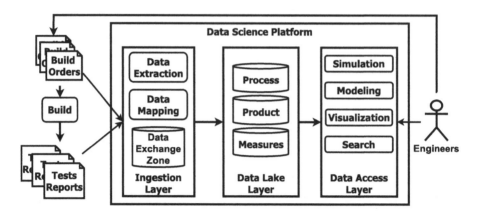

Fig. 1. The collected data are stored temporarily in the Data Exchange Zone, which provides several APIs for data transfers. The Data extraction and mapping processes transform the data to conform to the Datalake schema. The access layer provide Engineers and Analysts with tools to Search Visualize and Model the data in the Datalake

A set of data input processes update the data exchange zone continuously. In the case of file based ingestion of semi-structured documents which constitutes the majority of ingestion for the design cycle use-case described in Sect. 3, data is refreshed every 24h, by taking all modified files in that interval. This delay was chosen as acceptable for the users. Incoming data in the platform are from heterogeneous sources that can be separated in two main classes, based on their structuration level:

Database Extractions: These data sources provide a well-structured data schema that can be easily mapped to the target Datalake schema.

Document Files A large quantity of data is stored in semi-structured tables inside work spreadsheets, PDF, or Word documents. These data sources may have no structure at all and require a specific extraction process.

While the first kind of data is well structured, data coming from document sources poses a heterogeneity problem. Therefore, the data extraction process has to account for several styles of data sources. The data extraction module supports this role.

Located in the extraction layer (Fig. 1) the data extraction module is a framework that allows the user to extract data from unstructured documents and transform it to various table model database, based on a set of customizable rules. Inspired by the works of Shigarov et al. [17] this module processes each document with the sequence of steps described in Fig. 2. After the document identification step, two types of rules are applied:

Segmentation Rules The first set of rules, called *segmentation* rules, allows users to transform each document's pages into multiple sections to create a tree-shaped object, which recursively subdivides the document into small sections of meaningful content. The developer defines what is considered as a meaningful content section. Each segmentation rule is composed of an identifier, a capture condition, a capture range, and a section type. A capture condition is a set of predicates that switches the file content capture on or off based on the current content of the file. Such predicates can be, for example: matching the content of a cell or a line with a regular expression, matching a line number or matching a column number. The capture range specifies the vertical range of capture, for example: full line or the number of columns in the case of spreadsheets. Each rule associates the captured data with the specified section type, which reflects the nature and basic structure of the captured data (tabular data, text data, etc.).

Mapping Rules The second set of rules are the *mapping* rules. These rules associate each section or set of sections to a schema mapping function. The mapping function takes a set of sections as well as a target schema and returns a list of objects conforming to the target schema. The developer can define a schema for each mapping rule. This approach provided enough flexibility to extract the data in our use case.

Following the data extraction quality is essential for the good usage of the platform, especially since the input formats can evolve over time. Therefore, the platform administrators maintain a data extraction quality dashboard. The results of extraction for each document can be tracked and errors are recorded in order to establish a quick diagnostic when data is not available in the system. Interaction with the final user, as well as the repeating ingestion process, provide means to efficiently correct issues by re-typing documents with inaccurate formats and ingest them again post modification. The users monitor two main metrics:

Importation ratio Ratio of successfully recognized documents over the total number of documents in the Datalake. This ratio provides a good estimate of the amount of correct documents in the data set,

Extraction ratio For each table in the model, the ratio of documents that have an entry in it. This provides an overview of the completeness of the extraction process.

Extraction reports are created to enable users to follow and improve data input. With these reports, users can check whether the documents they expect to find were loaded in the Datalake or not. If the data extraction failed, the user can identify the root cause of importation failure. Thanks to the continuous importation process, users can update failed documents to correct it so that it can be re-imported at the next scheduled data collection.

4.2 Data Lake

The Datalake is a big data storage facility, that stores data post extraction. Data are stored in progressively more structured formats, from the raw extraction of the various data sources to the target data model for analysis. The first category

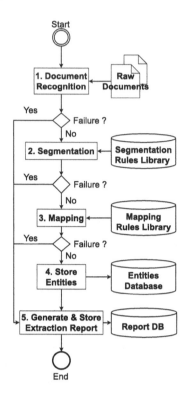

Fig. 2. Rule-based extraction process overview. Each document goes through two phases: a segmentation phase and a mapping phase, then extracted objects are stored in the target database and the system creates and stores an extraction report

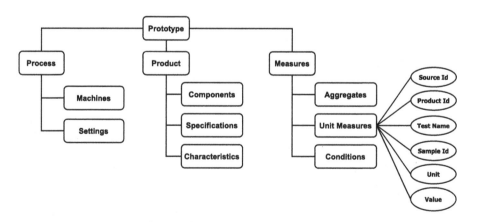

Fig. 3. Data Model: Collection of tables describing Process, Product and Measures data.

of tables consists in sets of entities extracted from input sources. These entities are then mapped and aggregated into a common data model that is more suitable for analysis and retrieval by the users. This data model, visible in Fig. 3 is based on the high-level taxonomy of data for machine learning applications in industrial context describe by Tercan and Meisein in [20]. Data is stored in multiple collections of tables, one per element of the taxonomy:

Measurements: This collection of table is a set of fact tables including all measurements done on all finite or semi-finite products in the chain. These data can come from quality monitoring systems or qualification tests results. Data sources include MES systems, manually filled spreadsheets or manufacturing quality monitoring systems.

Process: This table collection is a set of dimension tables related to the configuration settings used for a given machine and Fabrication Order (FO). Sources can be structured such as Supervisory Control And Data Acquisition (SCADA) or Manufacturing Execution Systems (MES) data or semi-structured data such as spreadsheets or images.

Products: This collection is another set of dimension tables containing the requirements and technical specifications of the products. Sources include Product Lifecycle Management systems, Product Design systems and fabrication order documents.

Each of these collections of tables include tables with similar schema as highlighted for the Unit Measures collection in Fig. 3. All tables in the Unit Measure collection have a similar set of fields, prefixed with the name of the value. This results in a star schema centered on the measurements tables. Advantages of such schema is a more efficient query execution as well as understandability of the tables by the users. On the other hand, the quantity of data is bigger because of the schema denormalization.

4.3   Access Layer

The data access layer is designed to provide production engineers the means to search, visualize, analyze, and model their data.

Data Retrieval. To enable engineers to search and extract data, we chose the open-source component Metabase[3]. It was selected because of its user interface that enables non expert users to build queries efficiently in a What You See is What You Get fashion. Users can create, record, and share dashboards and queries. The system is Open Source and can be deployed easily. It also allows for data virtualization, which permits modifications to underlying tables and data models to be transparent for the final users. Its administration interface also allows to document the created views extensively.

---

[3] https://www.metabase.com/, seen December 5, 2023.

Visualization. The visualization tool is a specific web interface developed in Python to enable exploration and discovery of relations between variables in a given dataset.

The tool retrieves existing queries from the data catalog through the Metabase API, and provides users with the opportunity to build an understanding of the data through automatic data selection and visualization. This provides Data Understanding and Data Preparation tasks based on the CRISP-DM process [21]. As a first step, users can retrieve data from queries stored in the Datalake. Then, through the tool, users provide additional details such as the columns that should be considered as variables, as well as the nature of each of those variables.

The first visualization the tool provides is a correlogram. Shown in Fig. 4, the correlogram is an interactive heat-map where variables are listed from top to bottom while response variables are listed from left to right. The color level indicates the correlation direction as well as the intensity of the correlation, which is proportional to the R-coefficient of the computed correlation. We chose to use the Spearman Rank Correlation [1] coefficient to cover a larger number of relationships while keeping the results easy to interpret for users. Some cells have no color and correspond to variable pairs where the correlation coefficient is not statistically significant. The statistical significance of the correlation is verified by checking the p-value as well as confidence intervals on the correlation coefficient. The user can select a cell of the heat-map to visualize the corresponding scatter plot. This tool enables users to rapidly validate their intuition against data with an easy to interpret visualization.

5 Discussion

In this section we discuss the impacts and outcomes of usage of the data platform. The first impact is a significant gain of time for reporting and information gathering about product prototypes. Thanks to the single point of entry for accessing data provided by the platform, some users were able to find relevant data for reporting on current designs in a few minutes or hours. The same process used to take several days before the deployment of the platform. This gain of time for information gathering affects the iterative engineering cycle described in Sect. 3 by accelerating the feedback loop between prototype fabrication and data analysis phases.

The second impact is the quality improvement of data after deployment of the platform. Users observed that the amount of data collected and available in the platform depends on how input files and documents are filled. As developing rules for the many possibilities of filling a line or cell in a documents is infeasible, and the time and resources required for building large annotated databases is not always available, platform users started an internal process for more strict document filling and checking rules. We hope these efforts lead to better data importation success rate in the future.

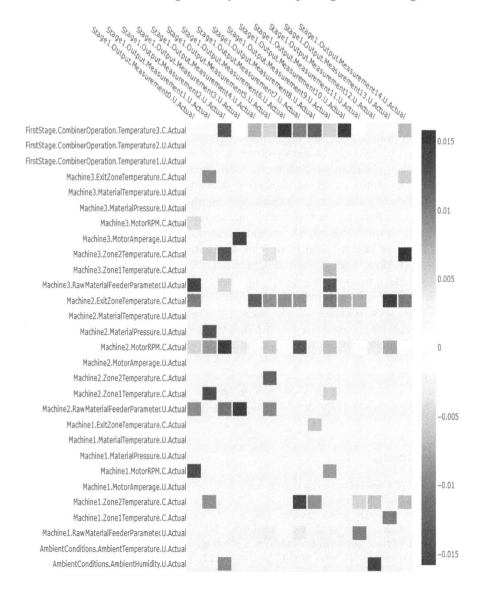

Fig. 4. Interactive Correlation heat-map example, data is from [13]

Another concern was the ease of access to data, which raises concerns against data leakage risks. As the data contains and correlate design data as well as measurements, the risk is the leakage of company knowledge, know-how and intellectual property. Therefore for the acceptability of the approach, it is important to enforce best practices such as end-to-end encryption, provide strict access control, and demonstrate these aspects to stake-holders.

6   Conclusion and Future Works

In this work, we addressed several challenges related to Industry 4.0 implementation for the improvement of product design phase. First, by deploying a continuous data collection system based on historical data and sources already available in the company IT systems, we are able to demonstrate the feasibility of a data-based approach for modeling product features with a lower material cost. We also developed a document extraction framework for tabular data extraction to address the diversity of data sources in the various documents stores of the company. The platform use resulted in a significant time gain according to users, providing the ability to extract analyze product tests results in a matter of hours instead of days previously. This may also result in qualitative improvement of the process by initiating better data input and control. Through continuous data collection and quality feedback, users can improve data quality daily.

In future works, we plan to develop the number of supported data sources, and use Natural Language Processing techniques in order to improve the robustness of the data extraction process and collect more various sources samples. In another part of the work, developing predictive models based on extracted data will enable users to anticipate the impact of design changes on future product. More specifically the study of graph-based techniques for these approaches seems promising to address the variety of data in input sources.

Acknowledgements. Funding for this work was provided by ACOME (https://www. acome.com/en) as part of the *Data Architecture for ACOME Factory 4.0* chair established between ACOME and the L@bISEN research laboratory (https://isen-brest.fr/ labisen/).

References

1. Dodge, Y.: Spearman rank correlation coefficient. In: Dodge, Y. (ed.) The Concise Encyclopedia of Statistics, pp. 502–505. Springer, New York (2008). https://doi. org/10.1007/978-0-387-32833-1_379
2. Bonnard, R., Arantes, M.D.S., Lorbieski, R., Vieira, K.M.M., Nunes, M.C.: Big data/analytics platform for industry 4.0 implementation in advanced manufacturing context. Int. J. Adv. Manuf. Technol. **117**(5–6), 1959–1973 (2021)
3. Dogan, A., Birant, D.: Machine learning and data mining in manufacturing. Expert Syst. Appl. **166**, 114060 (2021). https://doi.org/10.1016/j.eswa.2020.114060
4. Fricke, A., Schöneberger, J.: Industrie 4.0 with MS-excel? Chem. Eng. Trans. **43**, 1303–1308 (2015). https://doi.org/10.3303/CET1543218
5. Hubauer, T., Lamparter, S., Haase, P., Herzig, D.M.: Use cases of the industrial knowledge graph at siemens (2018)
6. Janík, S., Szabó, P., Mĺkva, M., Mareček-Kolibiský, M.: Effective data utilization in the context of industry 4.0 technology integration. Appl. Sci. **12**(20), 10517 (2022). https://doi.org/10.3390/app122010517
7. Kabugo, J.C., Jämsä-Jounela, S.L., Schiemann, R., Binder, C.: Industry 4.0 based process data analytics platform: a waste-to-energy plant case study. Int. J. Electr. Power Energy Syst. **115**, 105508 (2020). https://doi.org/10.1016/j.ijepes.2019. 105508

8. Kagermann, H., Wahlster, W., Helbig, J.: Recommendations for implementing the strategic initiative industrie 4.0 - securing the future of German manufacturing industry. Final report of the industrie 4.0 working group, acatech - National Academy of Science and Engineering, Munchen (2013). http://forschungsunion. de/pdf/industrie_4_0_final_report.pdf

9. Kahveci, S., Alkan, B., Ahmad, M.H., Ahmad, B., Harrison, R.: An end-to-end big data analytics platform for IoT-enabled smart factories: a case study of battery module assembly system for electric vehicles. J. Manuf. Syst. **63**, 214–223 (2022). https://doi.org/10.1016/j.jmsy.2022.03.010

10. Kalaycı, E.G., et al.: Semantic integration of Bosch manufacturing data using virtual knowledge graphs. In: Pan, J.Z., et al. (eds.) ISWC 2020. LNCS, vol. 12507, pp. 464–481. Springer, Cham (2020). https://doi.org/10.1007/978-3-030-62466-8_29

11. Kebisek, M., Tanuska, P., Spendla, L., Kotianova, J., Strelec, P.: Artificial intelligence platform proposal for paint structure quality prediction within the industry 4.0 concept. IFAC-PapersOnLine **53**(2), 11168–11174 (2020). https://doi.org/10.1016/j.ifacol.2020.12.299. 21st IFAC World Congress

12. Lavasani, M.S., Ardali, N.R., Sotudeh-Gharebagh, R., Zarghami, R., Abonyi, J., Mostoufi, N.: Big data analytics opportunities for applications in process engineering. Rev. Chem. Eng. (2021). https://doi.org/10.1515/revce-2020-0054

13. Liveline Technologies: Multi-stage continuous-flow manufacturing process (2020). https://www.kaggle.com/supergus/multistage-continuousflow-manufacturing-process/metadata. Accessed 01 Oct 2022

14. Patel, P., Ali, M.I., Sheth, A.: From raw data to smart manufacturing: AI and semantic web of things for industry 4.0. IEEE Intell. Syst. **33**, 79–86 (2018). https://doi.org/10.1109/MIS.2018.043741325

15. Rädler, S., Rigger, E.: A survey on the challenges hindering the application of data science, digital twins and design automation in engineering practice. Proc. Des. Soc. **2**, 1699–1708 (2022). https://doi.org/10.1017/pds.2022.172

16. Sanz, E., Blesa, J., Puig, V.: Bidrac industry 4.0 framework: application to an automotive paint shop process. Control Eng. Pract. **109**, 104757 (2021). https://doi.org/10.1016/j.conengprac.2021.104757

17. Shigarov, A., Khristyuk, V., Mikhailov, A.: Tabbyxl: software platform for rule-based spreadsheet data extraction and transformation. SoftwareX **10**, 100270 (2019). https://doi.org/10.1016/j.softx.2019.100270

18. Song, G., Fu, D., Zhang, D.: From knowledge graph development to serving industrial knowledge automation: a review. In: 2022 41st Chinese Control Conference (CCC), pp. 4219–4226. IEEE (2022)

19. Sun, K., Li, Y., Roy, U.: A PLM-based data analytics approach for improving product development lead time in an engineer-to-order manufacturing firm. Math. Model. Eng. Probl. **4**, 69–74 (2017). https://doi.org/10.18280/mmep.040201

20. Tercan, H., Meisen, T.: Machine learning and deep learning based predictive quality in manufacturing: a systematic review. J. Intell. Manuf. **33**(7), 1879–1905 (2022). https://doi.org/10.1007/s10845-022-01963-8

21. Wirth, R., Hipp, J.: CRISP-DM: towards a standard process modell for data mining (2000)

22. Xu, X., Hua, Q.: Industrial big data analysis in smart factory: current status and research strategies. IEEE Access **5**, 17543–17551 (2017). https://doi.org/10.1109/ACCESS.2017.2741105

Non-Fungible Token (NFT) Platform for Digital Twin Trust Management and Data Acquisition

Pasindu Kuruppuarachchi$^{(\boxtimes)}$ and Alan McGibney

Munster Technological University, Cork, Ireland
p.kuruppuarachchi@mycit.ie, alan.mcgibney@mtu.ie
https://www.mtu.ie/

Abstract. Non-Fungible Tokens (NFTs) are blockchain-based digital assets that are unique and cannot be replicated. In most cases, NFTs are used to hold the unique value of an asset in a traceable manner. However, NFTs can also be leveraged to provide a unique digital identity, allowing for secure data storage, access, and sharing. These features provide important capabilities when managing data acquisition and digital twins. Additionally, using NFTs can create a decentralized trust management system, ensuring data is only accessed and shared with authorized parties. The NFT platform can also facilitate data acquisition from digital twins, providing a secure and trustworthy method for collecting and analyzing data. This paper proposes an NFT platform to strengthen the trust of DTs operating in a collaborative ecosystem and the provision of a data loyalty platform to acquire data from DT owners by rewarding them for participating in data sharing. An electric car manufacturing use case is discussed as a pilot case to highlight the capabilities of the proposed DT NFT platform.

Keywords: Digital Twin · NFT · Trust · Web3.0

1 Introduction

The metaverse is a term used to describe a virtual world entirely online and can be accessed by anyone with an internet connection. It is a shared space where people can interact with each other using virtual objects and environments. The metaverse concept has been around for several decades, but it has gained renewed attention recently as virtual reality and augmented reality technologies have advanced [7].

NFTs (non-fungible tokens) are expected to play a significant role in developing the metaverse. An NFT is a type of digital asset that is unique and cannot

This research work is supported by Science Foundation Ireland Centre for Research Training focused on Future Networks and the Internet of Things (AdvanceCRT), under Grant number 18/CRT/6222.

be exchanged for other purchases on a one-to-one basis. NFTs are stored on a blockchain, which provides a secure and transparent record of ownership and transaction history. NFTs are currently famous for representing a variety of assets, such as digital art, collectables, and virtual real estate [19,20]. In addition, some research studies explore the possibility of other application domains, such as manufacturing [9] and supply chain traceability [6]. In these studies, the main reason for using NFTs is their ability to track and protect ownership which is vital in these application domains.

Considering the metaverse, Digital Twin (DT) is used to describe and implement virtual objects and ecosystems. A DT is a virtual replica of a physical asset or a process that uses its data to enhance its physical counterpart's capabilities [2,12,13]. DTs are interconnected in a virtual world to create digital ecosystems that replicate real-world ecosystems. Currently, DTs are implemented in manufacturing [2,12,13], energy management [1,11], healthcare [16], smart cities [3], etc. to improve its efficiency and performance.

DTs and NFTs are two concepts that can be coupled to enhance existing processes in various industries. For example, NFTs can be used to represent ownership and track the ownership history of DTs. This can be useful in various industries, such as manufacturing, logistics, and real estate [7].

A DT heavily depends on data, and the quality of this data will determine a DT's value. To get quality data from various sources, trust is a vital consideration. If data providers are untrusted, reliable decisions can not be made as data may be incorrect and inconsistent. Hence, trust and data quality are essential to any DT implementation. This paper proposes an NFT-based trust management and data acquisition platform to improve DT operational conditions in a collaborative ecosystem.

The remainder of the paper is organized as follows. Section 2 will discuss related work concerning the application of NFT in digital ecosystems. Next, Sect. 3 will present the proposed NFT platform, and Sect. 4 will provide an implemented use case scenario in the electric car manufacturing domain. This section will describe DT asset governance and the data acquisition platform for data gathering. Finally, Sect. 5 will conclude the findings and future works.

2   Related Work

The most popular definition of trust in a digital ecosystem evolves around the premise that systems behave as expected [4,22]. Trust is achieved in two ways, trust by design [18] and trust by computation [15,21]. Trust by design is the first step in constructing a trusted ecosystem, as it aims to ensure all the participants will operate as expected at the lowest level possible. A trust-by-design architecture for the DT collaborative ecosystems was proposed [10]. Figure 1 presents an updated version of this architecture to include the NFT management component in the trust management service. This is motivated to facilitate asset ownership management and traceability of the asset owners. This will strengthen the overall trust posture in the ecosystem and provide more flexible ownership transfers in asset base DT scenarios.

Single point of failure, trust, single authorization, and data ownership concerns are some of the downsides of centralized systems. Because of these problems, more and more organizations are moving towards decentralized system architectures. Typically DT data flow involves collecting data from a physical counterpart and sending it to the virtual space for processing and interpretation. This shared data is then used to invoke changes to the physical counterpart to improve operational efficiency, safety or general operation. An alternative approach is proposed that feeds all collected data to a distributed ledger using device agents [5]. In the simplest definition, DT is a two-way communication channel between the physical and digital counterparts. However, [5] implementation is more like collecting the data from the physical asset and visualizing it in the client application. Nevertheless, this implementation uses a distributed hash table to support off-chain storage for larger data segments. This off-chain storage is an excellent addition to many decentralized information systems to accommodate larger files with the same level of integrity used in simpler data-sharing messages. In a multi-stakeholder environment, asset governance is essential, and this approach did not provide any functionality to address that requirement.

Creating a DT is a complex process requiring multiple parties to collaborate. A Blockchain-based DT creation framework suggested in [8] aims to help keep track of all the partner interactions and maintain transparency for the process. The proposed [8] DT creation framework consists of all the common functionalities of a decentralized information-sharing platform. However, this framework did not describe information-sharing between multiple parties or conflict resolution mechanisms. Which is essential in collaborative ecosystems. EtherTwin [14] is an extension of the [8], highlighting more on the implementation aspects of the proposed solution. To address previously highlighted governance and information-sharing concerns, hybrid access controlling system (role-based and attribute-based) was proposed.

The main downside of this approach is in a complex dynamic system like a collaborative ecosystem, it is hard to define and maintain access control using roles and attributes. Because requirements will change frequently. Even though there is merit to using blockchain to enable accountability, it still needs a proper asset governance mechanism to give permission to change the DT in a complex dynamic ecosystem.

Distributed attribute-based access control system is proposed to address centralized access control management [17]. There are many possible problems with a centralized access control system, such as a single point of failure and transparency. Authors in [17] suggest using smart contract based access control policies because they are immutable and distributed. This will allow participants to see the access control policies, and because of the distributed ledger, it is extremely difficult to make unauthorized edits. This proposed access control management system is a potential enabler for DT access control management. However, this approach is also not suitable for complex dynamic ecosystems that need flexibility in asset governance. Because it is costly to change smart contract logic as requirement changes and hard to deploy a dynamic smart contract.

Considering tokens, there are few standards that have emerged, and the most popular in use is from the Ethereum network [6]. ERC-20 is the general fungible token, meaning each token is identical and interchangeable. On the other hand, ERC-721 is used for NFTs, and it is indivisible. The newest ERC-1155 enabled the full potential by combining both ERC-20 and ERC-721. Developers can create a single contract to leverage fungible and non-fungible tokens. Considering the proposed NFT platform, the ERC-1155 token standard provides both types of token options for the collaborative ecosystem participants.

In summary, there are interesting approaches to supporting DT creation and access control of a digital asset, but still, there is no solution for complex dynamic DT ecosystem governance with multiple stakeholders. This paper addresses this issue with an ERC-1155 NFT token base asset management approach.

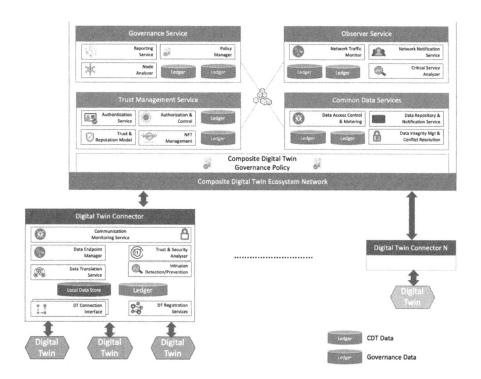

Fig. 1. Collaborative DT ecosystem architecture

3   Proposed NFT Management Platform

The NFT management platform component is an enhancement to a collaborative DT ecosystem architecture supporting trust management services as proposed in [10]. The primary function is to provide necessary services to facilitate NFT-based ownership and retain transparent asset management across its lifecycle to improve overall trustworthiness in the ecosystem.

As shown in Fig. 2, the core of the NFT management platform is the NFT management services which connect to all NFT-related functional blocks with the public and private blockchains used for NFT management. The NFT management services are also responsible for communicating with other ecosystem services, specifically ecosystem ledgers, to keep stakeholders updated with the NFT assets. The reason for designing an NFT management platform with multiple ledgers is to facilitate third-party observers to verify ownership and access relevant data without exposing internal ecosystem ledgers. This will improve ecosystem privacy while keeping transparency in asset ownership. In the current design, NFTs can be minted in public and private blockchains. If the DTs need public visibility, minting NFTs in a public blockchain will improve interoperability with other NFTs/blockchains and transparency relating to the asset information.

The token collection generator will configure the initial token parameters, such as the token type (ERC-721 or ERC-1155), token code, and token description. This enables ecosystem stakeholders to generate NFTs based on different scenarios. The token generator will then create NFTs and assign them to the asset. "Token info" is a service that helps to retrieve information about tokens. Token transfer service will facilitate token transfers between stakeholders. Finally, the transaction manager will record information related to the NFT and selected transactions, such as who minted NFTs, transfers, etc., to the ecosystem ledgers for internal records.

4   Implementation

In order to demonstrate the proposed NFT capabilities, a proof of concept implementation was carried out. The focus is a use case focused on electric car manufacturing and distribution. As shown in Fig. 3, in this use case, there are four parties involved: product owner, manufacturing stakeholders, car buyers, and other service providers. These four parties will participate in two ecosystems, namely, the electric car manufacturing ecosystem and the electric cars ecosystem. In the electric car manufacturing ecosystem, a number of stakeholders, alongside the product owner, will contribute to the manufacture of the electric car. As shown in Fig. 4, the product owner will initialise the ecosystem with stakeholders to produce these electric cars. Stakeholders will support the product owner's vision to build the product and record all the information related to the electric car using the NFT platform. This will ease the asset information traceability and trust between stakeholders because everyone can see how others are involved in the manufacturing process. Once the electric car is built, it will transfer to the asset buyer. From the asset buyer's point of view, because of NFT, it is easy to transfer ownership, and all the information related to the asset will have full traceability.

NFT Management Platform

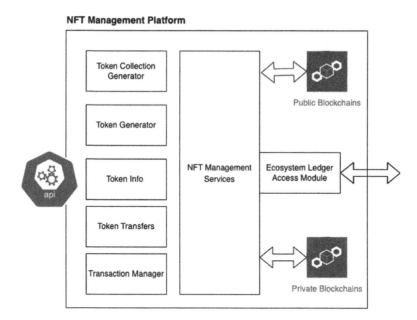

Fig. 2. Proposed NFT Platform

Considering the electric cars ecosystem, it is built with similar types of assets that consist of external and internal service providers that will provide capabilities such as part replacements, performance upgrades, etc. As shown in Fig. 5, data task creators will create data acquisition tasks in which asset buyers can participate. As mentioned earlier, data task creators can be original product owners or external service providers. Once the DT owner (asset buyer) completes the task, it will send the relevant data to the NFT platform and then to the data task creators. After evaluating the submitted data, data task creators will pass the rewards through the NFT platform. In this way, data task creators can acquire relevant data for future product improvements and enhance asset capabilities.

The current proof of concept is implemented using Unique Network[1], a Polkadot para chain specialized in NFTs. In Unique Network, it is possible to create non-fungible and re-fungible tokens. This proof of concept uses a non-fungible token for asset ownership, and the data acquisition loyalty platform uses a re-fungible token. Furthermore, the Unique Network is a public blockchain, and to create private blockchain-based NFTs, Substrate[2] can be used.

---

[1] https://unique.network/.
[2] https://substrate.io/.

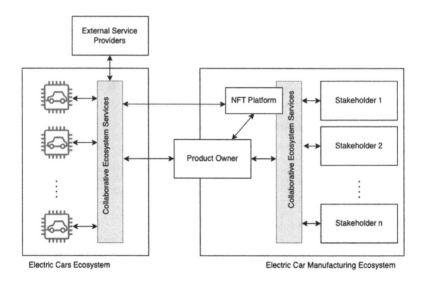

Fig. 3. Electric car manufacturing and distribution ecosystems

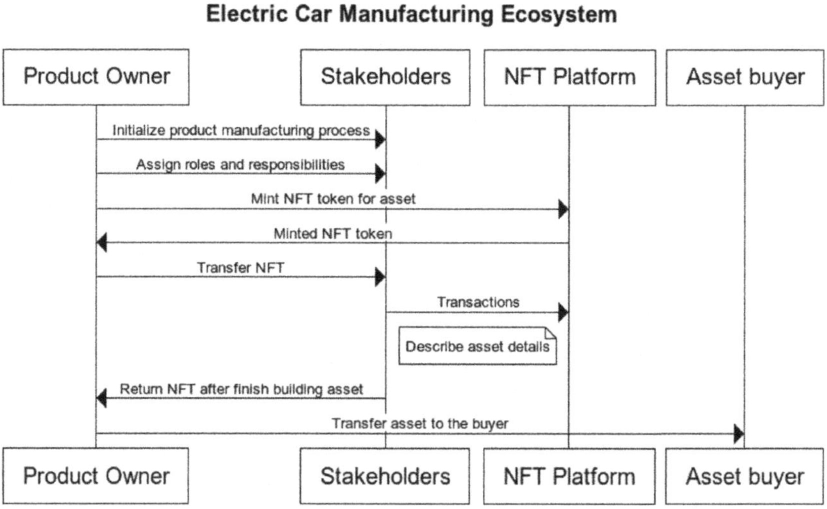

Electric Car Manufacturing Ecosystem

Fig. 4. Operational sequence electric car manufacturing ecosystem

4.1 Digital Twin Governance Using NFT

In the electric car manufacturing ecosystem, the product owner will initiate the process by creating an NFT collection, as shown in Fig. 6. This will set the collection's basic details and token type. In this instance, it is an ERC-721 token.

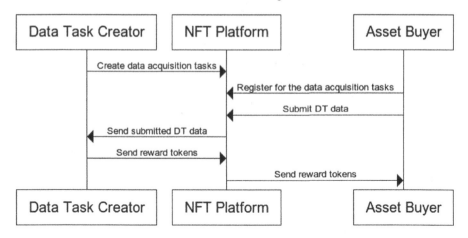

Fig. 5. Operational sequence electric cars ecosystem

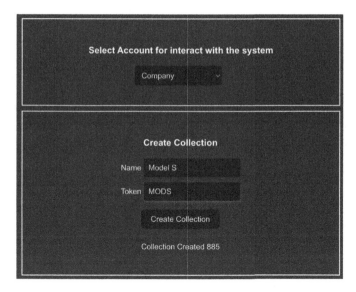

Fig. 6. Creating NFT Collection

After creating an NFT collection product owner can start minting NFTs for all built cars. For example, Fig. 7 shows a minted NFT token representing an electric car. Once done, the product owner can transfer the minted NFT to respective stakeholders to add capabilities to the asset DT.

As shown in Fig. 8, stakeholders can add transactions representing DT. In this case, it added a motor type for the electric car.

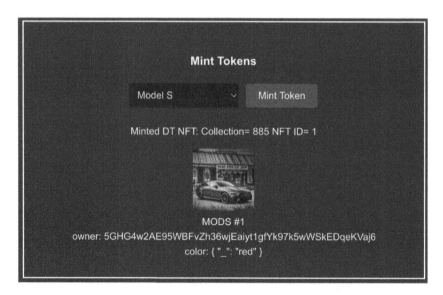

Fig. 7. Minting NFT token

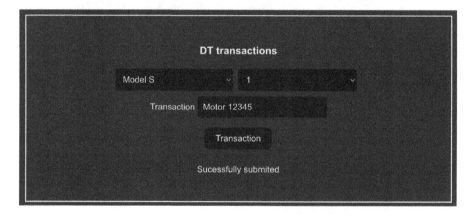

Fig. 8. NFT transactions

Once done, the product owner will transfer the car to the owner, as shown in Fig. 9. This is the end of the electric car manufacturing ecosystem, and then it will operate in the electric cars ecosystem.

4.2 Data Acquisition Using NFT Platform

After the electric car is released to the owner, it starts to operate in the real world and generates data that can be valuable for improving its capabilities. Product owners and external service providers can create data collection tasks to acquire this data. When car owner completes this task, they will be rewarded

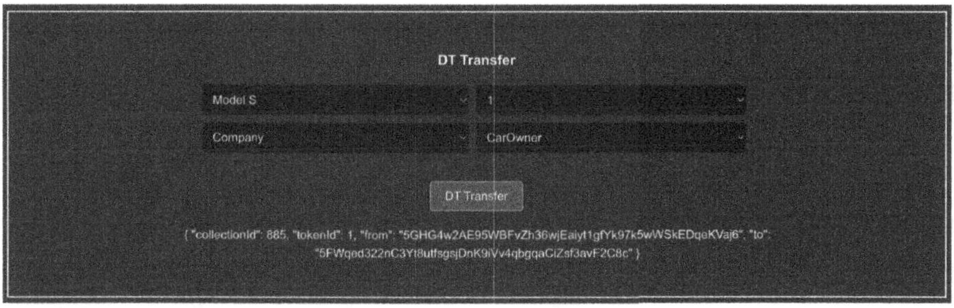

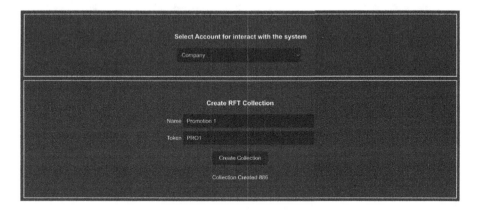

Fig. 9. NFT transfers

for completing it. In another way, NFTs can use to create a data acquisition loyalty platform.

To start the process, a product owner or external service providers will create a promotional Re-fungible token (RFT) collection as shown in Fig. 10. RFTs can group together and create a complete token collection. Each data collection task will be assigned to an RFT, and upon completion, RFTs will be grouped to create a complete token. To make promotional tokens, external service providers and product owners must go through the electric cars' collaborative ecosystem services because it will then record it in the ecosystem ledger and grant access to the NFT platform in the electric car manufacturing ecosystem.

Fig. 10. Data acquisition RFT collection creation

When minting an RFT data collection task, the promotion owner needs to specify how many tasks need to complete to get the reward. For example, as shown in Fig. 11, three RFT tokens will be minted for 3 data collection tasks. These data collection tasks will help service providers and product owners to get DT data about specific scenarios, such as battery state of charge throughout a long journey, motor conditions, etc. Once the task is completed, as shown in Fig. 12, RFTs will be transferred to the DT owner's account. After completing all the tasks, the user will get a reward.

Fig. 11. Minting RFT tokens based on the number of tasks

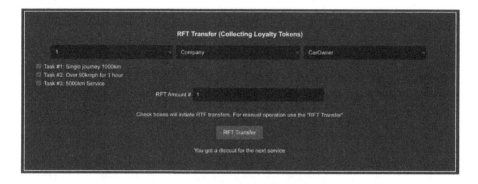

Fig. 12. RFT transfers based on the task completion

Nesting NFTs will allow the bundling of multiple tokens together. For example, as shown in Fig. 13, Main NFT will have one nested token from the task completion. This can also be leveraged to showcase added items to the asset, such as new motors, battery pack changes, etc.

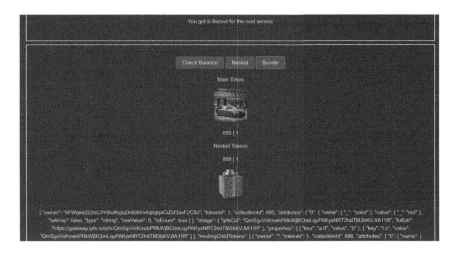

Fig. 13. Nesting NFT tokens to create token bundles

5   Conclusion

NFTs are gaining significant attention as an investment opportunity in the digital world. However, the base of NFTs is much more capable as NFTs can hold a unique value as a one-of-a-kind asset that can use to manage ownership and traceability of an asset. In the current state of the art, incorporating NFTs with DTs is still yet to be explored. This paper investigated the possibilities of using NFTs to strengthen trust in collaborative ecosystems and data acquisition using an NFT data loyalty platform. To facilitate this, a collaborative DT architecture with an NFT management platform is proposed. Finally, a representative use case with multiple DT ecosystems was discussed to highlight the proposed NFT platform capabilities. The next step will be to integrate with the complete collaborative DT ecosystem architecture and evaluate the scalability and performance of the proposed approach.

References

1. Digital Twins Debunking the Myths. https://www.ge.com/digital/blog/digital-twins-debunking-myths. Accessed 08 July 2020
2. Ayani, M., Ganebäck, M., Ng, A.H.: Digital twin: applying emulation for machine reconditioning. Procedia CIRP **72**, 243–248 (2018). https://doi.org/10.1016/j.procir.2018.03.139
3. Chaturvedi, K., Kolbe, T.H.: Towards establishing cross-platform interoperability for sensors in smart cities. Sensors **19**(3), 562 (2019). https://doi.org/10.3390/s19030562
4. Cioroaica, E., et al.: Towards creation of automated prediction systems for trust and dependability evaluation. In: 2020 28th International Conference on Software, Telecommunications and Computer Networks, SoftCOM 2020 (2020). https://doi.org/10.23919/SoftCOM50211.2020.9238329

5. Dietz, M., Putz, B., Pernul, G.: A distributed ledger approach to digital twin secure data sharing. In: Foley, S.N. (ed.) DBSec 2019. LNCS, vol. 11559, pp. 281–300. Springer, Cham (2019). https://doi.org/10.1007/978-3-030-22479-0_15

6. Gebreab, S.A., Hasan, H.R., Salah, K., Jayaraman, R.: NFT-based traceability and ownership management of medical devices. IEEE Access **10**, 126394–126411 (2022). https://doi.org/10.1109/ACCESS.2022.3226128

7. Ghirmai, S., Mebrahtom, D., Aloqaily, M., Guizani, M., Debbah, M.: Self-sovereign identity for trust and interoperability in the metaverse (2023). https://doi.org/10.48550/ARXIV.2303.00422. https://arxiv.org/abs/2303.00422

8. Hasan, H.R., et al.: A blockchain-based approach for the creation of digital twins. IEEE Access **8**, 34113–34126 (2020). https://doi.org/10.1109/ACCESS.2020.2974810

9. Jaribion, A., Knapen, A., Xamin, A., Holmström, J., Haghighat Khajavi, S.: Non-fungible tokens (NFTS) in additive manufacturing: a digital tool for enhancing IPR protection. International Conference on Design Science Research in Information Systems and Technology, DESRIST; Conference date: 01-06-2022 Through 03-06-2022 (2022)

10. Kuruppuarachchi, P.M., Rea, S., McGibney, A.: Trusted and secure composite digital twin architecture for collaborative ecosystems. IET Collab. Intell. Manuf. **5**(1), e12070 (2023). https://doi.org/10.1049/cim2.12070. https://ietresearch.onlinelibrary.wiley.com/doi/abs/10.1049/cim2.12070

11. Laaki, H., Miche, Y., Tammi, K.: Prototyping a digital twin for real time remote control over mobile networks: application of remote surgery. IEEE Access **7**, 20235–20336 (2019). https://doi.org/10.1109/ACCESS.2019.2897018

12. Malakuti, S., et al.: Digital twins for industrial applications, pp. 1–19 (2020). https://www.iiconsortium.org/pdf/IIC_Digital_Twins_Industrial_Apps_White_Paper_2020-02-18.pdf

13. Padovano, A., Longo, F., Nicoletti, L., Mirabelli, G.: A digital twin based service oriented application for a 4.0 knowledge navigation in the smart factory. IFAC-PapersOnLine **51**(11), 631–636 (2018). https://doi.org/10.1016/j.ifacol.2018.08.389

14. Putz, B., Dietz, M., Empl, P., Pernul, G.: EtherTwin: blockchain-based secure digital twin information management. Inf. Process. Manage. **58**(1), 102425 (2021). https://doi.org/10.1016/j.ipm.2020.102425

15. Qureshi, B., Min, G., Kouvatsos, D.: Collusion detection and prevention with fire+ trust and reputation model. In: Proceedings - 10th IEEE International Conference on Computer and Information Technology, CIT-2010, 7th IEEE International Conference on Embedded Software and Systems, ICESS-2010, ScalCom-2010, pp. 2548–2555 (2010). https://doi.org/10.1109/CIT.2010.433

16. Rasheed, A., San, O., Kvamsdal, T.: Digital Twin: Values, Challenges and Enablers, pp. 1–31 (2019). http://arxiv.org/abs/1910.01719

17. Rouhani, S., Belchior, R., Cruz, R.S., Deters, R.: Distributed attribute-based access control system using a permissioned blockchain. arXiv (2020)

18. Serov, I., Leitner, M.: An experimental approach to reputation in e-participation. In: Proceedings - 2016 International Conference on Software Security and Assurance, ICSSA 2016, pp. 37–42 (2017). https://doi.org/10.1109/ICSSA.2016.14

19. Wang, M., Lau, N.: NFT digital twins: a digitalization strategy to preserve and sustain miao silver craftsmanship in the metaverse era. Heritage **6**(2), 1921–1941 (2023). https://doi.org/10.3390/heritage6020103

20. Wang, Q., Li, R., Wang, Q., Chen, S.: Non-fungible token (NFT): overview, evaluation, opportunities and challenges (2021). https://doi.org/10.48550/ARXIV.2105.07447. https://arxiv.org/abs/2105.07447

21. Zong, B., Xu, F., Jiao, J., Lv, J.: A broker-assisting trust and reputation system based on artificial neural network. In: Conference Proceedings - IEEE International Conference on Systems, Man and Cybernetics, pp. 4710–4715 (2009). https://doi.org/10.1109/ICSMC.2009.5346098

22. Özalp Özer, Zheng, Y., Ren, Y.: Trust, trustworthiness, and information sharing in supply chains bridging china and the U.S. SSRN Electron. J. (2014). https://doi.org/10.2139/SSRN.1961774. https://papers.ssrn.com/abstract=1961774

Trust and Security Analyzer for Digital Twins

Pasindu Kuruppuarachchi$^{(\boxtimes)}$, Susan Rea , and Alan McGibney

Munster Technological University, Cork, Ireland
p.kuruppuarachchi@mycit.ie, {susan.rea,alan.mcgibney}@mtu.ie
https://www.mtu.ie/

Abstract. Connecting multiple digital twins aids in creating collaborative ecosystems that provide all participants with a holistic view of systems, products or components. Trust and security are always crucial in a collaborative environment. This work proposes a trust and security analyzer to evaluate individual digital twins in the ecosystem and classify their behaviour based on their actions. This classification will help ecosystem participants to make decisions about other digital twins, such as if it meets specific security criteria or interaction can lead to additional risk for the overall system operation. To validate the proposed analyzer accuracy, this paper implemented a digital twin simulator that can be used to emulate digital twin interactions. The proposed analyzer uses statistical analysis for the digital twin type classification, showing more than 94% accuracy for detecting malicious digital twins while maintaining low false-positive rates.

Keywords: Digital Twin · Collaborative Ecosystems · Trust and Security

1 Introduction

Virtual replicas of physical assets, systems, and processes that may be utilized for analysis, simulation, and optimization are known as Digital Twins (DTs) [4,17,19]. They can be developed using data feeds from sensors, IoT devices, and other sources that are useful for modelling the behaviour of complex systems in real time by combining them. Stakeholders in a collaborative ecosystem can better understand how a system operates, discover areas for development, and make informed decisions to optimize performance by deploying DTs [14,23,24].

DTs can also facilitate communication and collaboration among partners, suppliers, and customers by providing a common language and a shared understanding of the system. DTs can help stakeholders work together more effectively

This research work is supported by Science Foundation Ireland Centre for Research Training focused on Future Networks and the Internet of Things (AdvanceCRT), under Grant number 18/CRT/6222.

and efficiently in these collaborative ecosystems by providing insights about operational conditions. DT will also enable stakeholders to test and experiment with different scenarios and solutions without disrupting the physical system operations. Overall, DTs have the potential to transform collaborative ecosystems by improving communication between stakeholders, increasing overall ecosystem efficiency, and driving innovation. As the use of DTs becomes more widespread, we can expect to see new opportunities for collaboration and value creation in a variety of industries and domains such as manufacturing [4,17,19], energy management [1,15], healthcare [22], smart cities [5], etc.

Creating a successful Digital Twin Ecosystem (DTE) requires a range of factors to be considered and managed effectively. Here are some of the key factors that can contribute to the success of a DTE [9,12,23,24]:

- **Trust**: To confidently interact with other stakeholders in the ecosystem, trust is vital. Without trusting each other, it is impossible to create an ecosystem.
- **Data quality and availability**: A DT's value heavily depends on the data it is based on. To ensure the accuracy and reliability of the DT, it is essential to have high-quality, comprehensive data availability. Technology performance issues, requirements changes, unauthorized access and uncertainty in networks are some of the factors that can impact data quality and availability in the DT.
- **Interoperability**: By design, DTE consists of multiple stakeholders with their systems and technologies. Therefore, it is important to have interoperability standards and protocols that allow different systems to work together to ensure seamless communication and collaboration.
- **Security and privacy**: Various types of data are shared between DTs, and in some cases, as with mission-critical systems, sensitive data will be shared with other systems. Considering such ecosystems, security and privacy are critical to its operation. Therefore, it is essential to have robust security measures in place to protect data and prevent unauthorized access.
- **Governance and management**: A DTE requires effective governance and management to ensure all stakeholders and entities work towards the same goals and utilise resources reasonably and efficiently.
- **Scalability**: As the ecosystem grows and evolves, it is essential to scale the DT technology and infrastructure to meet changing needs without compromising security.
- **Continuous improvement**: A DTE is an evolving entity. Therefore, it is important to have a process and system of procedures in place for continuous improvement, which includes ongoing monitoring, analysis, and feedback.

An architecture was proposed that encapsulates critical functionality by design to address these key factors that facilitate creating a collaborative DT ecosystem [14]. A vital element of this architecture is the ability to assess trust, mainly focused on the interaction between DT. This paper will present the implementation of a trust and security analyzer as proposed in [13]. The evaluation of the proposed analyzer will be based on its accuracy in detecting malicious behaviour of DTs across the ecosystem. The evaluation of this was supported by the creation of a DT simulation environment to emulate various behaviours that can occur in collaborative DTE.

The remainder of the paper is organized as follows: Section 2 will discuss related works for trust and security analysis; Sect. 3 will present the proposed trust and security analyzer, and Sect. 4 will present the implementation of the trust and security analyzer and DT simulator. Section 5 will discuss the results, and finally, Sect. 6 will draw conclusions from the presented work and outline future directions.

2   Background

Trust is a core characteristic of successful collaboration. However, the definition of trust can often be subjective. In its simplest form, trust is defined as behaving as expected [6,29]. Considering the Internet of Things (IoT), Industrial IoT Consortium (IIC) defined trust using five categories [11]. Namely, these five trust categories are safety, security, privacy, reliability, and resilience. These categories map well to how DTs and more over DTE operate. As such, it is a good representation of trust in collaborative DTE.

Current literature categorises trust into two categories. Namely, trust by design [25], and trust by computation [21,28]. Trust by design is a way of implementing systems to ensure they will work as expected from the beginning rather than trying to embed additional features for trust as an afterthought. Examples include access control and authorisation techniques, the most commonly used tools to prevent unauthorised data modifications. They will improve data security, data quality and accuracy. Distributed ledgers can be used to keep the ecosystem transparent and enhance the accountability of the participants [9,10,20,24,26]. However, it is impossible to make any system perfectly secure. As such, trust by computation aims to evaluate and maintain trusted system behaviour during operation. Quality of Service (QoS) based trust evaluations are widespread in the literature as it is easy to quantify and define acceptable limits for various system characteristics [7,8,16,18,28]. Ranking and reputation models are also utilised to keep track of past behaviours [2,8,25,27,28], and once the system builds its reputation, participants will always try to maintain this. However, to be comprehensive, there is a need for a holistic trust and security analyser, adopting both parameter based-based analysers (QoS) and reputation-based trust evolution.

Despite the advancements in trust analysers for collaborative ecosystems, several challenges remain. These include the lack of standardised trust metrics, the difficulty in predicting trustworthiness in dynamic environments, and the need for more robust and scalable trust analysers. Additionally, these ecosystems' increased complexity and interconnectivity present new challenges for trust management. To address these research gaps, a comprehensive trust and security analyser is presented in this paper.

3   Proposed Trust and Security Analyzer

There are four abstract layers of the functionality of a DT [3] that have an impact on how security can be managed.

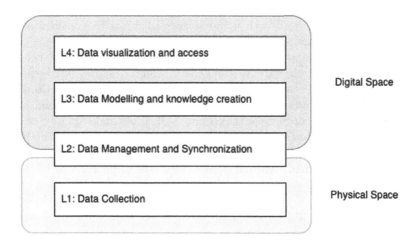

Fig. 1. Digital Twin functional layers

As shown in Fig. 1, these layers can be grouped into two segments, digital space and physical space. Based on these segments, the nature of the security threats also varies. Considering DT security threats, there are three types of security threat groups [3]. *Tampering, physical damage, and information extraction* are these three threat groups that DT need to be safeguarded. All of these threat groups possibly occur at any level, and based on the level, severity can be changed.

Considering L1, tampering can happen in the physical space by changing the settings of a physical asset or using external forces such as electromagnetic force to interrupt system workflow. In upper levels such as L2, L3, and L4, tampering can achieve by getting access to the systems such as PLC controllers, servers, etc. However, tampering attacks can even happen outside the organization's control, such as man-in-the-middle attacks. The expected outcomes of these attacks are either service disruption or producing incorrect data for further processing. These attacks will have a cascade effect, and other systems will also be affected.

Like tempering, L1 physical damage will also disrupt the services and produce incorrect values. However, considering upper levels, physical damages can happen due to natural disasters such as earthquakes, flooding, etc. or intruder actions to service hosts. The most noticeable effect is going to be service unavailability. But in some cases, incorrect data will be generated.

Information extraction is always required to get access to the information repositories such as data storage, data lakes, file system, etc. This attack can be an internal attack as well as an external one. Intruders want to obtain confidential information about the system and expose it to unwanted parties to reduce the competitive advantage or disrupt operations.

However, considering the DTE perspective, it is challenging to consider all four layers to create a trust and security analyzer because multiple DTs from different domains, standards, and practices collaborate in the ecosystem.

The proposed trust and security analyzer [13] aims to consider as many common security threats and their consequences as possible.

Each DT will be evaluated based on five categories: security-related concerns, including API, system vulnerabilities and encryption techniques, will be analyzed to assess the overall *Security* of connecting DTs and systems. *Resilience* will be evaluated to determine how well DTs and systems can withstand security attacks such as Denial of Service (DoS) and SQL injections. Quality of service (QoS) will be used to determine the *Reliability* of the DT, where a higher QoS indicates a lower likelihood of untrusted actions within the ecosystem. *Uncertainty and dependability* will be used to evaluate the behaviour of DTs and their dependence on other systems within the ecosystem. If a DT relies on a DT with a low trust score, this will impact the trust score of that DT. A dependency graph of the systems will be created to calculate the trust score, and unacceptable fluctuations in shared values will affect the uncertainty score. Finally, the *Goal analysis* module will monitor how well individual DTs achieve the goals of the collaborative ecosystem. Trustworthy DTs will work towards achieving shared goals rather than their own disruptive goals when multiple stakeholders connect to create a collaborative ecosystem.

The following evaluations will be carried out in each category. However, it is noted that these can be extended based on specific use case requirements:

– *Security*:
  - *API Security assessment*: Since DTs will expose services to other parties using APIs, evaluating each of these services for vulnerabilities is important. Attackers can use these exposed endpoints to inject remote scripts to gain access to the servers.
– *Reliability* :
  - *QoS*: QoS will help to understand how well DT will perform in the DTE. The most common QoS tests are throughput, time per request, success rate, etc.
– *Resilience* :
  - *Backup locations QoS*: If a DT is unreachable, it is essential to provide alternative operating nodes to provide uninterrupted service. However, evaluating the QoS of these nodes that offer redundancy and protection to overall system operation is also important.
– *Dependability* :
  - *Dependency graph*: Since DTs will depend on each other, exploring each DT's dependability is beneficial. In some cases, even though DTs are not directly connected, there will be some behavioural impact on other DTs.

– *Uncertainty* :
  - *Value fluctuations*: In many cases, value ranges represent acceptable operational states. If a DT provides data that deviates outside of this range could indicate something is wrong with the DT. Value fluctuations also help to identify patterns in DT data and can help to detect anomalies efficiently.
– *Goal analysis* :
  - *Trend analysis*: Most of the DTE will have goals to achieve, such as maximizing production output, increasing the revenue, decreasing wastage, etc. Test cases can be developed based on these goals to check and validate DT's operational behaviours to achieve these goals. However, this heavily depends on the use case-specific needs, and as such, it isn't easy to generalize goal analysis the same as other categories.

4   Implementation

The remainder of this section will describe the creation of a DT environment used to emulate various DT behaviour characteristics (Sect. 4.1), trust and security analyzer individual category implementations (Sect. 4.3), and evaluation environment setup (Sect. 4.2).

4.1   Digital Twin Simulator

In order to evaluate the proposed trust and security analyzer, first, it needs a collection of DTs with normal and malicious behaviours. To facilitate this, a high-level DT simulator was implemented that can be used to generate and distribute a collection of DTs. As shown in Fig. 2, the DT simulator consists of a data source, behaviour configurations, and visualizations. The data source represents the physical twin and will generate data to share with other DTs. Each DT will randomly generate a mathematical function to represent DT internal processing. As an example, a robotic arm DT will have various functions inside, such as equating the angle of arm movement, server motor control logic, etc. In this function, there will be internal and external parameters to calculate the final angle or control logic. In the simulator, to mimic this DT internal function, a random mathematical function will be created with various mathematical operations and variables. This internal function will randomly determine how many variables are in this function and how many variables are dependent on external inputs. Based on the external input requirement, DT will subscribe to other DTs for values. Since we need to create a DTE, the connector will facilitate the connection of multiple DTs and provide services such as registration of DTs, maintaining the DT subscription list, and checking the execution status. In simple terms, the connector is the orchestrator in the DTE. On top of the connector, there is an application layer that can be used for various applications.

The behaviour configuration endpoint is used to define DT behaviour in the DTE. In the current implementation, three types of DTs will be defined. Normal,

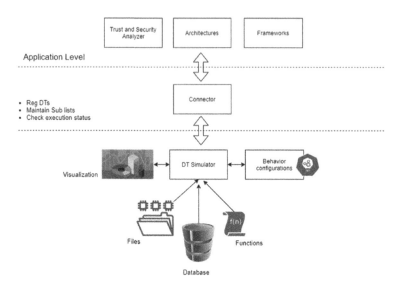

Fig. 2. Basic DT simulator for evaluations

malicious, and behavioural-changing DTs are also known as unpredictable DTs. The trust and security analyzer will be used to detect all of these three types of DTs.

The current simulation is configured as shown in Table 1, enabling the emulation of DT behaviours within the ecosystem. Based on the DT type, there is a probability that DT will behave as stated. As an example, Normal DT will have a 75% probability of fixing detected API vulnerabilities, while unpredictable DT will have on 50% probability of fixing API security issues. The API behaviour is utilized to simulate security issues associated with DT implementations, particularly the improper management of service endpoints (APIs). This vulnerability exposes the DT to external attackers, thereby jeopardizing the entire ecosystem. QoS simulation encompasses various aspects, including environmental conditions (e.g., inadequate infrastructure for service facilitation) and network traffic. Additionally, it can replicate external network attacks like man-in-the-middle attacks and DoS attacks. Consequently, these external attacks resulted in slower service and decreased overall QoS. The backup location feature exemplifies service quality and resilience in the face of network-related problems, ensuring uninterrupted service offerings. Value fluctuations serve as a means to simulate both internal and external issues. Internal problems may involve incorrect operational conditions and attacks on physical counterparts, while external activities can include man-in-the-middle attacks aimed at altering values exchanged between DTs.

4.2 Evaluation Environment

As shown in Fig. 3, a simulation script will generate DTs with randomly assigned behaviours, Digital Twin Trust and Security Analyzer (DTTSA), and Digi-

Table 1. Behavior configurations

Behavior	DT Type	Probability	Task
API	Normal	75%	Fix detected API vulnerbilities
	Unpredictable	50%	
	Malicious	25%	
QoS	Normal	25%	Delay in response 1 sec
	Unpredictable	50%	Delay response 1–2 s
	Malicious	100%	Delay response 2–4 s
Backup locations	Normal	75%	Have a backup service location
	Unpredictable	50%	
	Malicious	25%	
Value fluctuations	Normal		1 value range [min(1,10) to max(min,min+10)] and generate a value in this range
	Unpredictable		3 value ranges [min(1,10) to max(min,min+10)] and randomly pick one value range to generate a value.
	Malicious		generate a value in this range [min(1,10) to max(min+10)]

tal Twin Data Subscription Manager (DTDSM). DTTSA will determine DT's behaviour, while DTDSM will help to keep a record of all the DT subscriptions. The DTDSM will help DTTSA to generate a DT dependency graph based on the DT connections. As shown in Fig. 3, multiple evaluation cases can be carried out, but the focus of this paper is on accuracy.

In a real-world scenario, the control of DTTSA and DTDSM can be effectively managed by the ecosystem governance body, facilitating seamless interconnectivity among participants. This parallel can be drawn from the manufacturing industry, where a product owner (acting as the governance body) coordinates communication between smaller-scale suppliers and manufacturers to ensure smooth production processes. Similarly, in the ecosystem, suppliers and manufacturers initiate connectivity by linking their DTs to DTDSM and establishing connections with other participants. Once all stakeholders are on board, the dynamic evaluation of trustworthiness using DTTSA enhances overall ecosystem operations and serves as a mechanism to identify and eliminate bad actors. This approach significantly improves the efficiency and integrity of the ecosystem.

4.3   Trust and Security Analyzer

Initially, the DT evaluation environment was executed with the same behavioural types to define the statistical model and behavioural categories. This statisti-

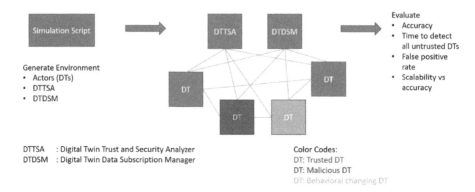

DTTSA   : Digital Twin Trust and Security Analyzer
DTDSM   : Digital Twin Data Subscription Manager

Color Codes:
DT: Trusted DT
DT: Malicious DT
DT: Behavioral changing DT

Fig. 3. DT evaluation environment

cal analysis helped to distinguish and group DT into relevant trust categories. The approach is that when DT analyzes an evaluation category, it groups its behaviour concerning the level of trustworthiness. Low means a low impact on trust, while high means trust impact is greater than other categories. As shown in Table 2, trust effect groups were created. For DT-generated values, the standard deviation of the output values is considered. If a DT fluctuates its values, the standard deviation will be higher than the normal operation conditions. For QoS, the average time per request is considered. API analysis based on the 22 known API vulnerabilities and the weighted average is considered to determine the trust effects group. More details on the API security evaluation is discussed in [13]. The backup service evaluates the DT resilience and QoS provided by the backup service endpoints.

Table 2. Statistical analysis categorizations (SD=Standard deviation, AVG = Average, WAVG= Weighted Average)

	Values (SD)	QoS (AVG)	API analysis (WAVG)	Backup service QoS (AVG)
Low	<1.499	<0.5	>25	<0.5
Mid	1.5–2	0.6–1	23.5–24.9	0.6–1
High	>2	>1	<23.5	>1

5   Evaluations

As shown in Fig. 3, the simulation script will deploy DTs and assign a type. This will define their behaviour and how they operate in the DTE. Currently, there are three types of DTs, Normal (n), Unpredictable (c), and Malicious (m). The number of DTs in the DTE also needs to determine how many variables need to be included in the DT internal function. A DT internal function is a representation of what DT will do in real operation conditions. As an example, a robotic arm will have a function to determine arm movement angle based on the other equipment it is connected with. In this case, other DTs are in the DTE. Therefore, as the number of DTs increases, the higher number of variables represent possible complex relationships with other DTs. Based on the number of external connections required to calculate the DT internal function, DTs make connections with other DTs to get values for the DT internal function.

As a first step, a DT will register with the DTTSA and submit its available services. The current implementation has two GET services and two POST services. Once it submits its services, it will also request services available from other DTs. Finally, once a full range of services is available, it will subscribe to other DTs to get values to calculate its internal function.

Once all the DTs register themselves with DTTSA and register for other DT services, the simulation begins. DTs will record all the values received from other DTs and request-response time. Later this data will be used to calculate the QoS and reliability of the DTs. Currently, DTTSA will carry out API security vulnerability tests, QoS, and backup service location QoS. A DT will submit received values from other DTs and their QoS values to DTTSA for further analysis. In addition, the DT-level trust value submission will enable future trust-related attack simulations such as bad-mouthing, self-promoting, etc.

Considering Table 2, DTTSA will analyze and categorise DTs into individual trust categories. Based on the low, mid, and high counts, the initial DT type will be determined. If the highest count is in a lower category, that evaluation category will be labelled as normal. This technique is referred to as the majority selection, and the same procedure will apply for mid and high, respectively, for changing and malicious. If low and mid or mid and high counts are equal, it will be labelled as changing, while all other possibilities are marked as malicious.

After labelling the category, all categories will pass to the DT-type predictor. This process will then determine the final DT type. First, it will check maximum label types, and if there is a clear maximum label, take it as the final predicted DT type. If not, two or more equals pick the final prediction as unpredictable DT behaviour, while all other cases are labelled as malicious.

After 60 simulation instances, Table 3 and 4 show that the proposed trust and security analyzer has high accuracy for detecting DT types and very low false positive rates. Since the DT simulator runs randomly, there is no guarantee it will create the same amount of DT types in each experiment. This is the reason in Table 3 has different numbers for each DT type deployment. In these 60 simulation instances, 290 times Normal DTs deployed and 258 times proposed trust and security analyzer correctly detected it as a normal DT. Specifically, only once analyzer detects a malicious DT as a normal DT, and only two occurrences for detecting a normal DT as a malicious DT.

Table 4 shows that the accuracy of detecting malicious DTs is 94%. Considering changing DT behaviour, false positive rates are slightly higher, but in all cases, it's less than 7%. Detecting normal DTs as malicious and vice versa is less than 1%. This shows that the proposed trust and security analyzer is capable of detecting multiple DT behaviours accurately.

Table 3. Each DT-type detection for 60 simulation runs

	Normal	Changing	Malicious	Deployments
Normal	258	30	2	290
Changing	18	250	16	284
Malicious	1	16	297	314

Table 4. Each DT type detection accuracy

	Normal	Changing	Malicious
Normal	88.97%	10.34%	0.69%
Changing	6.34%	88.03%	5.63%
Malicious	0.32%	5.10%	94.59%

6   Conclusions

Based on the state-of-the-art review, several challenges have been identified regarding the evaluation of trust in DT-based collaborative ecosystems. These challenges include the absence of standardized trust metrics, the difficulty in predicting trustworthiness in dynamic environments, and the requirement for more robust and scalable trust analyzers. The increasing complexity and interconnectivity of these ecosystems further compound the trust management challenges. To address these issues, a proposed trust and security analyzer has been introduced, employing five categories: security, resilience, reliability, dependency, uncertainty, and collaborative goals.

One primary limitation of the current trust and security analyzer is its reliance on statistical analysis to define malicious, changing, and normal behaviours. This poses a challenge when implementing new application scenarios due to limited data availability. However, the proposed DT trust analyzer offers independence through multiple evaluation categories. This allows for the independent evaluation of a DT, even if one or two evaluation categories are compromised or experiencing detection issues.

Simulated evaluations demonstrate that the proposed analyzer achieves a detection rate of over 94% for identifying malicious DTs while maintaining a false positive rate of less than 1%. Ongoing work involves assessing the accuracy of the proposed analyzer when scaling with a larger number of DTs.

References

1. Digital Twins Debunking the Myths. https://www.ge.com/digital/blog/digital-twins-debunking-myths. Accessed 08 July 2020
2. Albuquerque, R.D.O., Cohen, F.F., Mota, J.L.T., Sousa, R.T.D.: Analysis of a trust and reputation model applied to a computational grid using software agents. In: Proceedings - 2008 International Conference on Convergence and Hybrid Information Technology, ICHIT 2008, pp. 196–203 (2008). https://doi.org/10.1109/ICHIT.2008.182
3. Alcaraz, C., Lopez, J.: Digital twin: a comprehensive survey of security threats. IEEE Commun. Surv. Tutorials **24**(3), 1475–1503 (2022). https://doi.org/10.1109/COMST.2022.3171465
4. Ayani, M., Ganebäck, M., Ng, A.H.: Digital twin: applying emulation for machine reconditioning. Procedia CIRP **72**, 243–248 (2018). https://doi.org/10.1016/j.procir.2018.03.139
5. Chaturvedi, K., Kolbe, T.H.: Towards establishing cross-platform interoperability for sensors in smart cities. Sensors (Switz.) **19**(3), 562 (2019). https://doi.org/10.3390/s19030562
6. Cioroaica, E., et al.: Towards creation of automated prediction systems for trust and dependability evaluation. In: 2020 28th International Conference on Software, Telecommunications and Computer Networks, SoftCOM 2020 (2020). https://doi.org/10.23919/SoftCOM50211.2020.9238329
7. Cioroaica, E., Chren, S., Buhnova, B., Kuhn, T., DImitrov, D.: Reference architecture for trust-based digital ecosystems. In: Proceedings - 2020 IEEE International Conference on Software Architecture Companion, ICSA-C 2020, pp. 266–273 (2020). https://doi.org/10.1109/ICSA-C50368.2020.00051
8. Dessì, N., Pes, B., Fugini, M.G.: A distributed trust and reputation framework for scientific grids. In: Proceedings of the 2009 3rd International Conference on Research Challenges in Information Science, RCIS 2009, pp. 265–274 (2009). https://doi.org/10.1109/RCIS.2009.5089290
9. Dietz, M., Putz, B., Pernul, G.: A distributed ledger approach to digital twin secure data sharing. In: Foley, S.N. (ed.) DBSec 2019. LNCS, vol. 11559, pp. 281–300. Springer, Cham (2019). https://doi.org/10.1007/978-3-030-22479-0_15
10. Hasan, H.R., et al.: A blockchain-based approach for the creation of digital twins. IEEE Access **8**, 34113–34126 (2020). https://doi.org/10.1109/ACCESS.2020.2974810
11. Industrial Internet Consortium: The Industrial Internet of Things: Managing and Assessing Trustworthiness for IIoT in Practice, pp. 1–40 (2019)
12. Kuruppuarachchi, P., Rea, S., McGibney, A.: An architecture for composite digital twin enabling collaborative digital ecosystems. In: 2022 IEEE 25th International Conference on Computer Supported Cooperative Work in Design (CSCWD), pp. 980–985 (2022). https://doi.org/10.1109/CSCWD54268.2022.9776073
13. Kuruppuarachchi, P., Rea, S., McGibney, A.: Trust and security analyzer for collaborative digital manufacturing ecosystems. In: Margaria, T., Steffen, B. (eds.) ISoLA 2022 Part IV. LNCS, vol. 13704, pp. 208–218. Springer, Cham (2022). https://doi.org/10.1007/978-3-031-19762-8_15
14. Kuruppuarachchi, P.M., Rea, S., McGibney, A.: Trusted and secure composite digital twin architecture for collaborative ecosystems. IET Collaborative Intell. Manuf. **5**(1), e12070 (2023). https://doi.org/10.1049/cim2.12070. https://ietresearch.onlinelibrary.wiley.com/doi/abs/10.1049/cim2.12070

15. Laaki, H., Miche, Y., Tammi, K.: Prototyping a digital twin for real time remote control over mobile networks: application of remote surgery. IEEE Access **7**, 20235–20336 (2019). https://doi.org/10.1109/ACCESS.2019.2897018

16. Ma, W., Wang, X., Hu, M., Zhou, Q.: Machine learning empowered trust evaluation method for IoT devices. IEEE Access **9**, 65066–65077 (2021). https://doi.org/10.1109/ACCESS.2021.3076118

17. Malakuti, S., et al.: Digital twins for Industrial Applications (February), pp. 1–19 (2020). https://www.iiconsortium.org/pdf/IIC_Digital_Twins_Industrial_Apps_White_Paper_2020-02-18.pdf

18. Mayoral, A., et al.: Control orchestration protocol: unified transport API for distributed cloud and network orchestration. J. Opt. Commun. Netw. **9**, A216–A222 (2017). https://doi.org/10.1364/JOCN.9.00A216

19. Padovano, A., Longo, F., Nicoletti, L., Mirabelli, G.: A digital twin based service oriented application for a 4.0 knowledge navigation in the smart factory. IFAC-PapersOnLine **51**(11), 631–636 (2018). https://doi.org/10.1016/j.ifacol.2018.08.389

20. Putz, B., Dietz, M., Empl, P., Pernul, G.: EtherTwin: blockchain-based Secure Digital Twin Information Management. Inf. Process. Manag. **58**(1), 102425 (2021). https://doi.org/10.1016/j.ipm.2020.102425

21. Qureshi, B., Min, G., Kouvatsos, D.: Collusion detection and prevention with fire+ trust and reputation model. In: Proceedings - 10th IEEE International Conference on Computer and Information Technology, CIT-2010, 7th IEEE International Conference on Embedded Software and Systems, ICESS-2010, ScalCom-2010, pp. 2548–2555 (2010). https://doi.org/10.1109/CIT.2010.433

22. Rasheed, A., San, O., Kvamsdal, T.: Digital Twin: values, challenges and enablers, pp. 1–31 (2019). http://arxiv.org/abs/1910.01719

23. Rasor, R., Göllner, D., Bernijazov, R., Kaiser, L., Dumitrescu, R.: Towards collaborative life cycle specification of digital twins in manufacturing value chains. Procedia CIRP **98**, 229–234 (2021). https://doi.org/10.1016/j.procir.2021.01.035

24. Sahal, R., Alsamhi, S.H., Brown, K.N., O'shea, D., McCarthy, C., Guizani, M.: Blockchain-empowered digital twins collaboration: smart transportation use case. Machines **9**(9), 1–33 (2021). https://doi.org/10.3390/machines9090193

25. Serov, I., Leitner, M.: An experimental approach to reputation in e-participation. In: Proceedings - 2016 International Conference on Software Security and Assurance, ICSSA 2016, pp. 37–42 (2017). https://doi.org/10.1109/ICSSA.2016.14

26. Suhail, S., Hussain, R., Jurdak, R., Hong, C.S.: Trustworthy digital twins in the industrial internet of things with blockchain. IEEE Internet Computing **7801**(c), 1–8 (2021). https://doi.org/10.1109/MIC.2021.3059320

27. Sun, W., Xu, N., Wang, L., Zhang, H., Zhang, Y.: Dynamic digital twin and federated learning with incentives for air-ground networks. IEEE Trans. Netw. Sci. Eng. **4697**(c), 1–13 (2020). https://doi.org/10.1109/TNSE.2020.3048137

28. Zong, B., Xu, F., Jiao, J., Lv, J.: A broker-assisting trust and reputation system based on artificial neural network. In: Conference Proceedings - IEEE International Conference on Systems, Man and Cybernetics, pp. 4710–4715 (2009). https://doi.org/10.1109/ICSMC.2009.5346098

29. Özer, Ö., Zheng, Y., Ren, Y.: Trust, trustworthiness, and information sharing in supply chains bridging china and the U.S. SSRN Electron. J. (2014). https://doi.org/10.2139/SSRN.1961774. https://papers.ssrn.com/abstract=1961774

Architecture Technologies

Architecture for Ubiquitous Agents for Digital Ecosystem

Alexander Suleykin[1] (ID) and Peter Panfilov[2]([✉]) (ID)

[1] V.A. Trapeznikov Institute of Control Sciences of Russian Academy of Sciences,
Profsoyuznaya ul. 65, 117997 Moscow, Russia
[2] HSE University, Myasnitskaya ul. 20, 101000 Moscow, Russia
ppanfilov@hse.ru

Abstract. In this paper, we present the high-level architecture of an integrated resource management system for the digital ecosystem of a modern enterprise. The proposed system configuration implements the CONSORTS concept – a new kind of architecture for ubiquitous intelligent agents that provide services for modeling and forecasting the dynamics of changes in the resources of a modern enterprise. The other part of the digital ecosystem is made up of auxiliary agents for data processing, their integration and merging, normalization and filtering, converting data to a single model. We illustrate an idea of CONSORTS-based resource management system using the example of digital ecosystem of the real production enterprise. Considerations of special issues of stability design of an integrated control system in digital ecosystem accompany and complement the design issues of the semantic grounding and cognitive resources of the CONSORTS-based architectural style.

Keywords: Production Management System · Digital Ecosystem · Resource Management · Multi-Agent System

1 Introduction

The development and management of the production digital ecosystems (PDES) is becoming increasingly important along with the development of information technology, an increase in the amount of data in a manufacturing enterprise, the emergence of new sensors and equipment, and global industrial digitalization. The management of such complex production systems is essential for the stable and sustainable functioning of a modern manufacturing enterprise [1].

In the context of an ever-increasing amount of data and their fragmented nature (discreteness, formats, protocols, data scheme, type of loading, etc.), building an integrated production resource management system in an enterprise's PDES is a difficult task, which includes both the integration of disparate data from different levels of a manufacturing enterprise, building a modern fault-tolerant scale-out storage system and managing this data, as well as building intelligent services for predicting the dynamics of changes in all resources, which is the core of an integrated management system [2].

© The Author(s), under exclusive license to Springer Nature Switzerland AG 2024
R. Chbeir et al. (Eds.): MEDES 2023, CCIS 2022, pp. 293–302, 2024.
https://doi.org/10.1007/978-3-031-51643-6_21

For efficient and flexible control of the production process, it is necessary to integrate a lot of data from different sources, such as sensors of production equipment, process control systems, production management systems of the MES class, production resource planning like MRP, as well as enterprise credentials from the ERP level, general corporate directories of the enterprise, analytical reports of BI systems, external open data sources, data of competitors and partners from external digital ecosystems, etc.

Many studies consider digital ecosystems as a combination of social networks and knowledge [1] or digital twins and data transmission infrastructure [2]. In some studies authors agree that data and its constant transmission becomes a key resource [3]. Some works devoted to problems of integrated management and planning are focused on the development of cyber-physical production systems and the use of digital twins to optimize the production process. For example, the work [4] presents a basic solution for decentralized and integrated decision-making to change the schedule of a cyber-physical production system. In [5], the authors present the structure of a digital twin, synchronized with the field, for production planning under conditions of uncertainty. The viability of this structure demonstrated in a production line application in a laboratory environment. In paper [6], the current state of integrated production-distribution system has been reviewed and conclusion was made, that the real-time and data decision in production and supply chain are in trends and will continue to grow in popularity. Another approach to the management of production processes dynamics is described in [7], where an approach to manage production dynamics through the configuration changes of the products is presented. However, the approach does not consider and accounts for computing infrastructure level stability factors.

For such complex and dynamic digital ecosystem framework, we have been developing a multi-agent architecture of a digital ecosystem which is based on concept of cognitive resource management with physically-grounding agents or CONSORTS that represent a new kind of architecture for ubiquitous agents. CONSORTS agents have grounding to the physical world through sensory information and are conscious of physical resources in a cognitive way. Agents in CONSORTS realize services that extend conventional services using information about the physical world such as position, and can recognize, reorganize, and operate physical resources as cognitive resources [8].

In our previous works [9–12], we considered the issues of architecture modeling and intelligent algorithms for the tasks of production planning data processing [9], managing digital ecosystems of power grids [10], as well as an approach to the architecture design of a digital manufacturing ecosystem management system [11] and supply chains [12]. It has been shown that digitalization and digital ecosystem governance play an important role in the modern manufacturing enterprise.

In this work, it is proposed to use an integrated resource management system in the PDES of a modern manufacturing enterprise, which is capable of solving problems of different levels of management. Merging of data of different levels will allow achieving a synergistic effect and revealing new, deep dependencies between processes and objects of different levels. These control systems are intelligent services implemented as ubiquitous agents in CONSORTS architecture [13–15]. By CONSORTS agents we mean the intelligent services of the digital ecosystem, that, in the process of adapting to the natural conditions of existence, receive an additional advantage of entering into numerous relationships with each other. Agents in this architecture can provide both services directly aimed at solving management problems and auxiliary and supporting services to ensure the reliability, stability, scalability of intelligent services.

This work provides an expanded view of the architecture of such systems and considers the integrated management of production resources in the PDES of an enterprise as part of a management system for the entire enterprise information system. In this article we discuss the issues of constructing the high-level architecture of an integrated resource management system for the enterprise production digital ecosystem, the functional architecture of the CONSORTS service layer of the system, as well as stability of the control in the proposed management system. Proposed approach allows management to make real-time decisions, as well as consolidate all needed data from different production levels.

2   An Integrated Resource Management System

The top-level architecture of the resource management system in the PDES of a manufacturing enterprise is shown in Fig. 1.

The architecture of the system depicts various levels of control, the performance of which determines whether the resource management system will function effectively and stable. The lower level of control corresponds to the physical infrastructure layer that includes storage disks, RAM, processor cores, GPUs, networking hardware, etc. It is recommended to use the fastest disks for data storage in terms of write and read operations (Optane or NVME class), a large number of modern processor cores for data processing, with the ability to use several logical threads on a single physical core, a large number of GPUs (for a certain class of computational tasks), fast fiber-optic network for data transmission, with switches and buses to provide the required network bandwidth (usually 100Gb/s).

The next level of control is the operating system (OS), cloud, and virtualization layer. At this layer, it is important to ensure the stable operation of the operating system, virtual machines (VMs) and the functioning of the cloud - private or public.

Next comes the level of computing infrastructure management, in which the deployment of the main distributed scalable systems for processing and storing big data is carried out. All services in this layer can be divided into Stateful (stateful databases) and Stateless (stateless data processing services). These include:

- Messaging systems. This class of systems is designed for online storage and processing of data received from any external systems in streaming mode. If data is loaded in batch mode, then this class of systems may not be used.
- Data processing engines. A set of systems that help to run heavy computational tasks in a distributed manner. The systems support horizontal scaling and fault tolerance, which improves performance and stability, respectively.
- Engines for modeling and training. These are systems intended to be used in solving some computationally intensive tasks of processing images, video and other data in a distributed mode.
- Data storage systems: In-Memory storage; Relational storage; Time Series Storage; Object storage; Fast Data Marts storage.

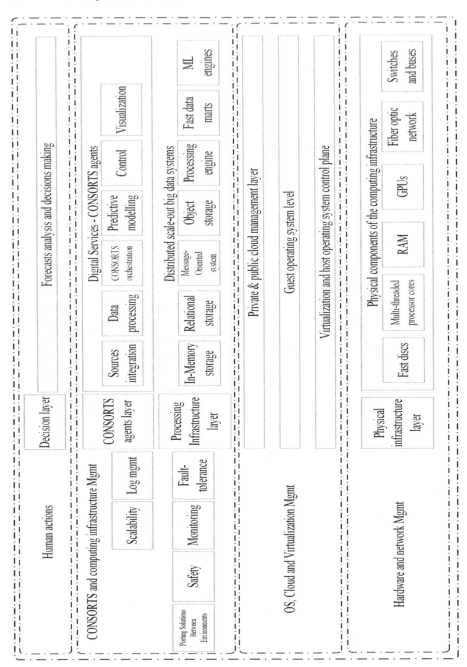

Fig. 1. A high-level architecture of the integrated resource management system for the Production Digital Ecosystem (PDES).

Level of control of CONSORTS agents and services. This layer includes all digital services for managing the digital ecosystem, services for integrating data from all sources, services for processing data in the warehouse, modeling services for predictive control models.

Management of the services and computing infrastructure is an important function in the entire architecture of a system. Efficient management of CONSORTS agents and computing infrastructure is achieved through containerization technology, where each intelligent agent or storage or processing computing service runs from container, which allows for better manageability, resilience and easier support. Management of agents and computing infrastructure includes health monitoring, security, event logging, fault tolerance management by ensuring high availability of services and automatically raising similar services on other machines, orchestrating containers among themselves, scaling them with increasing data volumes, as well as issues of automatic transfer and deploying solutions between environments.

3   Functional Architecture of the CONSORTS Agent Layer

The functional architecture (Fig. 2) of the CONSORTS agents and services layer depicts a set of agents/services that perform basic operations with data. It uses the services from infrastructure layer and all underlying layers.

CONSORTS agents perform the following tasks:

- Integration and Exchange agent offers services of loading data from various sources. Sources can be both internal transactional systems of the ERP class, MES, etc., internal systems of production processes and equipment that transmit data in streaming mode, as well as external systems. The task of this agent is to integrate the necessary data into a single repository, primary filtering, and validation of the data schema for compliance with the declared types.
- Data processing agent consists of services for processing data in the storage, normalizing, applying various business logic, etc. Also, to provide own system of unique primary keys, it is needed to ensure the rekeying of data coming from sources.
- Modeling agent realizes services for modeling intelligent predictive models. These services also help to improve forecasting accuracy and performance.
- Control Action agent renders control services based on real-time production data and provides direct management service of the production facility.
- Visualization agent of forecasting models represents a set of services for visualization of forecasts, their storage and management of notifications.
- Orchestration agent handles synchronization of agents and services with each other to ensure synchronization of transformations on data including data loading, schema validation, filtering, normalization, re-keying, modeling, control and visualization. Each CONSORTS agent and service should only be started within a certain period of time, sequentially or in parallel with other services.

It is assumed that external ecosystems will be data consumers for the control system of the digital ecosystem. These external ecosystems include:

- Supply chain ecosystems. They exchange forecasts with production suppliers.

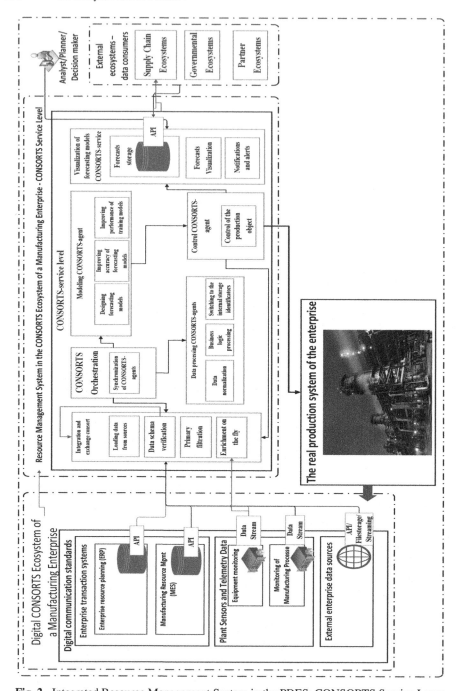

Fig. 2. Integrated Resource Management System in the PDES: CONSORTS Service Layer.

- State (Governmental) ecosystems. Send forecasts for the implementation of plans for the production of vital goods, their prices and quantities.
- Partner ecosystems. These systems exchange forecasts with partners.

The number of such external ecosystems will increase with the increase in the number of working forecast models. Interaction with external systems is implemented through the Application Programming Interface (API).

4 Control System Stability

4.1 Stability of CONSORTS Service Layer

The stability of the entire control system will consist of the stability of all levels of the control in an architecture. Of particular interest are the levels of control at computing infrastructure layer and CONSORTS agents and services layer, as well as layer of management systems for computing infrastructure and CONSORT agents. By using proper management system, it is possible to increase the stability of the control system by organizing fault-tolerant software components of both the computing infrastructure and CONSORTS service layer, to make CONSORTS agents with automatic "seamless" switching between different computers if necessary.

The computing infrastructure layer will include all software tools running on top of the operating system that are required to implement any CONSORTS agent service. For example, to implement the integration agent, it is necessary to consider a data source, which must also be taken into account in the analysis, a database for loading data, as well as the software frameworks, on the basis of which the integration agent is developed. If a framework written in Java is chosen as the basis, then when analyzing stability, it is necessary to take into account both the stability of the framework itself and the Java Virtual Machine, which is used "under the hood" of the framework. Thus, the CONSORTS service layer stability can be formalized by means of some signs:

$$S_i = IS * OS * SF * SE * SA * SM, \tag{1}$$

where: S_i is CONSORTS service layer stability ($S_i \leq 1$),

IS is Inbound Stability, i.e., stability of incoming data streams and source systems $IS \leq 1$),

OS is Outbound Stability, i.e., stability of data receiving systems for the CONSORTS services ($OS \leq 1$),

SF is Stability of the frameworks on the basis of which the CONSORTS service was developed ($SF \leq 1$),

SE is Stability of the engine on the basis of which the framework is implemented ($SE \leq 1$),

SA is Stability of the CONSORTS service itself ($SA \leq 1$),

SM is a mathematical stability of the intelligent service agent, if any ($SM \leq 1$).

The stability of the engine on the basis of which the framework is written can be neglected, since its stability can already be included in the stability of the framework.

When analyzing the formula, one can come to the conclusion that for each CON-SORTS agent the stability of adjacent receiver systems, which are the computing infrastructure of the architecture, will be taken into account. The stability of this infrastructure has already been taken into account in the general formula (1). However, in order to increase the importance of some services over others, with which the agents interact fewer times, it is proposed to introduce a weight coefficient that help to determine the importance of the service of computing infrastructure.

Thus, for CONSORTS agent services that interact with external ecosystems, the stability will look like:

$$S_i = SF * SE * SA * SM, \tag{2}$$

where: S_i is CONSORTS service layer stability ($S_i \leq 1$), SE is external (for the control system) system and communication channels ($SE \leq 1$), SF is Stability of the frameworks or libraries, on the basis of which the CONSORTS service works ($SF \leq 1$), SA is Stability of the CONSORTS agent service ($SA \leq 1$), SM is Mathematical stability of the intelligent service CONSORTS agent, if any ($SM \leq 1$).

4.2 Stability of Infrastructure Layer

The computational infrastructure of the control system is the stability of all components of the infrastructure and their connection with each other. To achieve the stability of the control system, it must be distributed by definition, since otherwise the failure of one machine will lead to the failure of the entire control system, which, obviously, is not a stable state of the system.

In general, such infrastructure components will include various database management systems (DBMS), distributed data processing services and training forecasting models, as well as visualization services. Stability of Infrastructure is the following:

$$S_i = \frac{\sum_1^N LnSdb}{N} \frac{\sum_1^M LmSpr}{M} \frac{\sum_1^K LkSvis}{K}, \tag{3}$$

where: S_i is General Infrastructure stability ($S_i \leq 1$),

N is Number of databases in the control system,

L_n - Coefficient (weight) of the significance of the n-th database in the system,

Sdb - Stability of functioning of the N-th database ($Sdb \leq 1$),

M - The number of distributed services for data processing and training models,

Lm - Coefficient (weight) of the significance of the m-th distributed data service,

Spr - Stability of functioning of the n-th distributed data processing service $Spr \leq 1$.

K - Number of visualization services,

Lk - The coefficient (weight) of significance of the k-th data visualization service,

$Svis$ - Stability of the k-th data visualization service ($Svis \leq 1$).

4.3 Stability of the Control System

The overall stability of the control system will be calculated as the logical product of variables at all levels of the control system architecture:

$$Se = Sh * Sv * Sg * Sc * Si * Sa, \tag{4}$$

where: *Se* - the overall stability of the control system,

Sh - the stability of the physical equipment and network in the control system,

Sv - the stability of the virtualization system and the host operating system,

Sg - stability of the guest operating system,

Sc - stability of the cloud infrastructure/service,

Si - infrastructure stability,

Sa - the application stability of the CONSORTS services, calculated using the formula above.

5 Conclusion

In this article, the high-level and functional architectures for an integrated production resource management system were proposed as a component of production digital ecosystems based on CONSORTS multi-agent architecture - a control system engine. A model of the CONSORTS service layer of the digital ecosystem and its interaction with internal and external ecosystems was discussed.

Special attention in the architecture is given to the CONSORTS service layer and the computing infrastructure layer, thanks to which it is possible to increase the overall stability of the control and management system in digital ecosystem, making the CONSORTS agent services and infrastructure services fault-tolerant and scalable. Improving the reliability of the control system through infrastructure and CONSORTS services will make it possible to minimize the dependence of the control system on the physical components of the computing infrastructure and machine failures.

Acknowledgments. The reported study was partially funded by HSE University according to the GSB's Project Group Competition in 2022–2023.

References

1. Nachira, F., Dini, P., Nicolai, A.A.: Network of digital business ecosystems for Europe: roots, processes and perspectives. digital business ecosystems. European Commission, Bruxelles (2007)
2. Dong, H., Hussain, F.K., Chang, E.: An integrative view of the concept of digital ecosystem. In: Proceedings of the Third International Conference on Networking and Services, Washington, DC, USA, pp. 42–44. IEEE Computer Society (2007)
3. Saleh, M., Abel, M.-H.: Moving from digital ecosystem to system of information systems. In: IEEE 20th International Conference on Computer Supported Cooperative Work in Design (CSCWD), Nanchang, China, pp. 91–96 (2013)
4. Villalonga, A., et al.: A decision-making framework for dynamic scheduling of cyber-physical production systems based on digital twins. Annu. Rev. Control **51**, 357–373 (2021). https://doi.org/10.1016/j.arcontrol.2021.04.008
5. Negri, E., Pandhare, V., Cattaneo, L., Singh, J., Macchi, M., Lee, J.: Field-synchronized digital twin framework for production scheduling with uncertainty. J. Intell. Manuf. **32**, 1207–1228 (2021). https://doi.org/10.1007/s10845-020-01685-9

6. Darvish, M., Kidd, M.P., Coelho, L.C., Renaud, J.: Integrated production-distribution systems: trends and perspectives. Pesquisa Oper. **41**(s1), e246080 (2021). https://doi.org/10.1590/0101-7438.2021.041s1.00246080

7. Dhungana, D., Falkner, A., Haselböck, A., Taupe, R.: Enabling integrated product and factory configuration in smart production ecosystems, pp.266–273 (2017). https://doi.org/10.1109/SEAA.2017.26

8. Suleykin, A., Bakhtadze, N.: Agent-based architectural models of supply chain management in digital ecosystems. In: Arai, K., Kapoor, S., Bhatia, R. (eds.) IntelliSys 2020. AISC, vol. 1252, pp. 115–127. Springer, Cham (2021). https://doi.org/10.1007/978-3-030-55190-2_9

9. Suleykin, A.S., Panfilov, P.B.: Designing data-intensive application system for production plans data processing and near real-time analytics. In: 2022 8th International Conference on Control, Decision and Information Technologies (CoDIT), pp. 1495–1500 (2022). https://doi.org/10.1109/CoDIT55151.2022.9804133

10. Suleykin, A., Bakhtadze, N., Pavlov, B., Pyatetsky, V.: Digital energy ecosystems. IFAC PapersOnLine **52**(13), 30–35 (2019)

11. Bakhtadze, N., Suleykin, A.: Industrial digital ecosystems: predictive models and architecture development issues. Annu. Rev. Control **51**, 56–64 (2020). ISSN 1367-5788

12. Suleykin, A., Bakhtadze, N.: Agent-based architectural models of supply chain management in digital ecosystems. In: Arai, K., Kapoor, S., Bhatia, R. (eds.) IntelliSys 2020. AISC, vol. 1252, pp. 115–127. Springer, Cham (2021). https://doi.org/10.1007/978-3-030-55190-2_9

13. Sashima, A., Izumi, N., Kurumatani, K.: CONSORTS: a multiagent architecture for service coordination in ubiquitous computing. In: Kurumatani, K., Chen, Shu-H., Ohuchi, A. (eds.) MAMUS 2003. LNCS (LNAI), vol. 3012, pp. 190–216. Springer, Heidelberg (2004). https://doi.org/10.1007/978-3-540-24666-4_12

14. Sashima, A., Kurumatani, K., Izumi, N.: Physically-grounding agents in ubiquitous computing. In: Proceedings of Joint Agent Workshop and Symposium 2002, pp. 196–203 (2002)

15. Kurumatani, K.: Chapter X: Social coordination with architecture for ubiquitous agents - CONSORTS. In: Intelligent Agents for Data Mining and Information Retrieval, pp.154–164. Idea Group Publishing, Hershey (2004). https://doc.lagout.org/Others/Data%20Mining/Intelligent%20Agents%20for%20Data%20Mining%20and%20Information%20Retrieval%20%5BMohammadian%202003-07-01%5D.pdf

Trick or Treat: Centralized Data Lake Vs Decentralized Data Mesh

Anton Dolhopolov[(✉)], Arnaud Castelltort, and Anne Laurent

LIRMM, Univ. Montpellier, CNRS, Montpellier, France
{anton.dolhopolov,arnaud.castelltort,anne.laurent}@lirmm.fr

Abstract. Over the course of the last few years, the augmentation of processed data and an increase in the need for fast product release cycles led to the emergence of bottlenecks in information and knowledge flows within large organizations. Recent research works attempted to resolve these issues from several perspectives, which span from the data platform architectures to the storage technologies. In this positional paper, we start by comparing the well-established methods of designing analytical data platforms and make a review of existing problems inherent to them, namely centralization of storage and ownership. It continues by analyzing the principles of a data mesh proposal and by providing an examination of unresolved challenges, such as metadata centralization. We further consider the business domain dependencies and platform architecture of our running example. The final section presents our vision for solving the identified metadata management issues in large enterprises via data decentralization and offers potential directions for future work.

Keywords: Big Data Platforms · Data Mesh · Metadata Management

1 Introduction

In the 21st century, the information technology community highly popularized the term *big data* [9]. This notion does not differ much from the original data definition. It is rather used to reflect properties such as the amount of data, processing speed, or heterogeneity. Commonly cited big data 5 V's classification [10] describes the following characteristics: the operated data volume; the processing velocity; the variety of structured (e.g., relational), semi-structured (e.g., XML, JSON), and unstructured (e.g., audio, video) data; the veracity - meaning truthfulness, correctness, or validity of data; and the value - the hidden insights or knowledge present in data. Though it is difficult to determine who coined the term, we can easily observe the relevant growth of both scientific research[1] and industrial solutions[2] in this domain.

Historically, *data warehouses* [8] were the first generation of solutions to deal with enterprise analytical data. While being oriented on managing the structured

---

[1] Analytics from app.dimensions.ai. Available at https://bit.ly/3I5p3N1.
[2] Big data and analytics software revenue worldwide. https://bit.ly/2Gt8VFt.

© The Author(s), under exclusive license to Springer Nature Switzerland AG 2024
R. Chbeir et al. (Eds.): MEDES 2023, CCIS 2022, pp. 303–316, 2024.
https://doi.org/10.1007/978-3-031-51643-6_22

data, it provided tools for business schema enforcement on the collected data, user query processing engines, and analytical data processing. These solutions are still successfully applied in OLAP-related scenarios, but they struggle with other big data requirements, namely velocity and variety. To overcome the limitations, in [3], James Dixon proposed the second generation platform called *data lake*. Its core idea is to provide a schema-on-read functionality, which is opposite to schema-on-write in the data warehouse. The need to pre-process the data is delayed until the future when the analyses are done by business analysts, data scientists, or other competent users. This facilitates the velocity of batch and real-time acquisition directly from the data generating process (application logs, user operations, crawling) to the data variety support in the underlying platform thanks to the storage in a raw format. Some noteworthy data lake architectures are data reservoir [1], Constance [6], lambda [17], and AUDAL [15]. Although data lakes can resolve the initial big data challenges, it is still seen as a centralized solution. It brings such issues as data silos, modules inter-dependencies, and long product delivery cycles [2]. We believe that platform decentralization will better benefit the large organization in comparison to widespread lake platform centralization. We thus consider the data mesh concept.

In this position paper, we make a further review of the existing data lake problems, describe the four main principles of a data mesh, present our vision for improving this architecture by decentralizing metadata and product catalogs of a data platform, and conclude with the remaining open scientific questions.

2   Data Lakes: Current Issues

In general, the existing data lake architecture models are built around centralized data storage and data ownership [5,14]. Modern cloud computing technologies provide physical data distribution and fault-tolerant access guarantees across different geographical regions. It is essential for providing highly available services to end users. However, from a logical point of view, data is still centralized and controlled by data engineering teams. Such centralization can create bottlenecks in large enterprises.

In the rest of this section, we are going to review such issues as data silos, team friction, and changing environments.

2.1   Hidden Data

A *data silo* is a good example that often happens in companies. Back in the days of using data warehouses, different departments would curate their master data sets and use them internally. Refining and improving data quality and the analytical pipelines within the business departments isn't something wrong. Nevertheless, in the modern days of advanced analytics, like machine learning, harvesting the value of data in big enterprises requires accessing all existing datasets. As soon as the matter comes to sharing the data, problems arise. Data lakes did not masterfully escape this fate too. Instead of putting the walls in

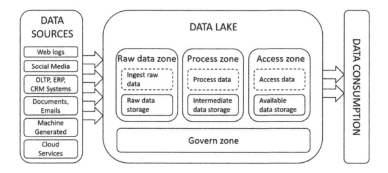

Fig. 1. Simplified Data Platform View from [13].

front of the analysts, the lake approach puts everything in one logical place for applying transformations later in time [11]. As a result, it can easily degrade into *data swamps* where it is impossible to understand and meaningfully process all of the available data [7]. A widely acknowledged solution for avoiding data garbage is a metadata management system. We shall provide a more detailed view of metadata in the Sect. 3.3.

2.2   Teams Communication

Developing monolithic applications in big companies becomes evidently problematic over time [12]. Monolith applications create intolerably many cross-team dependencies. It means that the implementation and release of new functionality or a product from one team are in direct reliance on the work of another one. Thus the main issues arise in efficiently managing inter-team communications and speeding up the product release cycle.

Unfortunately, the same limitations are faced in data platforms. Figure 1 displays a typical data lake architecture taken from [13]. It contains three main data handling zones, namely "raw data zone" (no processing but data ingestion that can be stream or batch), "process zone" (transformed data), and "access zone" (self-service data consumption for data exploitation - querying, reporting, machine learning serving, etc.). The governance zone is responsible for having a view of all the other zones and is in charge of ensuring data security, data quality, data life-cycle, data access, and metadata management.

Oftentimes data engineers (who build these zones) require close collaboration with application developers from the operational (data sources) plane, including, but not limited to data quality checks, new data attributes, or new source integration requests. The responsibility of managing and improving the data platform, in this case, is put on the shoulders of data engineers and data scientists who are detached from the day-to-day business operations of the company.

It means that engineers who work on the same product need to have high cohesion inside a single team.

2.3 Changing Organization Environment

Today, organizations rarely stay in a static environment, meaning that there are always new working requirements. The provided service or product is always subject to modifications or even cancellation. It forms a dynamic nature of all organizational processes, impacting IT teams.

To cope with it, the analytical teams should also be dynamic, agile, and flexible. The teams should fulfill the new requirements at an acceptable time without compromising the present functionalities and should adapt to changes arising from the operational plane.

In reality, it has been shown difficult to achieve in the current circumstances of large organizations. Highly specialized data platform engineers are grouped by skills and expertise and divided by functional modules at the same time. Their primary objective is to harvest and employ the value from data, but instead, they become a bottleneck in delivering innovations[3].

We have seen that the current state of analytical systems can not resolve all exigent challenges, such as data silos, team friction, and dynamic working environment. The following sections assess a Data Mesh architecture, which promises to deal with the aforementioned issues.

3 Towards Decentralized Data Platforms with Mesh Architecture

As was stated in the introduction, we advocate for the decentralization of data platforms. This section describes the concepts of the most recent works around platform decentralization and continues with its application on top of our running example. In the last part, we highlight the main ongoing difficulties that are not completely addressed.

3.1 Data Mesh 4 Pillars

Zhamak Dehghani proposed a novel architecture called *data mesh* [2]. It summons to make a paradigm shift in the way of building big data platforms. The shift is based on 4 main principles, and each one is essential on its own. Without proper implementation of all principles, it will only exacerbate the existing problems inside the organization.

Distributed Data Domains. The basic ideas for successfully implementing data mesh architecture take their origin from the domain-driven design (DDD) [4]. Similarly, way as the monolithic operational plane is broken up into small, independent components like microservices so that we can divide the analytical platform into self-contained business domains. *Distributed domains architecture*

---

[3] Break Through the Centralized Platform Bottlenecks with Data Mesh. Available at https://thght.works/40YM6Sj.

represents the first principle of a mesh. Instead of forcing centralized data owner-ship onto the narrowly specialized teams, one can benefit from forming domains aware groups of interdisciplinary employees. Each group would contain appli-cation developers, designers, data engineers, data scientists, business analysts, and product owners. This way, groups would be focused on developing both operational and analytical parts of a single product.

Data Product Design. As with the software products in domain-driven meth-odology, the systematic approach of building the *data-oriented products* within the domain is also required. Most of the time the users would include not only the payable clients but other teams of the same organization too. Providing a great service takes designing, delivering, measuring, and constantly improving the provided data, be it A/B testing results or machine learning models. It creates a new zone of responsibility for product owners since they also need to take care of how the data products perform. Guaranteeing SLAs, publishing trustworthy data, and helping the users to discover, understand and consume the product are some of the key indicators of a successful product.

Reusable Infrastructure. To avoid re-implementation of similar or even iden-tical data acquisition, processing, and serving functionality, one must benefit from a shared *self-serve infrastructure platform*. Its main goal would be a set of common and interchangeable tools like data source connectors and sinks, trans-formation jobs, automatic logs, data lifecycle configuration, and so on. Eliminat-ing the basic day-to-day engineering operations behind an easy-to-use abstrac-tion layer will help to unlock the fast release cycle.

Federated Computational Governance. The importance of providing gov-erning policies and mechanisms can not be overstated. It is the only way how a lot of independent, distributed, interconnected, and dynamic data domains will work efficiently together. Policies help to determine how the individual domain or product should behave in the mesh. For instance, interoperability standards would describe the data publishing formats (e.g., JSON, Protobufs), schema integrity checks, information security, and privacy rules. At the same time, enforcement mechanisms will allow leveraging the verification, monitor-ing, or alerting processes automatically. Defining and enforcing the governance elements is not easy, but it must not be centralized. The mechanisms must be incorporated directly into the infrastructure platform, and the policies could be defined by the committee of data domain representatives and other experts (e.g. legal team).

3.2 Running Example

We experimented with our running example by applying the mesh principles. We consider different departments in a video-streaming platform: Human Resources (HR), Sales, Finance, and content production Studios. In Fig. 2 (left part) we

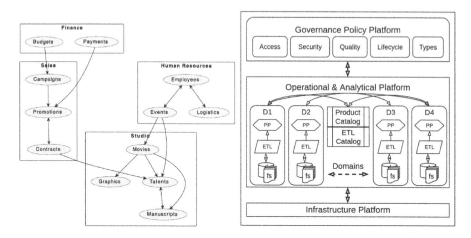

Fig. 2. Data mesh cross-domain dependencies (left) and functional architecture (right).

can easily notice that these departments inevitably have inter-dependencies, even when performing different day-to-day operations. For example, contracts issued by Sales would be related to creating new content and signing up partnerships with actors or directors (talents entity).

If we would like to integrate some analytical pipelines, it would be natural to proceed with extending the existing departmental technical modules. The Studio representatives may be interested in planning the load schedule. To deliver such an estimation, the Studio engineers will have to consume the information on contracts that the directors and actors have signed (an external data source provided by the Sales team), as well as the movie schedules (an internal source).

An important aspect of building the analytics here is not to be inclined with just another warehousing solution. One has to remember to provide the data product, not merely the statistical calculations. Our Studio product would include the metadata about data freshness, running transformation history, and semantic info on parties, costs, and jurisdictions in case we would like to filter the data further. In plus, the product could be consumed via different means: asynchronous message queues, HTTP requests, or even direct disk mounting in case of large blobs and supported data fabric functionality.

Overall, these interactions form a net of dependencies on the analytical plane in a similar way as on the operational one. The net would directly affect the design of the functional platform architecture, as is shown in Fig. 2 (right part), where different departments or domains pass the data to each other directly.

In addition, the specialized data (product) and extract-transform-load (ETL) catalogs can help in data discovery, development automation, etc., as is often done in the literature. Such catalogs can be implemented in metadata management systems by using, for instance, graph databases that provide efficient processing of graph structures (that naturally arise in our running example).

We shall consider the benefits of graphs in more detail in Sect. 4.2.

3.3 Challenges

It may not be obvious at first look, but the principal part of building the decentralized platform stems from changing the organizational hierarchy. Companies and institutions have to update their framework for creating engineering teams, zones of responsibility, and, finally, the rendered products. One of the data mesh paradigm objectives is to unite the once-divided operational and analytical planes together across different distributed data domains. Now we shall look into left open questions.

User Profile. We have mentioned previously that users operating in a centralized environment have to understand the business domain processes. It is necessary to know how the data was generated, processed, and stored in the operational plane, as well as the meaning, semantics, and relationships between attributes, tables, datasets, etc. Since all of the data is available to the end user as a huge chunk of files in one place, it becomes challenging to analyze it. Commonly, the data lake user profile is a technically knowledgeable person who has to use specific software (e.g., Apache Spark, Flink, Beam) to get the utility from data. It constrains the adaption and digital transformation of the organization which tries to implement big data managing solutions.

When adopting a decentralized platform architecture, special care should be taken to support multiple consumer profiles. Needless to say that if the advertised domain data is a chunk of files, it won't generate much utility. It means that consumption interfaces should provide and publish the data in multiple formats (datasets, analytical models, reports, etc.). There is a clear need to adapt the data product attitude to unlock the underlying value.

Such an approach will expand the list of end users - from data engineers and data scientists to analysts, marketing teams, or business owners. The latter would be able to find the required information via metadata and product catalog search or relationship traversal and plug it directly into visualization tools such as Grafana, Tableau, Data Studio, etc. The growth in the number of active data users will accelerate the transformation of the organization into a data company.

Technology State. On one side, decentralized approaches are still maturing, and there are no settled models and tools for implementing them across the integrated planes. On the other side, we should briefly note that: a) the operational teams have already established practices of DDD via microservices architecture (and later via service mesh paradigm), use of distributed computational platforms (e.g., Docker, Kubernetes), configuration tools (e.g., Ansible, Chef, Terraform), continuous integration and delivery services (e.g., Jenkins, GitLab); b) analytical teams also have a wide range of tools which support distributed technologies, including Apache Spark and Apache Beam for real-time and batch data processing; HDFS, Apache HBase, Apache Cassandra for non-relational and MySQL, PostgreSQL for relational data storage; Grafana or Tableau for data visualization. But mentioned data platform technologies provide the distribution only for scalability, fault-tolerance, and disaster recovery. It is quite complicated to apply it in terms of complete data ownership decentralization.

Metadata Management. There is a consensus in the research that a metadata system is an essential part of any big data platform [13,14,18]. Its main role is to prevent the formation of a data swamp. It is achieved by providing supplementary, descriptive information to the collected and processed data. For instance, having the data type annotations helps to avoid creating bugs in the code; marking the date and time stamps ensures the data freshness; directed acyclic graph of transformation jobs provides the data lineage, which is in turn important for failure detection. The author of the data mesh architecture puts metadata management as part of the federated computational governance but does not provide clear details on how to build it. The governance is described in a somewhat blurred state between centralization and decentralization.

4   Research Proposal

Deriving from our running example and challenges sections, we conclude to have a high impact of the mesh paradigm on the overall data platform transformation.

In the following section, we analyze and present our position regarding domain design and metadata management as part of federated governance.

4.1   Data Lake Architecture Layers

As a first attempt, we reconsider the architecture of data lakes in order to integrate a layer-oriented vision. Figure 3 shows this revision, where data sources are placed on the operational layer, while the analytic layer contains the three zones from [13], namely raw data, process, and access zones (presented in Sect. 2.2).

The governance layer contains a single metadata catalog organized in a flat or advanced manner and is responsible for having a view of all the other zones. It is in charge of ensuring data security, data quality, data life-cycle, data access, and metadata management.

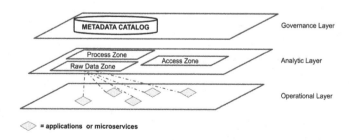

Fig. 3. Data Lake Architecture Layers revisited from [13]

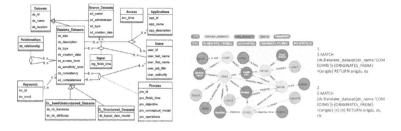

Fig. 4. Conceptual model (left) and Neo4j implementation (right) from [19]

As presented above, this metadata catalog is crucial and has attracted a lot of work in the literature. Also, it should be noted that such a catalog is more and more often implemented with property graphs. For instance, the DAMMS model [19] shown in Fig. 4 uses Neo4j, which is an ACID-compliant transactional database with native graph storage and processing.

4.2   Data Mesh Architecture Layers

In this section, we focus on the role of metadata in the context of data mesh. In existing mesh architectures metadata are often stored in XML/JSON format.

We claim that metadata cannot be easily and efficiently modelized with flat or tree representations. It is due to the fundamental principle of how the data is stored and the limited ability to construct and process real-world graph structures (e.g. cross-domain relationships) when using these representations.

Therefore, we first propose more advanced models below.

Centralized Metadata Catalog. In the Data Mesh architecture, the governance is seen as a federation. Within that federated governance, the metadata layer is the part where the metadata catalog is considered.

Figure 5 shows that applications from operational layers publish data that are then exposed by the data products. Those data products offer communication interfaces (e.g., REST API, Message Queue) to allow the consumption of data.

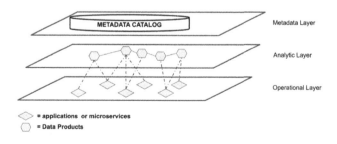

Fig. 5. Centralized Metadata Catalog

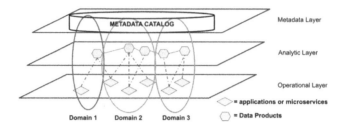

Fig. 6. Domains Perspective in Data Mesh

Every time a data product changes, it publishes its metadata to the centralized metadata repository from which clients can discover the available data.

However, this architecture has some drawbacks. Indeed, the data mesh can deliver data products that are inconsistent, and the data can be seen as non-reproducible (e.g. phantom reads).

If we take the data mesh architecture from the perspectives of business domains as shown in Fig. 6, we can see those data products operate as a vertical view to serve the end users' needs. For instance, such a domain can be dedicated to HR, Sales, Finance, etc., as presented in our running example in Sect. 3.2.

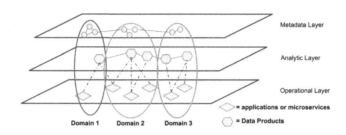

Fig. 7. Disjoint Metadata Graphs

In this architecture domains are disjoint and this is reflected in the metadata (which are represented as graphs) as shown by Fig. 7.

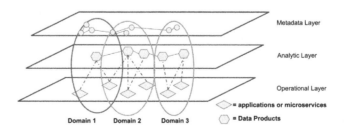

Fig. 8. Metadata Overlapping

On the opposite, Fig. 8 shows the case where domains and metadata overlap. In such a case, metadata entities are shared between several domains.

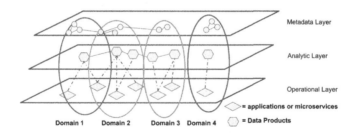

Fig. 9. Overlapping and Disjoint Metadata Graphs

As for disjoint domains, there is no obligation that all metadata graphs are connected, as in the example of Domain 4 from Fig. 9.

Given a data mesh composed of n_s data sources and n_d data domains, we consider that the metadata can be formalized as:

- a global graph $\mathcal{G}$ such that;
- $\mathcal{G} = \bigcup_{i=1,\ldots,n_d} G_i$ where G_i is metadata graph associated with Domain D_i;
- There may exist $i, j \in [1, n_d]$ where $G_i \bigcap G_j = \emptyset$.

Decentralized Metadata Catalog Proposal. The previous section highlights that the metadata layer can be seen as a graph and that each data product should provide metadata where entities lie in one or several business domains.

Generally, data mesh has a federation tier where centralized governance is meant to determine what semantic to use, who defines new vocabulary, and also to have a centralized catalog to allow the discovery of all metadata in one place.

In this era of decentralization, there are some pros and cons of this approach, for instance, the fact that centralized architectures lead to single points of failure.

Nevertheless, we would like to highlight the consequences of the centralized metadata repository on the delivery process. Indeed, one of the advantages of data mesh is that data products are not beholden to a single release cycle to make the improvements needed. This is improving time-to-market, end-user services, agility, etc. A data product does not have to wait to deploy everything together. Data or features can be added or transformed without waiting for the next release cycle, as it would be with most data lake architectures.

We claim that a centralized metadata catalog can break this assumption. For instance, updating a centralized metadata catalog should be added to the deployment process of each data product to avoid the side effects of an eventual consistency system. Also, if a Data Product needs to publish data about a term that has not previously been defined in the federation governance, then the release may be stalled.

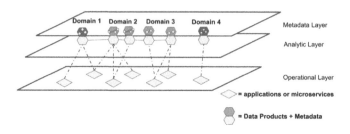

Fig. 10. Data Products with Metadata

Thus, our proposal is to treat the metadata catalog as a decentralized and distributed system. Each data product should provide its own metadata (business metadata, technical metadata, operational metadata, physical schema, semantic metadata, local and full lineage, and, quality metrics). Figure 10 illustrates that data products should be both in analytical and metadata layers.

In our proposal, we go beyond and consider that there is no more centralized metadata catalog where clients can browse the data, but a distributed and decentralized catalog accessible via discoverability, just as in the modern Web.

To go further, we consider that our metadata graph can be seen as a union of Labeled Property Graphs (LPG), each of them being hosted on a data product and representing its metadata as a graph and not as a tree or document (such as in XML or JSON format).

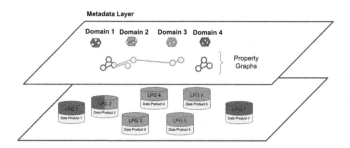

Fig. 11. Integrating Labeled Property Graphs

Figure 11 illustrates our proposition to have for each data product an LPG. An LPG can be defined as an extension of a property graph where 0 to N labels can be applied to nodes (or vertices). A property graph, as presented in [16], can be defined as a tuple $PG = \{V, E, S, P, h_e, t_e, l_v, l_e, p_v, p_e\}$, where:

- V is a non-empty set of vertices;
- E is a set of edges;
- S is a set of strings;
- P contains all $p = \{k, v\}$ key-value pairs describing properties;

- $h_e : E \rightarrow V$ is a function that yields the source of each edge (head);
- $t_e : E \rightarrow V$ is a function that yields the target of each edge (tail),
- $l_v : V \rightarrow S$ is a function mapping each vertex to label;
- $l_e : E \rightarrow S$ is a function mapping each edge to label;
- $p_v : V \rightarrow 2^P$ is a function used to assign vertices to their multiple properties;
- $p_e : E \rightarrow 2^P$ is a function used to assign edges to their multiple properties.

Given a data mesh composed of n_d data domains, we consider that the metadata can be formalized as:

- a global labeled property graph $\mathcal{LPG}$ such that
- $\mathcal{LPG} = \bigcup_{i=1,\ldots,n_d} LPG_i$ with LPG_i the labelled property graph of meta data associated with Domain D_i.
- There may exist $i, j \in [1, n_d]$ where $LPG_i \cap LPG_j = \emptyset$

This approach solves the issues of eventual consistency and non-reproducible environments (e.g., phantom reads), but of course, it generates new challenges to address, such as labeled-property graphs partitioning, discoverability and querying, networking issues (routing), etc., that will be discussed in further works.

5 Conclusions

The state-of-the-art centralized data lake architectures do not solve all modern big data platform challenges. Organizational scaling becomes an innovation bottleneck in companies with segregated operational and analytical platforms. To address these issues, some promising paradigms like data mesh were proposed.

However, new difficulties arise. Available metadata management systems which attempt to prevent the creation of data swamps are also designed as a centralized remedy. The mesh proposal does not offer any explicit guidelines for distributed domain implementation or evolution within the institutions. Moreover, the available technologies are still maturing and do not support the complete data decentralization capabilities for both operational and analytical planes.

Therefore, there is an open demand for developing the technology for building decentralized and interoperable data mesh with distributed metadata system.

In our research proposal, we introduce the main goals necessary to achieve for building a successful big data platform based on the data mesh principles, and we present and discuss centralized and decentralized architectures for disjoint and overlapping data domains.

Our future work will focus on refining our new metadata model and defining a logical structure based on property graphs and its decentralized technology implementation.

References

1. Chessell, M., Jones, N.L., Limburn, J., Radley, D., Shank, K.: Designing and operating a data reservoir. In: IBM Redbooks (2015)
2. Dehghani, Z.: Data Mesh: Delivering Data-Driven Value at Scale. O'Reilly Media Inc., Sebastopol (2022)
3. Dixon, J.: Pentaho, hadoop, and data lakes (2010). https://jamesdixon.wordpress.com/2010/10/14/pentaho-hadoop-and-data-lakes. Accessed 14 Aug 2022
4. Evans, E., Evans, E.J.: Domain-Driven Design: Tackling Complexity in the Heart of Software. Addison-Wesley Professional, Boston (2004)
5. Giebler, C., Gröger, C., Hoos, E., Eichler, R., Schwarz, H., Mitschang, B.: The data lake architecture framework. BTW 2021 (2021)
6. Hai, R., Geisler, S., Quix, C.: Constance: an intelligent data lake system. In: Proceedings of the 2016 International Conference on Management of Data, pp. 2097–2100 (2016)
7. Inmon, B.: Data Lake Architecture: Designing the Data Lake and Avoiding the Garbage Dump. Technics Publications, Denville (2016)
8. Inmon, W.H., Strauss, D., Neushloss, G.: DW 2.0: The Architecture for the Next Generation of Data Warehousing. Elsevier, Amsterdam (2010)
9. Stefanowski, J., Krawiec, K., Wrembel, R.: Exploring complex and big data. Int. J. Appl. Math. Comput. Sci. **27**(4), 669–679 (2017)
10. Laurent, A., Laurent, D., Madera, C.: Data Lakes, Chapter 1, Introduction to Data Lakes: Definitions and Discussions, vol. 2. STE Ltd and John Wiley & Sons Inc., Hoboken (2020)
11. Miloslavskaya, N., Tolstoy, A.: Big data, fast data and data lake concepts. In: 7th Annual International Conference on Biologically Inspired Cognitive Architectures (BICA 2016). Procedia Computer Science, 2016
12. Newman, S.: Building Microservices. O'Reilly Media Inc., Sebastopol (2015)
13. Ravat, F., Zhao, Y.: Data lakes: trends and perspectives. In: Hartmann, S., Küng, J., Chakravarthy, S., Anderst-Kotsis, G., Tjoa, A.M., Khalil, I. (eds.) DEXA 2019. LNCS, vol. 11706, pp. 304–313. Springer, Cham (2019). https://doi.org/10.1007/978-3-030-27615-7_23
14. Sawadogo, P., Darmont, J.: On data lake architectures and metadata management. J. Intell. Inf. Syst. **56**(1), 97–120 (2021). Springer
15. Sawadogo, P.N., Darmont, J., Noûs, C.: Joint management and analysis of textual documents and tabular data within the AUDAL data lake. In: Bellatreche, L., Dumas, M., Karras, P., Matulevičius, R. (eds.) ADBIS 2021. LNCS, vol. 12843, pp. 88–101. Springer, Cham (2021). https://doi.org/10.1007/978-3-030-82472-3_8
16. Tomaszuk, D.: RDF data in property graph model. In: Garoufallou, E., Subirats Coll, I., Stellato, A., Greenberg, J. (eds.) MTSR 2016. CCIS, vol. 672, pp. 104–115. Springer, Cham (2016). https://doi.org/10.1007/978-3-319-49157-8_9
17. John, T., Misra, P.: Data Lake for Enterprises Leveraging Lambda Architecture for Building Enterprise Data Lake. Packt Publishing Ltd., Birmingham (2017)
18. Zgolli, A., Collet, C., Madera, C.: Data Lakes, Chapter 4, Metadata in Data Lake Ecosystems, vol. 2. STE Ltd and John Wiley & Sons Inc., Hoboken (2020)
19. Zhao, Y.: Metadata Management for Data Lake Governance. PhD thesis, Toulouse 1 (2021)

A Taxonomy for Cloud Storage Cost

Akif Quddus Khan[1], Nikolay Nikolov[2], Mihhail Matskin[3], Radu Prodan[4],
Christoph Bussler[5], Dumitru Roman[2], and Ahmet Soylu[6(✉)]

[1] Norwegian University of Science and Technology – NTNU, Gjøvik, Norway
`akif.q.khan@ntnu.no`
[2] SINTEF AS, Oslo, Norway
[3] KTH Royal Institute of Technology, Stockholm, Sweden
[4] University of Klagenfurt, Klagefurt, Austria
[5] Robert Bosch LLC, Ontario, CA, USA
[6] OsloMet – Oslo Metropilotan University, Oslo, Norway
`ahmet.soylu@oslomet.no`

Abstract. The cost of using cloud storage services is complex and often an unclear structure, while it is one of the important factors for organisations adopting cloud storage. Furthermore, organisations take advantage of multi-cloud or hybrid solutions to combine multiple public and/or private cloud service providers to avoid vendor lock-in, achieve high availability and performance, optimise cost, etc. This complicated ecosystem makes it even harder to understand and manage cost. Therefore, in this paper, we provide a taxonomy of cloud storage cost in order to provide a better understanding and insights on this complex problem domain.

Keywords: Cloud · Storage cost · StaaS · Taxonomy

1 Introduction

Cost is one of the important factors for organisations while adopting cloud storage; however, cloud storage providers offer complex pricing policies, including the actual storage cost and the cost related to additional services (e.g., network usage cost) [19]. Given the increasing use of storage as a service (StaaS) and its rapidly growing economic value [18], cost optimisation for StaaS has become a challenging endeavour for industry and also for research. Furthermore, while it is rare, deploying an application in a multi-cloud environment, which involves utilising multiple public cloud service providers (CSPs), can add further complexity to the cost structure. The goal is to minimise cost of data storage under complex and diverse pricing policies coupled with varying storage and network resources and services offered by CSPs [23]. Organisations take advantage of multi-cloud or hybrid solutions [40] to combine multiple public and/or private cloud storage providers to avoid vendor lock-in, to achieve high availability and performance, optimising cost, etc. [37]. An application deployed using multiple public and/or private cloud providers distributed over several regions can enhance the application's performance while reducing the cost. Nevertheless, the cost of using

R. Chbeir et al. (Eds.): MEDES 2023, CCIS 2022, pp. 317–330, 2024.
https://doi.org/10.1007/978-3-031-51643-6_23

cloud storage services is complex and often unclear structure, particularly in a multi-cloud or hybrid ecosystem.

The cloud storage providers tout ostensibly simple use-based pricing plans when it comes to pricing; however, a practical cost analysis of cloud storage is not straightforward [12], and there are a limited number of studies that focus on cost optimisation across multiple CSPs with varying price policies [16]. Comprehensive models and mechanisms are required to optimise the cost of using cloud storage services and storage service selection for data placement, for which it is essential to understand this complex cost structure. In this context, we collected and analysed data from the documentation of three major cloud service providers to find commonalities and differences, to provide a comprehensive taxonomy of cloud storage cost, and to provide a systematic and comprehensive framework for analysing and comparing the cost of different cloud storage solutions. It fills this gap by providing a structured approach, which can be used to develop a software tool for cost optimisation. It also provides a basis for more meaningful cost comparisons between cloud storage providers, which can help organisations to make more informed decisions about their cloud storage strategy. We aim that the work presented in this paper will provide researchers and practitioners working on cost optimisation, cost modelling, cloud provider selection in a multi-cloud or hybrid setting, etc., with a better understanding and insights regarding this complex problem domain.

The rest of the paper is structured as follows. Section 2 provides an overview of the key concepts, while Sect. 3 presents a taxonomy along with the related work. Finally, Sect. 4 concludes the paper and presents the future work.

2   Overview

Data intensive applications processing large amounts of data are ideal candidates for cloud deployment due to the need for higher storage and computing resources [26]. A single cloud storage provider with multiple regions or, as discussed earlier, due to concerns about cost, scalability, availability, performance, vendor lock-in, etc., a (geo-)distributed approach through a multi-cloud or hybrid solution could be opted for. In this paper, we will focus on a few of the major cloud service providers worldwide, such as Amazon Web Services (AWS), Microsoft Azure (Azure), and Google Cloud, among others like Alibaba Cloud and IBM Cloud. However, there is no guarantee that one of these multinational CSPs alone is optimal for an organisation's needs.

In cloud storage, data is stored in the form of objects (files, blobs, entities, items, records), which are pieces of data that form a dataset (collection, set, grouping, repository). Every object in cloud storage resides in a bucket. The term "bucket" is used by AWS and Google Cloud, whereas Azure refers to it as a "container". Data could be stored and accessed in various structures, abstractions, and formats [26,27]; users can choose the location where the storage bucket will be placed. Data could be distributed over multiple data stores to exploit the advantages of a multi-cloud and multi-region environment. It also plays an essential role in data compliance issues, where data must be stored in particular geographical locations, e.g., GDPR [38], but it can also increase the cost. Yet, realising distributed data intensive applications on the cloud is not straightforward. Sharding and data replication [7] are the key concepts for data distribution. Sharding refers to splitting and distributing data across different nodes in a system, where each node holds a single copy of the data; it provides scalability in terms of load balancing and storage capacity and high availability. Data replication refers to continuous synchronisation of data or parts of it by copying it to multiple nodes in a system; it provides high availability and durability. However, data replication increases the cost and introduces the issue of data consistency due to synchronisation issues between the nodes under network partitioning; therefore, a trade-off between availability and consistency emerges [36]. CSPs offer storage services from datacenters located all around the world; therefore, communication and coordination among nodes could be hindered due to network issues in both cases, causing increased latency [8]. Data replication and sharding with an adequate data distribution strategy could also provide data locality and hence low latency by placing data closer to the computation early-on rather than moving it as needed later [3].

The location of a cloud storage server is characterised by continent, region, and availability zones (it is termed as zone by Google Cloud, replication zones by Azure, and availability zone by AWS). A continent is a geographical region such as North America, South America, the Middle East, etc. Each continent can have one or more regions, and each region features availability zones deployed within a latency-defined perimeter. They are connected through a dedicated regional low-latency network. Availability zones are physically separate locations within each region that are tolerant of local failures. A high-performance network connects the availability zones with extremely low round-trip latency. Each region often has three or more availability zones. Availability zones are designed so that if one zone is affected, regional services, capacity, and high availability are supported by the remaining two zones. Network infrastructure constitutes a major and integral part of the cloud continuum. Users are charged for using network services, reading and writing data to and from cloud storage (for most CSPs, data transfer-in is free). These are linked with data egress and ingress, while the former refers to data leaving the data container, and the latter refers to data entering a data container. Reading information or metadata from a cloud storage bucket is an example of egress. Uploading files to a cloud storage bucket or streaming data into a cloud-based data processing service are examples of data ingress in the cloud. Especially when data is distributed over multiple geographical areas over a distributed infrastructure managed by multiple third parties and transferred over the network, security and privacy concerns also need to be addressed. This is particularly challenging in complex multi-cloud and hybrid settings, as approaches that work seamlessly over multiple providers are required, apart from the additional cost introduced. In multi-cloud and hybrid settings, therefore, several challenges need to be addressed [8], such as multi-cloud management, security, workload and workflow management and cost optimisation under different contexts and parameters.

Cloud storage services offer a simple pay-as-you-go pricing plan; however, they do offer various pricing models as well [43]. In the block-rate pricing model, data ranges are defined, and each range has a different per GB price for storing data. Some CSPs, such as Azure, also offer a reserved pricing plan that helps lower the data storage cost by committing to and reserving storage for one year or three years. In addition to all these, with almost all the CSPs, there is an opportunity to directly contact the sales team and get a custom offer according to the requirements. A cloud service provider offers several different services with more or less the same functionality, but they cost differently because there's a difference in performance. For example, Amazon S3 and Reduced Redundancy Storage (RRS) are online storage services, but the latter compromises redundancy for lower cost [26]. An even more relevant example of this scenario is the model of storage tiers or classes that are offered not only by AWS but also by Google Cloud and Azure, i.e., the division or categorisation of storage services within AWS S3. Another strategy that the CSPs use is the bundling of services. It is not a strategy adopted recently, and not just by CSPs; it is being used intensively by a wide variety of other economic sectors as well [6]. Although the ultimate purpose of bundling is cost-effectiveness and increased customer satisfaction [39], it is also a strategy that can discourage new competitors from entering a market [31]. Following this strategy, CSPs bundle storage services with other related services. For example, network services have lower costs if data transfer between storage and other services is within the cloud environment, which means computing resources must also be from the same CSP.

3   A Taxonomy of Storage Cost

Cloud computing cost can be broken down into three groups: 1) storage cost concerns the amount of data stored in the cloud and its duration; 2) data transport cost concerns the amount of data moved over the cloud network; and 3) compute cost concerns the use of computing resources from the cloud continuum (e.g., VMs rented and duration). In this paper, we focus on storage cost and data transfer cost. Figure 1 shows the proposed cloud cost structure taxonomy. Storage costs comprise data storage, data replication, transaction, and network usage costs, whereas data transfer costs comprise data replication, transaction and network usage costs. In addition to that, storage cost also incorporates optional data security cost. We discuss the elements of the cloud storage cost structure based on how CSPs charge their users, including data storage, data replication, transaction, network usage, and data encryption costs. Storage and data transfer costs vary by storage tier, as discussed below. The taxonomy presented in this section is extracted by analysing the official pricing information provided publicly by AWS[1], Google Cloud[2], and Azure[3] in November 2022.

---

[1] https://aws.amazon.com/s3/pricing/.

[2] https://cloud.google.com/storage/pricing.

[3] https://azure.microsoft.com/en-us/pricing/details/storage/blobs/.

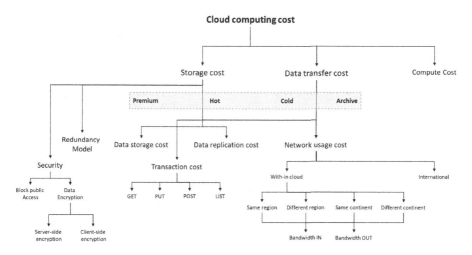

Fig. 1. Cloud computing cost taxonomy.

3.1 Storage Tiers

Every chunk of data stored in cloud storage uses a piece of information known as a "storage tier", specifying its availability level and pricing structure. Storage servers on tiers don't need to be connected to a virtual machine to store and read data. For example, AWS Elastic Block Storage can only be used with AWS EC2 instances; however, data stored on AWS S3 (tiered storage) can be accessed using a standard data transfer protocol. We collect storage tiers under four categories: premium, hot, cold, and archive. A summarised comparison of tiers offered by three different providers is shown in Table 1, whereas definitions and key characteristics of each storage tier are explained in the followings.

Premium tier is better suited for data that is frequently accessed and/or is only stored for short periods of time. This tier is called "Premium" in Azure, "Standard" in Google cloud, and "S3 Standard" in AWS. The premium tier costs more than the other tiers to store data but less to access the data. *Hot tier* is suggested for storing the data that is frequently accessed and modified. In Azure it is known as "Hot", in Google cloud as "Nearline", and in AWS as "S3 Standard – Infrequent Access". This tier also has a higher cost as compared to the cold and archive storage tiers, but the associated network usage costs are comparatively lower. *Cold tier* is designed for storing data that is accessed and modified occasionally. For this tier, all cloud storage providers recommend that data must be stored for a specific minimum amount of time. Storage costs are less than premium and hot tiers, but network usage costs are higher. This tier is referred to as "Cool" in Azure, "Coldline" in Google cloud, and "S3 Glacier - Instant Retrieval" in AWS. *Archive tier* is designed for storing data that is rarely accessed and is stored for a longer period of time – basically an offline tier. Mostly, the data that is stored cannot be accessed immediately, but it varies from CSP to CSP. That is why it is recommended to store data that has

Table 1. Storage tiers comparison.

Tier	Azure	AWS	Google Cloud	Characteristics
Premium	Premium	S3 Standard, S3 Intelligent Tiering	Standard	Frequent data access; Data stored briefly; Expensive storage; Less network usage cost; No minimum storage time
Hot	Hot	S3 Standard Infrequent, S3 One Zone-IA	Nearline	Infrequent data access; Lower cost than Premium tier; Storage duration requirement may vary
Cold	Cool	S3 Glacier Instant Retrieval	Coldline	Less frequent data access; Cheaper than Premium and Hot tier storage; Higher network usage cost; Storage duration requirement may vary
Archive	Archive	S3 Glacier (Flexible or Deep Archive)	Archive	Rare data access; Long-term storage; Flexible latency required; Minimum storage time

flexibility in terms of latency requirements, i.e., on the order of hours. Unlike the cold tier, the minimum storage time is not just recommended but required; e.g., for Azure, it is 180 days. Azure and Google cloud term this tier as "Archive", whereas AWS term the similar tiers as "S3 Glacier Flexible" and "S3 Glacier Deep Archive".

Storing a data object in only one tier at all times can be costly and inefficient. Mansouri and Erradi [24] present an example where storing 30 GB of data (with a large number of objects) and having 10K reads and 10K writes incur 1 GB of data retrieval in the US-South central region of Azure blob storage. Based on the pricing in January 2018, the cost in the cool tier is 79.55% more than that in the hot tier. However, as the data size increases to 60 GB, while the number of read and write requests approaches to zero, the cost of storing the blob in the cool tier becomes 84% less than the cost in the hot tier. Other studies also provide cost optimisation by moving data between different tiers during the data life cycle [10]. Krumm and Hoffman [12] developed a tool designed specifically for cost and usage estimation for laboratories performing clinical testing. It provides a way to explore storage options from different CSPs, cost forecasts, data compression, and mechanisms for rapid transfer to the cold tier. Jin et al. [11] developed a framework for cost-effective video storage in cloud storage, while Mansouri and Erradi [5] developed a cost optimisation algorithm for data storage and migration between different storage tiers. Nguyen et al. [33] proposed a cost-optimal two-tier fog storage technique for streaming services. Liu et al. [18–20] developed multiple algorithms presented in various studies for cost optimisation using multi-tier cloud storage.

Storage tiers can be effectively used to achieve high data durability and availability. For example, Liu et al. [17] developed an algorithm (PMCR) and did extensive numerical analysis and real-world experiments on Amazon S3.

Extending the work on high availability, Wiera et al. [35] presents a unified approach named Wier to achieve high availability and data consistency. Wier makes it possible to set data management policies for a single data centre or for a group of data centres. These policies let the user choose between different options and get the best performance, reliability, durability, and consistency. In this kind of situation, it finds the best place to store user data so that one can quickly find the best way to balance different priorities, such as cost, availability, durability, and consistency. Similarly, Zhang et al. [44] presents a bidding algorithm for tiered cloud storage to achieve low latency.

3.2 Cost Structure

The cost structure for cloud storage can be broken down into four main groups: 1) data storage, 2) data replication, 3) transaction, and 4) network usage. Figure 2 shows the cost taxonomy. The four elements mentioned above and those shown in Fig. 2 with solid lines are mandatory cost elements that a user can optimise but cannot altogether avoid. The other three elements, which are data management, data backup, and data security, are optional. CSPs do not provide these for free, but they are not mandatory. A user might have to pay for third-party data management services as well in the context of a multi-cloud environment.

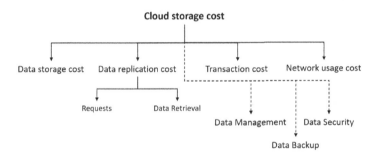

Fig. 2. Cloud storage cost taxonomy.

Data storage cost refers to storing data in the cloud. It is charged on a per-GB-per-month basis. Each storage tier has different pricing. It also depends on the amount of data that is being stored. Some CSPs offer block-rate pricing, i.e. the larger the amount of data; the lower the unit costs are [30]. When it comes to big data, data storage costs could be huge. However, data compression techniques can reduce the size of the data by efficiently compressing the data, hence reducing the storage cost. Hossain and Roy [9] developed a data compression framework for IoT sensor data in cloud storage. In their two-layered compression framework, they compressed the data up to 90% while maintaining an error rate of less than 1.5% and no bandwidth wastage. On the other hand, distributed data storage comes with its own challenges. One of the challenges of storing data in a distributed environment is the efficient repair of a failed node, i.e., minimising the data required to recover the failed node. Coding theory has evolved to overcome these challenges. Erasure encoding is used for reliable and efficient storage of big data in a distributed environment [14]. Several erasure coding techniques developed over time; Balaji et al. [2] present an overview of such methodologies (Table 2).

Table 2. Storage cost terminology comparison for the three providers.

Cost element	Definition	Azure	AWS	Google Cloud
Storage cost	It refers to data storage costs and is charged per GB per month.	Data storage	Storage	Data storage
Data replication cost	It refers to the process of replicating data from on-premises storage to the cloud or from one cloud zone to another. It is charged on a per GB basis	Data replication	Replication	Operation charges
Transaction cost	Cost for requests made against storage buckets and objects. They are charged on the quantity of requests. DELETE and CANCEL requests are free. Types of requests include PUT, COPY, POST, LISTS, GET, SELECT. Data retrieval is charged on a per GB basis	Operations & data transfer	Requests & data retrieval	Operation charges and retrieval fees
Network usage cost	Cost of all bandwidth, into and out of the cloud storage server. It is also charged on a per GB basis	Data transfer	Data transfer	Network egress

Data replication cost refers to replicating data from on-premises storage to the cloud or from one cloud zone to another. Data storage systems adopt a 3-replicas data replication strategy by default, i.e., for each chunk of data that is uploaded, three copies are stored, to achieve high data reliability and ensure better disaster recovery (AWS S3[4], Azure Blob Storage[5], Google Cloud Storage[6]). This means that for users to store one gigabyte of data, they have to pay for the cost of three gigabytes as well as the cost of making data copies, known as "data replication". This significantly affects the cost-effectiveness of cloud storage [15]. The cost of data replication is charged on a per-GB basis. Several data replication strategies are available to achieve various objectives. For example, Mansouri et al. [25], Liu et al. [17], and Edwin et al. [4] developed data replication strategies to achieve optimal cost. Mansouri and Javidi [22] and Nannai and Mirnalinee [32] focused on achieving low access latency by developing dynamic data replication strategies. Ali et al. [1] presented a framework

---

[4] https://aws.amazon.com/s3/faqs/.

[5] https://docs.microsoft.com/en-us/azure/storage/blobs/storage-redundancy.

[6] https://cloud.google.com/storage/docs/redundancy.

(DROP) to pull off maximum performance and security, whereas Tos et al. [41] and Mokadem et al. [29] developed approaches to attain high performance and increase providers' profit.

Transaction cost refers to the costs for managing, monitoring, and controlling a transaction when reading or writing data to cloud storage [34]. Cloud storage providers charge not only for the amount of data that is transferred over the network but also for the number of operations it takes. Both READ and WRITE operations have different costs. They are charged based on the number of requests. DELETE and CANCEL requests are free. Other requests include PUT, COPY, POST, LISTS, GET, and SELECT. On the other hand, data retrieval is charged per GB basis. Google Cloud has a different term for transaction costs, which is "operation charges", defined as the cost of all requests made to Google cloud storage.

Network usage cost refers to network consumption or usage based on the quantity of data read from or sent between the buckets. Data transmitted by cloud storage through egress is reflected in the HTTP response headers. Hence, the term network usage cost is defined as the cost of bandwidth into and out of the cloud storage server. It is charged on a per-GB basis. Google Cloud has two tiers of network infrastructure: premium and standard. These differ from Azure and AWS, as they only offer a single network tier. Although network performance varies by storage tier, meaning CSPs have multiple network tiers, users cannot explicitly choose between them. For Google Cloud, the cost to use the premium network tier is more than the standard network tier, but it offers better performance. The network usage cost is a complex combination involving several factors, such as the route of data transfer, whether within the same cloud or outside. In the case of the same cloud, the cost varies depending on whether data is moved in regions within and across continents. Figure 3 shows the taxonomy for the network usage cost.

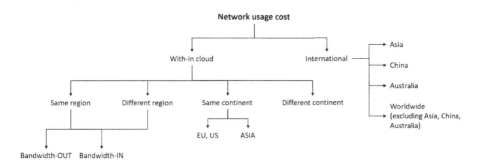

Fig. 3. Network usage cost taxonomy.

Data encryption cost is an essential element of the security costs. Cloud storage providers encrypt data using a key managed by the provider or the client, with no extra cost for the server-managed key. However, customer-managed keys incur charges as they are stored on the provider's infrastructure. The cost of key management is categorised into monthly billed key cost, number of operations using the key, and per hour billed HSM (hardware security module, a physical device that provides extra security for sensitive data). Key rotation is an additional cost. Though optional, data encryption affects the total cost of cloud storage. The cost of encryption and encryption/decryption keys is pretty much similar for all providers, while HSM costs vary.

3.3   Redundancy Model

Redundancy implies the service provider replicates valuable and important data in multiple locations. A client should ideally have several backups so that large server failures won't impair their ability to access information [21]. Cloud storage providers offer to store data with three different redundancy options. In single-region, data is stored in a single geo-graphic location such as *eu-west*. In a dual-region mode, a user can store data in two geo-graphical locations of his choice. For example, this mode can be a suitable option if the data is frequently accessed in two different regions, such as Europe and the US. A multiple-region mode can be selected if the data is frequently accessed from different regions. The redundancy model not only improves the durability of the data, but also the availability [28]. A summary of cloud storage redundancy models for three providers is given in Table 3.

Table 3. Cloud storage redundancy options accross the three providers.

Region	Azure	AWS	Google Cloud
Single	Locally redundant storage (LRS), Geo-redundant storage (GRS)	AWS Region	Single
Dual	Read-Access Geo Redundant Storage (RA-GRS)	Cross-region. Replication (CRR) (one way replication)	Dual-region
Multi	Zone-redundant storage (ZRS), Geo-zone-redundant storage (GZRS)	Cross-region, Replication (CRR) (two way replication)	Multi-region

Moving from single-region to dual or multiple regions can reduce access latency but comes at a cost. The higher the data redundancy, the higher the cost of data storage, both storage and replication costs. To determine which redundancy solution is ideal, it is advised to weigh the trade-offs between reduced costs and higher availability. Azure offers two types of replication in dual and multi-region replication. Using geo-replication, data is replicated to a secondary region remote from the primary region to protect against local disasters. The data in the secondary region can only be used for disaster recovery and has no read access. Using geo-replication with read access, a secondary region also provides read access. Waibel et al. [42] formulated a system that incorporates multiple cloud services to determine redundant yet cost-efficient storage by considering factors such as storage and data transfer costs in different cloud providers. The system recommends the most cost-effective and redundant storage solution. To increase application performance, different parts of the dataset can be stored and loaded from different availability zones or regions to ensure that the application's performance is not compromised due to network throughput bottlenecks.

Single-Region: A single geographic area, like Sao Paulo, is referred to as a single-region. For data consumers, e.g., analytics pipelines [13], operated in the same region, a single-region is utilised to optimise latency and network capacity. Since there are no fees levied for data replication in regional locations, single-regions are a particularly advantageous alternative for short-lived data. In comparison to data kept in dual and multi-region, single-region has the lowest cost. *Dual-region*: A particular pair of areas, such as Tokyo and Osaka, is referred to as a dual-region. When single-region performance benefits are required but improved availability from geo-redundancy is also desired, a dual-region is employed. High-performance analytics workloads that can run active-active in both regions at once are very well suited for dual-regions. This indicates that users will enjoy good performance while reading and writing data in both regions to the same bucket or data container. Due to the high consistency of dual-regions, the view of the data remains constant regardless of where reads and writes are occurring. Dual-region data storage is more expensive than single-region, but less expensive than multi-region and provides better availability and low latency. *Multi-region*: A vast geographic area, like the United States, that encompasses two or more geographic locations is referred to as a multi-region. When a user has to provide content to data consumers dispersed across a wide geographic area and not connected to the cloud network, a multi-region approach is employed. Generally, the data is kept near where the majority of the users are. The multi-region model is the most expensive model of data storage; however, it also addresses a wide range of security, privacy, availability, and data durability issues.

4   Conclusions

In this paper, we presented a storage cost taxonomy for the cloud to guide practitioners and researchers. Our taxonomy confirms that storage cost for the cloud is a complex structure, especially in a multi-cloud setting, where a broad spectrum of differences may exist between CSPs. Furthermore, cost needs to be considered inline with other quality of service (QoS) attributes and service level agreements (SLAs), which may also affect the cost directly or indirectly (e.g., availability, consistency, etc.). Our future work will include analysis of cost in relation with other QoS attributes, trade-offs between different cost elements (e.g., computing vs. storage), as well as review of existing literature for cost optimisation. These will provide a deeper understanding of cloud storage cost and uncover the existing literature's limitations and weaknesses.

Acknowledgments. This research is partially funded by DataCloud project (EU H2020 101016835).

References

1. Ali, M., Bilal, K., Khan, S.U., et al.: DROPS: division and replication of data in cloud for optimal performance and security. IEEE Trans. Cloud Comput. **6**(2), 303–315 (2018). https://doi.org/10.1109/TCC.2015.2400460
2. Balaji, S., Krishnan, M.N., Vajha, M., Ramkumar, V., et al.: Erasure coding for distributed storage: an overview. Sci. China Inf. Sci. **61**(10), 1–45 (2018). https://doi.org/10.1007/s11432-018-9482-6
3. Barika, M., Garg, S., Zomaya, A.Y., et al.: Orchestrating big data analysis workflows in the cloud: research challenges, survey, and future directions. ACM Comput. Surv. **52**(5) (2019). https://doi.org/10.1145/3332301
4. Edwin, E.B., Umamaheswari, P., Thanka, M.R.: An efficient and improved multi-objective optimized replication management with dynamic and cost aware strategies in cloud computing data center. Clust. Comput. **22**(5), 11119–11128 (2019). https://doi.org/10.1007/s10586-017-1313-6
5. Erradi, A., Mansouri, Y.: Online cost optimization algorithms for tiered cloud storage services. J. Syst. Softw. **160**, 110457 (2020). https://doi.org/10.1016/j.jss.2019.110457
6. Georgios, C., Evangelia, F., Christos, M., Maria, N.: Exploring cost-efficient bundling in a multi-cloud environment. Simul. Model. Pract. Theory **111**, 102338 (2021). https://doi.org/10.1016/j.simpat.2021.102338
7. Gessert, F., Wingerath, W., Friedrich, S., Ritter, N.: NoSQL database systems: a survey and decision guidance. Comput. Sci. Res. Dev. **32**(3–4), 353–365 (2017). https://doi.org/10.1007/s00450-016-0334-3
8. Hong, J., Dreibholz, T., Schenkel, J.A., Hu, J.A.: An overview of multi-cloud computing. In: Barolli, L., Takizawa, M., Xhafa, F., Enokido, T. (eds.) WAINA 2019. AISC, vol. 927, pp. 1055–1068. Springer, Cham (2019). https://doi.org/10.1007/978-3-030-15035-8_103
9. Hossain, K., Roy, S.: A data compression and storage optimization framework for IoT sensor data in cloud storage. In: Proceedings of the 21st International Conference of Computer and Information Technology (ICCIT 2018), pp. 1–6. IEEE (2018). https://doi.org/10.1109/ICCITECHN.2018.8631929
10. Irie, R., Murata, S., Hsu, Y.F., Matsuoka, M.: A novel automated tiered storage architecture for achieving both cost saving and QoE. In: Proceedings of the 8th International Symposium on Cloud and Service Computing (SC2 2018), pp. 32–40. IEEE (2018). https://doi.org/10.1109/SC2.2018.00012
11. Jin, H., Wu, C., Xie, X., Li, J., et al.: Approximate code: a cost-effective erasure coding framework for tiered video storage in cloud systems. In: Proceedings of the 48th International Conference on Parallel Processing (ICPP 2019), pp. 1–10. ACM (2019). https://doi.org/10.1145/3337821.3337869
12. Krumm, N., Hoffman, N.: Practical estimation of cloud storage costs for clinical genomic data. Pract. Lab. Med. **21**, e00168 (2020). https://doi.org/10.1016/j.plabm.2020.e00168
13. Lee, C., Murata, S., Ishigaki, K., Date, S.: A data analytics pipeline for smart healthcare applications. In: Resch, M.M., Bez, W., Focht, E., Gienger, M., Kobayashi, H. (eds.) Sustained Simulation Performance 2017, pp. 181–192. Springer, Cham (2017). https://doi.org/10.1007/978-3-319-66896-3_12

14. Li, J., Li, B.: Erasure coding for cloud storage systems: a survey. Tsinghua Sci. Technol. **18**(3), 259–272 (2013)
15. Li, W., Yang, Y., Yuan, D.: A novel cost-effective dynamic data replication strategy for reliability in cloud data centres. In: Proceedings of the 9th International Conference on Dependable, Autonomic and Secure Computing, pp. 496–502. IEEE (2011). https://doi.org/10.1109/DASC.2011.95
16. Liu, G., Shen, H.: Minimum-cost cloud storage service across multiple cloud providers. IEEE/ACM Trans. Netw. **25**(4), 2498–2513 (2017). https://doi.org/10.1109/ICDCS.2016.36
17. Liu, J., Shen, H., Narman, H.S.: Popularity-aware multi-failure resilient and cost-effective replication for high data durability in cloud storage. IEEE Trans. Parallel Distrib. Syst. **30**(10), 2355–2369 (2018). https://doi.org/10.1109/TPDS.2018.2873384
18. Liu, M., Pan, L., Liu, S.: To transfer or not: an online cost optimization algorithm for using two-tier storage-as-a-service clouds. IEEE Access **7**, 94263–94275 (2019). https://doi.org/10.1109/ACCESS.2019.2928844
19. Liu, M., Pan, L., Liu, S.: Keep hot or go cold: a randomized online migration algorithm for cost optimization in STaaS clouds. IEEE Trans. Netw. Serv. Manage. **18**(4), 4563–4575 (2021). https://doi.org/10.1109/TNSM.2021.3096533
20. Liu, M., Pan, L., Liu, S.: Effeclouds: a cost-effective cloud-of-clouds framework for two-tier storage. Futur. Gener. Comput. Syst. **129**, 33–49 (2022). https://doi.org/10.1016/j.future.2021.11.012
21. Expedient LLC: System Redundancy in Cloud Computing. https://www.expedienttechnology.com/blog/cloud/system-redundancy-in-cloud-computing/
22. Mansouri, N., Javidi, M.: A new prefetching-aware data replication to decrease access latency in cloud environment. J. Syst. Softw. **144**, 197–215 (2018). https://doi.org/10.1016/j.jss.2018.05.027
23. Mansouri, Y., Buyya, R.: To move or not to move: cost optimization in a dual cloud-based storage architecture. J. Netw. Comput. Appl. **75**, 223–235 (2016). https://doi.org/10.1016/j.jnca.2016.08.029
24. Mansouri, Y., Erradi, A.: Cost optimization algorithms for hot and cool tiers cloud storage services. In: Proceedings of the 11th International Conference on Cloud Computing (CLOUD 2018), pp. 622–629. IEEE (2018). https://doi.org/10.1109/CLOUD.2018.00086
25. Mansouri, Y., Toosi, A.N., Buyya, R.: Cost optimization for dynamic replication and migration of data in cloud data centers. IEEE Trans. Cloud Comput. **7**(3), 705–718 (2017). https://doi.org/10.1109/TCC.2017.2659728
26. Mansouri, Y., Toosi, A.N., Buyya, R.: Data storage management in cloud environments: taxonomy, survey, and future directions. ACM Comput. Surv. **50**(6), 1–51 (2017). https://doi.org/10.1145/3136623
27. Mazumdar, S., Seybold, D., Kritikos, K., Verginadis, Y.: A survey on data storage and placement methodologies for cloud-big data ecosystem. J. Big Data **6**, 15 (2019). https://doi.org/10.1186/s40537-019-0178-3
28. Melo, R., Sobrinho, V., Feliciano, F., Maciel, P., et al.: Redundancy mechanisms applied to improve the performance in cloud computing environments. J. Adv. Theor. Appl. Inform. **4**(1), 45–51 (2018)
29. Mokadem, R., Hameurlain, A.: A data replication strategy with tenant performance and provider economic profit guarantees in cloud data centers. J. Syst. Softw. **159**, 110447 (2020). https://doi.org/10.1016/j.jss.2019.110447

30. Naldi, M., Mastroeni, L.: Cloud storage pricing: a comparison of current practices. In: Proceedings of the 2013 International Workshop on Hot Topics in Cloud Services (HotTopiCS 2013), pp. 27–34. ACM (2013). https://doi.org/10.1145/2462307.2462315

31. Nalebuff, B.: Bundling as an entry barrier. Q. J. Econ. **119**(1), 159–187 (2004)

32. Nannai John, S., Mirnalinee, T.: A novel dynamic data replication strategy to improve access efficiency of cloud storage. Inf. Syst. e-Bus. Manage. **18**(3), 405–426 (2020). https://doi.org/10.1007/s10257-019-00422-x

33. Nguyen, S., Salcic, Z., Zhang, X., Bisht, A.: A low-cost two-tier fog computing testbed for streaming IoT-based applications. IEEE Internet Things J. **8**(8), 6928–6939 (2020). https://doi.org/10.1109/JIOT.2020.3036352

34. Nuseibeh, H.: Adoption of cloud computing in organizations. In: AMCIS 2011 Proceedings - All Submissions, p. 372 (2011)

35. Oh, K., Qin, N., Chandra, A., Weissman, J.: Wiera: policy-driven multi-tiered geo-distributed cloud storage system. IEEE Trans. Parallel Distrib. Syst. **31**(2), 294–305 (2019). https://doi.org/10.1109/TPDS.2019.2935727

36. Priya, N., Punithavathy, E.: A review on database and transaction models in different cloud application architectures. In: Shakya, S., Du, K.L., Haoxiang, W. (eds.) Proceedings of Second International Conference on Sustainable Expert Systems. Lecture Notes in Networks and Systems, vol. 351, pp. 809–822. Springer, Singapore (2022). https://doi.org/10.1007/978-981-16-7657-4_65

37. Ramamurthy, A., Saurabh, S., Gharote, M., Lodha, S.: Selection of cloud service providers for hosting web applications in a multi-cloud environment. In: Proceedings of the International Conference on Services Computing (SCC 2020), pp. 202–209. IEEE (2020). https://doi.org/10.1109/SCC49832.2020.00034

38. Shah, A., Banakar, V., Shastri, S., Wasserman, M., et al.: Analyzing the impact of GDPR on storage systems. In: Proceedings of the 11th USENIX Conference on Hot Topics in Storage and File Systems. USENIX Association (2019)

39. Simon, H., Wuebker, G.: Bundling-a powerful method to better exploit profit potential. In: Fuerderer, R., Herrmann, A., Wuebker, G. (eds.) Optimal Bundling, pp. 7–28. Springer, Heidelberg (1999). https://doi.org/10.1007/978-3-662-09119-7_2

40. Tomarchio, O., Calcaterra, D., Modica, G.D.: Cloud resource orchestration in the multi-cloud landscape: a systematic review of existing frameworks. J. Cloud Comput. **9**(1), 49 (2020). https://doi.org/10.1186/s13677-020-00194-7

41. Tos, U., Mokadem, R., Hameurlain, A., Ayav, T., et al.: Ensuring performance and provider profit through data replication in cloud systems. Clust. Comput. **21**(3), 1479–1492 (2018). https://doi.org/10.1007/s10586-017-1507-y

42. Waibel, P., Matt, J., Hochreiner, C., et al.: Cost-optimized redundant data storage in the cloud. Serv. Orient. Comput. Appl. **11**(4), 411–426 (2017). https://doi.org/10.1007/s11761-017-0218-9

43. Wu, C., Buyya, R., Ramamohanarao, K.: Cloud pricing models: taxonomy, survey, and interdisciplinary challenges. ACM Comput. Surv. **52**(6) (2019). https://doi.org/10.1145/3342103

44. Zhang, Y., Ghosh, A., Aggarwal, V., Lan, T.: Tiered cloud storage via two-stage, latency-aware bidding. IEEE Trans. Netw. Serv. Manage. **16**(1), 176–191 (2018). https://doi.org/10.1109/TNSM.2018.2875475

BKRSC-IoT: Blockchain-Based Key Revocation Using Smart Contracts for IoT Networks

Sami Bettayeb[1]([✉])[iD], Mohamed-Lamine Messai[2][iD],
and Sofiane Mounine Hemam[3][iD]

[1] ICOSI Laboratory, Abbes Laghrour University, 40004 Khenchela, Algeria
`sami.bettayeb@univ-khenchela.dz`
[2] Univ Lyon, Univ Lyon 2, ERIC, Lyon, France
`mohamed-lamine.messai@univ-lyon2.fr`
[3] Abbes Laghrour University, 40004 Khenchela, Algeria

Abstract. The growth of Internet of Things (IoT) networks has brought the crucial need for information and communication security to the fore. Since IoT devices exchange sensitive data, secure key management with its different phases and the key revocation phase especially is essential for IoT network security. However, existing IoT key management solutions need improvements because of the resource limitations of IoT devices. Despite considering these limitations, current key revocation solutions have several areas for improvement, including the high communication overhead of the limited-resource devices. Therefore, there is always a need for a decentralized and efficient solution to address these issues in IoT networks. This paper presents a new solution for key revocation based on Blockchain using smart contracts to minimize the communication overhead and the energy consumption in IoT networks. Furthermore, we assess the correctness of the proposed solution through security and performance analysis. The results show that our solution has reduced the communication overhead by 93.55%, 91.87%, and 99.75% compared to other solutions during the compromising, leaving, and draining cases, respectively, which proves that our solution is efficient and appropriate for IoT networks.

Keywords: Internet of Things (IoT) · Security · Wireless Sensor Networks (WSNs) · Blockchain · Key management · Key revocation

1 Introduction and Motivation

The Internet of Things (IoT) has revolutionized human interaction with technology, from smart homes to wearable devices and industrial automation. However, with the increasing number of connected devices, security, and privacy concerns have emerged as significant challenges. One of the critical security issues in IoT networks is key management in limited resource devices. In this context, the key revocation is one of the essential phases of key management schemes. In traditional systems, key revocation requires a central authority to manage and

R. Chbeir et al. (Eds.): MEDES 2023, CCIS 2022, pp. 331–344, 2024.
https://doi.org/10.1007/978-3-031-51643-6_24

distribute keys, which can lead to single points of failure vulnerability and significant communication overhead. In centralized systems, the entire system may be affected if the central authority becomes compromised or unavailable, leading to potential security breaches. Moreover, key revocation in centralized systems is energy-consuming. It requires a high communication overhead because of the need for communication between the devices and the central authority to manage their keys.

Blockchain was designed as a decentralized and distributed ledger technology to provide a trustless and tamper-proof environment for transactions and data management. However, blockchain's properties, such as decentralization, immutability, and security, make it a potential solution for various applications, including key management with its different phases, including key revocation in IoT networks.

This paper proposes a new solution called BKRSC-IoT, which stands for Blockchain-based Key Revocation using Smart Contracts for IoT networks. It uses blockchain to decentralize the process of the key revocation phase in IoT networks. It demonstrates the feasibility and effectiveness of using blockchain-based smart contracts for key revocation in limited resource devices in IoT networks. In addition, the paper aims to analyze the potential benefits of blockchain-based key revocation in IoT networks, including improved security, reduced communication overhead, and energy consumption.

The subsequent sections of this paper are organized as follows. Section 2 presents a brief background on Blockchain. Section 3 comprehensively reviews the related work in key management and revocation in IoT networks. Section 4 describes the proposed blockchain-based key revocation mechanism, including the smart contract design and implementation. Section 5 evaluates the performance and security of the proposed mechanism and compares it with existing approaches. Lastly, Sect. 6 concludes the paper and highlights the future research directions in this field.

2   Blockchain Background

From its name, Blockchain is a chain of blocks used as decentralized ledger technology. It appeared in 2008 when Satoshi Nakamoto published a paper that explained peer-to-peer cash transactions in a decentralized system [1]. The main idea of Blockchain is to create a distributed ledger that is shared among all the participants in the network. The database that contains all the transactions that have been made in the network is called a ledger. It is distributed among all the participants and synchronized using a consensus algorithm. The consensus algorithm is a protocol used to reach a consensus among these participants. Blockchain offers distribution, security, traceability, and immutability [2,3].

Different consensus algorithms have been proposed in the literature to solve the problem of reaching a common consensus among blockchain participants. The most famous consensus algorithms are Proof of Work (PoW) [1], Proof of Stake (PoS) [4], Delegated Proof of Stake (DPoS) [5] and Practical Byzantine Fault Tolerance (PBFT) [6]. These algorithms play a critical role in securing Blockchain.

There are three types of Blockchain: public, private, and consortium [7]. In public Blockchain, anyone can join the network and participate in the consensus algorithm. However, only a limited number of participants of the same organization can participate in private Blockchain. In consortium one, participants from different organizations can participate in the consensus algorithm. The advantages of private and consortium Blockchains are that they are faster and do not consume much energy like public Blockchain. However, they are limited regarding the number of participants compared to public Blockchain.

Smart contracts are autonomous programs that are executed on Blockchain. They are used to automate execution contracts between two or more parties. They appeared in 1994 when Nick Szabo proposed a digital contract [8]. They are used to reduce the cost and time in Blockchain without needing a trusted third party.

Several different applications have been proposed to use Blockchain in various fields. For example, it has been used to solve the key management and data integrity issues like in [2, 9–11].

3   Related Work

Several schemes have been proposed to address the key management security issues in IoT networks. Most of these schemes presented different phases of key management, such as key generation, key distribution, key refresh and key revocation.

In this section, we present a brief overview of the most relevant key revocation phases in the existing schemes.

According to [12], the authors distinguish two key revocation cases. The first case is when a gateway node detects some malicious activity of a sensor node. In this case, the gateway node deletes the pairwise key of the malicious node and updates its neighbors' matrix by removing the corresponding row and column of this node and by removing the node id from the neighbors' vector. The gateway node also reruns the group-wise key establishment phase to generate a new group key. It informs the neighbor nodes by sending a message containing the malicious node id, a nonce, and the newly calculated group key. Each node that receives this message responds with an acknowledgment message after checking the authenticity, and privacy of the received message and removing its related materials from its memory. The second case is when a node wants to leave the network with its willingness. In this case, the node sends a LEAVE message to its one-hop neighbors containing its id and a nonce. Each receiver deletes the related materials of the leaving node from its memory and replies with an acknowledgment message. In this case, the node sends a message to its neighbors containing its id and a nonce. The leaving node drains its memory after receiving the acknowledgment messages from all its neighbors and then leaves the network.

In [13], the authors proposed a node deletion phase in their scheme in which the neighboring nodes of a compromised or a leaving node delete it from their neighboring tables and update their polynomials by decreasing them by one term. They also delete its shared pairwise keys from their memory. However, the authors did not mention how the detection of a revoked node and the necessary communications happen in their scheme.

According to the authors of [14], the key revocation of a node is performed by its neighbors. Without sending any message to the neighbor nodes, each node revokes the key of every node that does not send a message within a predefined time interval. However, the nodes rerun the key generation phase each T_r, and the server sends a set of new one-one functions to all the nodes each $(2 * T_r)$. Furthermore, in the case of attack detection, the server sends a refresh message via the gateway node to all the nodes. The message contains the number of attacks to refresh the value of T_r. Therefore, receiving a refresh message from the server and replying to it makes the solution act like [12] regarding communication overhead.

Mesmoudi et al. [15] differentiate between two principal key revocation cases, as their scheme contains two node types: the cluster head (CH) and the cluster member (CM). The first case is when the base station (BS) detects a compromised cluster head (CH), it revokes the key of the compromised CH and its CMs and starts refreshing the keys of the remaining nodes. The second case is when a CH detects a compromised CM, it revokes the key of the compromised CM and notifies the other CMs of the cluster and starts the key renewal process. It should be noted that the scheme does not consider the key revocation in the case of leaving or draining the battery of a node.

In [10], the authors proposed a blockchain-based decentralized scheme. They have considered two layers, one for the key management and the other for the nodes' key management. They revoke the key of a leaving node by unicasting a refresh message to the node set of the leaving node containing its id and a randomly generated K_r, which is used to refresh the keys of the remaining nodes. It also broadcasts a refresh message to the other sets of nodes containing the id of the leaving node set and K_r. When the second layer of this scheme, composed of Blockchain participants (BP_s), receives the information about the leaving node, it creates a new transaction containing the id and the other information of the leaving node. Finally, all the BP_s verify this transaction by checking the signature, the hashes, and the transaction's validity by checking if the leaving node is a member of the set in the received information. The scheme decentralizes the key revocation process and resolves the centralized schemes' single point of failure problem. However, it has a high communication overhead because of the participation of all the constrained nodes in the key revocation process.

4   Proposed Solution

4.1   BKRSC-IoT Network Model

Our network model consists of three base components:

- **IoT devices:** These nodes are the main components of the IoT network. They are responsible for collecting data from the environment and sending them to the gateway nodes. These devices range from small sensor nodes to large industrial sensor-equipped machines and appliances.

- **Gateway nodes:** These nodes are responsible for receiving data from the sensor nodes and sending them to the remote server. Each of them is a blockchain participant.
- **Remote server:** This node is responsible for receiving data from the gateway nodes.

From another perspective, our network model consists of two layers like in [10], the first layer is responsible for the nodes' key management and consists of the IoT devices. The second layer is responsible for the blockchain and consists of the gateway nodes.

Figure 1 shows the network model of our proposed solution.

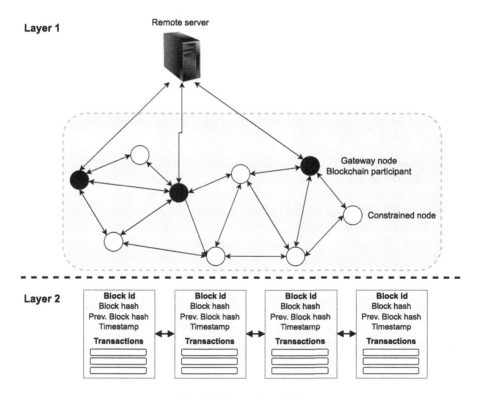

Fig. 1. Network model

4.2   Notations

Table 1 shows the notations used in this paper.

Table 1. Notations

Notation	Meaning
l_{ms}	The size of the sent message in bytes
l_{mr}	The size of the received message in bytes
d	Number of the neighbors of a node
n	Number of nodes in the network
n_s	Number of member nodes of a set
n_{gm}	Number of member nodes linked to the gateway g
n_c	Number of cluster members
$EPSB$	Consumed energy per a sent byte
$EPRB$	Consumed energy per a received byte

4.3   Assumptions

We assume that:

- The proposed solution is implemented on top of a base scheme that uses blockchain technology to manage at least its key distribution phase.
- The used consensus algorithm is Proof-of-Stake (PoS) as it is more energy efficient than Proof-of-Work (PoW) consensus [16].
- The used blockchain type is private as it is more efficient in energy consumption and transaction processing time than public blockchain.

4.4   BKRSC-IoT steps

In our proposed solution, a node can be revoked in three cases: (1) when a node is compromised, (2) when a node itself wants to leave the network, and (3) when a node's battery is drained.

Compromised Node. When one of the blockchain participants detects that one of its connected constrained nodes is compromised, it creates a transaction that contains the compromised node's information, including its id and its compromisation time. The transaction is then broadcasted to the other blockchain participants after signing its owner. The other participants validate the transaction and add it to the blockchain after receiving it by running the associated smart contract and checking that the node is already joined to the network. After successfully adding the transaction to the blockchain, the blockchain participants with the compromised node in their connected nodes list send a

KEY_REVOCATION message to them. The KEY_REVOCATION message contains the id of the compromised node. The receiving nodes then remove the compromised node and its key materials from their memories and reply with an ACK message to the sending blockchain participant.

Leaving Node. When a node wants to leave the network for any reason, like switching to idle mode to save energy, it sends a LEAVE message to its blockchain participant. The participant then creates a transaction that contains the leaving node's information, including its id, the time of the leaving request, and the reason for leaving. The transaction is then broadcasted to the other blockchain participants for validation. After successfully adding the transaction to the blockchain by running the associated smart contract that checks that the node is already connected to the network, the participants with the leaving node in their connected nodes list send a DISCONNECT message to their connected nodes. The DISCONNECT message contains the id of the leaving node. The receiving nodes then remove the leaving node from their connected nodes list and reply with an ACK message. When the leaving node receives the DISCONNECT message, it deletes all its keys except its pairwise key with the blockchain participant before disconnecting from the network.

Drained Node. When a node's battery is drained, it does not need to send a LEAVE message to inform the other nodes about its leaving. Instead, the blockchain participants execute the drain's smart contract and check the time of the last transaction in which the duration since the last time interaction of the node with the network is less than a predefined threshold. If the duration is less than the threshold, a transaction is created that contains the drained node's information, including its id and the time of its draining. Then, each blockchain participant with the drained node in the list of its associated nodes sends a KEY_REVOCATION message to its connected nodes. The KEY_REVOCATION message contains the id of the drained node. The receiving nodes then remove the drained node and its key materials from their memories and reply with an ACK message to the sending blockchain participant.

5   Evaluation

5.1   Security Analysis

In this part, we present the security analysis of our proposed solution.

Our proposed solution security is based principally on the base scheme's security in which this solution is implemented, as the exchanged messages between the different entities of the network are encrypted using it.

On the other hand, the transparency of the blockchain allows for an audit of the revocation process, and smart contracts allow automation. Moreover, our proposed solution does not store any key materials in the blockchain which makes it more secure.

5.2   Performance Analysis

This section presents the performance evaluation of our proposed solution. We first present a comparison of our solution with some of the existing solutions. Then we present the performance evaluation of our solution in terms of communication overhead and energy consumption of the constrained nodes.

Table 2. Comparison of our solution with some existing solutions for compromised node detection.

Solution	Node type	Communication	Energy consumption	nodes count	Total energy consumption
[15]	CH	$l_{ms} + (n_c - 1)*l_{mr}$	$EPSB*l_{ms} + EPRB*(n_c-1)l_{mr}$	1	$EPSB*l_{ms} + EPRB*(n_c-1)l_{mr}$
	CM	$l_{ms}+l_{mr}$	$EPSB*l_{ms}+EPRB*l_{mr}$	n_c	$n_c*(EPSB*l_{ms}+EPRB*l_{mr})$
[12,14]	Gateway	$l_{ms}+n*l_{mr}$	$EPSB*l_{ms}+n*EPRB*l_{mr}$	1	$EPSB*l_{ms}+n*EPRB*l_{mr}$
	Constrained	$l_{ms}+l_{mr}$	$EPSB*l_{ms}+EPRB*l_{mr}$	n	$n*(EPSB*l_{ms}+EPRB*l_{mr})$
BKRSC-IoT	Gateway	$l_{ms}+n*l_{mr}$	$EPSB*l_{ms}+n*EPRB*l_{mr}$	1	$EPSB*l_{ms}+n*EPRB*l_{mr}$
	Constrained	$l_{ms}+l_{mr}$	$EPSB*l_{ms}+EPRB*l_{mr}$	n_{gm}	$n_{gm}*(EPSB*l_{ms}+EPRB*l_{mr})$

Table 3. Comparison of our solution with some of the existing solutions in the case of a leaving node.

Solution	Node type	Communication	Energy consumption	nodes count	Total energy consumption
[12,14]	Leaving	$l_{ms}+d*l_{mr}$	$EPSB*l_{ms}+EPRB*d*l_{mr}$	1	$EPSB*l_{ms}+EPRB*d*l_{mr}$
	Others	$l_{ms}+lmr$	$EPSB*l_{ms}+EPRB*l_{mr}$	d	$d*(EPSB*l_{ms}+EPRB*l_{mr})$
[10]	Leaving	$(n_s-1)l_{ms}+(n-1)l_{mr}$	$(n_s-1)l_{ms}*EPSB+(n-1)l_{mr}*EPRB$	1	$(n_s-1)l_{ms}*EPSB+(n-1)l_{mr}*EPRB$
	Others	$l_{ms}+lmr$	$EPSB*l_{ms}+EPRB*l_{mr}$	n	$n*(EPSB*l_{ms}+EPRB*l_{mr})$
BKRSC-IoT	Gateway	$l_{ms}+(d+1)l_{mr}$	$EPSB*l_{ms}+EPRB*(d+1)l_{mr}$	1	$EPSB*l_{ms}+EPRB*(d+1)l_{mr}$
	Others	$l_{ms}+l_{mr}$	$EPSB*l_{ms}+EPRB*l_{mr}$	n_{gm}	$n_{gm}*(EPSB*l_{ms}+EPRB*l_{mr})$

Table 4. Comparison of our solution with some of the existing solutions in the case of a drained node.

Solution	Node type	Communication	Energy consumption	nodes count	Total energy consumption
[12,14]	Gateway	$l_{ms}+(n-1)l_{mr}$	$EPSB*l_{ms}+EPRB*(n-1)*l_{mr}$	1	$EPSB*l_{ms}+EPRB*(n-1)*l_{mr}$
	Constrained	$l_{ms}+(n-1)l_{mr}$	$EPSB*l_{ms}+EPRB*l_{mr}$	n	$n*(EPSB*l_{ms}+EPRB*l_{mr})$
BKRSC-IoT	Gateway	$l_{ms}+(n_{gm})l_{mr}$	$EPSB*l_{ms}+EPRB*(n_{gm})l_{mr}$	1	$EPSB*l_{ms}+EPRB*(n_{gm})l_{mr}$
	Constrained	$l_{ms}+l_{mr}$	$EPSB*l_{ms}+EPRB*l_{mr}$	n_{gm}	$n_{gm}*(EPSB*l_{ms}+EPRB*l_{mr})$

Comparison with Existing Solutions. Table 2, Table 3, and Table 4 show the comparison of our solution with some of the existing solutions in the case of compromised, leaving, and drained nodes, respectively. The comparison is based on the number of exchanged messages, the energy consumption of each node, the number of nodes involved in the communication, and the total consumed energy by the entire network. First, the communication overhead is calculated by summing each node's sent and received message length multiplied by the number of exchanged messages. Each node's energy consumption is then calculated by multiplying the communication overhead by $EPSB$ and $EPRB$. Finally, the total energy consumption is calculated by multiplying the obtained node's energy consumption by the number of the involved nodes. As we can see, the results demonstrate that our solution is more efficient than the existing solutions regarding the number of exchanged messages and energy consumption. In addition, the number of nodes involved in the communication is also less in our solution than in the existing ones.

Let us take an example. For the first scenario of node compromising, the number of the exchanged messages in all the compared schemes, including ours, is the same, and the difference is the number of involved nodes. It depends on the number of gateway member nodes and cluster members in BKRSC-IoT and [15], respectively. The number of these two variants is less than or equal in the worst case of one cluster and one gateway, respectively. The second scenario of the node leaving also has the same number of exchanged messages in all the compared schemes, including ours. However, the number of the involved nodes is different. It depends on the number of neighbors of the leaving node in [12,14] and the number of the gateway member nodes in ours. From another point of view, the number of the involved nodes in [10] is equal to the number of nodes in the network, which is the worst case. The third scenario of the node drained of energy is the same for the constrained nodes for all the compared schemes, including ours. In contrast, the number of the exchanged messages in our scheme is less than or equal to the other solutions' number of messages in the worst case of one gateway. The number of the involved nodes in our scheme also is less than or equal to the number of the involved nodes in the other solutions, making our scheme more efficient.

Experimental Results (Simulation). In this section, we present the simulation results of our proposed solution. We have used Rust programming language to implement a simulation of our solution, and [12,14]. The simulation is done according to the total communication overhead and energy consumption of the nodes in the network. We have 100 nodes randomly deployed in a 100 m^2 square area. The rate of the gateway member nodes is 10% of the total number of nodes. The number of neighbors of each node varies from 10 to 15. The simulation has been run 1000 times for the three scenarios of compromised, leaving, and drained nodes. It is based on [17] model, which considers an $EPSB = 59.2\,\mu J$ and $EPRB = 28.6\,\mu J$ for the transmission and reception of one byte, respectively.

Communication Overhead. Figure 2, Fig. 3, and Fig. 4 show the communication overhead required by all the constrained nodes in the network in the case of compromised, leaving, and drained nodes, respectively.

Our solution is more efficient than the existing solutions regarding the communication overhead, as shown in the results, due to Blockchain decentralization and delegating most of the communication overhead to the gateway nodes. Each gateway is responsible for communicating with its attached constrained nodes only. Therefore, unlike in [12] and [14], the number of involved nodes increases.

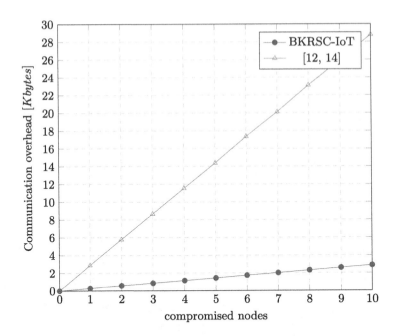

Fig. 2. Communication overhead required by all the constrained nodes in the network in the case of compromised nodes.

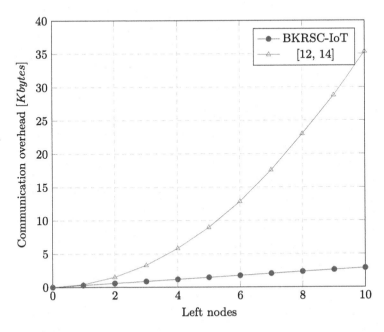

Fig. 3. Communication overhead required by all the constrained nodes in the network in the case of left nodes.

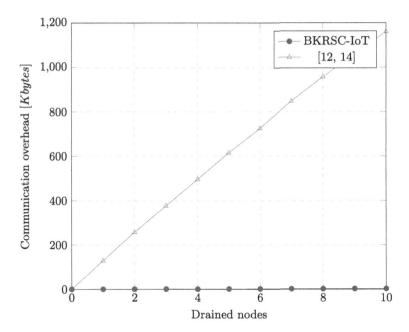

Fig. 4. Communication overhead required by all the constrained nodes in the network in the case of drained nodes.

Furthermore, most of the communication is done by the constrained nodes, where the gateway communicates with all the network nodes, which increases the communication overhead of the constrained devices. For the leaving case, in our proposal, the leaving node communicates with its gateway, which communicates with the other nodes to inform them, implying sending and receiving only one message. However, in [12], the leaving node must send and receive d ACK messages, leading to an increase in communication overhead.

Energy Consumption: Figure 5, Fig. 6, and Fig. 7 show the simulation results of the consumed energy by the constrained nodes due to their communications in the three scenarios of compromised, left, and drained nodes, respectively. The number of the affected nodes varies from 1 to 10. As we can see, our solution is more efficient than the existing solutions regarding the consumed energy by the constrained nodes in all three scenarios because of the number of the involved constrained nodes in the communication and due to delegating the communication to the gateway nodes. Figure 5, Fig. 6, and Fig. 7 are very similar to Fig. 2, Fig. 3, and Fig. 4, because of the direct relation between communication energy consumption and the number and the size of the messages.

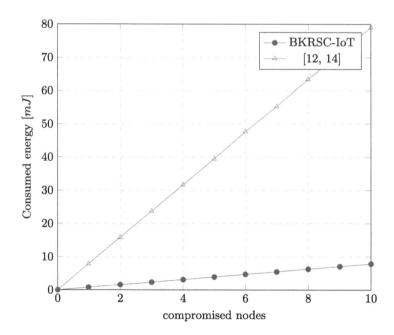

Fig. 5. Energy consumption of communication between all the constrained nodes in the network in the case of compromised nodes.

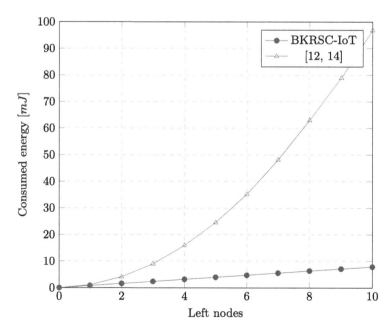

Fig. 6. Energy consumption of communication between all the constrained nodes in the network in the case of left nodes.

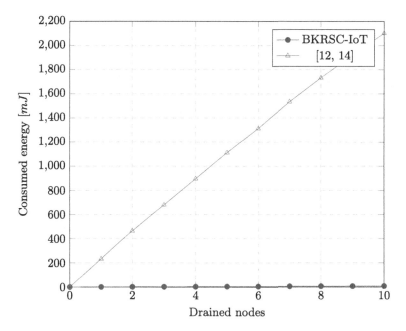

Fig. 7. Energy consumption of communication between all the constrained nodes in the network in the case of drained nodes.

6   Conclusion

Key revocation is an important issue in any key management solution. In this paper, a blockchain-based solution using smart contracts to address the key revocation problem in IoT networks is proposed. The proposal leverages blockchain technology's transparency and automation to decentralize and reduce communication overhead and energy consumption. Furthermore, the security analysis and the performance evaluation indicate that our proposed solution security is related to the security of the base scheme in which it is implemented. Furthermore, it does not store any key materials in the blockchain. Simulation results of our proposal show that it is more efficient than existing solutions. However, despite the valuable insights provided in this study, it is essential to acknowledge its limitations, particularly when it comes to the compromise of a blockchain participant. We plan to extend our proposed solution in future work to address key management challenges in IoT networks, such as key distribution and new node addition phases.

References

1. Nakamoto, S.: Bitcoin: a peer-to-peer electronic cash system. Decent. Bus. Rev. 21260 (2008)
2. Ma, M., Shi, G., Li, F.: Privacy-oriented blockchain-based distributed key management architecture for hierarchical access control in the IoT scenario. IEEE Access **7**, 34045–34059 (2019)

3. Viriyasitavat, W., Hoonsopon, D.: Blockchain characteristics and consensus in modern business processes. J. Ind. Inf. Integr. **13**, 32–39 (2019)

4. Vasin, P.: Blackcoin's proof-of-stake protocol V2, p. 71(2014). https://blackcoin.org/blackcoin-pos-protocol-v2-whitepaper.pdf

5. Larimer, D.: Delegated proof-of-stake (DPoS). In: Bitshare Whitepaper 81, p. 85 (2014)

6. Castro, M., Liskov, B., et al.: Practical byzantine fault tolerance. In: OsDI, vol. 99, pp. 173–186 (1999)

7. Zhang, A., Lin, X.: Towards secure and privacy-preserving data sharing in e-health systems via consortium blockchain. J. Med. Syst. **42**(8), 140 (2018)

8. Szabo, N.: Formalizing and securing relationships on public networks. First Monday (1997)

9. Lei, A., et al.: Blockchain-based dynamic key management for heterogeneous intelligent transportation systems. IEEE Internet Things J. **4**(6), 1832–1843 (2017)

10. Kandi, M.A., et al.: A decentralized blockchain-based key management protocol for heterogeneous and dynamic IoT devices. Comput. Commun. **191**, 11–25 (2022)

11. Hameedi, S.S., Bayat, O.: Improving IoT data security and integrity using lightweight blockchain dynamic table. Appl. Sci. **12**(18), 9377 (2022)

12. Nafi, M., Bouzefrane, S., Omar, M.: Matrix-based key management scheme for IoT networks. Ad Hoc Netw. **97**, 102003 (2020)

13. Nafi, M., Bouzefrane, S., Omar, M.: Efficient and lightweight polynomial-based key management scheme for dynamic networks. In: Bouzefrane, S., Laurent, M., Boumerdassi, S., Renault, E. (eds.) MSPN 2020. LNCS, vol. 12605, pp. 110–122. Springer, Cham (2021). https://doi.org/10.1007/978-3-030-67550-9_8

14. Nafi, M., et al.: IFKMS: inverse function-based key management scheme for IoT networks. J. Inf. Secur. Appl. **71**, 103370 (2022)

15. Mesmoudi, S., Benadda, B., Mesmoudi, A.: SKWN: smart and dynamic key management scheme for wireless sensor networks. Int. J. Commun Syst **32**(7), e3930 (2019)

16. Saleh, F.: Blockchain without waste: proof-of-stake. Rev. Financ. Stud. **34**(3), 1156–1190 (2021)

17. Wander, A.S., et al.: Energy analysis of public-key cryptography for wireless sensor networks. In: Third IEEE International Conference on Pervasive Computing and Communications, pp. 324–328. IEEE (2005)

Time and Text Management

Time-Series Estimation of the Best Time to View Seasonal Organisms Using Geotagged Tweets and Co-occurring Words

Yusuke Takamori[1] , Junya Sato[2(✉)] , Ryoga Sato[2(✉)] , Asahi Iha[2(✉)] ,
Masaki Endo[3(✉)] , Kenji Terada[3(✉)] , Shigeyoshi Ohno[3(✉)] ,
and Hiroshi Ishikawa[4(✉)]

[1] Japan Advanced Institute of Science and Technology, Nomi-shi, Ishikawa, Japan
y-takamori@jaist.ac.jp
[2] Electronic Information Course Polytechnic University, Kodaira-shi, Tokyo, Japan
{b19308,b20311,b20305}@uitec.ac.jp
[3] Division of Core Manufacturing Polytechnic University, Kodaira-shi, Tokyo, Japan
{endou,k-terada,ohno}@uitec.ac.jp
[4] Graduate School of Systems Design, Tokyo Metropolitan University, Kodaira-shi, Tokyo,
Japan
ishikawa-hiroshi@tmu.ac.jp

Abstract. The meteorological agency has reduced the scale of its biological seasonal observations because of requirements for maintaining observation targets and securing personnel. A low-cost, nationally applicable estimation method is being sought as a substitute. Earlier research has produced cherry blossom viewing estimates for a certain period in the future by predicting the transition of tweet counts on Twitter. One challenge of earlier research was the decline in prediction accuracy obtained in areas that produced few tweets. Additionally, it is difficult to estimate the viewing season in areas with few tweets, where previous methods cannot infer an increasing or decreasing trend. This paper therefore presents a proposal of a method to increase the number of data used for viewing season estimation for a certain period in the future using co-occurrence words. This method improves prediction accuracy compared to previous methods and demonstrates the possibility of estimating the viewing season in more areas than those estimated using previous methods.

Keywords: Co-occurrence · Seasonal Organisms · Time Series Estimation · Twitter

1 Introduction

The Japan Meteorological Agency makes biological seasonal observations to assess changes of plants' condition with the seasons. The purpose of these observations is to elucidate the overall meteorological situation [1] based on observed phenomena (data), while noting the delay or advancement of seasons, differences in climate, and changes.

R. Chbeir et al. (Eds.): MEDES 2023, CCIS 2022, pp. 347–360, 2024.
https://doi.org/10.1007/978-3-031-51643-6_25

This information is used as a reference for tourism and for predicting demand for tourism industry workers. The target organisms for biological seasonal observations are diverse, including plants and animals, with one target being cherry blossoms, with assessments of flowering and full bloom dates. In Japan, the observation targets have been reduced in scale for biological seasonal observations because of difficulties in maintaining the observation targets and in securing personnel for observations. As of 2022, the observation targets for the 34 species of plants and animals observed until 2021 have been reduced to only six species of plants [2]. Observations of cherry blossom blooming dates and full bloom dates are continuing, but they might be reduced in the future. Therefore, a need exists for a low-cost, real-time, and regionally applicable estimation method of blooming periods that can serve as an alternative to biological seasonal observations.

Twitter, a social networking service, has reached a monthly user count of 58.95 million in Japan [3], with information disseminated and accumulated widely and rapidly among its users. Among this information is tourism-related information. Research on tourism information is being conducted using Twitter. Sotiriadis et al. [4] elucidated the effects of online word-of-mouth on the decision-making of tourists by investigating the tourists' patterns of Twitter usage. Shimada et al. [5] proposed an analytical system for tourism information by analyzing the polarity of emotions expressed in extracted tweets. Olmedo et al. [6] conducted a comparative analysis of tourist density among three data sources. Twitter refers to user posts as "tweets" and displays the most recent tweets at the top of the feed. The benefits of using Twitter for tourism information analysis are threefold.

1. High real-time capability
2. Ability to explore where and what is happening using geotagged tweets
3. Low-cost data collection using Application Programming Interfaces (APIs) that are available for no fee or at a low price

Therefore, by collecting geotagged tweets from Twitter and analyzing them, one can develop a real-time and low-cost method for estimating the best time to visit. Moreover, the method is applicable in regions with different characteristics.

To date, several methods have been proposed for estimating the timing of cherry blossom viewing using geotagged tweets. Endo et al. [7] proposed estimation of cherry blossom viewing times using a method including a simple moving average of geotagged tweets. This method demonstrates that the timing of cherry blossom viewing can be estimated in prefectures or municipalities where some geotagged tweets are obtainable. Takahashi et al. [8] used a weighted moving average to estimate the timing of cherry blossom viewing. Specifically, they used a 5-day weighted moving average and a 7-day weighted moving average to improve the estimation accuracy. Furthermore, Horikawa et al. [9] demonstrated the possibility of estimating the timing of cherry blossom viewing for a certain period of time by combining the method of Takahashi et al. with time series prediction. Horikawa et al. performed estimation for each prefecture. Their method demonstrated that the estimation accuracy of prefectures with a small number of tweets decreases. Additionally, estimating the timing of cherry blossom viewing is difficult to do in regions for which only a few tweets can be collected and for which trends cannot be observed using the same method. Therefore, by increasing the number of tweets used for estimation, one can improve the estimation accuracy of prefectures that had low prediction accuracy using the method described earlier. It is also possible to estimate the timing of cherry blossom viewing in prefectures where estimation had not been possible because of the small number of tweets. It would be desirable to improve the accuracy without increasing the current amount of collected data, elegantly leveraging the existing data. However, since there are limitations in improving the accuracy from the limited amount of data used in previous studies, we conducted an attempt to enhance the accuracy by increasing the amount of data in this study. By increasing the number of tweets used for estimation, our proposed method can improve the estimation accuracy of prefectures that had low prediction accuracy using the method described earlier. It is also possible to estimate the timing of cherry blossom viewing in prefectures where estimation had not been possible because of the small number of tweets. Supported by results of this study, we propose a method for increasing the amount of tweet data used to estimate the timing of cherry blossom viewing for a certain period of time.

This paper is structured as follows: Sect. 2 describes our proposed method for increasing the amount of data used for estimating the best time for viewing cherry blossoms. Additionally, the differences between this method and previous methods are elucidated. Section 3 presents results obtained for estimating the best viewing time in the same region using both the conventional and proposed methods. Section 4 presents the conclusion of the study described herein.

2 Proposed Method

This section presents a description of our proposed method. First, we explain the overall process of our proposed procedure. Initially, we identify co-occurring words with "cherry blossom" in tweets, which were used in earlier studies. Then, after collecting tweets including any of the selected co-occurring words, we conduct a time-series prediction of the number of tweets collected within a certain period. Finally, we estimate the timing of the cherry blossom season based on the predicted number of tweets that were collected. These proposed methods intend to be implemented on a prefecture-by-prefecture basis. For this study, we conducted experiments in addition to the three prefectures of Tokyo, Kyoto, and Shizuoka, for which predictions have been made in earlier studies, by adding two prefectures, Miyagi and Fukuoka, to estimate the blooming season in areas where the blooming period falls during late March to early April, which is regarded as the usual blooming season. The specific procedures of the presented methods are outlined below.

Step 1. Collect tweets including the term "cherry blossom" in the text. The period of exploration was set as the period from February 2015, when the tweet collection began, through May 2022. The term used for the search was the Japanese characters "cherry blossom" in kanji, katakana, and hiragana.

Step 2. Using the MeCab [10] Japanese morphological analysis tool, the collected tweets from step 1 were subjected to morphological analysis to break down the tweet text into individual words. MeCab is an open-source tool for performing morphological analysis of Japanese language text. Morphological analysis involves separating text into words and parts of speech. MeCab is used widely for Japanese language morphological analysis because it can perform highly accurate analysis that incorporates examinations of factors such as part of speech and conjugation type. The following preprocessing steps were performed before conducting the morphological analysis: first, a cleaning process was performed to remove noise from the text, including the exclusion of URLs and symbols. Next, word normalization was performed to make the text easier to analyze. Japanese language tweets include a mixture of full-width and half-width characters. Therefore, full-width alphanumeric characters were converted to half-width, half-width kana characters were converted to full-width kana, all alphabetic characters were converted to lowercase, and all numbers were replaced with "0". After these preprocessing steps were performed, the tweets were broken down into individual words using MeCab. Furthermore, using the MeCab library and the IPAdic dictionary for morphological analysis, words corresponding to the three possible parts of speech "noun", "adjectival noun", and "verb", which are potential co-occurring words, were extracted. Then their frequency was counted. Here, "adjectival noun" refers to a large classification of part of speech introduced by UniDic [11], referring to the stem of an adjectival verb.

Step 3. The top 1% frequency of the collected words in "2" were subjected to co-occurrence judgment. Words with a frequency of less than 1% appeared in tweets including the keyword "cherry blossom" from February 2015 through May 2022 only in the single-digit range, indicating low relevance to the keyword "cherry blossom", and were therefore excluded from analyses. To determine co-occurring words, we calculated the skewness and kurtosis of the frequency distribution of each word and identified words that met the criteria as co-occurring words. Skewness and kurtosis are statistical measures that respectively indicate how much a distribution deviates from a normal distribution and how much it is peaked. We determined that they are appropriate indicators for identifying co-occurring words that share the same peak as the keyword in the annual trend of tweets. The judging criteria are shown in the following Eqs. (1) and (2), where S and K respectively represent the skewness and kurtosis of the frequency distribution of each word, and where Ss represents the skewness obtained from tweets including the keyword "cherry blossom".

$$(Ss - 1) \leq S \leq (Ss + 1) \tag{1}$$

$$K > 2 \tag{2}$$

Skewness and kurtosis were calculated as explained hereinafter. Skewness (Ske) and kurtosis (Kur) were computed based on tweets that included the target words within tweets extracted during January 1, 2018 – December 31, 2018. To obtain these measures, we used Eqs. (3) and (4) below, where n stands for the number of days within the specified time frame, x_i (i: 1, 2, ..., n) denotes the value of the measure for each day, x- represents the mean value for the period, and s signifies the sample standard deviation. For this study, n was set to 365 because we used a yearly time frame.

$$Ske = \frac{n}{(n-1)(n-2)} \sum_{i=1}^{n} \left(\frac{x_i - \bar{x}}{s} \right)^3 \tag{3}$$

$$Kur = \frac{n(n+1)}{(n-1)(n-2)(n-3)} \sum_{i=1}^{n} \frac{(x_i - \bar{x})^4}{s^4} - \frac{3(n-1)^2}{(n-2)(n-3)} \tag{4}$$

Examining the trend of tweets showing the same tendency as the cherry blossoms throughout the year was necessary for this study. For that reason, a period including all months from January through December had to be set. The tweets were collected by our research team or managed on a server, but there were periods during which the collection was stopped because of power outages and other issues. To avoid introducing bias into the calculated skewness and kurtosis values by including such periods, it was necessary to exclude, to the greatest extent possible, those periods during which data collection was limited. Therefore, the period of January 1, 2018 – December 31, 2018, which satisfies these two conditions, was adopted as the period for calculating the skewness and kurtosis values.

Step 4. We collected tweets that included words identified as co-occurring with "3" and used time-series forecasting to predict the number of tweets for a certain period in the future. Details of the data used in the collection are summarized in Table 1. We collected tweets including any of the co-occurring words from February 1, 2015 through February 28, 2022 by prefecture. Time-series forecasting was performed using the Forecast [12] service provided by Amazon Web Service, which has been used for earlier studies. Based on results of earlier studies, we used the Prophet algorithm to make predictions for the 60-day period from March 1, 2022 through April 29, 2022. The quartiles that must be set when using Forecast were 0.1, 0.5, and 0.9. Then we adopted the value at 0.5 as the predicted result.

Table 1. Details of data used.

Collection Period	February 1, 2015 through February 28, 2022
Tweet Type	Tweet with location information
Collection Condition	Tweets that were tweeted within the respective prefecture and one of the co-occurring words is included in the text

Step 5. We conducted time-series prediction of tweets that were identified as co-occurring terms in "4″" and estimated the period of the best viewing season based on the transition of the number of tweets calculated by time-series forecasting. Estimation of the best viewing season was conducted using the same moving average method as that used for the previous method. The simple moving average was used for moving average calculations. The n-day simple moving average is calculated using Eq. (5), where x represents the number of tweets per day, x_i denotes the number of tweets on reference day i, and $x_{(i-1)}$ denotes the number of tweets one day before reference day i.

$$\mathrm{Avg}n = \left(x_i + x_{i-1} + \cdots + x_{i-(n-2)} + x_{i-(n-1)}\right)/n \tag{5}$$

The period of peak viewing was determined by simultaneously satisfying Eqs. (6) and (7) for three or more consecutive days. Equation (6) identified periods with tweet counts higher than the average count over the course of one year, whereas Eq. (7) identified periods with a sudden increase in the tweet count. The period meeting both criteria was regarded as the peak viewing period. In Eqs. (6) and (7), xi represents the number of tweets on day i; Avg365, Avg10, and Avg20 represent 365-day, 10-day, and 20-day simple moving averages, respectively [9].

$$x_i > Avg\,365 \tag{6}$$

$$Avg10 < Avg\,20 \tag{7}$$

For the previous method, only tweets including the keyword "cherry blossom" were retrieved from the text body, resulting in approximately 30 tweets per day. However, when performing time series prediction using tweets including co-occurring words, the average value was around 400 tweets per day. If the moving average applied for the previous method is used, then even slight changes would be judged as the best viewing period, resulting in a marked decrease in estimation accuracy. Therefore, 10-day and 20-day moving averages were used as adjusted moving averages based on the number of tweets including co-occurring words. For this study, we specifically examined increasing the amount of data, which was a challenge when using the previous method. We aimed to solve it by changing only the data collection method. However, because of the difference in data volume, it became necessary to change the conditions for estimation. The final results were adjusted accordingly.

3 Results

This section presents results of the co-occurrence judgment and estimated results of the best time viewing cherry blossom analysis we conducted.

The co-occurrence words obtained from the detection are presented in Tables 2, 3, 4, 5 and 6, as collected for each of the five prefectures of Tokyo, Kyoto, Shizuoka, Miyagi, and Fukuoka. In Table 2 for Tokyo, it includes words related to cherry blossoms such as the famous Ueno Park, and petal-related words. Furthermore, in Table 3, the names of famous cherry blossom spots in Kyoto such as "Gion" and "Uji" are included. In Table 4, famous cherry blossom spots in Shizuoka such as "Kawazu" and "Sunpu" are listed. Table 5 presents the co-occurring words in Miyagi prefecture, including the names of cherry blossom spots such as "Shiogama Shrine" and "Funakoshi Castle Ruins Park," whereas Table 6 presents the co-occurring words in Fukuoka prefecture, which include the names of cherry blossom spots such as "Asai's single cherry blossom tree" and "Akizuki's cherry blossom avenue". From these findings, it can be inferred that the proposed method of co-occurring word detection can identify related words. Additionally, among the five prefectures surveyed, Tokyo had the highest number of co-occurring words detected compared to the other four locations. This result is likely to be attributable to the fact that the total number of tweets collected for co-occurring word detection was approximately ten times higher in Tokyo than in the other four prefectures, with 179,332 tweets collected for Tokyo, 15,596 for Shizuoka, 16,790 for Kyoto, 8,670 for Miyagi, and 11,512 for Fukuoka.

In Tables 2 through 6, the English translations of words and phrases are given in parentheses. Words that do not have English translations are those that do not make sense by themselves in Japanese, such as word stems. This is because these words are registered in the dictionary used in MeCab, a morphological analysis tool.

Table 2. List of co-occurring words in Tokyo prefecture (in Japanese).

cherry blossom	sakura	ueno park	さ く (cherry blossom)	ソ メ イ ヨ シ (Yoshino cherry)
ヒ ル ズ (building Name)	ミ ッ ド タ ウ ン (sightseeing place)	七 (seven)	五反田 (place name)	年 (year)
付着 (adhesion)	義	初 (first time)	咲い (bloom[missing words])	咲き (bloom[missing words])
国際 (international)	大学 (university)	大崎 (place name)	始め (start)	川沿い (riverside)
恩賜 (park name)	日和 (weather)	日野 (place name)	最後 (last)	本髪 (hair)
来年 (next year)	毎年 (every year)	江東 (place name)	皆 (every)	花 (flower)
花びら (petal)	花園 (place name)	見物 (sightseeing)	見頃 (best time to view)	調布 (place name)
開花 (blooming)	靖国 (name of shrine)			

Table 3. List of co-occurring words in Kyoto prefecture (in Japanese).

cherry blossom	割 (divide [missing words])	咲き (bloom [missing words])	宇治 (place name)	平野 (place name)
年 (year)	散っ (scatter [missing words])	淀川 (Yodo River)	疏水 (Place name)	祇園 (place name)
神社 (shrine)	蹴上 (name of shrine)	開花 (blooming)		

Next, Figs. 1, 2, 3, 4 and 5 represent the estimated peak blossom period of cherry blossoms based on time-series predictions for March 1, 2022 through April 30, 2022. The correct period shown in the figure refers to the duration from the announced date of blooming to the date of full bloom by the Japan Meteorological Agency, which was used to evaluate the prediction results. In each figure, a stacked bar graph was used to display the number of tweets that included the word "sakura" and the number of tweets that were determined to include co-occurring words in the text. The filled area was used to indicate the estimated period for each viewing time. Figure 1 portrays the estimated peak period for Tokyo, with the previous method shown in a darker shade and the proposed method in a lighter shade. Figure 2 displays the estimated peak period for Kyoto, whereas

Table 4. List of co-occurring words in Shizuoka prefecture (in Japanese).

みなみ (south)	並木 (row of trees)	分 (devide [missing words])	咲い (bloom [missing words])	咲き (bloom [missing words])
始め (start)	平 (place name)	新聞 (newsp-aper)	早咲き (early bloom)	梨子 (character name)
河津 (place name)	清水 (place name)	菜の花 (rape blosso-ms)	駿府 (place name)	

Table 5. List of co-occurring words in Miyagi prefecture (in Japanese).

sendai	がわら(place name)	ござい	しばた (place name)	みやぎ (place name)
ココ	千 (thousand)	名所 (famous place)	咲い (bloom[missing words)	咲き (bloom[missing words])
城址 (castle ruins)	春 (spring)	満開 (full bloom)	百貨 (department store[missing words)	石川 (place name)
神 (god)	船岡 (place name)	開花 (blooming)	韮 (place name)	鹽竈 (name of shrine)

Table 6. List of co-occurring words in Fukuoka prefecture (in Japanese).

ござい	セコハン	今年 (this year)	修正 (fix)	写真 (photo-graph)
初 (first time)	咲き (bloom [missing words])	始め (start)	年 (year)	散っ (scatter [missing words])
散り (scatter [missing words)	散歩 (stroll)	新木 (place name)	浅井 (place name)	満開 (full bloom)
秋月 (place name)	花 (flower)	菜の花 (rape blossoms)	見頃 (best time to view)	開花 (blooming)

Fig. 3 shows the same for Shizuoka prefecture. Figures 4 and 5 respectively presents the estimated peak periods for Miyagi and Fukuoka prefectures. The predicted bloom periods estimated using the proposed method for Tokyo (Fig. 1), Kyoto (Fig. 2), and Fukuoka (Fig. 5) are respectively about two weeks, one week, and two weeks longer than the actual bloom periods. The actual bloom period is defined as the period from the day of blooming to the day when cherry blossoms are in full bloom. It is estimated that about 10 days to two weeks must pass from full blooming to the end of the blooming period [13]. The estimated bloom period for cherry blossoms in Kyoto prefecture shown in Fig. 2 is from early March. Similarly, as shown in Fig. 3, it is estimated as being from early March in Shizuoka prefecture. A possible reason for this finding is the existence of early blooming cherry blossoms. Kawazu cherry blossoms, famous for their early blooming, can be viewed in Yodogawa and Uji City Botanical Park in Kyoto prefecture, and in the Kawazu River in Shizuoka prefecture. Kawazu cherry blossoms usually bloom in early January. They reach their peak in early March [14]. The estimated bloom period coincides with the period during which Kawazu cherry blossoms are in full bloom, which is believed to have led to the estimated bloom period from early March. Also, If we focus on the maximum value, Tokyo (Fig. 1) peaks behind the correct period both for predicted tweets containing co-occurring words and for predicted tweets containing the word "sakura". Kyoto (Fig. 2) and Shizuoka (Fig. 3) peaked in the correct period for predicted tweets containing co-occurring words, but peaked behind the correct period for predicted tweets containing the word "sakura". For Miyagi (Fig. 4) and Fukuoka (Fig. 5), the peaks for both predicted tweets containing co-occurring words and predicted tweets containing the word "sakura" appear within the correct answer period. We found that the predicted tweets with co-occurring words produced the maximum value in the period of correct answers, compared to the predicted tweets with the word "Sakura". This suggests that accuracy was improved by increasing the number of tweets to be predicted.

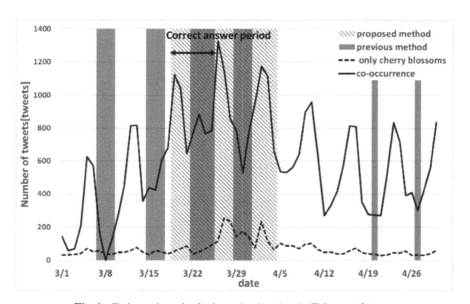

Fig. 1. Estimated results for best viewing time in Tokyo prefecture.

Using the previous method and the proposed method, we evaluated the results of estimating the cherry blossom season based on the temporal prediction of tweets collected from co-occurring words and using results obtained using the previous method.

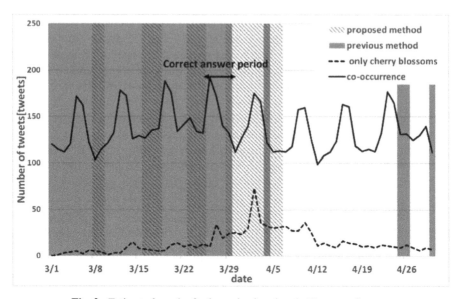

Fig. 2. Estimated results for best viewing time in Kyoto prefecture.

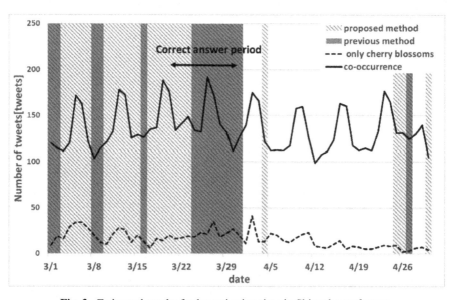

Fig. 3. Estimated results for best viewing time in Shizuoka prefecture.

Table 7 presents the evaluation metrics, including the recall and precision rates found for each method. The period from bloom to full bloom announced by the Japan Meteorological Agency is the correct period, and the reproduction rate is an indicator to evaluate how well the estimated results fall within that period. The proportion of the estimated results that are included in the correct period is calculated as the compliance

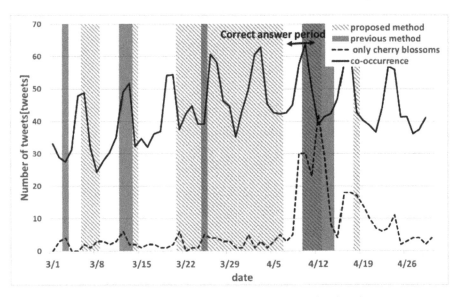

Fig. 4. Estimated results for best viewing time in Miyagi prefecture.

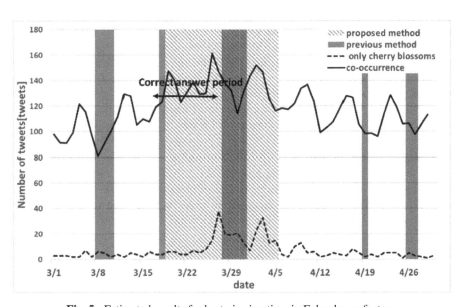

Fig. 5. Estimated results for best viewing time in Fukuoka prefecture.

rate. The previous method presented in Table 7 is based on the temporal change in the number of tweets including the word 'sakura' in their text to estimate the cherry blossom season, whereas the proposed method uses co-occurring words to predict the temporal changes in tweets and to estimate the cherry blossom season.

Table 7. Results of best viewing evaluation.

Prefecture	Method	Recall (%)	Precision (%)
Tokyo	Previous Method	50.0	26.7
	Proposed Method	100.0	47.1
Kyoto	Previous Method	57.1	23.5
	Proposed Method	85.7	18.2
Shizuoka	Previous Method	70.0	50.0
	Proposed Method	90.0	27.3
Miyagi	Previous Method	50.0	22.2
	Proposed Method	50.0	8.0
Fukuoka	Previous Method	9.1	9.1
	Proposed Method	81.8	50.0

As shown in Table 7, the previous method had a recall rate of 50.0% and a precision rate of 26.7% in Tokyo, whereas the proposed method had a recall rate of 100.0% and a precision rate of 47.1%. In Fukuoka, the recall and precision rates for the previous method were both 9.1%, whereas for the proposed method, the recall rate was 81.8% and the precision rate was 50.0%. Although bloom estimation for Fukuoka was not performed in earlier studies, the values of the recall and precision rates suggest that the previous method had low accuracy in bloom estimation and that the method was unable to estimate the bloom period. For these two prefectures, both the recall and precision rates for the proposed method are higher than those obtained using the previous method, indicating that the accuracy improved and that the bloom period can be estimated.

In addition, whereas the recall rate for the proposed method is higher than that of the previous method in Shizuoka and Kyoto prefectures, a decrease in the precision rate is apparent. This decrease might indicate that the proposed method is more agile in estimating the timing of early blooming cherry blossoms than the previous method, rather than a decline in prediction accuracy because of differences of a few days in the prediction period. For Miyagi prefecture, the recall rate and precision rate of the previous method were, respectively, 50.0% and 22.2%, whereas those of the proposed method were, respectively, 50.0% and 8.0%. The recall rate of the proposed method in Miyagi prefecture was equal to that of the previous method, but the precision rate was lower than that obtained using the previous method. The period from the flowering date observed by the Japan Meteorological Agency to the full bloom date in Miyagi prefecture is four days. The effect of the evaluation index per day of the predicted value is therefore greater than for other prefectures. This greater value is a phenomenon commonly observed in northern regions, where the switch to flowering within cherry blossoms occurs simultaneously when it becomes warmer because of the severity of cold weather in winter [15]. The small number of correct period days might have led to a decrease in precision because of the differences of a few days in the prediction period. In all five prefectures where cherry blossom blooming estimations were conducted, the proposed method demonstrated a 34.3% increase in the recall rate and a 4.0% increase in precision rate compared to previous methods, indicating the effectiveness of the proposed method. Therefore, accuracy can be improved using the proposed method instead of the previous method. Furthermore, the proposed method suggests that cherry blossom blooming estimation in regions where prediction is difficult can be conducted using the previous method.

4 Conclusion

This report outlines our study on estimating and predicting the cherry blossoms' blooming period using co-occurring words extracted from tweets. To enhance estimation accuracy, we propose increasing the data volume by incorporating cherry blossom-related co-occurring words. The proposed method takes time proportional to the number of words in the original data to collect data and determine co-occurring words. Applying our method resulted in a 34.3% increase in the recall rate and a 4.0% increase in the precision rate compared to the previous approach. This indicates the potential for improved accuracy using our proposed method. However, when estimating the blooming period in Miyagi prefecture, the recall rate of our method was comparable to the previous method, albeit with a lower precision rate. This challenge could be attributed to the short time between blooming and full bloom, emphasizing the need for further research to enhance accuracy in this region. Our approach also suggests the potential of estimating the blooming period in regions where the previous method struggles. In this study, we employed time-series prediction using the number of tweets as a single variable, but future research aims to enhance estimation accuracy by adopting multivariate time-series prediction and incorporating explanatory variables related to tweet transitions. Moreover, we anticipate verifying the effectiveness of our method for estimating the blooming period in regions beyond March–April, such as Hokkaido and Okinawa prefectures, thus making it a valuable tool for nationwide cherry blossom estimation.

Acknowledgments. This work was supported by JSPS KAKENHI Grant Number 20K12081, 22K13776, and the Telecommunication Advancement Foundation Research Grant.

References

1. Japan Meteorological Agency. Biological Seasonal Observation Guidelines (2021). https://www.data.jma.go.jp/sakura/data/shishin.pdf. Accessed 22 Feb 2023
2. Japan Meteorological Agency. Changes in the Disciplines and Phenomena of Biological Seasonal Observations (2020). https://www.data.jma.go.jp/sakura/data/shishin.pdf. Accessed 22 Feb 2023
3. Statista. Leading countries based on number of Twitter users as of January 2022 (2022). https://www.statista.com/statistics/242606/number-of-active-twitter-users-in-selected-countries/. Accessed 22 Feb 2023
4. Shimada, K., Inoue, S., Maeda, H., Endo, T.: Analyzing tourism information on Twitter for a local city. In: 2011 First ACIS International Symposium on Software and Network Engineering, pp. 61–66. IEEE (2011). https://doi.org/10.1109/SSNE.2011.27

5. Sotiriadis, M.D., van Zyl, C.: Electronic word-of-mouth and online reviews in tourism services: the use of twitter by tourists. Electron. Commer. Res. **13**, 103–124 (2013). https://doi.org/10.1007/s10660-013-9108-1

6. Salas-Olmedo, M.H., Moya-Gómez, B., García-Palomares, J.C., Gutiérrez, J.: Tourists' digital footprint in cities: comparing Big Data sources. Tour. Manage. **66**, 13–25 (2018). https://doi.org/10.1016/j.tourman.2017.11.001

7. Endo, M., Takahashi, M., Hirota, M., Imamura, M., Ishikawa, H.: Analytical method using geotagged tweets developed for tourist spot extraction and real-time analysis. Int. J. Inform. Soc. **12**(3), 157–165 (2021)

8. Takahashi, M., Endo, M., Ohno, S., Hirota, M., Ishikawa, H.: Automatic detection of tourist spots and best-time estimation using social network services. In: International Workshop on Informatics 2020, pp. 65–72 (2020). https://doi.org/10.1145/3405962.3405993

9. Horikawa, T., Takahashi, M., Endo, M., Ohno, S., Hirota, M., Ishikawa, H.: Estimating the best time to view cherry blossoms using time-series forecasting method. Mach. Learn. Knowl. Extract. **4**(2), 418–431 (2022). https://doi.org/10.3390/make4020018

10. Kudo, T.: MeCab: yet another part-of-speech and morphological analyzer. http://mecab.sourceforge.net/. Accessed 11 July 2022

11. National Institute for Japanese Language and Linguistics. Electronic Dictionary with Uniformity and Identity (2017). https://clrd.ninjal.ac.jp/unidic/. Accessed 22 Feb 2023

12. Amazon Web Service. Amazon Forecast Documentation (2019). https://docs.aws.amazon.com/en_us/forecast/?icmpid=docs_homepage_ml. Accessed 24 Feb 2023

13. Spring Season. What Month do Cherry Blossoms Bloom and When Do They Fall? Survey of cherry blossom season by prefecture (2020). https://nihonail.com/season/2195.html. Accessed 22 Feb 2023

14. Kawazuzakura. https://hanami.walk-erplus.com/special/kawazu/. Accessed 22 Feb 2023

15. Koiie, S., Shigeta, M., Higuchi, H.: Flowering time of cherry trees in Japan. In: 2012 AIRIES, pp. 15–20 (2012)

Semantic Similarity Between Medium-Sized Texts

Jacobo Farray Rodríguez[✉][ID], Antonio Jesús Fernández-García[ID],
and Elena Verdú[ID]

Universidad Internacional de La Rioja, Logroño, Spain
jacobofarray@gmail.com
https://gruposinvestigacion.unir.net/dds/

Abstract. Semantically comparing texts is a task that is useful in various fields, such as the automatic correction of exams and/or activities. Making use of Natural Language Processing (NLP) and deep learning techniques, the correction task can be facilitated for the teacher, so that a greater number of knowledge tests can be offered to the student. The objective of this work is to semantically compare texts in order to be able to evaluate the student's knowledge automatically. For this, models will be built based on Transformers architectures, specialized in the Spanish language and in 2 subjects. These models can be used and evaluated through an application. After using the different models to measure the similarity between a set of student's answers and the ideal answer provided by the teacher, a Pearson correlation coefficient greater than 80% is obtained when comparing the similarity measured and the teacher's grade. Given the Pearson correlation obtained, a MAE of 0.13 and an RMSE of 0.17, it is concluded that the models obtained would serve as an evaluation guide for both the teaching team and the students in the medium term, opening the door to further research to create an autonomous system in the long-term.

Keywords: deep learning · automatic correction · automatic short answer grading · semantic comparison · semantic similarity · transformers

1 Introduction

Semantically comparing texts involves analyzing their meaning in different contexts and can be very useful for a variety of applications such as sentiment analysis, plagiarism detection, or content analysis, among others. Education is not unfamiliar with this field. We find ourselves with the need to correct exams and/or activities, this being a necessary activity to validate the knowledge of the examinees.

Current natural language processing techniques allow us to obtain a semantic meaning of sentences, in such a way that we can find similarities of sentences written differently, but with similar semantics. While English may be more advanced in terms of Natural Language Processing (NLP) technologies due to the availability of large amounts of data used to create large models, there is a growing body of work in other languages like Spanish or Portuguese, and we can expect to see continued progress in this area in the coming years [4,6,10].

This study aims to make a contribution to the field of Education and NLP in the Spanish language, the second most spoken language in the world. Specifically, we focus on the automatic correction of exams/activities. The purpose of this research paper is to investigate the effectiveness of using NLP for the corrections of questions whose answers are around 200–250 words. These answers will be compared with the ideal answer provided by the teacher. To perform the comparison task our proposal is based on an architecture of Siamese Transformers models [9], architecture that reduces dimensionality and makes efficient use of resources when training the model.

This context led us to pose the following research question:

RQ How accurate can current models based on Transformers architectures be for semantically comparing Spanish language texts in the context of educational assessment?

For this study, a question/answer dataset from 2 subjects delivered at Universidad Internacional de La Rioja was used. Using them, specialized NLP models were created, which were benchmarked both quantitatively and qualitatively.

The rest of this communication is organized as follows. Section 2 reviews some related projects that involve measuring the similarity of texts. Section 3 provides an overview of the approach methodology. Section 4 shows the quantitative and qualitative results obtained, which are discussed in Sect. 5. Finally, some conclusions and further considerations are summarised in Sect. 6.

2   State of Art

This chapter presents the recent progress in the calculation of semantic similarity between texts, from the more classical approaches, such as those based on the similarity of vectors created from a latent probabilistic semantic analysis, generally using the cosine distance as a similarity metric [13] or variants of word embeddings models [3], to new approaches with the advent of machine learning. With machine learning, a lot of work has been done taking into account the context of the text to carry out NLP tasks. The calculation of semantic similarity is not immune to this trend. That is why the first approaches applied recurrent networks as long short-term memory (LSTM) ones [13], which were able to learn long-term dependencies in the text until the presentation of the Transformers architecture [11]. Transformers architecture has meant a turning point within the NLP, where the models have the novelty of the replacement of the recurrent layers by the so-called attention layers. These layers remove the recursion that LSTM has, so sentences are processed as a whole (positional encoding) instead of word by word. With this, it reduces the complexity and allows parallelization, thus improving the efficiency of the calculation.

In a study [12] of semantic comparison of English texts in the clinical environment using Transformers, good results are obtained using pre-trained models like Bert [5] and Roberta [7], obtaining a Pearson coefficient of 0.9010 for the second when comparing clinical texts, being able to apply them for clinical applications such as deduplication and summary of clinical texts.

Nowadays, most of the models are trained for the English language, but more and more multilingual models or models trained for different tasks in other languages are appearing recently [8]. Below, we list some of the NLP models that are used in this study:

- **BERT** [5]: Model that represented a turning point in NLP [3], in which Transformer architecture was used to obtain a better semantic meaning of the whole text.
- **mBERT** [5]: Extension of the initial Bert to which multilanguage support has been given for a total of 104 languages.
- **BETO** [4]: NLP model that has been prepared exclusively for Spanish. In the study by Cañete et al. [4] better results have been obtained than using mBert [5].

Continuing the progress, Reimers and Gurevych [9] presented a more advanced architecture based on the Transformers architecture, which uses two joined Transformers models. This has the main advantage of being able to work with larger texts when comparing them semantically, as it is not necessary to join the two texts as done with a classic Transformer model. This architecture reduces dimensionality, making efficient use of resources when training the model. Given the advantages offered by this architecture and the size of the text with which we have worked, this architecture is selected for the present study. Figure 1 shows the architecture proposal based on 2 Transformer models instead of 1.

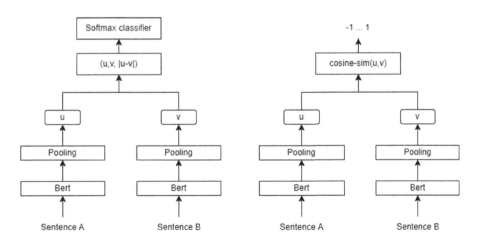

Fig. 1. SBert architectures for classification tasks (left) and semantic comparison tasks (right). Source: [9]

The aforementioned models are open-source, but there are applications on the market for calculating semantic similarity. We have selected 2 to make a comparison with them.

– Retina API [2]: API from the company Cortical with support for 50 languages, which provides different measures of similarity, such as cosine, Euclidean, Jaccard, and some own distance metrics.
– Dandelion API [1]: Product of a startup based in Italy, which offers different APIs for natural language processing, such as language detection or semantic similarity.

3   Methodology

In order to achieve the objective of automatically grading open responses of no more than 250 words, measuring their semantic similarity with an ideal response, a SCRUM methodology has been followed. The main tasks carried out have been:

1. Analysis of the data source to be used in the project. This is a set of questions/answers from two subjects delivered at Universidad Internacional de La Rioja (UNIR). The total number of records in the dataset is 240, with an average response length of the teacher of 130 words and the student of 150 words, there being cases in which the student's response is 405 words.
2. Identification of NLP Transformers models to use. Although the architecture used to specialize the models has always been that of sentence transformers, we have used four existing conjoined transformer models and two occurrences that create the Siamese architecture from scratch defined as shown in Fig. 2. A maximum input size of 256 words has been defined.
   For the choice of these models, support for Spanish or multilanguage and/or the number of tokens the models allow has been taken into account. Table 1 shows the selected models, where the S-ST type means new siamese transformer from the scratch and E-ST means existing Siamese Transformer models. Although in our datasets we have an average student response greater than 128 words, models with this number of tokens have been chosen, since they were multilingual models and the teacher's average response is 130 words. It is also worth mentioning that in the event that a sentence exceeds the maximum input size allowed by the model, the sentence will be truncated, affecting the training of the models. In this study we have prioritized the average size of the teacher's response, understanding that every response should be correct with that approximate size.
3. Specialization of NLP models, to which a fine-tuning phase has been applied. For the training process of the models, the open-source library Hugging Face (https://huggingface.com) has been used. For each of the Siamese models described above, the training will be done for epochs 1, 5, 10, 30, 50 and 100. In addition to the number of epochs, the other parameters used are:
   – train_loss: As a loss evaluation function we selected the cosine similarity.

Table 1. Selected Transformer Models.

Id	Model	Type	Tokens n°
A	sentence-transformers/all-distilroberta-v1	E-ST	512
B	sentence-transformers/distiluse-base-multilingual-cased-v1	E-ST	128
C	sentence-transformers/paraphrase-multilingual-MiniLM-L12-v2	E-ST	128
D	sentence-transformers/paraphrase-multilingual-mpnet-base-v2	E-ST	128
E	bert -base- multilingual - uncased [5]	S-ST	256
F	dccuchile/bert -base- spanish - wwm -uncased [4]	S-ST	256

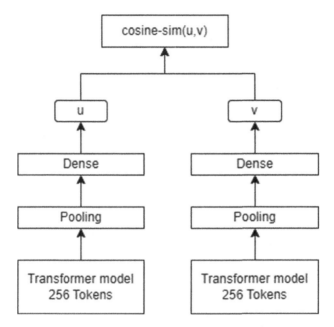

Fig. 2. Architecture followed in Siamese Transformers

- train_dataloader: In order to make better use of memory, we did the training in batches, defining the size of each batch as 10% of the size of the training data set.
- steps_per_epoch: The default value has been taken, so the number of training steps per epoch will be the size of the training data set.
- warmup_steps: Represents the number of training steps in which the learning rate will be maximum, after which the learning rate decreases linearly until it reaches zero. It is defined as the number of steps until reaching 10% of the training data.
- evaluation_steps: We gave it the value of 10% of the size of the training dataset.
- save_best_model: set with the value True, in order to save the best model evaluated.

4. Application development. To facilitate the task, an application was developed using the gradio SDK (https://gradio.app), whose main purpose is to make use of the obtained models. This application allows one to compare one pair of texts or a battery of texts. This second point serves as a support tool for evaluation for both teachers and students.
5. Evaluation and comparison of the different NLP models.
   - Quantitative comparative evaluation. On the one hand, we have chosen the Pearson, Spearman, and Kendall correlations to measure the correlation between the teacher's grade and the grade awarded (semantic similarity) by the model. The purpose is to measure the relationship between the teacher's grade and the grade obtained using the models, regardless of the error that we can obtain with the generated models. On the other hand, the MAE, MSE, RMSE, RMSLE and R2 metrics are used to evaluate the error made compared to the teacher's grade. See Evaluations 1 and 2 in Sect. 4.
   - Qualitative evaluation with random examples, where we have also wanted to test extreme cases such as negations and antonyms. See Evaluation 3 in Sect. 4.
   - Comparative evaluation between the best model obtained in this study and 2 existing applications in the market (Retina API [2] and Dandelion API [1]). See Evaluation 4 in Sect. 4.

4   Results

Evaluation 1. Considering the Pearson correlation (See Table 2), better results are obtained in the models previously trained with the Spanish language, and even better if we look at the Beto model, which is a model specifically designed for the Spanish language and not multilingual.

Observing the Spearman correlation (See Table 3), although the coefficients of this correlation are not so close to 1, a behavior similar to that with the Pearson coefficient is observed, having better results when we use multilingual models and even better in the case of the model based on Beto.

Table 2. Pearson correlation of the models obtained.

Epochs	A	B	C	D	E	F
1	0.76	0.72	0.67	0.76	0.77	0.80
5	0.75	0.81	0.66	0.76	0.77	0.81
10	0.76	0.79	0.69	0.81	0.77	0.78
30	0.77	0.81	0.72	0.78	0.80	0.80
50	0.76	0.78	0.73	0.75	0.82	0.81
100	0.77	0.81	0.74	0.77	0.77	0.82

Table 3. Spearman correlation of the models obtained.

Epochs	A	B	C	D	E	F
1	0.39	0.32	0.13	0.31	0.44	0.52
5	0.35	0.56	0.15	0.45	0.43	0.50
10	0.36	0.49	0.15	0.59	0.51	0.43
30	0.43	0.63	0.32	0.52	0.59	0.51
50	0.37	0.48	0.33	0.44	0.63	0.56
100	0.38	0.66	0.37	0.48	0.43	0.54

Considering the models trained with 50 epochs as those that offer a better balance between results and computational cost, the correlation plots including Pearson, Spearman and Kendall coefficients for these models are shown in Fig. 3.

Evaluation 2. MAE, MSE, RMSE, RMSLE, R2

It is observed that the models that present the best metrics are those trained with 50 epochs (Table 4), behaving better the models created with the Siamese architecture from scratch. The model with the best metrics is the one based on Beto [4] followed by mBert [5].

Evaluation 3. Negations

We studied the semantic similarity in those cases in which one of the texts to be compared semantically is the negation of the other. Since the goal is to rate an answer, a denial can mean a complete change in the rating. For example, for the question "Is Spain on the European continent?", the student's answer could be "Spain is on the European continent" or "Spain is not on the European continent". Both sentences are very similar but mean the complete opposite.

Analyzing the semantic similarity using the trained models based on BETO returns a semantic similarity of 0.783, a value that would tell us that these texts have a lot in common in terms of semantic meaning.

As an extension of this point, we can also include affirmation and denial in the same sentence.

Evaluation 4. Although in the quantitative evaluation, the models such as mBert or Beto had better results, the qualitative perception has been that the paraphrase-multilingual-MiniLM-L12-V2 model worked better. That is why this model has been chosen for carrying out certain random tests. In Table 5 we show some tested cases for the paraphrase-multilingual-MiniLM-L12-V2 model, comparing its results with 2 existing applications on the market such as Retina API [2] and Dandelion API [1]. In case 3, we wanted to test how the models would behave for **antonymous** words.

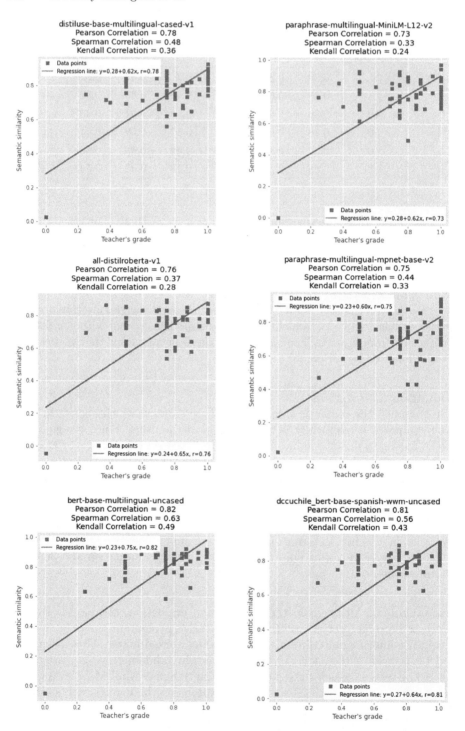

Fig. 3. Pearson, Spearman, and Kendall correlation for models trained with 50 Epochs

Table 4. Metrics MAE, MSE, RMSE, RMSLE, MAPE and R2 of the models obtained.

all-distilroberta-v1					
epochs	MAE	MSE	RMSE	RMSLE	R2
1	0.149	0.033	0.182	0.012	0.575
5	0.156	0.036	0.190	0.012	0.537
10	0.151	0.035	0.186	-	0.555
30	0.142	0.032	0.178	0.011	0.592
50	0.149	0.033	0.182	-	0.573
100	0.145	0.032	0.180	0.011	0.585

distiluse-base-multilingual-cased-v1					
epochs	MAE	MSE	RMSE	RMSLE	R2
1	0.177	0.044	0.209	-	0.438
5	0.137	0.028	0.167	-	0.642
10	0.144	0.030	0.173	0.011	0.616
30	0.129	0.027	0.165	-	0.652
50	0.141	0.030	0.175	0.011	0.609
100	0.129	0.027	0.164	-	0.653

paraphrase-multilingual-MiniLM-L12-v2					
epochs	MAE	MSE	RMSE	RMSLE	R2
1	0.170	0.045	0.213	0.016	0.418
5	0.172	0.046	0.213	0.016	0.415
10	0.165	0.043	0.207	0.015	0.450
30	0.153	0.039	0.197	-	0.503
50	0.149	0.037	0.193	0.013	0.524
100	0.152	0.037	0.191	-	0.529

paraphrase-multilingual-mpnet-base-v2					
epochs	MAE	MSE	RMSE	RMSLE	R2
1	0.153	0.037	0.191	0.014	0.531
5	0.158	0.035	0.186	0.012	0.556
10	0.141	0.029	0.169	-	0.633
30	0.148	0.033	0.182	-	0.575
50	0.154	0.037	0.193	0.013	0.520
100	0.143	0.033	0.182	-	0.576

mbert					
epochs	MAE	MSE	RMSE	RMSLE	R2
1	0.183	0.060	0.244	-	0.235
5	0.188	0.064	0.252	-	0.182
10	0.191	0.062	0.249	-	0.201
30	0.134	0.029	0.171	0.010	0.626
50	0.133	0.028	0.169	-	0.635
100	0.186	0.063	0.251	0.021	0.190

beto					
epochs	MAE	MSE	RMSE	RMSLE	R2
1	0.154	0.033	0.182	0.012	0.574
5	0.139	0.027	0.165	0.009	0.652
10	0.139	0.032	0.179	0.012	0.586
30	0.139	0.030	0.173	-	0.614
50	0.130	0.027	0.164	0.010	0.654
100	0.154	0.034	0.185	0.011	0.562

Table 5. Cases tested at random.

	semantic similarity	Cortical IO	dandelion
CASE 1			
Colón discovered America			
Colón discovered Japan	0.645	0.71	0.64
Colón discovered India	0.749	1	0 .69
Colón discovered the American continent	0.966	0.79	1
Colón found the American continent	0.952	0.58	1
CASE 2			
The numbers being multiplied are known as factors, while the result of the multiplication is known as the product			
The factors are the numbers that are multiplied and the result is the product	0.87	0.79	1
The factors are not the numbers being multiplied and the result is not the product	0.659	0.79	1
The factors are the numbers that are multiplied and the result is the dividend.	0.639	0.59	0 .92
CASE 3 (ANTONYMS)			
Solving algorithm problems is easy			
Solving algorithmic problems is not difficult	0.847	0.71	1
Solving algorithmic problems is easy	0.972	0.66	0 .85
Solving algorithmic problems is difficult	0.686	0.71	1
CASE 4			
The cell is the morphological and functional unit of all living things. The cell is the smallest element that can be considered alive. Living organisms can be classified according to the number of cells they have: if they only have one, they are called unicellular; if they have more, they are called multicellular			
The cell is the morphological and functional unit of living beings. It is the smallest living element. Living organisms are classified according to the number of cells into unicellular, if they only have one, or multicellular, if they have more.	0.973	0.78	0 .95
The cell is the functional unit of living beings. Living organisms are classified as unicellular, when they have one cell, or multicellular, when they have more.	0.917	0.65	0.82
The cell is the functional unit of living beings. Living organisms are classified as unicellular, when they have one cell, or multicellular, when they have more.	0.92	0.65	0 .82
The cell is the smallest unit of living things. Cells are classified into univocal and multicellular.	0.878	0.59	0 .68
The cell is the morphological and functional unit of all living things. The cell is the largest element that can be considered alive.	0.832	0.59	1

5   Discussion

The models trained with 50 epochs are the ones with better metrics. Within these, the best ones are the Siamese models built from scratch, being first the one based on Beto [4] followed by mBert [5]. This may be because they were built with a more complex architecture, adding an extra dense layer (see Fig. 2). In Fig. 3 we show Pearson, Spearman, and Kendall coefficients for these models. For the Pearson coefficient, a linear dependence between the teacher's qualification and the semantic similarity of at least 0.81 is obtained. Considering the rank correlation, values of at least 0.56 are obtained for Spearman and 0.49 for Kendall. This Kendall value is obtained for the siamese model based on mBert, so we can conclude that if we order the students' answers according to the grade given by the teacher, we find that this order is respected in 49% of the cases.

Analyzing correlations from Fig. 3 we see 2 important points:

- The models are not able to give good similarities, even when the teacher's grade is high. This is mainly because for the model to give a 1 as semantic similarity, the 2 texts must be exactly the same.
- We see quite a few cases in the intermediate zone of the graphs, in which the models give a better semantic similarity or "mark" than the one assigned by the teacher.
- In addition, we observed that better results are obtained with the mBert model than with the Beto model (model trained specifically for Spanish), although this may be due to the size of the corpus used to train said models. For this reason, the translation between semantic similarity and note could not be done directly, so it would be necessary to investigate a mechanism to carry out the said translation. To carry out this translation, other factors that may influence the qualification must also be taken into account, such as misspellings.

It is worth mentioning that the qualitative evaluation carried out by the human expert shows that our best model is paraphrase-multilingual-MiniLM-L12-V2, having performance comparable to that of commercial applications. In the qualitative test, we worked with short texts, with no truncation. The model chosen by the human evaluator seems to have better results than one of the models that work with 128 tokens, so truncation could have affected these models and led to lower performance in the quantitative evaluation.

6   Conclusion

Starting from an architecture of Siamese Transformers models, a relatively modern architecture and very useful for the case at hand, where we want to measure the similarity of two medium-size text inputs, this study delves into:

- Dealing with medium-sized texts leads to greater complexity and dimensionality of the models, which is why the architecture adopted is very important, directly impacting the performance of the models and mainly their training.
- Working with texts in Spanish since most research work is in English.

Putting emphasis on these 2 challenges, the relevance of the study lies in the union of both, that is working with medium-sized texts in Spanish for the semantic comparison between them. Analyzing the results obtained in detail, we see that the models obtained, although they have an acceptable performance (Pearson correlation around 82% for the best two), are far from being a solution that can be used autonomously without human review. In relation to this, it is necessary to take into account the volume of data that has been used to train the models, with a total of 240 labeled question-answers. With this volume of data, it has been possible to assess, in a certain way, if the proposed architecture solution would be valid, but it would be advisable to train the models with the largest volume of labeled data. In addition to starting with a larger volume of data, it would be interesting if we had the teacher's response and equally valid alternatives to it. This could help a better calibration of the model while training.

Although we still cannot use the models autonomously, it has been a starting point to detect and delve into possible branches of future work, such as:

- Studying the possibility of resolving the problem of comparing medium-sized texts breaking the text into smaller sentences and using these to obtain semantic similarity.
- Deepen into how the truncation of texts affects the calculation of semantic similarity
- Deepen into how negations and antonyms affect the calculation of semantic similarity.
- Integrate semantic similarity models with other models, each of them with the purpose of evaluating a specific point (spelling mistakes, semantic similarity, writing style, denials, etc.).
- Investigate the possibility of not only giving a mark on an exam but also giving feedback to the student with which they can know where they have failed and how to improve both the completion of an exam and their study techniques.

Acknowledgements. This Work is partially funded by the PLeNTaS project, "Proyectos I+D+i 2019", PID2019-111430RB-I00/AEI/10.13039/501100011033, and by the EVATECO-PLN project, Proyecto PROPIO UNIR, projectId B0036.

References

1. Dandelion API. https://dandelion.eu/semantic-text/text-similarity-demo. Accessed 28 Feb 2023
2. Retina API. https://www.Cortical.Io/Retina-Api-Documentation. Accessed 28 Feb 2023
3. Babić, K., Guerra, F., Martinčić-Ipšić, S., Meštrović, A.: A comparison of approaches for measuring the semantic similarity of short texts based on word embeddings. J. Inf. Organ. Sci. **44**(2) (2020). https://doi.org/10.31341/jios.44.2.2, https://jios.foi.hr/index.php/jios/article/view/142
4. Cañete, J., Chaperon, G., Fuentes, R., Ho, J.H., Kang, H., Pérez, J.: Spanish pre-trained BERT model and evaluation data. Pml4dc ICLR **2020**(2020), 1–10 (2020)
5. Devlin, J., Chang, M.W., Lee, K., Toutanova, K.: BERT: pre-training of deep bidirectional transformers for language understanding (2018). https://doi.org/10.48550/ARXIV.1810.04805, https://arxiv.org/abs/1810.04805
6. Gonçalo Oliveira, H., Sousa, T., Alves, A.: Assessing lexical-semantic regularities in portuguese word embeddings. Int. J. Interact. Multimed. Artif. Intell. **6**, 34 (03 2021). https://doi.org/10.9781/ijimai.2021.02.006
7. Liu, Y., et al.: RoBERTa: a robustly optimized BERT pretraining approach (2019). https://doi.org/10.48550/ARXIV.1907.11692, https://arxiv.org/abs/1907.11692
8. Qiu, X., Sun, T., X.Y., et al.: Pre-trained models for natural language processing: a survey. Sci. China Technol. Sci. **63**, 1872–1897 (2020). https://doi.org/10.1007/s11431-020-1647-3

9. Reimers, N., Gurevych, I.: Sentence-BERT: sentence embeddings using Siamese BERT-networks. In: Proceedings of the 2019 Conference on Empirical Methods in Natural Language Processing and the 9th International Joint Conference on Natural Language Processing (EMNLP-IJCNLP), pp. 3982–3992. Association for Computational Linguistics, Hong Kong (2019). https://doi.org/10.18653/v1/D19-1410, https://aclanthology.org/D19-1410

10. de la Rosa, J., Ponferrada, E., Villegas, P., González de Prado Salas, P., Romero, M., Grandury, M.: BERTIN: Efficient pre-training of a Spanish language model using perplexity sampling. Procesamiento Lenguaje Nat. **68**, 13–23 (2022). http://journal.sepln.org/sepln/ojs/ojs/index.php/pln/article/view/6403

11. Vaswani, A., et al.: Attention is all you need. In: Guyon, I., et al. (eds.) Advances in Neural Information Processing Systems, vol. 30. Curran Associates, Inc. (2017). https://proceedings.neurips.cc/paper/2017/file/3f5ee243547dee91fbd053c1c4a845aa-Paper.pdf

12. Yang, X., He, X., Zhang, H., Ma, Y., Bian, J., Wu, Y.: Measurement of semantic textual similarity in clinical texts: comparison of transformer-based models. JMIR Med. Inform. **8**(11), e19735 (2020). https://doi.org/10.2196/19735, http://medinform.jmir.org/2020/11/e19735/

13. Zhang, L., Huang, Y., Yang, X., Yu, S., Zhuang, F.: An automatic short-answer grading model for semi-open-ended questions. Interact. Learn. Environ. **30**(1), 177–190 (2022). https://doi.org/10.1080/10494820.2019.1648300

The Medium is the Message: Toxicity Declines in Structured vs Unstructured Online Deliberations

Mark Klein[1,2(✉)]

[1] Massachusetts Institute of Technology, Cambridge, MA 02139, USA
m_klein@mit.edu
[2] School of Collective Intelligence, University Mohammed VI Polytechnic, Ben Guerir, Morocco

Abstract. Humanity needs to deliberate effectively *at scale* about highly complex and contentious problems. Current online deliberation tools - such as email, chatrooms, and forums - are however plagued by levels of discussion toxicity that deeply undermine their utility for this purpose. This paper describes how a structured deliberation process can substantially reduce discussion toxicity compared to current approaches.

Keywords: collective intelligence · crowd-scale deliberation · toxicity

1 Introduction

Deliberation processes have changed little in centuries, perhaps even millennia. Typically, small groups of powerful stakeholders and designated experts craft solutions behind closed doors. Most people affected by the decisions have limited input, so important ideas and perspectives do not get incorporated, and there is often substantial resistance to *implementing* the ideas from those who were frozen from the process.

Humanity now however needs to deliberate effectively about highly complex, contentious, and existentially important problems – such as climate change, security, and poverty – where a small-circle process is no longer adequate. We need to find a way to effectively integrate the expertise and preferences of tens, hundreds or even thousands of individuals in our most consequential deliberations.

This paper addresses one important barrier to creating this capability: toxicity[1] in online deliberations. Online technology seems to represent our best hope for scaling up deliberations, but it has been plagued by debilitating levels of toxic comments. How can we fix that? As part of that discussion, we will cover:

- Goal: defining deliberation, and why scale is so important
- Challenge: the toxicity trap of existing deliberation technologies

---

[1] We define toxicity as the presence of rude, disrespectful, or unreasonable comments that are likely to make people leave a discussion.

R. Chbeir et al. (Eds.): MEDES 2023, CCIS 2022, pp. 374–381, 2024.
https://doi.org/10.1007/978-3-031-51643-6_27

- Solution: an introduction to deliberation mapping, a solution to online toxicity:
- Assessment: an evaluation of how well deliberation mapping reduces toxicity
- Conclusions: lessons learned and next steps

2   The Goal: Effective Deliberation at Scale

Let us define deliberation as the activity where groups of people (1) *identify* possible solutions for a problem, (2) *evaluate* these alternatives, and (3) *select* the solution(s) that best meet their needs (4).

Research from the field of collective intelligence has shown that engaging crowds in the way has the potential to unleash such powerful benefits as:

- *many hands*: the advent of cheap digital communication and ubiquitous personal computing has revealed the existence of a massive cognitive surplus: very large numbers of people with deep and diverse skill sets are eager to participate in collective tasks, driven by such non-monetary incentives as contributing to problem or communities they care about. (20) (22) Wikipedia is an excellent example of this.
- *casting a wide net:* frequently, solutions for difficult problems can be found by consulting outside of the usual small circle of conventional experts in that field (7). Innocentive is one example of a company that has been very successful exploiting this phenomenon.
- *idea synergy:* out-of-the-box solutions can often be achieved by bringing together many individuals and engaging them in *combining* and *refining* each other's ideas. The Matlab Coding Coopetition is a spectacular example of the power of this effect (12)
- *wisdom of crowds:* large numbers of suitably diverse, motivated and independent raters have been shown to produce assessment accuracy - e.g. for prediction and estimation tasks - that exceeds that of experts (21). Prediction markets are a powerful example of the value of this phenomenon.
- *many eyes:* our ability to detect possible problems in solution ideas increases dramatically by simply engaging more people in the task. This has been one of the key reasons for the success of such volunteer-created open-source software tools as Linux (the dominant operating system for supercomputers), Apache (the most widely-used web server), MySQL (the most widely-used relational DB) and the web toolkits used by Chrome, Firefox (the most popular web browsers in the world). These open source tools have decisively out-competed software developed by massive software companies with thousands of highly-paid engineers (16).

Engaging the relevant stakeholders in making decisions also has the great advantage of reducing the resistance and confusion that can occur when trying to actually *implement* the solutions developed by the deliberation engagement.

3   The Challenge: Limitations of Existing Technologies

While existing collective intelligence tools (i.e. email, wikis, chatrooms, forums, blogs, micro-blogs, and so on) have become very successful in some domains, they almost invariably produce poor outcomes when applied to large-scale deliberations on com-plex and contentious topics. This problem is inherent to the approach they take. These tools move conversations into the digital world, but they incorporate no model of what *kind* of conversations will lead crowds to quickly and efficiently find good solutions for complex problems. This frequently results in haphazard and highly inefficient de-liberations that produce large disorganized "comment piles" made up of frequently low-value content (Klein & Convertino, 2014).

We will focus, in the paper, on one piece of this problem. Participants in conversation-centric tools frequently contribute toxic postings which enormously undercuts the willingness and ability of other participants to engage in thoughtful, meaningful, deliberations (2; 18) (23) (5) (11) (19) (17) (14) (6) (13) (1). All too often, such toxicity makes online discussions all but useless for deliberation, leading many organizations to either shut down their forums or invest in expensive and ethically fraught manual moderation of people's contributions to their forums. More recently, techniques for *automatically* detecting (and potentially filtering out) toxic posts have emerged. Perhaps the leading example of this is the Google Perspective API, which developed a set of toxicity-assessment rules by applying machine learning to a large corpus of manually-classified forum posts (8). While this approach represents a substantial advancement, it is far from perfect. The sarcastic phrase "I can see that you are a quote unquote *expert*" gets a very low toxicity score of 4/100, while a genuinely empathic comment like "Wow, it's terri-ble that someone called you a big fat jerk" gets a high toxicity score of 76/1000. It is also a *band-aid* solution, in the sense that it does nothing to address the underlying **cause** of the generation of toxic comments. Can we change the deliberation process in a way that prevents toxicity from happening in the first place?

4   A Solution to Toxicity: Deliberation Mapping

Deliberation mapping (Shum, Selvin, Sierhuis, Conklin, & Haley, 2006) is an alternative to unstructured online conversations that engages participants in co-creating logically-organized knowledge structures rather than conversation transcripts. As we will see below, the introduction of this structure fundamentally changes the participant incentives and results in a substantial reduction in toxicity.

The work reported in this paper uses a form of deliberation mapping called the "Deliberatorium" (9). It represents the simplest form of deliberation map that, in our experience, enables effective crowd-scale deliberation. Our map schema is built of "QuAACRs", i.e. *questions* to be answered, possible *answers* for these questions, *criteria* that describe the attributes of good answers, *arguments* that support or rebut an answer or argument, and *ratings* that capture the importance of questions and criteria, the value of answers, and the strength of arguments:

Deliberation maps have many important advantages over conversation-centric approaches. All the points appear in the part of the map they logically belong, e.g. all answers to a question are attached to that question in the map. It is therefore easy to find all the crowd's input on any given question, since it is collocated in the same branch. It's also easy to check if a point has already been contributed, and therefore to avoid *repeating* points, radically increasing the signal-to-noise ratio. Detecting and avoiding redundancy can in fact be mostly automated by the use of semantic similarity assessment

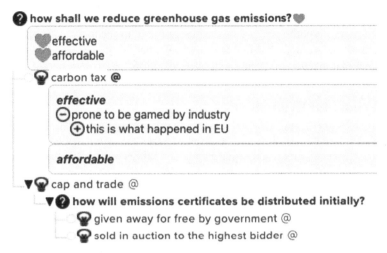

Fig. 1. An example of a deliberation map.

tools based on text embedding technology (15). *Gaps* in the deliberation - e.g. questions without any answers, or answers without any arguments - are easy to identify, so we can guide crowd members to fill in these gaps and foster more complete coverage. Making arguments into first-class map entities implicitly encourages participants to express the evidence and logic for or against competing answers (3), and means that arguments can be critiqued individually. Users, finally, can easily collaborate to refine proposed solutions. One user can, for example, propose an answer, a second raise a question about how that answer can achieve a given requirement, and a third propose possible answers for that sub-question (see Fig. 1).

Why should this approach reduce toxicity? As was pointed out by media theorist Marshall McLuhan in his 1964 book *Understanding Media* (10), the nature of the discussion medium we use can have a profound impact on *what* we communicate. In a sense, as he points out, the medium *is* the message. How, then, do online discussion media shape what we say? In such tools, one of the key questions for participants is: how do I win the **attention war** as new posts pile on? Our inputs can easily be overlooked unless we frame them in ways that are likely to gather more attention. One guaranteed way to do that is to be more *extreme/toxic* than the others in the discussion. But if most people follow this individually rational strategy, the result is an upward toxicity spiral as contributors become more extreme in order to compete with other people using the same strategy.

Deliberation maps have different rules that in turn change the incentive structures (and thus typical behaviors) for contributors. Participants no longer need to engage in extremization in order to make themselves visible. Everybody's points on a given topic are co-located, right next to each other, and every unique idea appears just once, regardless of when or how often they were contributed. Deliberation maps make it immediately visible whether an individuals' postings have underlying (PRO or CON) arguments from the original poster and other crowd members. The "game" therefore changes *from* simply trying to get attention in a massive growing comment pile *to* creating points that people find compelling. In this context, less extremized and more carefully-argued points, we hypothesize, are instead more likely to receive positive evaluations. Based on this, we hypothesized that toxicity in deliberation maps will be significantly less than that in conventional (conversation-centric) forums.

5 Experimental Evaluation

We assessed the toxicity of the posts contributed in a random controlled trial consisting of two demographically matched experimental conditions of over 400 participants each:

- *Forum*: Participants used a forum (AKA threaded discussion) to submit posts as well as reply to other posts The posts and subsequent multiple levels of replies were viewed as an indented outline. Since users can contribute any kind of posts at any time, we considered this the "unstructured" condition.
- *Deliberatorium:* Participants used the Deliberatorium system, described above, to post questions answers and arguments in response to the newspaper articles. Since users are asked to contribute posts in a specific format (i.e. as questions answers and arguments in a logically-organized "map"), we considered this the "structured" condition.

Participants in each condition were asked to discuss, using their assigned tools, the content of the following eight newspaper articles (used with permission from the New York Times):

- Finding Compassion for 'Vaccine-Hesitant' Parents By Wajahat Ali
- We've All Just Made Fools of Ourselves—Again By David Brooks
- Why Are Young People Pretending to Love Work? By Erin Griffith
- New Zealand Massacre Highlights Global Reach of White Extremism By Patrick Kingsley
- The India-Pakistan Conflict Was a Parade of Lies. By Farhad Manjoo
- The West Doesn't Want ISIS Members to Return. Why Should the Syrians Put Up With Them? By Abdalaziz Alhamza 3/14/2019 at 10:52:22 pm
- Britain Is Drowning Itself in Nostalgia By Sam Byers 3/24/2019 at 4:34:26 pm
- If Stalin Had a Smartphone. By David Brooks 3/13/2019 at 0:19:42 am

The group participants were recruited using ads on a range of social media platforms including Facebook and others, and almost exclusively were based in the UK.

Neither of these conditions were moderated: so participants were free to take any tone they chose in their postings.

We used the Google Perspective API (https://www.perspectiveapi.com/) to assess the toxicity of the posts from the two conditions on a scale from 0 (non-toxic) to 1 (highly toxic). While, as noted above, the Perspective API is imperfect, it is the acknowledged state-of-the-art tool for this purpose and is widely used.

The average toxicity for the posts generated in the two conditions was as follows:

Platform	# posts	Average Toxicity
forum	915	0.19
deliberatorium	812	0.14

While the overall toxicity levels were relatively low in our community, the average toxicity of the forum posts was 30% higher than the deliberation map posts: this difference was highly significant statistically ($p < 1.5 * 10^{-10}$). We also found that high toxicity posts (i.e. with toxicity scores above 0.3) were twice as common in the forums than in the deliberation maps (Fig. 2):

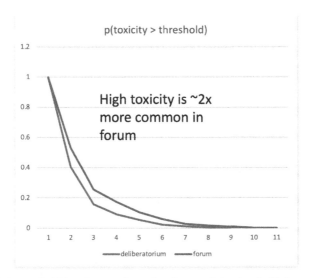

Fig. 2. Cumulative probability of posts above the given toxicity threshold, forum vs Deliberatorium.

6 Discussion

Toxicity has emerged as one of the major challenges for those who hope to enable useful crowd-scale online deliberations around complex and contentious topics. Our work has demonstrated that the level of toxicity in online discussions is deeply affected by the *way in which the discussions take place*. The structured nature of deliberation mapping, we believe, changes the rules of the game in a way that makes toxic comments no longer part of a winning strategy. Our data provides initial support for this hypothesis based on a carefully designed randomized control trial experiment involving a total of over 800 participants.

For future work, we would like to reproduce these experiments with communities and topics where the base toxicity level in the online forums is substantially higher, so we can assess the power of structuring conversations on reducing toxicity in more severely challenging contexts.

Acknowledgements. The author would like to acknowledge the contributions of Arnab Sircar and Paolo Spada to this work.

References

Almerekhi, H., Kwak, H., Jansen, B.J.: Investigating toxicity changes of cross-community redditors from 2 billion posts and comments. PeerJ Comput. Sci. **8**, e1059 (2022). https://peerj.com/articles/cs-1059/?via=indexdotco

Aroyo, L., Dixon, L., Thain, N., Redfield, O., Rosen, R.: Crowdsourcing subjective tasks: the case study of understanding toxicity in online discussions. In: Proceedings from World Wide Web Conference (2019)

Carr, C.S.: Using computer supported argument visualization to teach legal argumentation. In: Kirschner, P.A., Shum, S.J.B., Carr, C.S. (eds.) Visualizing argumentation: software tools for collaborative and educational sense-making, pp. 75–96. Springer-Verlag, Cham (2003). https://doi.org/10.1007/978-1-4471-0037-9_4

Eemeren, F.H.V., Grootendorst, R.: A Systematic Theory of Argumentation: The Pragma-dialectical Approach. Cambridge University Press, Cambridge (2003)

Hede, A., Agarwal, O., Lu, L., Mutz, D.C., Nenkova, A.: From toxicity in online comments to incivility in American news: proceed with caution. arXiv preprint: arXiv:2102.03671 (2021)

Jakob, J., Dobbrick, T., Freudenthaler, R., Haffner, P., Wessler, H.: Is constructive engagement online a lost cause? Toxic outrage in online user comments across democratic political systems and discussion arenas. Communication Research, 00936502211062773 (2022). https://doi.org/10.1177/00936502211062773

Jeppesen, L.B., Lakhani, K.R.: Marginality and problem-solving effectiveness in broadcast search. Organ. Sci. **21**(5), 1016–1033 (2010). http://dash.harvard.edu/bitstream/handle/1/3351241/Jeppesen_Marginality.pdf?sequence=2

Jigsaw: Reducing toxicity in large language models with perspective API (2023). https://medium.com/jigsaw/reducing-toxicity-in-large-language-models-with-perspective-api-c31c39b7a4d7

Klein, M.: How to harvest collective wisdom for complex problems: an introduction to the MIT Deliberatorium (2007). Retrieved

McLuhan, M.: Understanding Media: The Extensions of Man. Signet Books, New York (1964)

Mohan, S., Guha, A., Harris, M., Popowich, F., Schuster, A., Priebe, C.: The impact of toxic language on the health of Reddit communities (2017)

Gulley, N.: Patterns of innovation: a web-based MATLAB programming contest. In: CHI '01 Extended Abstracts on Human Factors in Computing Systems, pp. 337–338 (2001). https://doi.org/10.1145/634067.634266

Park, J.S., Seering, J., Bernstein, M.S.: Measuring the prevalence of anti-social behavior in online communities. Proc. ACM Hum.-Comput. Interact. **6**(CSCW2), 1–29 (2022).

Pelzer, B., Kaati, L., Cohen, K., Fernquist, J.: Toxic language in online incel communities. SN Soc. Sci. **1**, 1–22 (2021). https://doi.org/10.1007/s43545-021-00220-8

Ravichandiran, S.: Getting Started with Google BERT: Build and Train State-of-the-Art Natural Language Processing Models using BERT. Packt Publishing Ltd., Birmingham (2021). https://play.google.com/store/books/details?id=CvsWEAAAQBAJ&source=gbs_api

Raymond, E.: The cathedral and the bazaar. Knowl., Technol. Policy **12**(3), 23–49 (1999).

Rossini, P.: Toxic for whom? Examining the targets of uncivil and intolerant discourse in online political talk (2019)

Rossini, P.: Beyond toxicity in the online public sphere: understanding incivility in online political talk. Res. Agenda Digit. Polit., 160–170 (2020). https://www.elgaronline.com/display/edcoll/9781789903089/9781789903089.00026.xml

Salminen, J., Sengün, S., Corporan, J., Jung, S.-g., Jansen, B.J.: Topic-driven toxicity: exploring the relationship between online toxicity and news topics. PloS One **15**(2), e0228723 (2020). https://doi.org/10.1371/journal.pone.0228723

Shirky, C.: Here Comes Everybody: The Power of Organizing Without Organizations. Penguin, London (2009)

Surowiecki, J.: The Wisdom of Crowds. Anchor, New York (2005)

Tapscott, D., Williams, A.D.: Wikinomics: How Mass Collaboration Changes Everything. Portfolio Hardcover, Brentford (2006)

Xia, Y., Zhu, H., Lu, T., Zhang, P., Gu, N.: Exploring antecedents and consequences of toxicity in online discussions: a case study on Reddit. Proc. ACM Hum.-Comput. Interact. **4**(CSCW2), 1–23 (2020). https://doi.org/10.1145/3415179

XAI for Time-Series Classification Leveraging Image Highlight Methods

Georgios Makridis[1]([✉]) [iD], Georgios Fatouros[1,2] [iD], Vasileios Koukos[1],
Dimitrios Kotios[1], Dimosthenis Kyriazis[1] [iD], and John Soldatos[2,3] [iD]

[1] University of Piraeus, 185 34 Pireas, Greece
`gmakridis@unipi.gr`
[2] Innov-Acts Ltd, City Business Center Office SF09, 27 Michalakopoulou St. 1075,
Nicosia, Cyprus
`info@innov-acts.com`
[3] Netcompany-Intrasoft S.A, 2b, rue Nicolas Bové L-1253, Luxembourg City,
Luxembourg

Abstract. Although much work has been done on explainability in the computer vision and natural language processing (NLP) fields, there is still much work to be done to explain methods applied to time series as time series by nature can not be understood at first sight. In this paper, we present a Deep Neural Network (DNN) in a teacher-student architecture (distillation model) that offers interpretability in time-series classification tasks. The explainability of our approach is based on transforming the time series to 2D plots and applying image highlight methods (such as LIME and Grad-Cam), making the predictions interpretable. At the same time, the proposed approach offers increased accuracy competing with the baseline model with the trade-off of increasing the training time.

Keywords: XAI · Time-series · LIME · Grad-Cam · Deep Learning

1 Introduction

The current day and age, also known as the Digital or Information Age, is characterized by complex computing systems which generate enormous amounts of data daily. The digital transformation of industrial environments leads to the fourth industrial revolution -Industry4.0 [15], with Artificial Intelligence (AI) being the key facilitator of the Industry4.0 era by enabling innovative tools and processes [27]. At the same time, there has been a growing interest in eXplainable Artificial Intelligence (XAI) towards human-understandable explanations for the predictions and decisions made by machine learning models.

The notion of explaining and expressing a Machine Learning (ML) model is called interpretability or explainability [5]. This need for interpretability mainly exists in Deep Neural Networks (DNN), which are defined by large levels of complexity, thus appearing to be "black boxes" [30]. To address this issue, researchers

---

Supported by University of Piraeus Research Center.

R. Chbeir et al. (Eds.): MEDES 2023, CCIS 2022, pp. 382–396, 2024.
https://doi.org/10.1007/978-3-031-51643-6_28

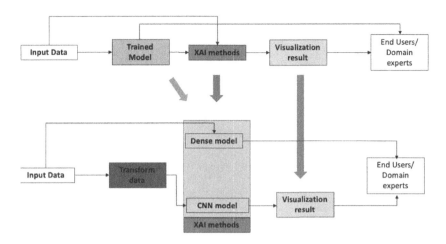

Fig. 1. The proposed high-level architecture. The above pipeline represents the "traditional" way of applying XAI methods, while the lower one depicts the proposed model.

have proposed various methods for explaining the predictions made by deep learning models for image classification tasks, known as XAI for images [31]. These methods include visualizing the features learned by the model, feature attribution techniques, and model distillation [25]. For example, visualizing the features learned by the model can provide insights into which parts of the input image the model uses to make its prediction, while feature attribution techniques can highlight the regions of the input image that are most important for making a prediction. Model distillation, on the other hand, attempts to convert a complex model into a simpler, more interpretable one that still preserves the accuracy of the original model. A knowledge distillation system consists of three principal components: the knowledge, the distillation algorithm, and the teacher-student architecture [9]. Model distillation is a technique where a smaller, simpler model is trained to mimic the predictions of a larger, more complex model. This allows for the smaller model to be more easily interpretable and can help to provide insight into the workings of the larger model. For example, in [3] authors proposed a method called "DeepTaylor" that uses a Taylor series approximation to distill a deep neural network into a linear model that is more interpretable.

Although much work has been done on explainability in the computer vision and Natural Language Processing (NLP) fields, there is still much work to be done to explain methods applied to time series. This might be caused by the nature of time series, which we can not understand at first sight. Indeed, when a human looks at a photo or reads a text, they intuitively and instinctively understand the underlying information in the data [22]. Although temporal data is ubiquitous in nature, through all forms of sound, humans are not used to representing this temporal data in the form of a signal that varies as a function of time. We need expert knowledge or additional methods to leverage the under-

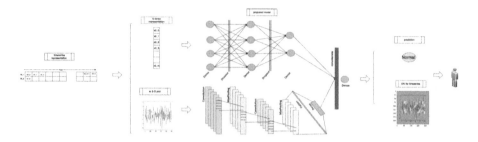

Fig. 2. Schematic explanation of the data aspect to the end-to-end approach including the main steps to the process, from raw data to the user.

lying information present in the data [13]. Despite this drawback, timeseries approach play a key role in industry 4.0 so does XAI for these cases (e.g., XAI for timeseries can enhance transparency in Industry 4.0 by providing clear and interpretable explanations for how the predictive maintenance tool works, or for identifying patterns and anomalies in time series data, providing early detection of potential issues, and insights into how to mitigate risks).

This paper addresses the emerging challenge of explainability of the "black-box" DNN models concerning time series as input data by introducing a teacher-student (distillation model) approach to facilitate user explainability and reasoning. In this context, the operational objective is twofold:

(i) Time series categorization, providing a sound approach leveraging unstructured image data (i.e., 2D plot), facilitating the exploitation of the image XAI methods.

(ii) Systematically providing visualization of XAI by applying various XAI methods on the CNN part of the proposed model.

In terms of added value, the scientific contributions can be briefly summarized as:

(i) Combination of the strengths of both networks to achieve better performance.

(ii) Handling of both time series as arrays and as images, which provides more flexibility for data inputs and potentially enhances the interpretability of the model.

(iii) Explainability by visualizing the important parts of the plot for time series, which is an open research field with limited state-of-the-art solutions.

In this context, the proposed approach presents a novel approach to XAI for time series data, in which image highlight techniques are used to visualize and interpret the predictions of a time series model as depicted in Fig. 1. While a more detailed view of the proposed approach is provided in Fig. 2, which depicts the data handling pipeline, in an approach, to apply both the time series classification and XAI methods. In the first step, the raw data are pre-processed and fed into the distillation model. Then the model is trained and finally, the output comprises the predicted "class" and the heatmap of the time-series representation to be utilized for explainability purposes. Our approach aligns with the local post-hoc interpretability section of the XAI taxonomy, focusing on providing instance-level explanations of model decisions. This places our work within a specific niche of interpretability techniques, targeting the temporal aspects of model understanding [28].

The remainder of the paper is organized as follows: Sect. 2 presents related work done in the areas of study of this paper, while Sect. 3 delivers an overview of the proposed methodological approach, introduces the overall architecture, and offers details regarding the datasets used and how these are utilized within the models. Section 4 dives deeper into the results of the conducted research and the implemented algorithms, with the performance of the proposed mechanisms being depicted in the results and evaluation section. Section 5 concludes with recommendations for future research and the potential of the current study.

2   Related Work

Time series classification is a challenging task, where DNNs have been shown to achieve state-of-the-art results in various fields such as finance [8], and industry [16]. However, the internal workings of these models are often difficult to interpret. To address this issue, researchers have proposed various methods for explaining the predictions made by deep learning models for time series classification, known as XAI for time series. These methods include attention mechanisms [18] and visualization techniques [6]. For example, attention mechanisms allow the model to focus on specific parts of the input time series that are important for making a prediction, while visualization techniques can provide a graphical representation of the input time series and the model's decision-making process.

Attention mechanisms allow the model to focus on specific parts of the input time series, providing insight into which regions of the input are most important for making a prediction. For example, in [1] authors proposed an attention-based LSTM model that learns to weigh different parts of the input time series when making a prediction.

Furthermore there are post-hoc methods that approach the behavior of a model by exporting relationships between feature values and predictions, in this case, feature lags of time series also play a role. While the ante-hoc methods incorporate the explanation in the structure of the model, which is therefore already explainable at the end of the training phase. The first category includes variants of the widely used LIME, k-LIME [11], DLIME [29], LIMEtree [26], and SHAP (e.g., TimeSHAP [2]), as well as Anchors [21], or LoRE [10]. Surrogate models are built for each prediction sample in most of these techniques, learning the behavior of the reference model in the particular instance of interest by adding perturbations (or masking) to the feature vector variables. The numerous feature disturbance techniques for assessing the contribution of features to the projected value when they are deleted or covered are nearly a distinct research topic in this context. These XAI models may be used for DNN since they are unaffected by the underlying machine-learning model. The CAM, ConvTimeNet [12], which belongs to this group but intervenes in the model structure, is particularly interesting. Apart from these, it is worth mentioning approaches such as RETAIN [4] (Reverse Time Attention) with application to Electronic Health Records (EHR) data. RETAIN achieves high accuracy while remaining clinically interpretable and is based on a two-level neural attention model that detects previous visits. Finally, NBEATS [19] focuses on an architecture based on residual back-and-forth connections and a very deep stack of fully connected layers. The architecture has a number of desirable properties, as it is interpretable and applicable without modification to a wide range of target areas. In line with the comprehensive review [28], our method contributes to the emerging body of time-series XAI research, particularly targeting interpretability in IoT applications.

One limitation of XAI models for time series data is that the outputs and explanations they provide may be difficult for end users to understand. The models' complexity and the explanations' technical nature may make it challenging for non-experts to interpret the results and take appropriate actions. Additionally, the effectiveness of XAI models can depend on the end user's level of domain knowledge and familiarity with the data. To address these limitations, it is important to design XAI models with the end user in mind and provide explanations that are tailored to their needs and level of expertise. This involve proper visualizations to help users explore and understand the model's predictions, as well as providing contextual information about them following the "human-centricity" perspective that is the core value behind the evolution of manufacturing towards Industry 5.0 [23].

3   Method

3.1   Proposed Model Architecture

The main research challenges addressed in this paper enable the accurate classification of time series and the generation of interpretable XAI visualizations. These two topics are interconnected as the XAI model is based on the classification results. To facilitate the usage of a DNN model by making it explainable, we introduce a form of distillation model (i.e., teacher-student architecture) where the teacher is the complex DNN model that yields state-of-the-art performance while the student model is a CNN model that can be interpretable by human end users when LIME and Grad-Cam methods are applied to it. Figure 3 depicts the architecture of the proposed model, where the Dense model represents the "teacher" while the CNN represents the "explainable"-"student". In the rapidly evolving landscape of IoT, the proposed method offers a tangible pathway to enhance transparency and trust in autonomous decision-making systems. By providing graphical interpretations of time-series data, users across various domains of IoT can gain clearer insights into model behavior. The adoption of the distillation model in our approach is motivated by its capability to synthesize complex models into more interpretable forms, without a significant loss of predictive accuracy. Furthermore, we employed LIME for its model-agnostic interpretability, paired with Grad-Cam for its detailed visual explanations. This combination ensures a versatile and comprehensive explanation model, adapting to the varying needs of different stakeholders.

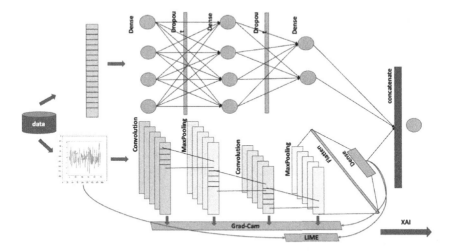

Fig. 3. The architecture of the proposed model, where the Dense model represents the "teacher" while the CNN represents the "explainable"-"student". The data are fed as an array to the Dense network while the CNN as 2D plots.

Regarding the DNN model, its layers can be summarized as follows:

- Input layer: This layer will take an image as input.
- Rescaling layer.
- Convolutional layers: to extract features from the input image. In our experiments, we used 32 filters of size 3×3, and a stride of 1.
- Pooling layers: to reduce the spatial dimensions of the feature maps and reduce the computational requirements of the network. A common choice is to use max pooling with a pool size of 2×2 and a stride of 2.
- Flattening layer: to convert the high-dimensional feature maps into a 1D vector that can be input into a fully connected layer.
- Dense layer: One or multiple dense (fully connected) layers can be added to make predictions based on the extracted features.
- Output layer: this can be a dense layer with a single node and a sigmoid activation function for binary classification or with as many nodes as the number of classes in your data for multi-class classification.

3.2 Datasets

In the frame of our research, the utilized datasets have been retrieved by [7] composed of labeled time series. Specifically, we used 2 of the available datasets with more than 1000 training and test samples:

– Wafer: This dataset was formatted by R. Olszewski at Carnegie Mellon University, 2001. Wafer data relates to semiconductor microelectronics fabrication. A collection of inline process control measurements recorded from various sensors during the processing of silicon wafers for semiconductor fabrication constitute the wafer database; each data set in the wafer database contains the measurements recorded by one sensor during the processing of one wafer by one tool. The two classes are normal and abnormal. There is a large class imbalance between normal and abnormal (10.7% of the train are abnormal, 12.1% of the test). The best performance in terms of Accuracy till now is 99,8% by using the ST algorithm [14].
– FordA: This data was originally used in a competition at the IEEE World Congress on Computational Intelligence, 2008. The classification problem is to diagnose whether a certain symptom exists or does not exist in an automotive subsystem. Each case consists of 500 measurements of engine noise and a classification. For FordA the train and test data set were collected in typical operating conditions, with minimal noise contamination. The best performance in terms of Accuracy till now is 96,54% by using the ST algorithm.

3.3   Time-Series to Image Explainability

In order to make the time series interpretable we chose the most comprehensive representation of a time series (i.e., a 2D plot with the time axis on the x-axis and the value of the time series on the y-axis.) We first plot the time series as an image and then input the image into the CNN for classification. In all of our experiments, we plotted the time series as line-plot figures with (224,244,1) dimensions.

Once we have plotted the time series as an image, we use them as inputs into a CNN for classification. The CNN will process the image and use its learned features to make a prediction about the time series.

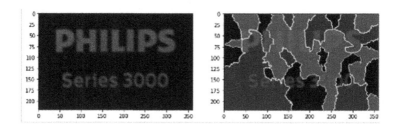

Fig. 4. Example of LIME important super-pixels

When dealing with image data, feature importance can be translated into the importance of each pixel to the output forecast. The latter can also be visualized into a heatmap where the importance of each feature (pixel) can be displayed with different colors and can work as an excellent explanation for the human operator. In our approach, we have chosen 2 notable methods of XAI on image data as the more appropriate for time series plots. The LIME model is a model-agnostic method based on the work of [20]. While, the Gradient-weighted Class Activation Mapping (Grad-Cam) model [24] was used as one of the SotA methods for interpreting the top features (parts of the image) concerning the "Label" when the underlying model is a CNN.

In Fig. 4, we see the output of an XAI model that has been applied based on the LIME method in the study [17], where we can see the green and red areas of the image. This means that the ML/DL model classifies the underlying image to a specific category because of these parts of super-pixels; the size of super-pixels colored in green are the ones that increase the probability of our image belonging to the predicted class, while the super-pixels colored in red are the ones that decrease the likelihood. LIME is a technique for explaining the predictions of any machine learning model by approximating it locally with an interpretable model. It does this by perturbing the input data and creating a new, simpler model that is fit only to the perturbed data. This process is repeated many times, each time with a different set of perturbations, and the results are aggregated to create a global explanation of the model's prediction. In the case of image data, LIME can be used to explain the prediction of a CNN or other image classification model by creating a heatmap that shows which parts of the image are most important for the model's prediction. The heatmap is created by perturbing the pixels of the image and creating a new, simpler model that is fit only to the perturbed data. This process is repeated for different parts of the image, and the results are aggregated to create the final heatmap.

Fig. 5. Grad-Cam heatmap examples in the last layer of the CNN model

An example of applying the Grad-Cam method is depicted in Fig. 5. We can see the original image and the explanation of Grad-Cam methods where there are highlighted parts of the image that the CNN model is focusing on in each layer. This is a technique for visualizing the regions in an image that are most important for a convolutional neural network (CNN) to classify an image correctly. It does this by overlaying a heatmap on top of the original image, where the intensity of the color in the heatmap indicates how important that region is for the classification. To create the heatmap, Grad-Cam first computes the gradient of the output of the CNN with respect to the feature maps of a convolutional layer. It then weighs these gradients by the importance of the feature maps to the class prediction and produces a weighted combination of the feature maps. Finally, it resizes the resulting map to the size of the input image and overlays it on top of the original image to produce the heatmap. Overall, the heatmap produced by Grad-Cam can be used to understand which regions of an image are most important for a CNN's prediction and to identify potential areas of the image that may be causing the CNN to make incorrect predictions.

The mapping of LIME's super-pixels and Grad-Cam's heatmaps to relevant time segments in univariate time-series provides an interpretable link between the visual explanations and underlying temporal patterns. This allows us to identify specific intervals of time that significantly influence the predicted class, although there are challenges, such as interpretations involving axes and numbers on the axes. A comparative evaluation with other time-series explanation methods is also presented to provide a comprehensive perspective on the strengths and weaknesses of the generated explanations.

4 Evaluation

4.1 Experimental Setup

We evaluate the performance of our model on a classification task, using a train, validation, and test dataset split. The task involves classifying a set of time series into one of two classes. Our distillation model consists of a teacher network, which is a Dense network, and a student network, which is a CNN. The goal of the distillation is to transfer the knowledge from the teacher network to the student network, resulting in an explainable and more efficient model with similar or better performance. One limitation of model distillation is that it may not always be feasible to distill a complex model into a simpler, more interpretable one. To this end, we provide the results of the teacher-student network, the teacher-only and the student-only results.

We use the training dataset to train the models, and a validation dataset to tune the hyperparameters of the network, such as the learning rate and the number of layers. We perform early stopping if the validation accuracy does not improve for a certain number of epochs. Finally, we evaluate the performance of the teacher and student networks on the test dataset.

We compare the performance of the teacher network, the student network, and our distillation model. We report the accuracy, precision, recall, F1-score for each model. Additionally, we showcase the interpretability of the student network using LIME and Grad-Cam, which highlight the important parts of the input images that contribute to the classification decision.

We use the TensorFlow deep learning framework to implement the models and train them in an environment with 20 CPU cores of 2.3GHz, and 64GB of RAM. The hyperparameters are chosen based on a grid search over a range of values, and the best set of hyperparameters are chosen based on the validation accuracy. The models are trained for a maximum of 300 epochs, with early stopping if the validation accuracy does not improve for 20 epochs. The code and the trained models are publicly available for reproducibility. Moreover, we make a qualitative evaluation regarding the interpretability of the XAI result of our approach. Finally, we present a more fine-grained view of the performance of the examined method in terms of time. The results are the average outcomes of ten independently seeded runs for each measurement.

4.2   Experimental Results

The Dense model achieved a precision of 0.86 for class 0 in the FordA dataset, indicating that it correctly identified 86% of instances belonging to class 0. However, its precision for class 1 (0.82) suggests that it had a slightly lower accuracy in identifying instances of class 1. The CNN model achieved a precision of 0.70 for class 0 in the FordA dataset, which is lower than the Dense model's precision for the same class. This suggests that the CNN model may have faced challenges in correctly identifying instances of class 0. The Proposed model achieved the same precision (0.86) as the Dense model for class 0 in the FordA dataset, indicating its effectiveness in correctly classifying instances of class 0. Additionally, it achieved a precision of 0.75 for class 1, suggesting a reasonably accurate classification for this minority class. The F1-scores for class 0 are high across all models and datasets, indicating a good balance between precision and recall for the majority class. Both the Dense and Proposed models achieved perfect precision (1.0) for class 0 in the Wafer dataset, demonstrating their ability to accurately classify instances of the majority class. The CNN and Proposed models achieved perfect precision (1.0) for class 1 in the Wafer dataset, indicating their strong performance in correctly identifying instances of the minority class. The accuracy values across all models and datasets are consistently high, with all models achieving perfect accuracy (1.0) on the Wafer dataset. However, the accuracy of the CNN model (0.73) on the FordA dataset is slightly lower than the other models. Based on these observations, it appears that the Proposed model performs well across both datasets, achieving high precision and accuracy for both majority and minority classes. The Dense model also shows good performance, particularly in correctly classifying instances of the majority class. However, the CNN model seems to struggle in accurately identifying instances of both classes in the FordA dataset (Table 1).

Given that, time performance can impact the scalability and cost-effectiveness of AI systems, as slower models may require more computational resources or increased processing time, leading to increased costs. Thus, optimizing the performance of AI models in terms of time is a crucial aspect of AI development and deployment. To this end, in Table 2 we present the execution time of each model for the training task as well as how many epochs took each model to converge. We should highlight that the configurations of the models were identified as mentioned in the previous subsection. It should also be mentioned that concerning the inference time (i.e., the time taken by the model to produce a prediction for a single input) there is no significant discrepancy.

Table 1. Results of the classification tasks with different models

Model	(FordA) Dense	(FordA) CNN	(FordA) Proposed
Precision (Class 0)	0.86	0.70	0.86
Precision (Class 1)	0.82	0.75	0.84
F1-Score	0.84	0.73	0.86
Accuracy	0.84	0.73	0.85
Model	(Wafer) Dense	(Wafer) CNN	(Wafer) Proposed
Precision (Class 0)	1.0	1.0	1.0
Precision (Class 1)	0.98	1.0	0.99
F1-Score	1.0	1.0	1.0
Accuracy	1.0	1.0	1.0

Table 2. Execution time of each model for the training task as well as how many epochs took each model to converge. The RAM column refers to the MB needed for loading the training datasets to the RAM

	training time (sec)	early stopping (epochs)	train-set RAM (MB)
Dense (FordA)	31	67	1.16
CNN (FordA)	643	76	1148.44
Dense + CNN (FordA)	5106	102	1149.6
Dense (Wafer)	186	300	13.74
CNN (Wafer)	3539	300	4135.52
Dense + CNN (Wafer)	3048	257	4149.26

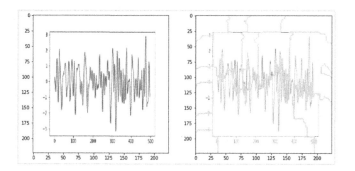

Fig. 6. Example of LIME important superpixels where we can notice the red areas that seem not relevant to the predicted class (Color figure online)

Moving to the "explainability" part of the model, the model has integrated the process to provide LIME and Grad-Cam heatmaps helping the interpretation for a non-data scientist user. LIME helps to understand why a machine learning model made a certain prediction by looking at the most important parts of the input data that the model considered when making the prediction. While

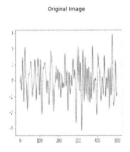
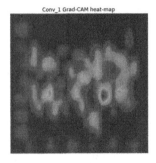

(a) Example of Grad-Cam heatmap and the original image where we can notice the areas of the image that the model focused

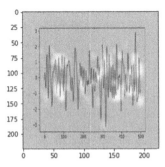

(b) Example of Grad-Cam heatmap and the overlap of heatmap to the original image where we can notice the areas of the image that the model focused

Fig. 7. Grad-Cam example in the last convolution layer of the CNN

Grad-Cam generates a heatmap that shows which areas of an image were most important for a machine learning model to make a prediction. This helps us to see which parts of the image the model focused on to make its prediction. In Fig. 6 and Fig. 7 we can see some indicative examples of the respective XAI visualizations.

5   Conclusion

In conclusion, this paper examines an XAI-enhanced DNN for addressing the problem of interpretability of DNN models when it comes to time series classification tasks. Specifically, this paper presents a novel distillation model for time-series classification that leverages image highlight methods for XAI. The model takes in both the time series data as an array and a 2D plot, providing a unique approach to time-series classification. The student model is specifically designed for XAI images, demonstrating the potential of this method for improving interpretability in time-series classification tasks. The results of the experiments conducted show that the proposed model outperforms existing methods and has the potential to be applied to a wide range of time-series classification problems. A teacher-student architecture was developed where the student part has as inputs the 2D plot of the time series where LIME and Grad-Cam model is applied offering XAI capabilities. Regarding the future steps, we have 2 main objectives to make the model more human-centered by applying a model to translate the XAI visualizations to text, of course, we plan to apply the model to time series forecasting tasks while at the same time examining visual analytics approach, where the human would inspect the figures and provide some kind of feedback.

Acknowledgements. The research leading to the results presented in this paper has received funding from the Europeans Union's funded Projects MobiSpaces under grant agreement no 101070279 and STAR under grant agreement no 956573.

References

1. Bach, S., Binder, A., Montavon, G., Klauschen, F., Müller, K.R., Samek, W.: On pixel-wise explanations for non-linear classifier decisions by layer-wise relevance propagation. PLoS ONE **10**(7), e0130140 (2015)
2. Bento, J., Saleiro, P., Cruz, A.F., Figueiredo, M.A., Bizarro, P.: TimeSHAP: explaining recurrent models through sequence perturbations. In: Proceedings of the 27th ACM SIGKDD Conference on Knowledge Discovery & Data Mining, pp. 2565–2573 (2021)
3. Chiu, M.T., et al.: The 1st agriculture-vision challenge: methods and results. In: Proceedings of the IEEE/CVF Conference on Computer Vision and Pattern Recognition Workshops, pp. 48–49 (2020)
4. Choi, E., Bahadori, M.T., Sun, J., Kulas, J., Schuetz, A., Stewart, W.: RETAIN: an interpretable predictive model for healthcare using reverse time attention mechanism. In: Advances in Neural Information Processing Systems, vol. 29 (2016)
5. Choo, J., Liu, S.: Visual analytics for explainable deep learning. IEEE Comput. Graphics Appl. **38**(4), 84–92 (2018)
6. Dahl, M., et al.: Private machine learning in TensorFlow using secure computation. arXiv preprint: arXiv:1810.08130 (2018)
7. Dau, H.A., et al.: The UCR time series archive. IEEE/CAA J. Automatica Sinica **6**(6), 1293–1305 (2019)
8. Fatouros, G., Makridis, G., Kotios, D., Soldatos, J., Filippakis, M., Kyriazis, D.: DeepVaR: a framework for portfolio risk assessment leveraging probabilistic deep neural networks. Digit. Finan., 1–28 (2022)
9. Gou, J., Yu, B., Maybank, S.J., Tao, D.: Knowledge distillation: a survey. Int. J. Comput. Vision **129**, 1789–1819 (2021)
10. Guidotti, R., Monreale, A., Ruggieri, S., Pedreschi, D., Turini, F., Giannotti, F.: Local rule-based explanations of black box decision systems. arXiv preprint: arXiv:1805.10820 (2018)
11. Hall, P., Gill, N., Kurka, M., Phan, W.: Machine learning interpretability with H2O driverless AI. H2O. AI (2017)

12. Kashiparekh, K., Narwariya, J., Malhotra, P., Vig, L., Shroff, G.: ConvTimeNet: a pre-trained deep convolutional neural network for time series classification. In: 2019 International Joint Conference on Neural Networks (IJCNN), pp. 1–8. IEEE (2019)
13. Lim, B., Zohren, S.: Time-series forecasting with deep learning: a survey. Phil. Trans. R. Soc. A **379**(2194), 20200209 (2021)
14. Lines, J., Davis, L.M., Hills, J., Bagnall, A.: A shapelet transform for time series classification. In: Proceedings of the 18th ACM SIGKDD International Conference on Knowledge Discovery and Data Mining, pp. 289–297 (2012)
15. Makridis, G., Kyriazis, D., Plitsos, S.: Predictive maintenance leveraging machine learning for time-series forecasting in the maritime industry. In: 2020 IEEE 23rd International Conference on Intelligent Transportation Systems (ITSC), pp. 1–8. IEEE (2020)
16. Makridis, G., Mavrepis, P., Kyriazis, D., Polychronou, I., Kaloudis, S.: Enhanced food safety through deep learning for food recalls prediction. In: Appice, A., Tsoumakas, G., Manolopoulos, Y., Matwin, S. (eds.) DS 2020. LNCS (LNAI), vol. 12323, pp. 566–580. Springer, Cham (2020). https://doi.org/10.1007/978-3-030-61527-7_37
17. Makridis, G., et al.: XAI enhancing cyber defence against adversarial attacks in industrial applications. In: 2022 IEEE 5th International Conference on Image Processing Applications and Systems (IPAS), pp. 1–8. IEEE (2022)
18. Mitchell, M., et al.: Model cards for model reporting. In: Proceedings of the Conference on Fairness, Accountability, and Transparency, pp. 220–229 (2019)
19. Oreshkin, B.N., Carpov, D., Chapados, N., Bengio, Y.: N-BEATS: neural basis expansion analysis for interpretable time series forecasting. arXiv preprint: arXiv:1905.10437 (2019)
20. Ribeiro, M.T., Singh, S., Guestrin, C.: why should i trust you? Explaining the predictions of any classifier. In: Proceedings of the 22nd ACM SIGKDD International Conference on Knowledge Discovery and Data Mining, pp. 1135–1144 (2016)
21. Ribeiro, M.T., Singh, S., Guestrin, C.: Anchors: high-precision model-agnostic explanations. In: Proceedings of the AAAI Conference on Artificial Intelligence, vol. 32 (2018)
22. Rojat, T., Puget, R., Filliat, D., Del Ser, J., Gelin, R., Díaz-Rodríguez, N.: Explainable artificial intelligence (XAI) on timeseries data: a survey. arXiv preprint: arXiv:2104.00950 (2021)
23. Rožanec, J.M., et al.: Human-centric artificial intelligence architecture for industry 5.0 applications. Int. J. Prod. Res., 1–26 (2022)
24. Selvaraju, R.R., Cogswell, M., Das, A., Vedantam, R., Parikh, D., Batra, D.: Grad-CAM: visual explanations from deep networks via gradient-based localization. In: Proceedings of the IEEE International Conference on Computer Vision, pp. 618–626 (2017)
25. Shrikumar, A., Greenside, P., Kundaje, A.: Learning important features through propagating activation differences. In: International Conference on Machine Learning, pp. 3145–3153. PMLR (2017)
26. Sokol, K., Flach, P.: LIMEtree: interactively customisable explanations based on local surrogate multi-output regression trees. arXiv preprint: arXiv:2005.01427 (2020)
27. Soldatos, J., Kyriazis, D.: Trusted Artificial Intelligence in Manufacturing: A Review of the Emerging Wave of Ethical and Human Centric AI Technologies for Smart Production. Now Publishers, Hanover (2021)

28. Theissler, A., Spinnato, F., Schlegel, U., Guidotti, R.: Explainable AI for time series classification: a review, taxonomy and research directions. IEEE Access (2022)
29. Zafar, M.R., Khan, N.M.: DLIME: a deterministic local interpretable model-agnostic explanations approach for computer-aided diagnosis systems. arXiv preprint: arXiv:1906.10263 (2019)
30. Zahavy, T., Ben-Zrihem, N., Mannor, S.: Graying the black box: understanding DQNs. In: International Conference on Machine Learning, pp. 1899–1908. PMLR (2016)
31. Zeiler, M.D., Fergus, R.: Visualizing and understanding convolutional networks. In: Fleet, D., Pajdla, T., Schiele, B., Tuytelaars, T. (eds.) ECCV 2014. LNCS, vol. 8689, pp. 818–833. Springer, Cham (2014). https://doi.org/10.1007/978-3-319-10590-1_53

Invited Paper

Parallel and Distributed Data Series Processing on Modern and Emerging Hardware

Panagiota Fatourou[1,2]($\boxtimes$) (iD)

[1] Foundation for Research and Technology, Institute of Computer Science, Heraklion, Greece

[2] Department of Computer Science, University of Crete, Crete, Greece
faturu@csd.uoc.gr
http://www.ics.forth.gr/~faturu

Abstract. This paper summarizes state-of-the-art results on data series processing with the emphasis on parallel and distributed data series indexes that exploit the computational power of modern computing platforms. The paper comprises a summary of the tutorial the author delivered at the 15th International Conference on Management of Digital EcoSystems (MEDES'23).

Keywords: Data series · Time series · Indexing · Similarity search · Query answering · Multi-core architectures · Parallelization · GPU processing · Disk-based index · In-memory index · Distributed processing

1 Introduction

Ordered sequences of data points, known as *data series*, are one of the most common types of data. They are heavily produced by several applications in many different domains, including finance, astrophysics, telecommunications, environmental sciences, engineering, multimedia, neuroscience, and many others [24,36]). Similarity search is a fundamental building block in data series processing, as many types of complex analytics, such as, clustering, classification, motif and outlier detection, etc., are heavily dependent on it. A similarity search query is also useful in itself. It searches for the data seires in the collection that has the smallest distance to the query series, given some distance metric (which can be e.g., Euclidean distance [2] or Dynamic-Time Warping [32]).

As data series collections grow larger, sequential data series indexing technologies turn out to be inadequate. For example, the state-of-the-art such index, ADS+ [35], requires more than 4min to answer a single query on a moderately

Supported by the Hellenic Foundation for Research and Innovation (HFRI) under the "Second Call for HFRI Research Projects to support Faculty Members and Researchers" (project number: 3684).

sized 250 GB sequence collection. Thus, ADS is inefficient in processing the enormous sequence collections that are produced in many domains.

We briefly present a sequence of state-of-the-art indexes that take advantage of multiple nodes and modern hardware parallelization in each node, in order to accelerate processing times and achieve scalability.

We focus on a specific family of indexes, namely the *iSAX indexes* [27–31, 35]. An iSAX index first computes the *iSAX summary* [33] of each data series in the collection (*summarization phase*). Then, it builds a tree storing all summaries (*tree construction phase*), and uses it to answer similarity search queries. Given a query q, the similarity search algorithm first traverses a path of the tree to find a first approximate answer to q. This approximate answer is called *Best-So-Far (BSF)*. Then, it traverses the collection of data series to prune those whose summaries have higher distance to q's summary than the value stored in BSF. The distance between the summaries of two data series is called *lower bound distance*. It has been proved that if the lower bound distance of a series DS from q is higher than BSF, the real distance of DS from q is also higher than BSF. Then, DS can be pruned. Finally, the actual (real) distances between each data series that cannot be pruned and q is calculated. Whenever a real distance computation results in a lower value than that of BSF, then BSF is updated. Eventually, the answer to q is the value stored in BSF. If the pruning degree is high, a vast amount of expensive real distance computations are avoided. This results in good performance.

We first discuss ParIS+ [29, 31], a *disk-based* concurrent index, capable to manipulate big data series collections stored in secondary storage. We then continue to present MESSI [26, 27], the state-of-the-art *in-memory* concurrent index. Next, we discuss the challenges originating from the utilization of Graphics Processing Units (GPUs) [28] for further improving performance during query answering. We also discuss SING [28], an index that utilizes GPUs for query answering to perform better than MESSI. These indexes improve performance drastically in comparison to ADS+, the state-of-the-art sequential index [35]: to answer a similarity search query on a 100 GB (in memory) data series collection, SING requires 35 msec whereas ADS+ requires several tens of seconds.

Finally, we discuss Odyssey [7], a *distributed* data-series (DS) indexing and processing framework, that efficiently addresses the challenges for efficient and highly-scalable *multi-node* data series processing.

All the indexes that we discuss in the next sections, exploit the Single Instruction Multiple Data (SIMD) capabilities of modern CPUs to further parallelize the execution of individual instructions inside each core.

2   ParIS+

ParIS+ [29, 31] is a disk-based index that takes advantage of the computational power of multi-core architectures in order to execute in parallel the computations needed for both index creation and query answering. ParIS+ makes careful design choices in the coordination of the computational and I/O tasks, thus managing to completely hide the CPU cost during index creation under I/O.

ParIS+ is 2.6x faster than ADS+ [35] in index creation, and up to 1 order of magnitude faster in query answering. This makes ParIS+ a very efficient solution for disk-resident data. However, its answering time to a search query on a 100 GB dataset is 15 s. This performance not only does not support interactive analysis (i.e., 100msec) [19], but also it is above the limit for keeping the user's attention.

To move data from disk to main memory, ParIS+ uses a double buffering scheme. While a coordinator thread moves data to one part of the buffer, a number of worker threads compute the iSAX summaries for the data series stored into the other part, and store them in a set of *iSAX buffers*. The use of the double buffering scheme enables ParIS+ to hide CPU computation under I/O.

The worker threads traverse the iSAX buffers storing pairs of iSAX summaries and the pointers to the corresponding data series, into the leaves of the index tree. The iSAX buffers are needed to ensure some form of data locality. All data series found in an iSAX buffer are stored in the same subtree of the index tree. ParIS+ uses a dedicated thread to build each subtree. This eliminates the need for costly synchronization and communication between the threads.

During query answering, ParIS+ first calculates BSF using the index tree (and never uses the tree again). Then, a number of threads concurrently traverse different parts of an array, called SAX, which contains the iSAX summaries of all data series of the collection, in order to create a list (*candidate list*) of those series that are good candidates to be the query's answer (i.e., those whose lower bound distance is smaller than BSF and cannot be pruned). Finally, a number of threads perform in parallel, using SIMD, the real-distance computations needed to find the closest data series to the query, among the candidate series.

3   MESSI

The second index, called MESSI [26, 27], provides an efficient indexing and query answering scheme for *in-memory* data series processing. Fast in-memory data series computations often appear in real scenaria [9, 25]. For instance, Airbus stores petabytes of data series, reasoning about the behavior of aircraft components or pilots [21], but requires experts to run analytics only on subsets of the data (e.g., on those relevant to landings from Air France pilots) that fit in memory. MESSI features a novel solution for answering similarity search queries which is 6-11x faster than an in-memory version of ParIS+, achieving for the first time interactive exact query answering times, at ~60msec. It also provides redesigned algorithms that lead to a further ~4x speedup in index construction time, in comparison to (in-memory) ParIS+.

The design decisions in ParIS+ were heavily influenced by the fact that its performance cost was mostly I/O bounded. Since MESSI copes with in-memory data series, no CPU cost can be hidden under I/O. Therefore, MESSI required more careful design choices and coordination of the parallel workers. This led to the development of a more subtle design for the index construction and new algorithms for answering similarity search queries on this index.

For query answering, in particular, the MESSI paper shows that an in memory version of ParIS+ is far from being optimal. Thus, MESSI proposes new solutions to achieve a good balance between the amount of communication among the parallel worker threads, and the effectiveness of each individual worker.

MESSI uses concurrent priority queues for storing the data series that cannot be pruned, and for processing them in order, starting from those that have the smallest lower bound distance to the query series. In this way, the worker threads achieve a better degree of pruning. Moreover, MESSI assigns an iSAX summary to each node of the index tree. Then, it traverses the tree to decide which data series cannot be pruned based on these iSAX summaries. If the lower bound distance of a node from the query series is lower than BSF, the entire subtree rooted at the node can be pruned. In this way, the number of lower bound distance calculations performed is significantly reduced. To achieve load balancing, MESSI ensures that all priority queues have about the same number of elements, and workers use randomization to choose the priority queues they will work on.

4   SING

Although ParIS+ [29,31] and MESSI [27,30] exhibit advanced performance by exploiting the parallelism opportunities offered by the multi-core and SIMD architectures, they ignore the computational power of Graphics Processing Units (GPUs). SING [28] is the first (in-memory) data series indexing scheme that combines the GPU's parallelization opportunities with those of multi-core architectures (and SIMD), to further accelerate exact similarity search. SING outperforms MESSI in a variety of settings, reducing the MESSI cost for query answering to (almost) half.

Data series processing with GPUs is challenging for several reasons. First, the GPU memory is rather limited, so storing the entire raw data set in it is impossible. Moreover, the slow interconnect speeds disallows processing raw data in the GPU memory, as moving even small subsets of such data (i.e., those data series that are not pruned) in the GPU memory incurs a prohibitively high cost. Last, GPUs employ non-sophisticated cores, which are not readily suited to processing tree indexes and algorithms on top of them that frequently involve branching. These considerations imply that it is just (parts of) the query answering computation that can be performed efficiently in the GPU. Furthermore, the SING paper provides experimental evidence that simple GPU adaptations of the techniques employed by previously-presented tree-based indices for implementing those parts cannot outperform state-of-the-art solutions, such as MESSI.

To address these challenges, SING provides a new similarity search algorithm that runs on top of the tree structure created by MESSI. The algorithm ensures the efficient collaboration of both the CPU and GPU cores to answer queries. The main ideas on which it is based are the following. SING stores in the GPU memory, an array of (just) the iSAX summaries of the data series in the collection. This array is sorted in the order the data series appear in the leaves of the index tree. SING performs an inital pruning phase to prune entire root subtrees, thus reducing the number of lower bound distance computations that the GPU executes. Moreover, it employs a simple polynomial function to compute lower bound distances. This enables the computation of lower bound distances in their entirety within the GPU. SING employs streaming to effectively synchronize the parallel execution of CPU and GPU threads.

5   Odyssey

The data series indexes discussed in the previous sections, operate on a single node. Thus, they do not take advantage of the full computational power of modern distributed systems comprised of multiple multi-core nodes. Odyssey [7] is a state-of-the-art *distributed* data-series processing framework, which ensures good speedup and high scalability, thus addressing two major challenges of distributed data series indexing. An *ideal* distributed data series index should achieve linear speedup or be able to process data collections whose size is proportional to the number of nodes in the system. Experiments show [7] that Odyssey does not notably depart from this ideal behavior.

Odyssey provides a collection of scheduling schemes for query batches, which result in good performance under several different workloads. These schemes are based on predicting the execution time of each query. Odyssey provides a query analysis that shows correlation between the total execution time of a query and its initial best-so-far value. This analysis enables the calculation of the predictions.

Odyssey achieves a good degree of load-balancing among the nodes even in settings where the execution time predictions are not accurate. Odyssey's load balancing algorithm illustrates how to efficiently implement the work-stealing approach [1,3,5,6,13,17,18] in distributed data series indexing settings. In the work-stealing approach, nodes sitting idle may steal work from busy nodes. The difficulty here is how to achieve this without ever moving any data around, as moving data between nodes would be prohibitively expensive. In Odyssey, this is esured by employing a (partial) replication scheme, which is flexible enough to allow Odyssey to navigate through a fundamental trade-off between data scalability, and good performance during query answering. Specifically, no data replication would minimize space overhead, but it would disallow a cheap load-balancing solution, thus resulting in higher execution times for answering queries. In Odyssey, a user may choose the replication degree that is the most relevant to its application based on its scalability and performance needs.

Odyssey is the first data series index that supports parallelization outside the boundaries of a single node, without sacrificing the good performance of state-of-the-art indexes [27,28,30] within a node. This was not a trivial task, as experiments show that simple solutions of using as many instances of a state-of-the-art data series index as the number of nodes would not result in good performance, mainly due to severe load balancing problems. Supporting work-stealing on top of a state-of-the-art index would require moving data around.

Odyssey *single-node* indexing algorithm borrows techniques from MESSI [27,30], but it also provides new mechanisms to allow a node v to rebuild parts of the index tree of another node v' needed for executing the load that v steals from v'. This requires the utilization of a different pattern of parallelism in traversing the index tree to produce the set of data series that cannot be pruned, and new implementations for populating and processing the data structures needed for efficient query answering.

Experiments show that Odyssey's index creation exhibits perfect scalability as both the dataset size and the number of nodes increase. Moreover, Odyssey exhibits up to 6.6x times faster exact query answering times than other state of the art parallel or distributed data series indexes.

6   Conclusion and Open Problems

We discussed state-of-the-art parallel and distributed indexes for answering similarity search queries on big collections of data series in a fast and scalable way. We started with concurrency techniques for disk-based indexes. We continued with efficient parallelization techniques for indexes built to work on in-memory data. We also focused on techniques for data series processing that utilize GPUs to further speed up computation. Finally, we touched upon the main challenges that are introduced when moving from a single multi-core node to a distributed system with many multi-core nodes, and summarized state-of-the-art techniques for addressing these challenges.

We focused on solving the problem of *exact* similarity search on big collections of *fixed-length* data series. Exact similarity search is a core operation needed in many critical data analytics tasks (including outlier detection, frequent pattern mining, clustering, classification, and others) [25]. An interesting open problem is whether the discussed techniques can be easily extended to efficiently support other types of similarity search queries, such as approximate search, without or with (deterministic or probabilistic) guarantees [11]. Also, it is interesting to study how these parallelization techniques can be extended to indexes that handle data series of variable length [23].

Concurrent iSAX indexes are *locality-aware*. They maintain some form of data locality, and achieve high parallelism with low synchronization cost by having threads working, independently, on different parts of the data as much as possible, to avoid the need of frequent communication between threads. However, they all employ locks, thus, they are blocking. If a thread holding a lock becomes slow (or crashes), the entire index blocks without being able to make any further progress. *Lock-freedom* [22] is a widely-studied property when designing concurrent trees [4,12,16] and other data structures [14,20,22]. It avoids the use of locks, ensuring that the system, as a whole, makes progress, independently of delays (or failures) of threads. A recent study [15] presented the first lock-free iSAX index, FreSh, together with Refresh, a generic approach that can be applied on top of any iSAX index to provide lock-freedom without adding any performance cost. An interesting open problem is to study the fundamental performance properties that govern other families of data series indexes, and come up with generic schemes for achieving locality-aware, lock-free synchronization on top of them.

The tree employed by an iSAX index has big root fan-out and its root subtrees are leaf-oriented binary trees. This type of trees support locality-aware parallelization, using locks, in a relatively easy way. Experimental work [10] has shown that no single indexing method is an overall winner in exact query answering. For this reason, recent indexing schemes [8] incorporate key ideas from more than one data series indexing families with the goal of exhibiting the combined performance power of the different incorporated approaches. It would be interesting to see what kind of parallelization techniques would be suitable to types of indexes that are not in the iSAX family [34], or for indexes that follow combined approaches [8].

Acknowledgements. This work has been supported by the Hellenic Foundation for Research and Innovation (HFRI) under the "Second Call for HFRI Research Projects to support Faculty Members and Researchers" (project number: 3684).

References

1. Cilk: an efficient multithreaded runtime system. J. Parallel Distrib. Comput. **37**(1), 55–69 (1996)
2. Agrawal, R., Faloutsos, C., Swami, A.: Efficient similarity search in sequence databases. In: Lomet, D.B. (ed.) FODO 1993. LNCS, vol. 730, pp. 69–84. Springer, Heidelberg (1993). https://doi.org/10.1007/3-540-57301-1_5
3. Arora, N.S., Blumofe, R.D., Plaxton, C.G.: Thread scheduling for multiprogrammed multiprocessors. In: Proceedings of the Tenth Annual ACM Symposium on Parallel Algorithms and Architectures, SPAA '98, pp. 119–129. Association for Computing Machinery, New York (1998). https://doi.org/10.1145/277651.277678
4. Attiya, H., Ben-Baruch, O., Fatourou, P., Hendler, D., Kosmas, E.: Detectable recovery of lock-free data structures. In: Proceedings of the 27th ACM SIGPLAN Symposium on Principles and Practice of Parallel Programming, PPoPP '22, pp. 262–277 (2022)
5. Blelloch, G.E., Gibbons, P.B., Matias, Y., Narlikar, G.J.: Space-efficient scheduling of parallelism with synchronization variables. In: Proceedings of the Ninth Annual ACM Symposium on Parallel Algorithms and Architectures, SPAA '97. Association for Computing Machinery (1997)
6. Blumofe, R.D., Leiserson, C.E.: Scheduling multithreaded computations by work stealing. J. ACM **46**(5), 720–748 (1999). https://doi.org/10.1145/324133.324234
7. Chatzakis, M., Fatourou, P., Kosmas, E., Palpanas, T., Peng, B.: Odyssey: a journey in the land of distributed data series similarity search. Proc. VLDB Endow. **16**(5), 1140–1153 (2023). https://doi.org/10.14778/3579075.3579087
8. Echihabi, K., Fatourou, P., Zoumpatianos, K., Palpanas, T., Benbrahim, H.: Hercules against data series similarity search. In: PVLDB (2022)
9. Echihabi, K., Zoumpatianos, K., Palpanas, T.: Big sequence management: on scalability (tutorial). In: IEEE BigData (2020)
10. Echihabi, K., Zoumpatianos, K., Palpanas, T., Benbrahim, H.: The lernaean hydra of data series similarity search: an experimental evaluation of the state of the art. Proc. VLDB Endow. **12**(2), 112–127 (2018). https://doi.org/10.14778/3282495.3282498

11. Echihabi, K., Zoumpatianos, K., Palpanas, T., Benbrahim, H.: Return of the ler-
    naean hydra: experimental evaluation of data series approximate similarity search.
    Proc. VLDB Endow. **13**(3), 403–420 (2019). https://doi.org/10.14778/3368289.
    3368303, http://www.vldb.org/pvldb/vol13/p403-echihabi.pdf
12. Ellen, F., Fatourou, P., Helga, J., Ruppert, E.: The amortized complexity of non-
    blocking binary search trees. In: ACM Symposium on Principles of Distributed
    Computing, PODC '14, Paris, France, 15–18 July, 2014. pp. 332–340 (2014).
    https://doi.org/10.1145/2611462.2611486
13. Fatourou, P.: Low-contention depth-first scheduling of parallel computations with
    write-once synchronization variables. In: Proceedings of the Thirteenth Annual
    ACM Symposium on Parallel Algorithms and Architectures. SPAA '01, Associa-
    tion for Computing Machinery, New York (2001). https://doi.org/10.1145/378580.
    378639
14. Fatourou, P., Kallimanis, N.D., Ropars, T.: An efficient wait-free resizable hash
    table. In: Proceedings of the 30th on Symposium on Parallelism in Algorithms and
    Architectures, SPAA '18, pp. 111–120. Association for Computing Machinery, New
    York (2018). https://doi.org/10.1145/3210377.3210408
15. Fatourou, P., Kosmas, E., Palpanas, T., Paterakis, G.: Fresh: a lock-free data
    series index. In: International Symposium on Reliable Distributed Systems (SRDS)
    (2023)
16. Fatourou, P., Ruppert, E.: Persistent non-blocking binary search trees supporting
    wait-free range queries. CoRR abs/1805.04779 (2018). http://arxiv.org/abs/1805.
    04779
17. Fatourou, P., Spirakis, P.: A new scheduling algorithm for general strict multi-
    threaded computations. In: Jayanti, P. (ed.) DISC 1999. LNCS, vol. 1693, pp.
    297–311. Springer, Heidelberg (1999). https://doi.org/10.1007/3-540-48169-9_21
18. Fatourou, P., Spirakis, P.: Efficient scheduling of strict multithreaded computa-
    tions. Theory Comput. Syst. **33**, 173–232 (2000)
19. Fekete, J.D., Primet, R.: Progressive analytics: a computation paradigm for
    exploratory data analysis. CoRR (2016)
20. Fraser, K.: Practical lock-freedom. Tech. Rep. 579, University of Cambridge Com-
    puter Laboratory (2004). https://www.cl.cam.ac.uk/techreports/UCAM-CL-TR-
    579.pdf
21. Guillaume, A.: Head of operational intelligence department airbus. Personal com-
    munication. (2017)
22. Herlihy, M., Shavit, N.: The Art of Multiprocessor Programming. Morgan Kauf-
    mann, Burlington (2008)
23. Linardi, M., Palpanas, T.: Scalable data series subsequence matching with ULISSE.
    VLDBJ (2020)
24. Palpanas, T.: Data series management: the road to big sequence analytics. SIG-
    MOD Rec. (2015)
25. Palpanas, T., Beckmann, V.: Report on the first and second interdisciplinary time
    series analysis workshop (ITISA). SIGMOD Rec. **48**(3), 36–40 (2019)
26. Peng, B., Fatourou, P., Palpanas, T.: MESSI: in-memory data series indexing. In:
    ICDE (2020)
27. Peng, B., Fatourou, P., Palpanas, T.: Fast data series indexing for in-memory data.
    VLDB J. **30**(6), 1041–1067 (2021)
28. Peng, B., Fatourou, P., Palpanas, T.: SING: sequence indexing using GPUs. In:
    37th IEEE International Conference on Data Engineering, ICDE 2021, Chania,
    Greece, 19–22 April 2021, pp. 1883–1888. IEEE (2021). https://doi.org/10.1109/
    ICDE51399.2021.00171

29. Peng, B., Palpanas, T., Fatourou, P.: Paris: the next destination for fast data series indexing and query answering. In: IEEE BigData (2018)
30. Peng, B., Palpanas, T., Fatourou, P.: Messi: in-memory data series indexing. In: ICDE (2020)
31. Peng, B., Palpanas, T., Fatourou, P.: Paris+: data series indexing on multi-core architectures. TKDE (2020)
32. Rakthanmanon, T., et al.: Searching and mining trillions of time series subsequences under dynamic time warping. In: SIGKDD (2012)
33. Shieh, J., Keogh, E.: iSAX: indexing and mining terabyte sized time series (2008). https://doi.org/10.1145/1401890.1401966
34. Wang, Y., Wang, P., Pei, J., Wang, W., Huang, S.: A data-adaptive and dynamic segmentation index for whole matching on time series. Proc. VLDB Endow. **6**(10), 793–804 (2013). https://doi.org/10.14778/2536206.2536208
35. Zoumpatianos, K., Idreos, S., Palpanas, T.: ADS: the adaptive data series index. VLDB J. **25**(6), 843–866 (2016)
36. Zoumpatianos, K., Palpanas, T.: Data series management: fulfilling the need for big sequence analytics. In: ICDE (2018)

Author Index

Printed in the United States
by Baker & Taylor Publisher Services